VOLUME EIGHTEEN

ADVANCES IN TRANSPORT POLICY AND PLANNING

Health on the Move 3: The Reviews, Part 2

VOLUME EIGHTEEN

ADVANCES IN TRANSPORT POLICY AND PLANNING

Health on the Move 3: The Reviews, Part 2

Edited by

DENA KASRAIAN

Department of the Built Environment,
Eindhoven University of Technology,
Eindhoven, the Netherlands

AHMADREZA FAGHIH IMANI

Centre for Environmental Policy, Imperial College London,
London, United Kingdom

STEPHEN WATKINS

Transport and Health Science Group, 4, St Andrew's Place,
London, United Kingdom

ELSEVIER

ACADEMIC PRESS

An imprint of Elsevier

Academic Press is an imprint of Elsevier
125 London Wall, London, EC2Y 5AS, United Kingdom
50 Hampshire Street, 5th Floor, Cambridge, MA 02139, United States

First edition 2026

ISBN: 978-0-443-34403-9
ISSN: 2543-0009

For information on all Academic Press publications
visit our website at https://www.elsevier.com/books-and-journals

Publisher: Zoe Kruze
Acquisitions Editor: Mariana Kuhl
Editorial Project Manager: Rehan Ismail
Production Project Manager: Greetal Carolyn
Cover Designer: Arumugam Kothandan

Typeset by MPS Limited, India

Contents

Contributors

Jacob Albin Korem Alhassan
Community Health and Epidemiology, University of Saskatchewan, Saskatoon, SK, Canada

Paulo Anciaes
Centre for Transport Studies, University College London, London, United Kingdom

Zanna Buckland
Centre for Environmental Policy, Imperial College London, London, United Kingdom

Daniele Carrieri
Department of Public Health and Sport Sciences, Faculty of Health and Life Sciences, University of Exeter, Exeter, United Kingdom

Nick Cavill
Department of Social & Policy Sciences, University of Bath, Bath, United Kingdom

Karen Conduit-Turner
Public Health Scotland, Edinburgh, Scotland

Margaret Douglas
Public Health Scotland, Edinburgh; University of Glasgow, Glasgow, Scotland

Ahmadreza Faghih Imani
Centre for Environmental Policy, Imperial College London, London, United Kingdom

Daniel Fuller
Community Health and Epidemiology, University of Saskatchewan, Saskatoon, SK, Canada

Yegane Ghezelloo
Department of Architecture, Mie University, Tsu City, Japan

Thomas Gotschi
Institute of Transportation Studies, University of California, Berkeley, United States

Chima Casmir Ibeh
Community Health and Epidemiology, University of Saskatchewan, Saskatoon, SK, Canada

Sonja Kahlmeier
WHO European Centre for Environment and Health, Bonn, Germany; City Health, Zurich, Switzerland

Dena Kasraian
Department of the Built Environment, Eindhoven University of Technology, Eindhoven, the Netherlands

Tamiyo Kondo
Research Center for Urban Safety and Security, Kobe University, Kobe City, Japan

Eleanor Lyons
South West Public Health Training Programme, Exeter, United Kingdom

Gail E. McMillan
Public Health Scotland, Edinburgh, Scotland

Şeref Oruç
Department of Civil Engineering, Faculty of Engineering, Karadeniz Technical University, Trabzon, Turkey

Francesca Racioppi
WHO European Centre for Environment and Health, Bonn, Germany

William Riggs
Management, Urban Affairs and Public Administration University of San Francisco, San Francisco, CA, United States

Dorothea Schaffner
Faculty of Applied Psychology, University of Applied Sciences Northwestern Switzerland, Olten, Switzerland

Nino Sharashidze
WHO European Centre for Environment and Health, Bonn, Germany

Emily Wall
Centre for Environmental Policy, Imperial College London, London, United Kingdom

Stephen Watkins
Transport and Health Science Group, 4, St Andrew's Place, London, United Kingdom

Audrey de Nazelle
Centre for Environmental Policy, Imperial College London, London, United Kingdom

Michael A.B. van Eggermond
Faculty of Architecture, Construction & Geomatics, University of Applied Sciences Northwestern Switzerland, Muttenz, Switzerland

Kübra Çevrim
Department of Civil Engineering, Faculty of Engineering and Architecture, Batman University, Batman, Turkey

Preface

The Transport and Health Science Group (THSG) is an independent group of global public health and transport practitioners and researchers committed to understanding and addressing the links between transport policies and health, and to promoting a healthy transport system. One of the THSG's core objectives is to ensure that the expanding body of knowledge on the relationships between transport and health is regularly reviewed, critically assessed, and brought to the attention of professionals, decision-makers, and the wider public. Since its inception, *Health on the Move* has been a principal mechanism through which THSG has fulfilled this role.

The first *Health on the Move* volume was published in 1991. At that time, it was a slim volume, reflecting both the nascent state of the field and the limited availability of systematic evidence. Two decades later, the field had matured substantially. This was reflected in *Health on the Move 2* (2011), a significantly expanded and revised e-book that rapidly gained recognition as a comprehensive reference on transport and health. Since then, research activity at the intersection of transport and public health has grown at an unprecedented pace, driven by heightened concerns about climate change, physical inactivity, social exclusion, and widening health inequalities.

Against this backdrop, it is now time to revise and expand the series once again. *Health on the Move 3* comprises several volumes, including:

- *Health on the Move 3: The Reviews, Part 1* (published in 2024 as volume 13 of the *Advances in Transport Policy and Planning* series); and
- *Health on the Move 3: The Reviews, Part 2* (the present volume).

More complementary volumes of *Health on the Move 3* are also in preparation:

- *Health on the Move 3: Placemaking*, including reviews and articles and a portfolio of examples of good practice showing how placemaking contributes to healthy transport;
- *Health on the Move 3: The Policy Recommendations*, revisiting and updating THSG's policy positions;
- *Health on the Move 3: The Guidelines*, assembling good-practice guidelines; and
- *Health on the Move 3: The Update*, revising the existing e-book.

It is appropriate that this series of publications begins with literature reviews, for science must always be the driver of policy. It reflects the advances in the field that we have been able to prepare two full volumes of such reviews, and we are proud to present this – the second of those volumes. The present volume builds on Part 1 by extending the scope of reviewed policy instruments, health pathways, and contexts, and by addressing topics that have received comparatively less attention in earlier syntheses.

We are deeply grateful to the reviewers and editorial colleagues whose expertise, critical engagement and commitment have made this volume possible. Their contributions have helped ensure that the chapters are both scientifically robust and relevant to policy and practice. We would particularly like to thank Paula Barros, Nicole Cowell, Adrian Davies, Margaret Douglas, Ruth Gelletlie, Louis Goffe, Khashayar Kazemzadeh, Scarlet McNally, Bardia Mashhoodi, Jennifer Mindell, and Eleanor Roaf for their valuable support.

We are grateful to Elsevier for publishing *Health on the Move 3: The Reviews, Parts 1 and 2*. Elsevier also publishes, in collaboration with THSG, the *Journal of Transport and Health*, an award-winning peer-reviewed journal which has established itself as a major contributor to the development of knowledge on transport and health and the principal specialist journal in the field. However, it is indicative of the growing interest in the field that relevant publications are no longer limited to specialist transport and health journals but can now also be found across a wide range of disciplines, including public health, urban planning, and engineering.

CHAPTER ONE

Introduction - transport policy and health

Dena Kasraian[a,*], Ahmadreza Faghih Imani[b], and Stephen Watkins[c]
[a]Department of the Built Environment, Eindhoven University of Technology, Eindhoven, the Netherlands
[b]Centre for Environmental Policy, Imperial College London, London, United Kingdom
[c]Transport and Health Science Group, 4, St Andrew's Place, London, United Kingdom
*Corresponding author. e-mail address: d.kasraian@tue.nl

Contents

Abstract

This book is part of the *Health on the Move* series, which explores the relationship between transport and health. This chapter introduces the book and sets out its conceptual and policy context. It explains how transport policy influences health through multiple pathways, including access, physical activity, environmental exposures, road traffic injuries, stress and social exclusion. The chapter outlines key transport policy instruments, including infrastructure and service provision, land-use planning, pricing, regulation, information and communication technologies, and behavioural interventions, and provides examples of their health impacts. It presents the volume's scope, logic, and structure and then introduces its ten peer-reviewed chapters and the policy instruments and pathways they address. The chapter positions the volume as a contribution to understanding how transport policy instruments shape health outcomes and health equity through multiple pathways, expanding the evidence base to support both research and policy-making at the intersection of transport and public health.

1. Transport Policy and Health: Setting the Scene

Transport and transport policy influence health in multiple beneficial or detrimental ways. Transport policy decisions shape not only how people move, but also whether they can access essential services, engage in social

Advances in Transport Policy and Planning, Volume 18
ISSN 2543-0009, https://doi.org/10.1016/bs.atpp.2026.07.008

life, be physically active, breathe clean air, experience safe streets, and live in environments that support wellbeing across the life course.

Transport policy operates through a broad set of instruments, including infrastructure and service provision, land-use planning, pricing, regulation, information and communication technologies (ICT), and behavioural interventions (Table 1). These instruments influence health through a variety of pathways, i.e., changes in environmental exposures or lifestyles. For instance, pathways such as road traffic injuries, air pollution, and noise affect health through exposures to harmful physical hazards and environmental substances and stressors, whereas pathways such as physical activity, access, and social exclusion, and stress influence health by encouraging or discouraging certain behaviours and lifestyles.

Importantly, the resulting health impacts are not distributed equally. Transport-related health burdens and benefits tend to be socially and spatially

Table 1 Transport policy instruments adopted from van Wee (2009).

	Policy type	Explanation and example interventions
1	Infrastructure and service provision	Measures related to transport infrastructure, vehicles, equipment, and the operation of transport services (e.g., bus services, bike lanes, e-bike provision, shared mobility services, and transport network improvements)
2	Land-use planning	Urban planning and design measures (e.g., pedestrianization, transit-oriented development, public lighting, adding green spaces, parking place reduction)
3	Pricing	Financial (dis)incentives (e.g., public transport subsidies, levies on vehicles/fuels, prices for parking, road pricing)
4	Regulation	Legal and regulatory measures (e.g., speed limits, tailpipe emission standards, blood alcohol limits)
5	ICT	Information and communication measures (e.g., information provision for public transport, dynamic traffic management)
6	Behavioural	“Soft” measures aimed at behaviour change through nudging and awareness raising schemes (e.g. personalised travel apps, campaigns)

patterned, with vulnerable populations (e.g., children, older adults, people with disabilities, and lower socio-economic status groups) often experiencing disproportionate exposure to risks and reduced access to benefits. These inequalities are, in part, shaped and sometimes reinforced by how transport policies and interventions are designed and implemented. Thus, the importance of transport policy for advancing health equity is increasingly recognised.

Health framing has therefore become critical for justifying transport policy interventions and securing political and public support. However, while the effects of transport interventions on certain pathways—most notably air pollution and road traffic injuries—are well-documented, evidence on the health impacts of many transport policies remains fragmented. Reviews that explicitly connect transport policy instruments to less-investigated health pathways and health outcomes are therefore essential.

1.1 Conceptual pathways linking transport and health

Transport policy shapes the relationship between transport and health through a range of interconnected pathways, including changes in both environmental exposures and lifestyles. Several works have sought to conceptualize the relation between transport and health (Giles-Corti et al., 2020; Glazener et al., 2021; Hannah et al., 1991; Khreis et al., 2017; van Wee and Ettema, 2016; Widener and Hatzopoulou, 2016).

As the evidence base on the impacts of transport and health has expanded, transport-health frameworks have become increasingly comprehensive, and the range of recognized pathways has broadened. While earlier frameworks focused primarily on pathways such as access, physical activity, air quality, safety, and noise (Dannenberg and Sener, 2015; Lyons et al., 2014), more recent frameworks have incorporated a broader set of pathways, including exposure to green space and heat, community severance, social exclusion, climate change (Khreis et al., 2016), mobility independence, stress, roadway contamination and electromagnetic fields (see e.g. Glazener et al., 2021 for an overview of pathways linking transport to health outcomes).

In *Health on the Move 3: The Reviews, Part 1*, the pathways from transport to health are summarized as beneficial (the three A's) and harmful (the nine C's) (Mindell and Watkins, 2024). The three A's capture the primary health promoting aspects of transport: access, referring to opportunities to reach employment, education, people, services, goods, green and blue spaces, and other opportunities for recreation as well as social connectedness; activity, referring to the physical activity gained through active travel; and attractive environments, referring to green and blue spaces that can be saved/created through transport interventions, such as converting parking spaces into parklets.

The adverse impacts are captured by the nine C's. These include cacophony, or transport-related noise; carbon emissions, which contribute to climate change; community severance, the barrier effect created by transport and busy roads; concern, referring to transport-related stress and anxiety; congestion; contamination, or exposure to pollutants such as air pollution and road runoff; conurbation disruption, describing the environmental and social harms of car-oriented urban planning and design, including urban heat islands and urban sprawl; couch potatoes, reflecting sedentary lifestyles from excessive reliance on motorized transport; and crashes and casualties, referring to injuries and fatalities associated with transport.

The three A's and nine C's are useful because they show that transport policy is not only concerned with reducing harms but can also create conditions that promote health, for example by improving access or enabling active travel. The chapters included here examine how different transport policy instruments influence a wide range of health outcomes through both beneficial and detrimental pathways.

1.2 Types of transport policy instruments

Transport policy can influence health through a broad range of policy instruments. Importantly, these instruments shape accessibility, or the degree to which transport and land use systems allow people to reach activities or destinations using one or more transport modes (Geurs and van Wee, 2004). They also influence transport volumes, modal split, vehicle technologies and efficiency, energy sources, and travel behaviour (van Wee, 2009) all of which can affect health outcomes. By changing these factors, transport policy can enhance or diminish the health benefits of transport and mitigate or exacerbate its adverse effects.

Measures related to **transport infrastructure and service provision** have important health implications. For example, evidence indicates that investments in transport infrastructure, especially new infrastructure supporting walking, cycling, and public transport, are associated with higher levels of both overall and transport-related physical activity (Kärmeniemi et al., 2018). Conversely, poor operational performance of transport systems, including congestion and delays, has been shown to negatively affect individuals' mental wellbeing (Conceição et al., 2023).

Land-use planning, including urban planning and design interventions across regional, city, neighbourhood and street scales can influence travel behaviour and health outcomes. Coordinating land-use and transport planning through approaches such as transit-oriented development (TOD) and the 15-minute city can bring homes, jobs, and amenities closer together. By improving access to public transport and shortening travel distances, these strategies can reduce reliance on private cars while promoting active travel and public transport use, thereby reducing exposures to air and noise pollution and increasing physical activity and social interaction (Allam et al., 2022).

Reallocating road space from private vehicles to active modes and green and blue spaces can encourage physical activity, boost social interaction and reduce stress while contributing to climate change mitigation and resilience. Interventions such as "living streets" and green corridors, which prioritise walking, cycling, play, and community life, contribute to improved health and wellbeing (Mindell, 2015). Green and blue infrastructure can make walking and cycling routes more appealing, help lower temperatures and thus reduce energy demand for cooling, and mitigate flood risks. Such environments can also support mental wellbeing through exposure to nature (Chen et al., 2025), while indirectly contributing to lower transport emissions by encouraging shifts from motorised travel to walking and cycling.

Health promotion literature increasingly argues for more integrated interventions that connect urban planning and design with communication-based and participatory approaches (Lowe et al., 2022). Placemaking is one such collaborative approach: it involves communities and stakeholders in shaping public spaces in ways that support health, social connection and environmental sustainability. For instance, the Kool Routes to School program in Santiago, Chile, brought together children, schools, communities, and local government to improve school surroundings and support active school travel (Sagaris and Lanfranco, 2019).

Pricing measures can also influence travel behaviour and eventually health. Financial disincentives such as fuel taxes, parking fees, and road user charging, together with incentives for alternative transport modes have been shown to reduce car use (Graham-Rowe et al., 2011). For example, it is shown that higher fuel prices over the period 2003–2019 in the United States coincided with increased use of public transport, walking and cycling, mainly in urban areas (Belloc et al., 2024).

Regulations such as mandatory daytime running lights or speed limit zones (e.g. 30 km/h) can reduce road traffic crashes and injuries (Morrison and Petticrew, 2003). Emission standards for passenger and freight vehicles help improve air quality, thereby reducing the risk of respiratory and cardiovascular diseases. Regulations targeting transport noise, for instance restrictions on night-time deliveries and requirements for quieter vehicle technologies, can further enhance health by lowering noise exposure, which has been associated with stress, sleep disturbance, and increased cardiovascular risk (World Health Organization, 2024).

Finally, **information and communication technology (ICT)** and **behavioural** (or "soft") measures such as real-time public transport information and awareness campaigns, can encourage behaviour change towards healthy and sustainable travel behaviours. These measures primarily use information sharing, public education, and persuasive communication to influence travel behaviour and tend to achieve the greatest impact when implemented alongside infrastructure improvements (Roaf et al., 2024).

2. Scope, logic and structure of the volume

This volume reviews the evidence on a wide range of transport policies and interventions, examining their health outcomes, and the pathways through which these impacts arise. The volume includes systematic literature reviews, scoping reviews, rapid reviews, narrative syntheses and a forward-looking conceptual contribution. The chapters draw on (quasi-) experimental studies, observational studies, modelling and simulation studies, randomized controlled trials where available, and wider bodies of evidence relevant to transport policy and health.

The reviewed chapters address policies across the typology presented in Table 1 and examine outcomes spanning physical and mental health, social wellbeing and health equity. Particular attention is given to interventions that have been less extensively reviewed in earlier literature, including land-use planning interventions (place making, pedestrianisation, and Ciclovías), the psychological determinants of behaviour change, the potential health impacts of new mobility, and mobility planning in the context of disaster recovery.

The volume's logic is intentionally broad. It begins with measures regarding transport infrastructure and services, then moves to the design and allocation of urban space, pricing and regulatory instruments, behavioural interventions, exceptional and future mobility contexts, and finally health impact assessment. This structure reflects the fact that transport policy does not operate through one mechanism alone. Its health impacts emerge through different pathways, depending on the type of policy, the context in which it is implemented, and the populations affected.

2.1 Overview of chapters

The volume includes ten peer-reviewed chapters. Table 2 summarises these chapters, their aims and features, the transport policy instruments investigated and health outcomes. Chapters use different terminology to describe similar health pathways. For consistency, Table 2 groups related concepts under broader headings informed by Glazener et al. (2021). For example, the term social exclusion is used here to include related concepts such as participation, social engagement, social inclusion, social networks and community connectivity. The health pathway column should therefore be read as a synthesis of the main pathways considered in each chapter, rather than as a direct reproduction of each chapter's terminology. We briefly discuss each chapter in the following paragraphs.

We begin with measures related to transport infrastructure and service provision, examining how mobility systems influence health through access to opportunities, social participation, physical activity, environmental exposures, and safety. McMillan et al. illustrate these relationships through a rapid review of how bus services, bus use, and bus-related occupations relate to health. The chapter primarily examines buses as an **infrastructure and service provision** intervention, while also considering **pricing** through the effects of fare subsidies and concessionary travel schemes. It explores multiple pathways through which bus systems influence health, including **access to services**, **social exclusion**, **physical activity**, **road traffic injuries**, **stress**, **air pollution**, and **noise exposure**. Attention is paid to how bus service characteristics, such as affordability, reliability, accessibility, frequency, connectivity, and journey times, shape health outcomes and health inequalities, especially among low-income groups, women, older adults, people with disabilities, and other marginalized populations.

While transport infrastructure and services connect people to destinations, the design and allocation of urban space influence how people move within cities. The design of urban space can encourage more people to walk or cycle by creating a safe and supportive environment.

Anciaes' scoping review examines the outcomes of interventions designed to increase or improve the use of urban streets as places, primarily through **land-use planning** measures and complementary **infrastructure** improvements. The chapter focuses mainly on street-use outcomes, such as the number of people using streets, time spent in streets and the quality of place

Table 2 Overview of chapters.

Chapter in volume	Aim	Review characteristics	Health pathways	Policy instrument	Health and other outcomes
1. Buses McMillan et al.	Reviews the evidence on links between bus transport interventions, health and wellbeing outcomes.	Rapid review; 2015–2025; 62 studies; mostly North America and Europe.	Access; air pollution; noise; physical activity; road traffic injuries; social exclusion; stress (personal safety, occupational stress/ worker health).	Bus infrastructure and service provision; also fare subsidies and concessionary travel schemes.	Physical, mental, social and equity-related health outcomes; air pollution and noise exposure.
2. Street placemaking Anciaes	Integrates the scattered body of research related to outcomes of street placemaking interventions.	Scoping review; 2005–2025; 39 studies; mainly Global North.	Air pollution; community severance; noise; physical activity; road traffic injuries; social exclusion.	Street placemaking, including pedestrian spaces, shared spaces, plazas, parklets, street closures, and street redesign.	Physical, mental and social wellbeing; social interaction; social cohesion; perceived safety; physical activity; collisions; air and noise pollution.
3. Pedestrianisation Buckland et al.	Reviews worldwide pedestrianisation schemes, their impacts, their challenges and how to address them.	Systematic review; 1985–2025; 87 studies; worldwide evidence, with EU and UK most common.	Access; aesthetics; air pollution; greenhouse gases; heat; noise; physical activity; road traffic injuries; social exclusion.	Pedestrianisation and reallocation of street space from motor vehicles to pedestrians and cyclists, often with complementary regulation and infrastructure.	Physical health; mental wellbeing; quality of life; safety; social wellbeing; thermal comfort; accessibility; health equity; environmental and economic effects.

4. Ciclovías Lyons and Carrieri	Synthesises evidence on the health and equity impacts of Ciclovía initiatives.	Scoping review; 2004–2023; 13 studies; mainly Latin America, especially Colombia.	Access; physical activity; road traffic injuries; social exclusion.	Temporary reallocation of streets from motorised traffic to active and recreational uses through periodic road closures.	Physical health; health-related quality of life; self-perceived health; perceived safety; social cohesion; premature mortality; health equity.
5. Fare-free transport initiatives Alhassan et al.	Reviews the types, health impacts and equity impacts of fare-free transport initiatives.	Scoping review; 2000–2024; 27 studies; all but one from the Global North.	Access; community severance; physical activity; social exclusion; stress.	Pricing interventions that remove or reduce the financial costs of mobility.	Healthcare access; social exclusion; mental health and wellbeing; depressive symptoms; stress; quality of life; life satisfaction; physical activity; active travel; obesity; cognitive function; health equity.
6. Low Emission Zones Çevrim and Oruç	Reviews Low Emission Zone initiatives, their human health impacts and public perception.	Systematic review; 1996–2025; 24 studies; almost all in Europe.	Access; air pollution; physical activity; social exclusion; stress.	Regulatory measures restricting high-emitting vehicles from designated areas, often with associated pricing mechanisms.	Cardiovascular and respiratory conditions; pregnancy and birth outcomes; infant and child health; mortality; life expectancy; life satisfaction; anxiety; social exclusion; health equity; air pollution.

(continued)

Table 2 Overview of chapters. (*cont'd*)

Chapter in volume	Aim	Review characteristics	Health pathways	Policy instrument	Health and other outcomes
7. Behaviour change van Eggermond and Schaffner	Synthesises evidence on behavioural interventions to increase active travel, focusing on psychological mechanisms that mediate effects.	Systematic review; 2010–2025; 28 studies; mostly North America and Europe.	Physical activity (with attention to psychological determinants such as attitudes and self-efficacy).	Behavioural intervention functions including education, persuasion, goal setting, planning, training, social support, incentivisation, enablement, feedback, modelling and environmental restructuring.	Active travel behaviour; walking/cycling/physical activity; psychological determinants of behaviour change. Health outcomes are indirect.
8. Post-disaster mobility planning Ghezelloo and Kondo	Reviews the impact of mobility disruptions and mobility planning on post-disaster recovery and survivors' wellbeing.	Systematic review; mostly past 15 years; 61 studies; largely Japan, with examples from Thailand, USA and New Zealand.	Access; community severance; physical activity; social exclusion; stress.	Infrastructure and service provision, and land-use planning in disaster recovery contexts.	Physical, mental-emotional and social wellbeing; access to healthcare and essential services; social participation; equitable recovery.

9. New mobility Riggs	Develops a conceptual framework to explore the public health impacts of new mobility, its potential risks, and strategies to mitigate them.	Forward-looking conceptual chapter rather than a traditional review of an established policy intervention.	Access; air pollution; greenhouse gases; noise; mobility independence; physical activity; road traffic injuries; social exclusion; stress.	Innovations in infrastructure and service provision enabled through ICT and shaped by regulation, including shared (micro)mobility, automated and autonomous vehicles, rideshare, and urban air mobility.	Physical activity; mental health and psychosocial wellbeing; health equity; accessibility; environmental outcomes; labour conditions; wildlife disturbance.
10. HEAT Kahlmeier et al.	Reviews the development, application and policy uptake of the Health Economic Assessment Tool for walking and cycling.	Review/ methodological chapter; 2005–2025; primarily European applications, with wider international uptake.	Air pollution; greenhouse gases; physical activity; road traffic injuries.	Health impact assessment/ economic appraisal; decision-support tool for walking and cycling.	Premature mortality and economic valuation of health benefits associated with walking and cycling; contribution to evidence-informed transport appraisal.

activities, as well as health-related outcomes. The health-related outcomes here include primarily **physical activity** and **social exclusion**, and secondarily **air pollution**, **road traffic injuries and safety**, **stress**, **community severance**, and **noise**. It investigates outcomes such as physical activity, mental health, wellbeing, personal security, social interaction, social inclusion, collisions, air quality, and noise. The chapter reviews how street placemaking interventions such as pedestrianisation, shared spaces, plazas, parklets, street closures, and street redesigns can transform streets into healthier, safer, and more socially vibrant public spaces. This chapter is concerned with street placemaking as a broad family of interventions, rather than with pedestrianisation alone.

Buckland et al.'s systematic review examines pedestrianisation schemes, their impacts, and the challenges and enablers associated with their implementation. The chapter considers pedestrianisation as a **land-use planning** intervention that reallocates street space from motor vehicles to pedestrians, often supported by complementary **regulatory** and **infrastructure and service provision** measures such as street redesign, traffic restriction, greening and other public realm improvements. The chapter explores impacts primarily through **physical activity**, and secondarily through **air pollution**, **road traffic injuries and safety**, **stress**, **social exclusion**, **access**, and **community severance**. It investigates outcomes including physical health, mental wellbeing, quality of life, safety, social wellbeing, thermal comfort, and health equity. Attention is given to the potential of pedestrianisation to create healthier, safer, and more liveable urban environments, while also addressing concerns about accessibility, inclusion, and the distribution of benefits across population groups. The chapter highlights the importance of participatory planning, clear communication, and context-sensitive design to address concerns about car dominance, access and the distribution of benefits and burdens.

Lyons et al.'s scoping review examines the health and equity impacts of Ciclovía programmes. Ciclovías are regular open-street programmes, a form of **land-use planning** intervention, that temporarily close streets to motorised traffic and provide space for walking, cycling, running and other recreational activities. The chapter explores impacts primarily through **physical activity**, and secondarily through **social exclusion**, **access**, accompanied by some discussions on **road traffic injuries**, and **air pollution**. It investigates outcomes including physical health, health-related quality of life, self-perceived health, social cohesion, perceived safety, premature mortality, and health equity. The review examines Ciclovías as opportunities for physical activity and social interaction, while also considering equity in access and participation, including differences by gender and socioeconomic status.

Beyond the provision of infrastructure and services and shaping of urban environments, policy makers can also influence mobility through economic instruments that affect the affordability of travel.

Alhassan et al.'s scoping review examines the health and equity impacts of fare-free transport initiatives, a **pricing** intervention that removes or reduces the financial costs of travel. While most of these initiatives are embedded in public transport systems, some operate outside them, for example through community buses, dedicated vans or rideshare credits. The chapter explores impacts primarily through **access**, and **social exclusion**, and secondarily through **physical activity, stress,** and **community severance.** It investigates outcomes such as healthcare access, mental wellbeing, physical activity, obesity, social participation, cognitive function, and health equity. A key focus is on how fare-free transport initiatives affect vulnerable populations, such as older adults, youth, low-income populations, and racialized groups, and the extent to which these initiatives improve mobility and access to health-promoting resources.

Another important policy lever to shape health outcomes is **regulation**. Çevrim and Oruç's systematic review examines the physical and mental health impacts of Low Emission Zones (LEZs), a form of regulatory intervention that restricts or charges vehicles that do not meet specified emission standards. The chapter explores impacts primarily through the pathway of **air pollution**, and secondarily through **stress**, **social exclusion**, **physical activity**, and **access**. It investigates physical, mental, social, and equity-related health outcomes measured by a host of indicators (e.g., cardiovascular and respiratory diseases, mortality, life expectancy, birth outcomes, quality of life, and health equity). It also considers the distribution of benefits and burdens, including how LEZs may affect people living outside zone boundaries, lower-income households, diesel vehicle owners and those with limited access to alternative transport. The chapter therefore highlights both the public health potential of LEZs and the importance of equity-sensitive implementation, public engagement and integration with wider mobility policies.

While infrastructure and service provision, land-use planning, pricing, and regulation shape the contexts within which mobility occurs, behavioural interventions focus more directly on the psychological and social determinants of travel choices. Van Eggermond and Schaffner's systematic review examine **behavioural** interventions designed to promote active travel, focusing on how these interventions influence psychological factors that may explain changes in walking and cycling behaviour. The chapter explores impacts primarily through **physical activity.** The chapter considers intervention functions such as education, persuasion, goal setting, planning, training, social support, incentivisation, enablement, feedback and monitoring, and environmental restructuring. It also examines psychological factors including attitudes, motivation, self-efficacy, perceived control, social influence, planning, and information and skills. The review gives attention to the extent to which these psychological factors are measured as mediators of behaviour change, and highlights the need for more theory-driven and methodologically consistent research on how active travel interventions work.

The volume then moves beyond established policy instruments to consider mobility in both exceptional and future contexts. Addressing a topic that has received little attention, Ghezelloo and Kondo examine mobility planning in the context of disaster recovery, where the role of **infrastructure and service provision** in ensuring access and social connectivity becomes critical to the survivors' wellbeing and community recovery. The chapter focuses on how disrupted, poorly connected or relocated mobility environments can affect survivors' access to healthcare, essential services, daily activities and social networks. It considers these impacts across three dimensions of wellbeing: physical, mental-emotional and social. It highlights the importance of accessible, equitable and context-sensitive mobility planning, particularly for groups who may be disproportionately affected by post-disaster displacement and poor transport access, including older adults, people with disabilities and rural populations.

Looking towards the future of mobility, Riggs suggests a conceptual framework to explore the health implications of new mobility, including rideshare, shared micromobility, automated and autonomous vehicles, and urban air mobility. It primarily considers these innovations as **infrastructure and service provision** interventions (including vehicles and equipment) enabled through **ICT** systems and shaped by evolving regulatory frameworks. Rather than reviewing a single established intervention, the chapter develops a forward-looking framework for considering how these technologies may affect health through physical activity, environmental exposure, psycho-social wellbeing, safety, accessibility and equity. It highlights both opportunities and risks: new mobility may improve access, reliability and safety for some groups, but may also reduce active travel, increase environmental or noise exposure, create new forms of stress and exclusion, and raise concerns about labour conditions and uneven access. The chapter therefore emphasises the need for proactive governance, including health impact assessment, investment in active modes, clean and low-noise technologies, universal access, data sharing and equity-oriented planning.

The volume concludes with a chapter on health impact assessment, demonstrating how analytical tools can support evidence-informed transport planning and policy across the diverse interventions discussed throughout this volume. Kahlmeier et al. examine the Health Economic Assessment Tool (HEAT) for walking and cycling, a decision-support tool developed to estimate the economic value of health impacts associated with active travel. Rather than evaluating a specific transport intervention, the chapter reflects on more than ten years of HEAT development, dissemination and application in policy and practice. The tool primarily assesses the economic value of reductions in premature mortality associated with walking and cycling, considering **physical activity, air pollution**, **road traffic injuries** and **greenhouse gas emissions**. The chapter highlights the role of health economic assessment in making the benefits of active travel more visible within transport appraisal, while also discussing challenges related to data availability, usability, communication, equity, uptake beyond Europe, and the inclusion of wider health outcomes.

2.2 What is not Included?

This volume does not seek to cover every issue at the intersection of transport and health. Some topics are addressed in *Health on the Move 3: The Reviews, Part 1*, including disability and travel; interventions to increase active travel; the impacts of active travel to school on children; the impacts of area-wide 20 mph (30 km/h) speed limits; effectiveness of policies to reduce congestion; the economic and social impacts of public transport and how these relate to health; links between public transport use and the mobility and health of older adults; transport and loneliness; the impacts of the costs of transport on mental health; gender differences in travel patterns; cognitive biases; and impacts of transport interventions on inequality.

Nor have we addressed some topics, as reviews already existed or have become available since the publication of our last volume. These include broader approaches to behaviour change interventions in transport (Chatterjee and Carey, 2018), the implications of rurality for transport and health (Musselwhite, 2023), community severance (Vaughan et al., 2020), liveable streets (Appleyard and Appleyard, 2021), and the impact of air pollution exposure on rheumatic diseases (Zhang et al., 2023).

There are also important issues that are not addressed in either volume. These omissions do not mean that the topics are unimportant; rather, they reflect the necessary limits of the two volumes and point to priorities for future work. These include impact of freight transport on health, the impact of cycle helmet regulations, the relationship between business and finance and transport and health, and the impacts of rail transport, aviation and shipping on health.

2.3 Who can benefit from this volume?

This volume is of interest to a number of different groups. To academics interested in the intersection of transport and public health, it provides access to new review articles that should assist them in finding material relevant to their own work and identifying gaps in the evidence base. We have consciously aimed to include topics which evaluate what has been shown to work and this should make the volume valuable to transport planners, public health practitioners, urban designers and other transport professionals. Some of the issues we have addressed, such as pedestrianisation, free transport and LEZs are subjects of current political debate. This should make the volume of great value to decision makers, opinion formers and advocates seeking to understand how transport policy can support healthier, fairer, and more sustainable cities.

References

Allam, Z., Nieuwenhuijsen, M., Chabaud, D., Moreno, C., 2022. The 15-minute city offers a new framework for sustainability, liveability, and health. Lancet Planet. Health 6 (3), e181–e183. https://doi.org/10.1016/S2542-5196(22)00014-6.

Appleyard, B., Appleyard, D. (Eds.), 2021. Livable Streets 2.0 Elsevier. https://books.google.com/books?hl=en&lr=&id=fci2DwAAQBAJ&oi=fnd&pg=PP1&dq=Appleyard+B,+Appleyard+D+(2021)+Livable+streets+2.0.+Elsevier,+Amsterdam&ots=ZBSzy4Ddls&sig=P6R_mE44a1QR09J0-c_0pNtpHTE.

Belloc, I., Gimenez-Nadal, J.I., Molina, J.A., 2024. The gasoline price and the commuting behavior of US commuters: exploring changes to green travel mode choices. J. Transp. Geogr. 121, 104006. https://doi.org/10.1016/J.JTRANGEO.2024.104006.

Chatterjee, K., Carey, R.N., 2018. Special Issue on the theory, design and evaluation of behaviour change interventions in transport. J. Transp. & Health 10, 7–10. https://doi.org/10.1016/J.JTH.2018.08.009.

Chen, L., Yan, R., Greening, Y.H., 2025. City walk or nature walk? Evidence-based psycholo gical and physiological outcomes–A systematic review and meta-analysis. In: Chen, R., Yan, R., Hu, Y. (Eds.), Urban Forestry & Urban Greening, Elsevier, 128726. Retrieved June 30, 2026, from https://www.sciencedirect.com/science/article/pii/S1618866725000603.

Conceição, M.A., Monteiro, M.M., Kasraian, D., van den Berg, P., Haustein, S., Alves, I., et al., 2023. The effect of transport infrastructure, congestion and reliability on mental wellbeing: a systematic review of empirical studies. Transp. Rev. 43 (2), 264–302. https://doi.org/10.1080/01441647.2022.2100943.

Dannenberg, A.L., Sener, I.N., 2015. Why public health and transportation: setting the stage - TRID. TR. N. 299. https://trid.trb.org/View/1373978.

Geurs, K.T., van Wee, B., 2004. Accessibility evaluation of land-use and transport strategies: review and research directions. J. Transp. Geogr. 12 (2), 127–140. https://doi.org/10.1016/J.JTRANGEO.2003.10.005.

Giles-Corti, B., Lowe, M., Arundel, J., 2020. Achieving the SDGs: evaluating indicators to be used to benchmark and monitor progress towards creating healthy and sustainable cities. Health Policy (Amsterdam, Neth.) 124 (6), 581–590. https://www.sciencedirect.com/science/article/pii/S016885101830441X.

Glazener, A., Sanchez, K., Ramani, T., Zietsman, J., Nieuwenhuijsen, M.J., Mindell, J.S., et al., 2021. Fourteen pathways between urban transportation and health: A conceptual model and literature review. J. Transp. Health 21, 101070. https://doi.org/10.1016/j.jth.2021.101070.

Graham-Rowe, E., Skippon, S., Gardner, B., Abraham, C., 2011. Can we reduce car use and, if so, how? A review of available evidence. Transportation Res. Part. A: Policy Pract. 45 (5), 401–418. https://doi.org/10.1016/J.TRA.2011.02.001.

Hannah, J., Morton, S., Watkins, S.J., 1991. Health on the move: policies for health promoting transport. Policy Statement Transp. Health Study Group. https://scholar.google.nl/scholar?hl=en&as_sdt=0%2C5&q=Hannah%2C+J.%2C+Morton%2C+S.%2C+and+Watkins%2C+S.J.+%281991%29.+Health+on+the+Move%3A+Policies+for+Health+Promoting+Transport.&btnG=.

Kärmeniemi, M., Lankila, T., Ikäheimo, T., Koivumaa-Honkanen, H., Korpelainen, R., 2018. The built environment as a determinant of physical activity: a systematic review of longitudinal studies and natural experiments. Ann. Behav. Med. 52 (3), 239–251. https://doi.org/10.1093/ABM/KAX043

Khreis, H., May, A.D., Nieuwenhuijsen, M.J., 2017. Health impacts of urban transport policy measures: a guidance note for practice. J. Transp. & Health 6, 209–227. https://doi.org/10.1016/j.jth.2017.06.003

Khreis, H., Warsow, K.M., Verlinghieri, E., Guzman, A., Pellecuer, L., Ferreira, A., et al., 2016. The health impacts of traffic-related exposures in urban areas: Understanding real effects, underlying driving forces and co-producing future directions. J. Transp. & Health 3 (3), 249–267. https://doi.org/10.1016/j.jth.2016.07.002.

Lowe, M., Adlakha, D., Sallis, J.F., Salvo, D., Cerin, E., Moudon, A.V., et al., 2022. City planning policies to support health and sustainability: an international comparison of policy indicators for 25 cities. Lancet Glob. Health 10 (6), e882–e894. https://doi.org/10.1016/S2214-109X(22)00069-9.

Lyons, W., Morse, L., Nash, L., Strauss, R., 2014. Statewide Transportation Planning for Healthy Communities. United States Department of Transportation. https://doi.org/10.21949/1503647.

Mindell, J.S., 2015. Active travel is (generally) good for health, the environment and the economy. J. Transp. & Health 2 (4), 447–448. https://doi.org/10.1016/J.JTH.2015.10.006.

Mindell, J.S., Watkins, S.J., 2024. Transport, health and inequality. An overview of current evidence. J. Transp. & Health 38, 101886. https://doi.org/10.1016/J.JTH.2024.101886.

Morrison, D.S., Petticrew, M., 2003. What are the most effective ways of improving population health through transport interventions? Evidence from systematic reviews. J. Epidemiol. Community Health 57, 327–333. https://doi.org/10.1136/jech.57.5.327.

Musselwhite, C., 2023. Editorial - Rurality, sustainability and health. J. Transp. & Health 28, 101571. https://doi.org/10.1016/J.JTH.2023.101571.

Roaf, E., Larrington-Spencer, H., Lawlor, E.R., 2024. Interventions to increase active travel: a systematic review. J. Transp. & Health 38, 101860. https://doi.org/10.1016/J.JTH.2024.101860.

Sagaris, L., Lanfranco, D., 2019. Beyond "safe": Chilean "Kool" routes to school address social determinants of health. J. Transp. & Health 15, 100665. https://doi.org/10.1016/J.JTH.2019.100665.

van Wee, B., 2009. Transport policy: what can it and what can't it do? European Transport Conference (ETC), Association for European Transport (AET). https://aetransport.org/public/downloads/JjcOU/4183–514ec5ce6cdc9.pdf.

van Wee, B., Ettema, D., 2016. Travel behaviour and health: a conceptual model and research agenda. J. Transp. Health 3 (3), 240–248. https://doi.org/10.1016/j.jth.2016.07.003.

Vaughan, L., Anciaes, P.R., Mindell, J.S., 2020. Cars, conflict and community severance. In: Appelyard, B. (Ed.), Livable Streets Vol. 2. Elsevier, pp. 121–128. https://discovery.ucl.ac.uk/id/eprint/10073091/.

Widener, M.J., Hatzopoulou, M., 2016. Contextualizing research on transportation and health: a systems perspective. J. Transp. Health 3 (3), 232–239. https://doi.org/10.1016/j.jth.2016.01.008.

World Health Organization, 2024. Compendium of WHO and other UN guidance on health and environment, 2024 update. https://books.google.com/books?hl=en&lr=&id=NwgTEQAAQBAJ&oi=fnd&pg=PR5&dq=WHO+(2022),+Environmental+noise,+in+Compendium+of+WHO+and+other+UN+guidance+on+health+and+environment,+2022+update&ots=igPbOI4nyt&sig=HWPs8w9zuZaPYm3A_JykactpzA.

Zhang, R.D., Chen, C., Wang, P., Fang, Y., Jiang, L.Q., Fang, X., et al., 2023. Air pollution exposure and auto-inflammatory and autoimmune diseases of the musculoskeletal system: a review of epidemiologic and mechanistic evidence. Environ. Geochem. Health 45 (7), 4087–4105. https://doi.org/10.1007/S10653-023-01495-X.

CHAPTER TWO

Pathways between bus services, bus use and health: A rapid review

Gail E. McMillan[a,*], **Karen Conduit-Turner**[a], **and Margaret Douglas**[a,b]
[a]Public Health Scotland, Edinburgh, Scotland
[b]University of Glasgow, Glasgow, Scotland
*Corresponding author. e-mail address: gail.mcmillan2@phs.scot

Contents

Abstract

Transport can influence health through several complex pathways. Buses are a commonly used and important form of public transport due to their flexibility and low-cost compared to other modes. We conducted a rapid review to provide an overview of the ways buses affect health through several pathways: access to services and social inclusion, physical activity, road travel injury, personal safety, environmental exposures and air quality, noise pollution, health and wellbeing outcomes. Two bibliographic databases (Scopus and Transport Research International Documentation) were

Advances in Transport Policy and Planning, Volume 18
ISSN 2543-0009, https://doi.org/10.1016/bs.atpp.2026.07.001

searched to identify peer-reviewed evidence from systematic reviews, qualitative studies, and primary quantitative studies. Sixty-two studies met our inclusion criteria. We found that travelling by bus may have positive impacts through access to services, physical activity, social inclusion and mental wellbeing. Negative impacts may include exposure to air pollution, noise, injuries and harassment for passengers and drivers, and occupational hazards for drivers. Most studies were at moderate or high risk of bias for reasons including cross sectional design and lack of comparable controls, meaning the robustness of associations should be further assessed. We identified little evidence of the impacts of bus services on wider communities or studies comparing buses with other transport modes. The impacts varied by contextual factors including rurality, traffic density, proximity to stops and service characteristics like accessibility, frequency, reliability and journey duration. Low-income groups, women, disabled people and other marginalized groups were more affected by both positive and negative impacts. Improvements in bus service affordability, reliability, connectivity, accessibility and on-board conditions could help to reduce social and health inequalities.

1. Introduction

1.1 Background

The relationship between transport and health is complex and is exerted through multiple pathways. All forms of transport can affect health by influencing access to health-promoting services, amenities, social opportunities and employment. The links between transport and health have been illustrated in a conceptual model describing 14 pathways that can exert positive or negative effects on physical and mental health (Glazener et al., 2021). These 14 pathways are physical activity, access (to amenities, healthcare, employment opportunities), green and blue space aesthetics, mobility independence, contamination (from chemicals like oils, gasoline, heavy metals and lead), social inclusion, noise, heat, road travel injuries, air pollution, community severance, electromagnetic fields, stress, and greenhouse gases (Glazener et al., 2021). The pathways are influenced by intrinsic and extrinsic modifiers, such as socio-economic status, nutrition, and co-exposure. The model emphasizes the interaction between transport factors, urban planning and personal factors and highlights the intersection between transport and inequalities, particularly socio-economic deprivation. The Glazener et al. (2021) model acknowledged that different transport modes can have different impacts on health and inequalities. For example, while active travel is a beneficial source of physical activity (PA), private motorized transport has multiple adverse effects including – but not limited to - road travel injuries, pollution and physical inactivity (Miner et al., 2024).

Transport can also affect social and health inequalities (Glazener et al., 2021). There is growing research interest in the social and health impacts of transport poverty (Lucas, 2018), defined as the lack of transport options allowing people to meet their daily needs and achieve a reasonable quality of life that are: available, reliable, affordable, accessible and safe (Public Health Scotland, 2024). Factors contributing to transport poverty are the transport system, spatial planning, service provision and sociodemographic and household circumstances, which are ultimately underpinned by car culture and car-centric urban planning.

Populations can experience transport poverty for different reasons. Low-income groups may find transport costs are a barrier (Gates et al., 2019; Lucas, 2018). Disabled people may experience access barriers (Gates et al., 2019; Lucas, 2018). Women experience challenges including greater economic constraints, safety concerns and are more likely to trip-chain (combining a series of trips to multiple locations for different purposes), meaning public transport scheduling is a barrier (Borker, 2024). Rural communities may need to travel long distances and often have absent or infrequent public transport (Gates et al., 2019). Perceptions of safety and affordability may also influence mode choice and exacerbate transport poverty (Jamei et al., 2022).

In the following sections, we summarize previous studies demonstrating links between public transport and health, outline the rationale to focus on buses, and state the objectives for this paper.

1.2 Public transport, health and inequalities

Past research has provided evidence of associations between public transport and health for several of the pathways identified by Glazener et al. (2021), including travel associated physical activity (Anciaes and Alhassan, 2024; Barros et al., 2024), exposure to air and noise pollution (Nieuwenhuijsen et al., 2016), access to healthcare (Musselwhite, 2022), social inclusion (Williams et al., 2024) and traffic collisions (van Erpecum et al., 2024). For example, a previous review found evidence that public transport use can improve social participation (Anciaes and Alhassan, 2024). Research on physical activity gains found a range between 8–33 min of walking as part of public transport use (Rissel et al., 2012) and that built environment characteristics, like proximity to stops and stations, influences this association (Hirsch et al., 2014; Xiao et al., 2019).

Other studies have examined links with health outcomes. Research on public transport use by older adults (aged 60+) reported an association with reduced depressive symptoms, improved cognitive function, increased gait speed and decreased BMI (Body Mass Index) (Dilian et al., 2024). Conversely, another systematic review, not focused on older adults, found no evidence of a clinically significant impact of public transit use on weight loss (Janatabadi and Ermagun, 2022). Interventions to improve affordability of public transport were associated with improved mental health and wellbeing, especially for frequent users of public transport and low-income groups (Foster et al., 2024). Studies have highlighted that public transport accessibility particularly impacts on vulnerable and marginalized communities (Musselwhite, 2023).

Most previous reviews have combined all forms of public transport without considering whether impacts may vary for different public transport modes. Buses may be an important form of public transport for addressing transport poverty. Despite this, no previous reviews have brought together evidence of the positive and negative health impacts of bus services (Musselwhite, 2022). Our review will extend and add to the literature by focusing specifically on pathways between buses and health.

1.2.1 Buses and health

Buses are an important form of public transport. They offer more flexible routes than trains or trams that run on rails and account for a high proportion of public transport journeys, particularly for low-income populations (Gates et al., 2019; Lachapelle and Boisjoly, 2023; Noor et al., 2016). These characteristics mean that bus impacts may differ from other forms of public transport, such as rail and metro services, and have particular importance for transport poverty and inequalities. Despite this, buses often attract less public funding per head than other forms of public transport. For example, in Scotland national funding in 2023/24 was estimated to be £0.26 per passenger km for buses, £0.60 for trains and £2.29 for ferries (Transport Scotland, 2024). Buses may also have differing effects on bus passengers, wider communities and bus drivers or other staff. Understanding the health impacts arising from bus use and characteristics of bus services can enhance understanding of public transport needs and guide recommendations for funding and local planning.

Musselwhite (2022) identified several key links between buses and health in a proposed research agenda. These included physical activity, air pollution, road travel injuries, social connections and occupational stressors for bus drivers. Drawing on the Glazener et al. (2021) model, Musselwhite's (2022) research manifesto, and previous reviews combining impacts for all public transport, we identified hypothesized priority pathways through which bus use or characteristics of bus services could impact on passengers, communities or staff. We excluded some pathways from the Glazener et al. (2021) model relating to transport infrastructure, including loss of greenspace and heat islands, because buses share road infrastructure with other vehicles so the impacts are not solely attributable to buses. The hypothesized pathways are presented in Fig. 1.

1.3 Objectives

This review aimed to map evidence of the positive and negative links between buses and health, how or why they arise, and how people are differentially affected. We aimed to demonstrate evidence on the breadth of pathways through which health is impacted by buses rather than focusing in-depth on fewer pathways. The current study provides a conceptual foundation for understanding what knowledge gaps remain and informing the direction of further in-depth research. To this end we carried out a rapid review of the evidence on the relationships between bus services, bus use or bus related occupation and health. Our overall research question, and sub-questions, were:

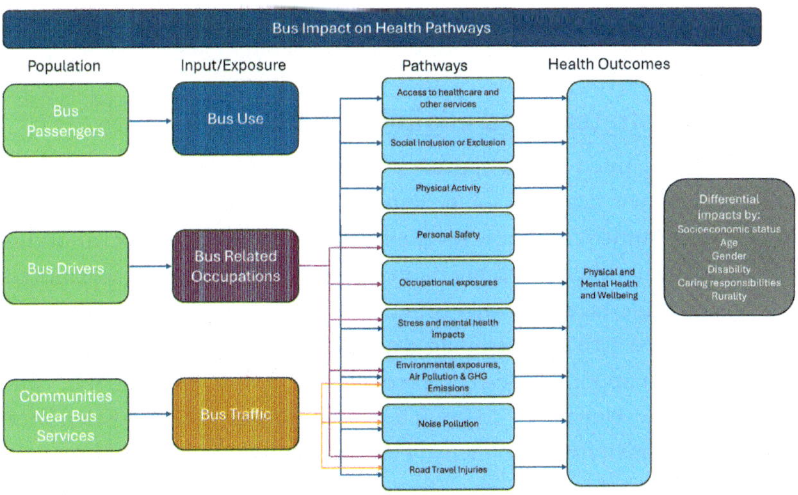

Fig. 1 Conceptual model of the pathways between buses and health.

1. What is the evidence that bus services and bus use influence health for bus users, bus staff, and communities?
   a. What are the associations between bus services, bus use or bus-related occupation (and their characteristics) and health determinants, impacts or outcomes?
   b. Why or how do health impacts of bus services, bus use or bus-related occupation occur?
   c. Are there differential health impacts of bus services, bus use or bus-related occupation between groups?

2. Methods

We undertook a rapid review according to a pre-specified protocol registered with PROSPERO (CRD42024629241) in line with Preferred Reporting Items for Systematic Reviews and Meta-Analysis (PRISMA) guidelines.

The protocol was updated, prior to extraction, to reflect two main changes. We originally included 'Mobility independence' as a search term and health pathway but the retrieved studies examined ability to access the bus without showing that this increased people's independence overall. Mobility independence also overlapped with the definitions of access and social inclusion, which aligned more closely to health outcomes. Secondly, due to the volume and complexity of the included studies, quantitative evidence is presented in narrative text format, rather than a table.

2.1 Search strategy and eligibility criteria

There was a planned staged approach to searching and identifying relevant studies. First, we searched for systematic reviews and primary qualitative studies. If no sufficient review level evidence was identified for an outlined health pathway, then a supplementary search for primary quantitative studies was undertaken for that topic.

We searched two bibliographic databases to identify published literature: Scopus and Transport Research International Documentation. The search strategy was developed in collaboration with an information scientist and piloted for sensitivity and specificity. The searches were developed by adapting from previous systematic reviews (Barros et al., 2024; Dilian et al., 2024) and from our eligibility criteria by combining terms using Boolean operators AND and OR. For the intervention/exposure we used terms including ("bus" OR "bus users" OR "bus travel"). We used AND to combine this with terms for each pathway. Searches were restricted to English language. Searches for systematic reviews and qualitative studies were undertaken in December 2024 to January 2025 and supplementary primary literature searches for physical activity and social inclusion in February 2025. Due to the accelerated nature of rapid reviews, search terms were specifically focused on bus terms rather than public transport terms and supplementary primary searches were restricted to the past 10 years (Garritty et al., 2024; Klerings et al., 2023). The full search strategy can be found in our protocol. Additionally, we identified further primary studies that met our inclusion criteria from systematic reviews that were excluded because they combined results for all public transport.

Identified studies were assessed for eligibility against the following inclusion criteria:

a) Participants were bus users, bus staff, or communities near, or affected by, bus routes (as defined by study authors).
b) The exposures of interest were public bus service use (or any population-level intervention that influenced availability, accessibility, frequency, reliability, affordability, safety, overcrowding, or journey length of public bus services), employment in a bus-related occupation, and living near or being affected by bus services.
c) The study reported outcomes on: social inclusion/exclusion or access to healthcare and essential amenities/services; physical activity; air pollution or greenhouse gases; noise pollution; personal safety; road travel injuries; health and wellbeing; or health equity.
d) In the first instance, we included systematic reviews or qualitative studies that synthesized data where conclusions could be drawn about the association between health and bus use, bus-related occupation, or bus-affected communities.
e) We included primary studies of the impact of bus use on physical activity and social exclusion, as insufficient review level evidence was identified for these pathways.
f) Studies published in the English language and where the full-text could be retrieved.

Exclusion criteria were studies about any other modes of public transport or cars (including those that combined results for buses with other transport modes), transport modes restricted to defined populations such as patient transport or school buses, interventions for individual behavior change, studies where the outcomes were about mode choice only with no link to health (including access to the bus), studies with only potential rather than actual bus users as the population or hypothetical scenarios. For primary quantitative studies identified by our bibliographic search, we excluded studies from before 2015.

2.2 Study selection and extraction

Citations retrieved in searches were imported into the online review screening tool Covidence, and de-duplicated automatically. Duplicates were manually checked. Each title and abstract was independently screened by two reviewers. Two reviewers then independently assessed potentially eligible full texts for final inclusion using a standardized screening form. All disagreements were resolved by discussion. The percentage agreement at title and abstract stage exceeded 80 % at all stages.

Data extraction was conducted in Covidence with a standardized form that included key study characteristics including objectives, study design and methods, sample details, description of intervention or exposure and comparator, outcomes, results. After piloting the form, extraction was conducted independently by one author with all extractions checked by a second author for accuracy and completeness. Disagreements were resolved by discussion.

2.3 Study quality assessment

Risk of bias assessment was undertaken using the JBI (formerly Joanna Briggs Institute) critical appraisal checklist relevant to the study design, with minor adaptations. The JBI checklists cover areas where bias may have been introduced in the study, tailored to the specific study design. Items are rated as 'Yes', 'No' or 'Unclear'. An overall judgement was made of risk of bias for each study. We did not exclude studies based on quality rating. Full details of our approach to critical appraisal can be found in our protocol on PROSPERO.

2.4 Synthesis

Due to heterogeneity of exposures, interventions, measurements, outcomes, study designs, and populations, narrative synthesis was most appropriate. A convergent segregated approach to synthesis and integration of findings from quantitative and qualitative evidence was used in line with previous research (Stern et al., 2020). Evidence was tabulated by health pathway, then by whether it was quantitative or qualitative. The findings for the pathways for 'access' and 'social inclusion' have been combined due to significant overlap in how these terms were operationalized within studies. Quantitative results are presented as a narrative summary of findings. A qualitative meta-synthesis was conducted where initial themes were coded by one author, and final themes were agreed by a second author. The meta-synthesis results are presented in a summary table with key themes.

3. Results

3.1 Selection process

The process of study selection is presented in a PRISMA flow diagram (Fig. 2). Searches identified a total of 2002 records, with 1908 studies for

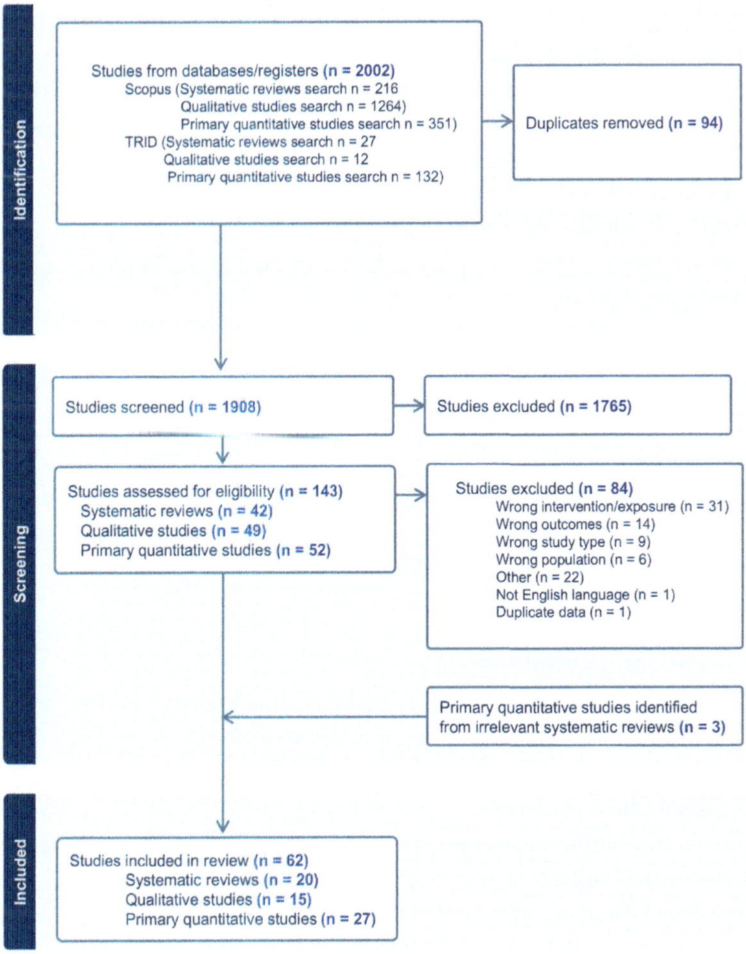

Fig. 2 PRISMA flow diagram.

screening after duplicate removal. After screening titles and abstracts, 143 studies were assessed for full-text eligibility. Following selection we included 20 systematic reviews, 15 qualitative studies, and 24 primary quantitative studies from database searches. We identified a further three primary studies from systematic reviews that didn't meet our inclusion criteria. This gave a total of 62 included studies. The characteristics of included studies are provided in Table 1.

3.2 Study quality

Of the 62 total studies, 48 were rated as moderate or high risk of bias. Weaknesses of the included studies included the use of multi-component interventions that didn't isolate the effects of the intervention, the use of cross-sectional designs that cannot provide conclusions on the directionality of effects, small sample sizes, self-reported (rather than objectively measured) exposure/outcome measures, lack of comparability with control groups, and inadequate accounting for the influence of confounding factors.

3.3 Main findings by health pathway

This section summarizes the quantitative and qualitative evidence for the following pathways:

- Access and social inclusion
- Physical activity
- Road travel injuries
- Personal safety
- Environmental exposures, air quality and greenhouse gas emissions
- Noise
- Health and wellbeing outcomes
- Health equity

3.3.1 Access and social inclusion

We found 2 systematic reviews, 6 primary quantitative studies and 15 qualitative studies on this pathway

3.3.1.1 Quantitative evidence

Bus use, better service provision or increased affordability (e.g. free bus travel) facilitated access to services and opportunities (Abe et al., 2023; Carney, 2021; Green et al., 2014; Hopson et al., 2022; Perez-Barbosa and Zhang, 2017; Starbird et al., 2018; Whitley et al., 2019) and was associated with lower odds of experiencing social isolation (Jackson et al., 2019).

Table 1 Summary of included study characteristics for each health pathway (number of studies for each in brackets).

Included studies	Contexts/settings	Populations	Intervention/ exposures	Methods	Outcomes	Risk of bias
Access and social inclusion						
2 systematic reviews (Hopson et al., 2022; Starbird et al., 2018)	26 Primary studies published 1947–2021, MICs and HICs (Hopson et al., 2022) 10 Primary studies published 1992 – 2014, all HICs (Starbird et al., 2018).	Children and adolescents (Hopson et al., 2022) Adults and adults with chronic health conditions (Starbird et al., 2018).	Bus travel to school (Hopson et al., 2022) Multicomponent interventions including transport (Starbird et al., 2018).	Narrative synthesis (Hopson et al., 2022; Starbird et al., 2018)	School attendance, academic achievement (Hopson et al., 2022) Healthcare utilization and chronic disease outcomes (Starbird et al., 2018).	Moderate (1) High (1)
6 Primary quantitative studies (Abe et al., 2023; Carney, 2021; Green et al., 2014; Jackson et al., 2019; Perez-Barbosa and Zhang, 2017; Whitley et al., 2019)	HIC (4) MIC (2)	Young people (2) Adults (1) Older people (3)	Free bus pass (3), number of weekday buses (1), minimum travel (1), travel mode choice (1), travel time to school (1).	Cross-sectional (4) CBA (1) Non-randomized experimental (1)	Perception of social isolation (1), frequency or likelihood of participation in social clubs, retail area, work, healthcare, education (5)	Moderate (5) High (1)

(continued)

Table 1 Summary of included study characteristics for each health pathway (number of studies for each in brackets). (*cont'd*)

Included studies	Contexts/settings	Populations	Intervention/exposures	Methods	Outcomes	Risk of bias
15 qualitative studies (Aceves-González et al., 2015; Alhassan et al., 2021, 2023; Del Rio et al., 2017; Goodman et al., 2013; Jahangir et al., 2021; Joseph et al., 2023; Lewinson et al., 2017; Mah and Mitra, 2017; Morris et al., 2017; Premkumar et al., 2024; Rambaldini-Gooding et al., 2022; Santana Palacios et al., 2020; Stafford and Tye, 2023; Stjernborg, 2024)	HICs (9) MICs (6)	Bus users, residents and key informants (7) Women (1) Older people (5) Young people (1) Disabled people (1)	Bus systems	Interviews (5) Focus groups (3) Combined methods (5) Observations (1) Online survey (1)	Experiences/observations	High (1) Moderate (9) Low (5)

Physical Activity

One systematic review (Delgado-Ron et al., 2000)	14 Primary studies published 2009 - 2018, MICs and HICs. Only 2 about PA	Bus users	Fixed-gateway transport systems (trains or buses)	Narrative synthesis	PA	Low
15 primary quantitative studies (Bartels et al., 2016; Collins and Agarwal, 2015; Grisé et al., 2019; Lemoine et al., 2016; Sharman et al., 2024; Webb et al., 2016)	12 HICs 3 MICs	Adults (8) Adults >59 years (6) Young people <18 years (1)	Free bus travel (6) BRT (3) Transport mode (6) Comparators were non-bus users/other transport modes (5), people without free bus travel (2), before-intervention (1), young adults (1), no comparator (5).	Cross-sectional (14) CBA (1)	Self-report PA (11) Objectively measured PA (2) Objectively measured walking distance (1) Self-reported number of walking trips (1).	High (4) Moderate (8) Low (4)

(continued)

Table 1 Summary of included study characteristics for each health pathway (number of studies for each in brackets). (*cont'd*)

Included studies	Contexts/settings	Populations	Intervention/ exposures	Methods	Outcomes	Risk of bias
Road travel injuries						
Two systematic reviews (Crizzle et al., 2017; Yendra et al., 2024)	41 Primary studies published 2004 – 2023, global (Yendra et al., 2024) Primary studies published 2000–2016, four studies on bus drivers (Crizzle et al., 2017)	Bus users, wider community (Yendra et al., 2024) and bus drivers (Crizzle et al., 2017)	Bus stop/built environment characteristics, road features, road users' behavior (Yendra et al., 2024) and occupational factors (Crizzle et al., 2017)	Narrative synthesis (Crizzle et al., 2017; Yendra et al., 2024)	Crashes, injuries, fatalities (Crizzle et al., 2017; Yendra et al., 2024)	High (2)
One primary quantitative study (Green et al., 2014)	UK (HIC)	Young people (<18 years)	Free bus travel	CBA	Road travel injury	Moderate
Five qualitative studies (Aceves-González et al., 2015; Del Rio et al., 2017; La et al., 2016; Morris et al., 2017; Nævestad et al., 2022)	HIC (5) MIC (6)	Mixed populations of bus users, bus drivers, key informants (5), Bus users (2), Women (2), Older people (3)	Bus systems	Semi structured interviews (4) Focus groups (2), mixed data collection (7)	Experiences/ observations	High (1), Moderate (9) Low (2)

Personal safety						
One primary quantitative study (Green et al., 2014)	UK (HIC)	Young people (<18 years)	Free bus travel	CBA	Road travel injury	Moderate
Twelve qualitative studies (Aceves-González et al., 2015; Alhassan et al., 2021, 2023; Del Rio et al., 2017; García et al., 2022; Jahangir et al., 2021; Joseph et al., 2023; Morris et al., 2017; Neupane and Chesney-Lind, 2013; Niboye, 2023; Premkumar et al., 2024; Santana Palacios et al., 2020)	HIC (5) MIC (6)	Mixed populations of bus users, bus drivers, key informants (5), Bus users (2), Women (2), Older people (3)	Bus systems	Semi structured interviews (4) Focus groups (2), mixed data collection (7)	Experiences/ observations	High (1), Moderate (9) Low (2)

(continued)

Table 1 Summary of included study characteristics for each health pathway (number of studies for each in brackets). (*cont'd*)

Included studies	Contexts/settings	Populations	Intervention/exposures	Methods	Outcomes	Risk of bias
Environmental exposures, air pollution and greenhouse gases						
Three systematic reviews (Cepeda et al., 2017; Ramel-Delobel et al., 2024; Singh et al., 2021)	Between 20–110 primary studies, published 1995–2022 Global	Bus users or drivers. Comparators: pedestrians and cyclists (Cepeda et al., 2017; Ramel-Delobel et al., 2024) or different transport modes (Singh et al., 2021)	Black Carbon (BC), course particulate matter (PM_{10}, $PM_{2.5}$), Ultrafine particles (UFP), Carbon monoxide (CO), Nitrous oxide (NO_2)	Meta-analysis (Cepeda et al., 2017; Ramel-Delobel et al., 2024) Narrative synthesis (Singh et al., 2021)	Exposure levels and inhalation dose (Cepeda et al., 2017; Singh et al., 2021). Exposure levels only (Ramel-Delobel et al., 2024)	Moderate (2) High (1)
One primary quantitative study (Kim et al., 2018)	HIC	Female non-smokers	Tobacco smoke	Cross-sectional	Urinary cotinine concentration	High

Noise pollution						
One systematic review (Kumari et al., 2024)	18 Primary studies, published 2002–2023. MICs (18) HIC (1).	Communities and businesses near bus terminals.	Noise pollution	Narrative synthesis	Noise levels at bus terminals	High
Health and wellbeing outcomes						
One systematic review (Delgado-Ron et al., 2000)	HIC	Bus users	BRT use	Narrative synthesis	Self-reported health and wellbeing	Low
Nine primary quantitative studies (Besser et al., 2020; Jackson et al., 2019; Laverty et al., 2018; Liu et al., 2020; Reinhard et al., 2018; Tao et al., 2019; Webb et al., 2016; Yin et al., 2024; Zamudio et al., 2015)	UK (4), East Asia (4) and Peru (1).	Older people (4) Adults (5)	Free bus travel (5) Commuting mode (4)	Cross-sectional (8) Case-control (1)	Objectively measured healthy weight/adiposity (5) Tuberculosis (1) Self-reported health and wellbeing (3)	High (3) Moderate (4) Low (2)

(continued)

Table 1 Summary of included study characteristics for each health pathway (number of studies for each in brackets). (*cont'd*)

Included studies	Contexts/settings	Populations	Intervention/ exposures	Methods	Outcomes	Risk of bias
Seven systematic reviews (Akinlotan and Drewry, 2024; Boffetta and Silverman, 2001; Cardoso and Matos, 2017; Cendales et al., 2024; Crizzle et al., 2017; Lawin et al., 2018; Reulen et al., 2015)	Between 20–130 primary studies, published 1968–2023 HICs (Boffetta and Silverman, 2001; Crizzle et al., 2017) Upper-MICs (Akinlotan and Drewry, 2024; Kim et al., 2018; Lawin et al., 2018) Global (Cendales et al., 2024) Not stated (Cardoso and Matos, 2017)	Bus drivers. Three reviews (Boffetta and Silverman, 2001; Lawin et al., 2018; Reulen et al., 2015) included non-exposed occupations or a different exposed population as comparators	Bus-driver occupation	Meta-analysis (Boffetta and Silverman, 2001; Lawin et al., 2018; Reulen et al., 2015). Narrative synthesis (Akinlotan and Drewry, 2024; Cardoso and Matos, 2017; Cendales et al., 2024; Crizzle et al., 2017).	Bladder cancer incidence (Boffetta and Silverman, 2001; Reulen et al., 2015). Pollutant exposure, health and disease outcomes (Lawin et al., 2018) Safety, health and mental health outcomes (Akinlotan and Drewry, 2024; Cardoso and Matos, 2017; Cendales et al., 2024; Crizzle et al., 2017).	High (6) Low (1)

Health equity

One primary quantitative study (Patterson et al., 2018)	HIC	Older people by ethnic group	Free bus pass	Cross-sectional	Bus use, active travel, walking 3+ times/week	Low
Seven qualitative studies (Alhassan et al., 2021, 2023; García et al., 2022; Premkumar et al., 2024; Neupane and Chesney-Lind, 2013; Niboye, 2023; Stafford and Tye, 2023)	HIC (4), MIC (3)	Women (3) Disabled people (1) Bus users, bus drivers, key informants (3)	Bus systems	Semi structured interviews (2) Mixed data collection methods (7)	Experiences/ observations	Moderate (4) Low (3)

Note: Classification of country income levels were made using the World Bank 2024–2025 ratings. HIC=high income country; MIC=middle income country CBA=controlled before and after, BRT=bus rapid transit, PA=physical activity

Examples included healthcare, schools, retail, or social participation (e.g. attendance at social clubs, leisure/hobbies). Multicomponent interventions that made bus travel more accessible or affordable (e.g. bus tickets mailed, bus travel reimbursed) were related to improvements in healthcare utilization and chronic disease management outcomes (e.g. blood pressure, cholesterol and diabetes control) (Starbird et al., 2018). Compared to older adults without a bus pass, there was a threefold increase in weekly travel for shopping and access to services when bus travel changed from half price to free, and significantly decreased odds following the withdrawal of free bus travel (Whitley et al., 2019).

Relationships between bus use, access and social participation are complex due to several inter-related reasons, which are confounded with sociodemographic factors (e.g. age, economic status). Reasons include whether individuals are travelling for necessary purposes or choosing to travel for better opportunities or leisure reasons (Green et al., 2014; Hopson et al., 2022; Perez-Barbosa and Zhang, 2017), whether other preferred travel options are available, the level of rurality/isolation of locations, and the length of journey times. For example, compared with urban students, there were poorer academic outcomes and perceived affordability of travel to school for students in rural or isolated areas with no alternative transport, long walks to the bus stop, long waits for the bus and/or long journey times to school (Hopson et al., 2022; Perez-Barbosa and Zhang, 2017).

Using the bus for access to opportunities and amenities, particularly when it was made more accessible or affordable, was associated with greater likelihood of engagement in social activities, accessing a larger area of retail activity, lower odds of feeling socially isolated, and better academic outcomes (Abe et al., 2023; Carney, 2021; Hopson et al., 2022; Jackson et al., 2019; Whitley et al., 2019). However, living in a less densely populated area, and being dependent on buses, was related to lower satisfaction with frequency of social participation (e.g. getting help from close family when needed, going to a park) (Perez-Barbosa and Zhang, 2017). There was no greater benefit from bus travel if individuals could access opportunities and leisure/recreation by other modes, particularly walking or cycling (Abe et al., 2023; Hopson et al., 2022; Perez-Barbosa and Zhang, 2017).

3.3.1.2 Qualitative evidence

A summary of main findings from the meta-synthesis of qualitative studies is provided in Table 2. Five main themes described how and why buses

Table 2 Qualitative meta-synthesis with summary of main findings.

References	Health pathway	Theme	Sub-theme (s)	Contributing factors	Main findings summary
Del Rio et al. (2017), Jahangir et al. (2021), Joseph et al. (2023), Lewinson et al. (2017), Rambaldini-Gooding et al., 2022, Santana Palacios et al. (2020), Stjernborg, (2024)	Access and social inclusion	Experiences of poor-quality bus services		Journey and waiting times Reliability and convenience Routes/service provision Overcrowding	Features of poor-quality services include: lack of connectivity to where people live and need to go, being overly complex, lack of availability at peak/early/late times of day, unreliability, lack of direct routes, overcrowding (messier, noisier, chaotic on-board conditions), inconvenient, expensive (particularly multi-trip journeys), insufficient seating, isolated stops/stations, desolate, drab, bare environments, lack of security and surveillance, poor lighting. Consequences: stress and physical discomfort, feeling unsafe, feelings of instability and inability to meet life's demands, longer travel times meaning less free time. Poor quality services resulted in reduced bus travel and participation in life. To be a preferred travel mode, bus services need to be as convenient, fast, reliable, comfortable, safe, available, affordable, and useful as other transport modes and connect to where people live and with other modes.

(continued)

Table 2 Qualitative meta-synthesis with summary of main findings. (*cont'd*)

References	Health pathway	Theme	Sub-theme (s)	Contributing factors	Main findings summary
Alhassan et al. (2021, 2023), Del Rio et al. (2017), Goodman et al. (2013), Jahangir et al. (2021), Lewinson et al. (2017), Morris et al. (2017), Rambaldini-Gooding et al. (2022), Stafford and Tye (2023)	Access and social inclusion	Social Connections	(a) Better social connections (b) Social isolation/feel marginalized	Bus use Affordability Reliability and convenience Routes/service provision Journey and waiting times Bus vehicle factors	Affordable and reliable bus services help to generate and maintain social connections and friendships, particularly for people of low socioeconomic status. Conversely, cost and unreliable services as barriers to bus use led to experiences of social isolation or loss of connections to friends or family, or social groups. More precarious journeys, inadequate service provision, longer journey times, and longer waiting times reduced social participation. More accessible buses (e.g. priority seating, handrails, designated space for older people, disabled people and prams) help sustain social connections. Conversely, cognitive/physical/digital inaccessibility reduced ability to participate in social activities.
Aceves-González et al. (2015), Alhassan et al. (2021, 2023), Goodman et al. (2013), Premkumar et al. (2024), Mah and Mitra (2017), Morris et al. (2017),	Access and social inclusion	Freedom/independence	(a) Access to recreation/non-necessary journey (b) Mobility independence (c) Empowerment	Bus use Affordability Routes/service provision Reliability/convenience Service information	Increased affordability of bus use facilitated freedom to make journeys for recreational, leisure or non-necessary purposes. Cost of the bus or needing to rely on others' time and resources were barriers to recreational activities and feelings of independence. The ability to travel without worrying about cost increased autonomy, independence and feelings of

Stafford and Tye (2023)			(d) Save money for other things	Bus vehicle factors	empowerment. Money saved by free bus travel allowed more financial freedom and ability to prioritize other health and social needs. Lack of accessible service information, long wait times, and needing to change buses were perceived as barriers to mobility. Cognitive, physical or digital accessibility challenges included obstructions, lack of handrails, boarding and alighting difficulties, driver and other passenger behavior, complex navigation, and lack of information to plan travel. Bus routes and services directly affected healthcare access. Infrequent buses or loss of bus services reduced access to recreational and leisure activities, causing a sense of dispossession
Goodman et al. (2013)	Access and social inclusion	Capabilities/skills/confidence		Affordability	Free bus travel for young people (<18 years old) allowed them to develop capabilities and confidence to travel independently. This was partly from having a 'safety net' so they wouldn't be 'stranded' if they had no money or got lost.

(continued)

Table 2 Qualitative meta-synthesis with summary of main findings. *(cont'd)*

References	Health pathway	Theme	Sub-theme (s)	Contributing factors	Main findings summary
Alhassan et al. (2021, 2023), Del Rio et al. (2017), Jahangir et al. (2021), Joseph et al. (2023), Lewinson et al. (2017), Santana Palacios et al. (2020)	Access and social inclusion	Access to services, health and opportunities		Bus use Affordability Journey and waiting times Routes/service provision Bus vehicle factors Congestion Other transport options	More costly and inflexible bus fares were a barrier to accessing economic and employment opportunities, necessary amenities and healthcare. Free bus travel increased access to opportunities including education and better employment, further facilitating financial independence. Removing cost barriers facilitates access to healthcare, amenities (e.g. markets, food, library), and promoted PA and better mental wellbeing. More accessible buses (e.g. providing priority seating, handrails, designated space for older people, disabled people and prams), improved access to healthcare appointments. Access to economic opportunities, healthcare and services were limited by more precarious and unreliable journeys, inadequate service provision, longer journey times, longer waiting times, congestion, system complexity and lack of connectivity. The removal of community bus services led to missed health appointments and foregone treatments, and forced car ownership. Other transport options were preferred if they were more convenient with better connectivity and access to economic opportunities, healthcare and services.

Aceves-González et al. (2015), Alhassan et al. (2021, 2023), Del Rio et al. (2017), García et al. (2022), Jahangir et al. (2021), Joseph et al. (2023), Morris et al. (2017), Neupane and Chesney-Lind (2013), Niboye (2023), Santana Palacios et al. (2020)	Personal safety	Personal Safety –Harassment and crime, risk behaviors	(a) Perceived safety (b) Actual safety	Bus use Routes/service provision Overcrowding Environmental factors	Negative impacts of bus use included lack of safety for women. Bus use and overcrowding were perceived to contribute to actual and feared harassment and crime. Buses were considered a convenient/risk free setting for perpetrators due to overcrowding and anonymity. Women, racially marginalized groups and older people were more likely to experience harassment and verbal abuse, with women also experiencing physical and sexual abuse. Harassment and unwanted touching were perpetrated by conductors and other passengers. More security and services provided at early or late times of the day were perceived to reduce likelihood of crime. Environmental features contributing to feelings of insecurity and unsafety were: isolated stops/stations (e.g. design and distances between stations/bus stops), desolate, drab, bare environments, lack of security and surveillance, poor lighting, travelling at night. Positive impacts of bus use on safety included reducing risky behaviors among young people.

(continued)

Table 2 Qualitative meta-synthesis with summary of main findings. (*cont'd*)

References	Health pathway	Theme	Sub-theme (s)	Contributing factors	Main findings summary
La et al. (2016), Nævestad et al. (2022), Stjernborg (2024)	Road travel injuries	Safety – Crashes and injuries	(a) Crashes (b) Injury	Bus vehicle factors Bus drivers Bus company regulation/ monitoring Road/transport environment Human factors	Bus use was perceived to increase road and pedestrian safety. Crashes were perceived to be more likely due to large buses (occupancy of lanes for motorcycles and pedestrians, blocked vision), poor safety conditions of buses and motorcycles, and road and environmental factors (e.g. poor transport infrastructure, weak law enforcement), and unsafe driving behaviors of others. Bus vehicle features that were perceived to contribute to falls or injuries for older people included: navigating boarding and alighting, prevention of steady walking, pushing and shoving caused by overcrowding. Features perceived to reduce risk of injuries were: lower bus floor, handrails, priority seating. Bus drivers' perceptions and behaviors perceived to contribute to crashes and injuries were: attitude toward safe driving, confidence in skills, heavy workloads, hostile behaviors and drink driving (of both bus drivers and other drivers).

					Bus drivers waiting for less mobile people to be seated before departing were perceived to reduce risk and fear of injuries. The rules, regulations, monitoring and oversight, safety culture, and service priority (e.g. cash flow, sustainability) of bus transit operators were perceived to impact likelihood of crashes and safety.
Alhassan et al. (2021, 2023), García et al. (2022), Premkumar et al. (2024), Neupane and Chesney-Lind (2013), Niboye (2023), Stafford and Tye (2023)	Health equity	Health equity	(a) Impacts of increased or decreased access to bus services (b) Impacts of harassment (c) Impacts of inaccessible buses	Affordability Routes/service provision Bus vehicle factors	The themes identified above impact more vulnerable people disproportionately. These differential impacts are summarized within this health equity theme. The impacts of harassment and gender violence were psychological (e.g. fear, distress), economic (e.g. thefts), physical (e.g. injuries), disempowerment, reductions in travel, denials, minimization, and victim blaming. Increasing affordability of buses for women in highly patriarchal cultures contributed to strategic empowerment by facilitating access to social and economic opportunities. While one negative impact was experiencing poor treatment from male passengers and bus drivers who disliked the scheme, positive impacts were: increased financial and mobility

(continued)

Table 2 Qualitative meta-synthesis with summary of main findings. (*cont'd*)

References	Health pathway	Theme	Sub-theme (s)	Contributing factors	Main findings summary
					independence and increased feelings of safety due to greater number of female passengers. The removal of an essential bus service caused decreased feelings of freedom, perceived safety and loss of access to social determinants of health. These impacts were disproportionately experienced by those living in rural/isolated areas, marginalized groups who are more vulnerable to crime and harassment, people with poorer mental health, people experiencing poverty, and disabled people. Physically and cognitively inaccessible bus services disproportionately impact older and disabled peoples' ability to be independently mobile – causing forced immobility due to inequity and exclusion throughout the transport system.

influence access and social inclusion: social connections; freedom/independence; capabilities/skills/confidence; access to services, health and opportunities; and experiences of (user-defined) poor-quality services. These themes largely converged with, and supplemented, the quantitative evidence.

While people perceived good quality bus services as facilitating access and social participation, poor-quality bus services created barriers to access and social participation. Negative experiences of the bus were caused by poor-quality service characteristics including: complexity, unavailability, unaffordability, inconvenience, unreliability, lacking connectivity and poor on-board or bus-stop conditions (Del Rio et al., 2017; Jahangir et al., 2021; Joseph et al., 2023; Lewinson et al., 2017; Rambaldini-Gooding et al., 2022; Santana Palacios et al., 2020; Stjernborg, 2024). These negative experiences included mental and physical discomfort, lack of perceived safety, less leisure time and inability to meet life's demands.

Greater feelings of freedom, autonomy, and empowerment were realized through: access to recreation and ability to make non-necessary journeys; mobility independence; and financial independence (Aceves-González et al., 2015; Alhassan et al., 2021, 2023; Goodman et al., 2013; Premkumar et al., 2024; Mah and Mitra, 2017; Morris et al., 2017; Stafford and Tye, 2023). More affordable, frequent, reliable, accessible bus services facilitated better social connections, greater freedom and access to education, employment, skills development, amenities and healthcare (Alhassan et al., 2021, 2023; Jahangir et al., 2021; Joseph et al., 2023; Lewinson et al., 2017; Santana Palacios et al., 2020). Free bus passes were perceived as providing a 'pass' to social relationships and social support, primarily through access to places to socialize, but also opportunities for socializing at bus stops and on buses (Goodman et al., 2013; Mah and Mitra, 2017). Free bus travel allowed people to travel without worry of financial strain and to prioritize spending on other health and social needs (Goodman et al., 2013; Premkumar et al., 2024; Mah and Mitra, 2017; Morris et al., 2017). Barriers to accessing opportunities, amenities and health care were bus services that were costly and unreliable, longer waiting and journey times, and lack of connectivity with places and other transport modes. Bus services that were cognitively/physically/digitally inaccessible, or lacked adequate provision, resulted in reduced access to leisure and social spaces, social isolation, feelings of dispossession and forced immobility (Alhassan et al., 2021, 2023; Del Rio et al., 2017; Lewinson et al., 2017; Stafford and Tye 2023).

3.3.2 Physical activity

One systematic review, 15 primary quantitative and no qualitative studies assessed associations with physical activity.

3.3.2.1 Quantitative findings

People who used the bus undertook physical activity (PA) as part of their journey, but estimates of PA gains varied widely (Bartels et al., 2016; Besser et al., 2020; Collins and Agarwal, 2015; Delgado-Ron et al., 2000; Du et al., 2022; Grisé et al., 2019; Jackson et al., 2019; Laverty et al., 2018; Lemoine et al., 2016; Patterson, et al., 2018; Patterson, et al., 2018; Sharman et al., 2024; Webb et al., 2016). Observational evidence found varying minutes or distances walked on days with bus travel (Bartels et al., 2016; Collins and Agarwal, 2015; Delgado-Ron et al., 2000; Du et al., 2022; Evans et al., 2024; Grisé et al., 2019; Lemoine et al., 2016; Patterson et al., 2019) and that more frequent bus users were more likely to walk (Besser et al., 2020). In some cases, this increased the likelihood of reaching daily PA targets of 30 min per day (Bartels et al., 2016; Collins and Agarwal, 2015; Delgado-Ron et al., 2000; Grisé et al., 2019; Lemoine et al., 2016; Patterson et al., 2018). Active travel as part of bus use contributed to greater overall PA levels (Bartels et al., 2016; Collins and Agarwal, 2015; Du et al., 2022). Though, where buses were less reliable with longer commute times, it was suggested that bus commuters had less free time for PA than other commuters (Yin, et al., 2024).

Some observational evidence found that bus travel is associated with more commuting and total PA than passive modes (i.e. cars), but less than other public transport modes such as trains or subway (Collins and Agarwal, 2015; Du et al., 2022; Grisé et al., 2019; Patterson et al., 2018; Yin et al., 2024). This may partly be explained by the distance needed to travel to access public transport, but the relationships may not be linear. For example, shorter average distances to bus stops than train and subway stops resulted in less PA by bus users, and a reduced walking distance of 5.7 m for every increase in number of bus stops (Grisé et al., 2019). Conversely, those who lived within 1 km of a Bus Rapid Transit (BRT) stop were twice as likely to achieve PA guidelines compared to those living further than 1 km from a stop (Bartels et al., 2016). One study reported decreased walking distances with more mode transfers (Grisé et al., 2019). Another reported increased steps walked with increased number of bus trips per day but also increased sedentary time (Evans et al., 2024). These differences may reflect differences in the distance individuals are willing to walk to reach public transport or their preference for walking to make fewer transfers.

Compared to controls, working adults and older adults with free bus passes made more bus journeys and were more physically active (Jackson et al., 2019; Laverty et al., 2018; Patterson et al., 2018; Sharman et al., 2024; Webb et al., 2016). However, observational study designs make the direction of causality uncertain, as more physically active people may be more likely to use their free bus pass. One exception is a study that demonstrated increased odds of engaging in more PA four years after becoming eligible for a free bus pass, even after accounting for baseline levels of PA (Laverty et al., 2018).

A controlled before-and-after study (Green et al., 2014) assessing free bus travel for young people (<18 years old) found that introduction of free bus travel was not associated with increases in PA overall. There was a relative decrease in the number and proportion of cycling trips and short walking trips and distances cycled in 12–17 year olds compared to 18–25 year-old controls. However, there was no change in total walking distances compared to before the introduction of free bus travel. This may partly be explained by modal shift in young people from active travel to bus use.

3.3.3 Road travel injuries

We identified 2 systematic reviews, 1 primary quantitative study and 5 qualitative studies on injury. Most of these considered the factors that increased or reduced the risk of road collision or injury on, or waiting for, a bus.

3.3.3.1 Quantitative findings

Factors identified that influenced road collisions were: road design, infrastructure design, bus-stop design and location, occupational factors for bus drivers, and mode choice (Crizzle et al., 2017; Green et al., 2014; Yendra et al., 2024). Pedestrian safety, in terms of bus driver awareness and reduced fatal crashes, improved with clear signage and road markings (e.g. vehicle stop signs at unsignalized junctions, rumble strips) and pedestrian crossings (e.g. presence of zebra marking) (Yendra et al., 2024). Pedestrian-vehicle crashes were reduced where footpaths had even surfaces and were sufficiently wide, continuous and unobstructed. Poorer pedestrian safety (e.g. more vehicle-pedestrian crashes) was associated with bus stops on a gradient, lack of median islands providing refuge for pedestrians crossing the road, wide roads or multiple lanes, blocked visibility and mixed vehicle traffic (Yendra et al., 2024). More pedestrian fatalities were associated with absent, obstructed or poor-quality bus shelters and absent or poor lighting conditions. Bus stops located near areas of high pedestrian activity or on high-speed roads were associated with more crashes. Bus-stop configurations, in relation to intersections, and bus-stop geometric design (e.g. safety of curbside vs bus bay stops) may also influence pedestrian safety but evidence was inconclusive.

Crash rates were higher under certain bus driver occupational conditions including: negative experiences with, or distractions by, passengers; driving route layout (e.g. narrow travel lanes, non-routine routes); vehicle design (e.g. blind spots from pillars, posts and mirrors); and fatigue (Crizzle et al., 2017). Additionally, being younger, more distracted, driving at a higher speed, and experiencing more stress contributed to near-misses or crashes.

A controlled before-and-after study (Green et al., 2014) compared trends among 12–17-year-olds and 18–25 year olds before and after introduction of free bus travel for young people under 18. Following the introduction, it found a relative decline in road injuries, cycling injuries, and car-occupant injuries among 12–17 year olds, compared to the trend in 18–25 year olds. There was no relative reduction in pedestrian injuries.

3.3.3.2 Qualitative findings

Converging with quantitative evidence, factors that were considered to contribute to crashes included bus vehicle factors, bus drivers, bus company regulations (e.g. monitoring and oversight, safety culture, and service priorities), road/transport environment (e.g. poor road infrastructure), and human factors (Aceves-González et al., 2015; La et al., 2016; Morris et al., 2017; Nævestad et al., 2022). Bus use was perceived to increase pedestrian safety (Del Rio et al., 2017). Factors that were considered to contribute to injuries occurring from falls were bus vehicle factors (e.g. ease of boarding and alighting, lower bus floor, handrails, priority seating), overcrowding, and bus drivers (e.g. skills, attitudes).

3.3.4 Personal safety

We identified no systematic reviews, one primary quantitative study and 12 qualitative studies on perceptions and experiences of harassment, abuse and assault.

3.3.4.1 Quantitative findings

The study of free bus travel for young people (Green et al., 2014) found slightly increased odds of being a victim of assault for 12–17-year-olds compared to 18–25-year-olds during the study period. The authors attributed this to a local secular trend as the highest increase had occurred before the introduction of free bus travel (Green et al., 2014).

3.3.4.2 Qualitative findings

Bus use factors such as routes/service provision, overcrowding, and environmental factors contributed to perceived and actual personal safety (Aceves-González et al., 2015; Alhassan et al., 2021, 2023; Del Rio et al., 2017; García, et al., 2022; Jahangir et al., 2021; Joseph et al., 2023; Morris et al., 2017; Neupane and Chesney-Lind, 2013; Niboye, 2023; Premkumar et al., 2024; Santana Palacios et al., 2020). Women, racially marginalized groups and older people reported experiencing harassment and verbal abuse, with women additionally experiencing physical and sexual abuse. Buses, particularly when overcrowded, were perceived to facilitate harassment, violence and other crimes by providing perpetrators with anonymity and enclosed access to potential victims (Jahangir et al., 2021; Niboye, 2023; Premkumar et al., 2024). Contributing factors to perceptions of safety at bus stops were: lack of security and surveillance, isolated or desolate conditions, poor lighting, and travelling at night (García et al., 2022; Niboye, 2023). Conversely, bus use was considered to reduce risk behaviors in young people (Del Rio et al., 2017).

3.3.5 Environmental exposures, air pollution and greenhouse gases

We included three systematic reviews and one primary quantitative study, but no qualitative studies on environmental exposures. These mostly compared exposure to air pollutants by mode. We found no studies of the impact of buses on greenhouse gas emissions.

3.3.5.1 Quantitative findings

Evidence was identified comparing exposure for bus users to active travelers (cyclists and pedestrians) but there was a lack of comparison to other modes. Bus users may be at increased risk of exposure to course particles (PM_{10} and $PM_{2.5}$) and may be at decreased risk of exposure to ultrafine particles compared to pedestrians and cyclists, but evidence was inconclusive (Cepeda et al., 2017; Ramel-Delobel et al., 2024). Bus users are at increased risk of exposure to carbon monoxide and nitrogen dioxide compared to cyclists (Cepeda et al., 2017; Ramel-Delobel et al., 2024). Bus users may be at increased risk of exposure to carbon monoxide and nitrogen dioxide compared to pedestrians, but evidence was inconclusive (Cepeda et al., 2017; Ramel-Delobel et al., 2024). There was no difference in exposure to black carbon between bus users and cyclists or pedestrians (Cepeda et al., 2017).

In terms of effects of air pollutants combined, evidence from a review of mostly European studies reported combined air pollution exposure was greatest for car and bus commuters, followed by commuters in a car with controlled ventilation settings, cyclists, and pedestrians (Cepeda et al., 2017). However, the difference in exposure for bus users compared to cyclists and pedestrians was not significant (Cepeda et al., 2017). Evidence from a review of studies of mostly Asian contexts reported that closed transport modes (car, bus, and metro) had lower concentration levels than open transport modes (motorcycle, cycling and walking), measured by particle penetration rate (Singh et al., 2021). Inhalation and uptake of pollutants were greatest for active travelers compared to other modes (including buses), due to respiration rates and trip times (Cepeda et al., 2017; Singh et al., 2021). Regardless of differences in relative risk of exposure for bus users compared to other modes, evidence consistently found that ambient levels of carbon monoxide, nitrogen dioxide, fine and coarse particles exceed air quality standards (Cepeda et al., 2017; Ramel-Delobel et al., 2024; Singh et al., 2021).

Contextual factors that modified the exposure and inhalation rates of travelers included proximity to vehicle exhausts and density of environment (Singh et al., 2021). There is some evidence that average exposures are similar across modes (e.g. walking, cycling, bus, taxi) in dense environments and that segregated paths and lanes for pedestrians, cyclists and bus commuters reduces exposure to air pollution (Singh et al., 2021). Air-conditioning in both cars and buses, and closing bus windows, reduced exposure (Singh et al., 2021).

A cross-sectional study (Kim et al., 2018) of non-smoking women in South Korea found no robust association between travel mode and environmental tobacco exposure (measured by urinary cotinine concentration).

3.3.6 Noise pollution

We identified one systematic review on noise at bus terminuses, but no primary quantitative or qualitative studies.

The systematic review (Kumari et al., 2024) identified sources of noise as bus engines, conductors, passengers, music from stores within bus terminuses, other vehicles, sirens, construction, loudspeakers, and horns. Noise at bus terminals at nearly all sites exceeded permissible levels, ranging from 47.8 dB(A) to 98.65 dB, compared to permissible levels of 60–85 dB(A). The potential health impacts of exceeded noise levels were not explored.

3.3.7 Health and wellbeing outcomes

We identified one systematic review and nine primary quantitative studies on health outcomes for bus users and seven systematic reviews of health outcomes for bus-related occupation. No qualitative studies were identified.

3.3.7.1 Bus user findings

Outcomes studied included healthy weight, self-reported health and wellbeing, and tuberculosis.

Five studies (Laverty et al., 2018; Liu et al., 2020; Tao et al., 2019; Webb et al., 2016; Yin et al., 2024) examined the association between bus travel and objectively measured healthy weight/adiposity, with conflicting findings. Two studies conducted in the same population of UK older adults found that free bus travel was not associated with BMI or waist circumference in men (Laverty et al., 2018; Webb et al., 2016). One of these was a cross-sectional study that found an association between having a free bus pass and faster gait speed, lower BMI, and smaller waist circumferences in women (Webb et al., 2016). However, the other longitudinal study accounting for baseline BMI, did not confirm this relationship (Laverty et al., 2018). Conversely, a study conducted in China (Liu et al., 2020) found some evidence of lower odds of overall obesity or abdominal obesity in men who used the bus compared to car or taxi, but no differences in women. However, the findings were not robust when adjusted for exposure to different air pollutants (Liu et al., 2020). Two further studies conducted in China had contradictory findings. One demonstrated an association between bus commuting and reduced odds of dyslipidemia and unhealthy cholesterol profile compared to other commute modes (Tao et al., 2019), and another reported that bus commuters had higher BMIs than those commuting by other transport modes (Yin et al., 2024). Overall, there is a lack of convergent evidence suggesting a relationship between bus use or free bus travel and healthy weight/adiposity, even accounting for different contextual factors.

There was some evidence of an association between bus use and self-reported health and wellbeing. There was no association between bus rapid transit (BRT) use and life satisfaction or self-reported physical and mental health (Delgado-Ron et al., 2000; Du et al., 2022). Increased bus use, resulting from free bus eligibility for older people, was associated with lower depression symptoms, higher life satisfaction and better quality of life (Jackson et al., 2019; Reinhard et al., 2018). Greater frequency of bus use was associated with better mental wellbeing (Jackson et al., 2019; Reinhard et al., 2018). The relationship between free bus pass eligibility and better wellbeing was partly explained by lower social isolation and higher levels of PA (Jackson et al., 2019).

One case-control study (Zamudio et al., 2015) in urban Peru found that regular bus/minibus users were almost 12 times more likely to have active tuberculosis than people who worked at home (Zamudio et al., 2015).

3.3.7.2 Bus-related occupation findings

Some evidence suggested bus drivers have a moderately increased risk of developing bladder cancer compared to other occupations (Boffetta and Silverman, 2001; Reulen et al., 2015). There was limited evidence of increased risk of lung cancer, bladder cancer, Hodgkins's lymphoma and mortality in bus drivers compared to controls (Lawin et al., 2018). The purported risk factors contributing to this increased risk of disease were exposure to diesel exhausts, Benzo[*a*]pyrene and carcinogenic Polycyclic Aromatic Hydrocarbons (PAHs). A review which examined this link did not find strong evidence that bus drivers are at increased risk of exposure to these risk factors compared to other occupations (Lawin et al., 2018).

There was limited evidence of high prevalence of musculoskeletal disorders (particularly neck and back pain) in bus drivers (Cardoso and Matos, 2017; Crizzle et al., 2017). Bus drivers reported that occupational factors, such as twisting when driving, seat posture and non-ergonomic conditions, contributed to musculoskeletal pain (Crizzle et al., 2017). Musculoskeletal disorders were reported to impact job performance with negative economic implications for bus drivers (Cardoso and Matos, 2017).

Two reviews examined prevalence of mental health conditions and factors contributing to poor mental health in bus drivers (Akinlotan and Drewry, 2024; Cendales et al., 2024). Drivers reported high prevalence of substance use, job stress, sleep problems, fatigue and need for recovery, burnout symptoms, post-traumatic stress disorder (PTSD), depression, anxiety, psychopathology, psychosomatic symptoms, and psychological stress (Akinlotan and Drewry, 2024; Cendales et al., 2024). These were related to poor working conditions including poor pay, precarity, long working hours and irregular shifts; occupational factors including safety culture and driving conditions; and driver-passenger interactions including offensive conduct, fare evasion and assault (Akinlotan and Drewry, 2024; Cendales et al., 2024).

3.3.8 Health equity

One primary quantitative study and seven qualitative studies identified differential impacts on population groups.

3.3.8.1 Quantitative findings

One primary quantitative study (Patterson et al., 2018) conducted in a large, representative sample of older people from England examined the differential impacts of a free bus pass on physical activity (PA) for different ethnic groups. Bus pass holders, compared to their ethnic group counterparts without a bus pass, were more likely to engage in bus use and active travel as part of a bus journey. Compared to White bus pass holders, South Asian bus pass holders were more likely to engage in active travel as part of a bus journey but less likely to engage in active travel outside of a bus journey. For those with a bus pass, the total amount of active travel accumulated (i.e. active travel as part of a bus journey and active travel not related to a bus journey) did not vary between ethnic groups. Minority ethnic groups were proportionately more likely to hold a bus pass than White people. Therefore, even accounting for factors such as socioeconomic status, holding a bus pass may be more important for facilitating active travel in South Asians than White people.

3.3.8.2 Qualitative findings

A theme from the qualitative studies was the impacts of buses on health equity (Alhassan et al., 2021, 2023; García et al., 2022; Premkumar et al., 2024; Neupane and Chesney-Lind, 2013; Niboye, 2023; Stafford and Tye, 2023). These studies examined the impacts of: increased or decreased access to bus services; harassment; and inaccessible buses for disabilities. The themes identified in the qualitative synthesis were found to disproportionately impact on vulnerable and marginalized groups. For example, while increasing affordability of buses for women improved health equity, their pervasive experience of harassment and fear contributed to inequity (Premkumar et al., 2024; Neupane and Chesney-Lind, 2013; Niboye, 2023).

The impacts of harassment and gender violence were psychological (e.g. fear, distress), economic (e.g. thefts), physical (e.g. injuries), disempowerment, reductions in travel, denial, minimization, and victim blaming. The removal of bus services can differentially impact vulnerable groups, who depend more on the bus to meet their daily and social needs (Alhassan et al., 2021, 2023). Buses that are unreliable or inaccessible for people with cognitive or physical disabilities prevent them from making journeys, greatly impacting their ability to participate in life (Stafford and Tye, 2023).

4. Discussion

4.1 Summary of findings in context

Most previous reviews have considered the impacts of all modes of public transport together. Our review focused specifically on links between buses and health, extending and adding to the previous literature. We identified and synthesized evidence on the breadth of pathways underpinning the relationship between buses and health, including positive and negative health impacts, how and why they arise, and how populations are differentially affected.

There was some evidence to support the links hypothesized in our conceptual model. Similar to past research on public transport (Anciaes and Alhassan, 2024; Goodman et al., 2013; Mah and Mitra, 2017; Musselwhite, 2017; Williams et al., 2024), bus use was associated with access to services, social participation, social connections, and less social isolation. We found some evidence of physical activity gains from walking to and from bus stops for adults and older adults, in line with previous research (Hirsch et al., 2014; Rissel et al., 2012; Xiao et al., 2019), but not for young people. Physical activity gains for bus users may be less than for other public transport users, but more than car users. The relationships between buses and access, social inclusion or physical activity varied by factors such as living in urban or rural areas and distance to bus stops.

Aligned with past research on public transport (Dilian et al., 2024; Foster et al., 2024; Janatabadi and Ermagun, 2022), subsidized bus travel was associated with better mental health outcomes, which were partly explained by reduced social isolation and increased physical activity from increased bus use. There was no association between bus use and healthy weight, despite the evidence that bus use is associated with physical activity.

The negative links between buses and health were identified as exposure to air and noise pollution, the potential for collisions and injuries, and women's experiences of harassment, on buses or at bus stops. As with past research (Singh et al., 2021), we identified contradictory findings from studies comparing air pollution exposure by mode. Bus users may have greater exposure than cyclists and pedestrians to some pollutants but not others, though inhalation and uptake of pollutants is greater for active travelers than bus users and other modes (Cepeda et al., 2017; Ramel-Delobel et al., 2024). Levels of both ambient air and noise pollution were greater than recommended safety levels (Cepeda et al., 2017; Kumari et al., 2024; Ramel-Delobel et al., 2024; Singh et al., 2021).

We found some evidence of increased odds of bladder cancer, some other cancers, musculoskeletal and mental health conditions in bus drivers. However, the evidence had a high risk of bias and the link to occupational exposure to diesel and other chemicals is unclear.

There were several common themes on how and why links between buses and health arise. The most common themes across both quantitative and qualitative evidence was the influence of affordability of bus travel (e.g. free bus travel schemes, provision vouchers or reimbursements) on physical activity, mental wellbeing, as well as access to essential services and amenities, social participation, and less social isolation. Other aspects of bus services that are important for access and inclusion include: journey length, reliability, interconnectivity with other modes, cognitive/physical accessibility and on-board conditions including overcrowding and safety. Importantly, bus services that are poor quality may contribute to barriers to access and participation. Therefore, we found some evidence that the dimensions of transport poverty (availability, reliability, affordability, accessibility, and safety) contribute to the links between buses and health. The road, transport, and built environments were also influential in how and why buses linked to physical activity, road travel injuries, personal safety, and exposure to noise and air pollution.

The impacts of contributing factors were experienced differentially, with vulnerable or marginalized populations most likely to benefit from positive impacts of improved services or affordability, but also more likely to bear negative impacts from absent, unreliable or overcrowded services. Our findings align with past research on the more pronounced impacts of public transport accessibility and quality on marginalized communities (Musselwhite, 2023).

Car culture and car-centric infrastructure are at the root of factors influencing how and why bus travel links to health. Car-centric infrastructure prioritizes traffic flow for cars and the allocation of public spaces to large road networks and parking facilities. This creates a car-dependent environment in which other modes are unavailable, inconvenient or not accommodated (Public Health Scotland, 2024). While the prioritization of car-centric infrastructure and policy has an impact on all forms of public transport, the impacts may be more pronounced for buses due to shared road infrastructure. Our findings from both quantitative and qualitative studies provide some evidence of the consequences of car-centric infrastructure for buses and the impacts on health and health inequalities.

4.2 Strengths and limitations

The breadth of pathways and types of research included in our review are both a strength and a limitation. We included quantitative and qualitative studies giving complementary evidence on the associations, how the impacts arise and some insight into how and why different populations may be differentially affected.

The breadth means we have not studied the associations for each pathway in-depth. Our rapid review methodology means that we likely have not identified all possible studies on the links between buses and health. In our search strategy, we used only bus-related search terms rather than public transport terms and we only sought primary studies for pathways where there were no systematic reviews. For pathways where we identified systematic reviews, gaps in evidence do not denote complete absence of evidence as there may be primary studies that fill the gaps. Finally, we restricted our search to English language and peer reviewed papers. Further studies, settings and perspectives may have been identified by including public transport search terms, non-English language papers, and grey literature. However, the accelerated nature of rapid reviews meant that a focused search was appropriate (Garritty et al., 2024; Klerings et al., 2023).

There are also gaps in the evidence. Most of the evidence concerns bus users or bus drivers, with few studies of impacts for wider communities. No evidence was identified on the relative contribution of buses to ambient pollution or greenhouse gas emissions. We excluded some pathways related to transport infrastructure, such as loss of greenspace and the heat island effect, because of the difficulty of attributing these impacts specifically to bus services. Our conceptual model identified occupational exposures affecting bus drivers but not the positive impacts of employment for bus drivers. There is evidence relating to some populations, such as older adults, young people and women, but less for other groups with specific transport needs, such as carers. For several pathways there is no evidence comparing bus use with other modes. We excluded modelling studies which may have provided some comparative estimates, for example for greenhouse gas emissions, and estimates of the impact of some pathways on health outcomes.

Most studies were rated as moderate or high risk of bias. Of particular note, the one systematic review that addressed noise pollution was high risk of bias and six of the seven studies on bus driver health were high risk of bias. The methodological weaknesses of the included evidence mean that conclusions on the directionality of effects and robustness of associations cannot be definitive.

4.3 Implications for policy and practice

Our findings suggest there is a need to prioritize and invest in spatial planning that is centered on sustainable transport rather than being car-centric. Sustainable transport policies aim to encourage public transport use through increased walkability, facilities (e.g. bike storage), connectivity, enhanced public transport infrastructure to improve access and travel times, as well as increased greenspace (Bozovic, 2025). Policies that are sustainable transport-oriented then may facilitate population mode shift from private car use to buses, with positive effects on transport poverty, traffic congestion, air pollution, noise and collisions affecting the wider community as well as individual travelers (Miner et al., 2024).

Specific recommendations identified from our study for bus systems that promote public health and address transport poverty are:

- Interventions to improve affordability of bus travel (like subsidized or free bus travel), particularly for low income and marginalized populations.
- Prioritize availability and frequency of bus services in communities that have less access to opportunities by other modes, such as walking or cycling.
- Infrastructure which segregates buses from other traffic to improve reliability, journey times, overcrowding and reduce exposure to collisions and air pollutants. This would benefit passengers and reduce stressors reported by bus drivers.
- Built environments that place bus stops and stations near residential areas and common trip destinations (e.g. commercial areas, employment hubs,

hospitals). Bus stops and stations should integrate links with other travel modes, particularly walking and cycling (e.g. planning should include attractive and safe footpaths and cycle lanes).

- Infrastructure that reduces risk of injuries at bus stops including clear signage, positioning footways and bus shelters to allow good visibility.
- Measures to improve personal safety could include reducing overcrowding and improved lighting and passive surveillance at bus stops/ stations.
- Buses that are physically and cognitively accessible (handrails, priority seating, digitally accessible, easy to understand routes and timetables) and are air-conditioned to reduce exposure to pollutants. Measures to avoid overcrowding and to reduce driver distraction or fatigue.
- Better ergonomic design of vehicles and improvements to working conditions including shift patterns, working hours and work culture for bus drivers to reduce musculoskeletal and mental health conditions.

4.4 Implications for research

Better quality research designs are needed with appropriate comparators, as this was frequently an evidence gap. This includes comparing impacts of bus travel with other public or private transport modes across the health pathways (e.g. road travel injuries), comparing bus drivers with other occupations, and exploring the relative contribution of buses to ambient pollution compared to other modes. Research should also compare impacts affecting different groups of bus users by age, gender and other characteristics.

Research is needed to further disentangle the complexities in the health pathways studied. Many of the identified associations are affected by context. For example, several studies reported experiences of harassment against women on buses that are likely to reflect wider attitudes to women in those settings. Future research should recognize and explore the contextual factors that influence these associations. This may help to clarify some inconsistencies in evidence identified in our review, such as the link between bus travel to healthy weight and exposure to pollutants.

There was a dearth of studies investigating the impacts of bus services on wider communities. Further research is needed to fill this gap and should also include the impacts of changes such as fleet electrification. Finally, a priority research gap is the impacts of population mode shift, to bus from other modes, on pathways such as air quality, noise, and road injuries affecting the wider community.

5. Conclusion

We found that bus travel may be positively linked to health through access to services, physical activity, social interaction and improved mental health. Negative links include exposure to air pollution, noise, injuries and harassment. Some low-quality evidence suggests that bus drivers have higher odds of some cancers and may have high rates of musculoskeletal and mental health conditions. The impacts differentially affect low income populations, women, older people, young people, disabled people and other marginalized groups. There is very little evidence comparing the associations between buses and health with users of other transport modes, so further research is needed. Investments to improve the affordability, availability, reliability, journey times, connectivity, cognitive/physical accessibility and safety of bus services could have important benefits for health and health inequalities.

References

Abe, T., Seino, S., Hata, T., Yamashita, M., Ohmori, N., Kitamura, A., et al., 2023. Transportation modes and social participation in older drivers and non-drivers: results from urbanised Japanese cities. J. Transp. Geogr. 109. https://doi.org/10.1016/j.jtrangeo.2023.103598.

Aceves-González, C., Cook, S., May, A., 2015. Bus use in a developing world city: implications for the health and well-being of older passengers. JTH 2, 308. https://doi.org/10.1016/j.jth.2015.04.001.

Akinlotan, O., Drewry, H., 2024. Factors that influence the mental health of bus drivers: a systematic review. Ment. Health Prev. 35. https://doi.org/10.1016/j.mhp.2024.200355.

Alhassan, J.A.K., Abonyi, S., Neudorf, C., Hanson, L., 2021. It feels like somebody cut my legs off: Austerity, transportation and the 'web of dispossession' in Saskatchewan, Canada. Soc. Sci. Med. 282. https://doi.org/10.1016/j.socscimed.2021.114147.

Alhassan, J.A.K., Hanson, L., Abonyi, S., Neudorf, C., 2023. Producing vulnerability: a qualitative analysis of health equity impacts of budget cuts to intercity public transportation - evidence from Saskatchewan, Canada. JTH 33. https://doi.org/10.1016/j.jth.2023.101715.

Anciaes, P., Alhassan, J.A.K., 2024. Chapter Seven - Economic and social impacts of public transport investments: a scoping literature review. In: Mindell, J.S., Watkins, S.J. (Eds.), Advances in Transport Policy and Planning. Academic Press, pp. 145–165.

Barros, P., Guerra, P.H., Khan, M., Fermino, R.C., 2024. Chapter Four - Impact of active travel to school on children's health: an overview of systematic reviews. In: Mindell, J.S., Watkins, S.J. (Eds.), Advances in Transport Policy and Planning. Academic Press, pp. 145–165.

Bartels, C., Kolbe-Alexander, T., Behrens, R., Hendricks, S., Lambert, E.V., 2016. Can the use of Bus Rapid Transit lead to a healthier lifestyle in urban South Africa? The SUN study. JTH 3, 200. https://doi.org/10.1016/j.jth.2016.04.003.

Besser, L.M., Chang, L.-C., Kluttz, J., 2020. Individual and neighborhood characteristics associated with neighborhood walking among US older adults. Prev. Med. Rep. 21. https://doi.org/10.1016/j.pmedr.2020.101291.

Boffetta, P., Silverman, D.T., 2001. A meta-analysis of bladder cancer and diesel exhaust exposure. Epidemiology 12 (1), 125–130.

Borker, G., 2024. Understanding the constraints to women's use of urban public transport in developing countries. World Dev. 180, 106589. https://doi.org/10.1016/j.worlddev.2024.106589.

Bozovic, T., 2025. Urban walkability and equity in the car-centric city. In: Bailey, A., Otsuki, K. (Eds.), Inclusive Cities and Global Urban Transformation: Infrastructures, Intersectionalities, and Sustainable Development. Springer Nature Singapore, Singapore, pp. 77–85.

Cardoso, A., Matos, M.L., 2017. The prevalence of work-related musculoskeletal disorders (WMSDs) in professional bus drivers-a systematic review. Occupational Safety and Hygiene V, 211–214.

Carney, F., 2021. Linking loyalty card data to public transport data to explore mobility and social exclusion in the older population. Sustainability 13. https://doi.org/10.3390/su13116217.

Cendales, B.E., Gómez-Ortiz, V., Useche, S.A., Cedillo, L., Stephenson, D.W.H., Landsbergis, P., 2024. Mental health outcomes among urban public transport workers: a systematic literature review. JTH 36. https://doi.org/10.1016/j.jth.2024.101804.

Cepeda, M., Schoufour, J., Freak-Poli, R., Koolhaas, C.M., Dhana, K., Bramer, W.M., et al., 2017. Levels of ambient air pollution according to mode of transport: a systematic review. Lancet Public. Health 2, e23–e34. https://doi.org/10.1016/S2468-2667(16)30021-4.

Collins, P.A., Agarwal, A., 2015. Impacts of public transit improvements on ridership, and implications for physical activity, in a low-density Canadian city. Prev. Med. Rep. 2, 874. https://doi.org/10.1016/j.pmedr.2015.10.001.

Crizzle, A.M., Bigelow, P., Adams, D., Gooderham, S., Myers, A.M., Thiffault, P., 2017. Health and wellness of long-haul truck and bus drivers: a systematic literature review and directions for future research. JTH 7, 90. https://doi.org/10.1016/j.jth.2017.05.359.

Del Rio, M., Hargrove, W.L., Tomaka, J., Korc, M., 2017. Transportation matters: a health impact assessment in rural new Mexico. Int. J. Environ. Res. Public. Health 14. https://doi.org/10.3390/ijerph14060629.

Delgado-Ron, J.A., Iroz-Elardo, N., Frank, L., 2000. Health effects of fixed-guideway transit: a systematic review of practice-based evidence. JTH 26. https://doi.org/10.1016/j.jth.2022.101476.

Dilian, O., Beckers, C., Davidovitch, N., Martens, K., 2024. Chapter Eight - Physical and mental health outcomes of public transport use among older adults: a systematic review. In: Mindell, J.S., Watkins, S.J. (Eds.), Advances in Transport Policy and Planning. Academic Press, pp. 255–282.

Du, Y., Sun, G., Kwan, M.-P., 2022. Transit-oriented development for older people: does using multiple public transport options improve their physical and mental health? J. Transp. Land. Use 15, 729. https://doi.org/10.5198/jtlu.2022.2152.

Evans, J.T., Stanesby, O., Blizzard, L., Greaves, S., Timperio, A., Jose, K., et al., 2024. Is public transport a promising strategy for increasing physical activity? Evidence from a study of objectively measured public transport use and physical activity. Int. J. Behav. Nutr. Phys. Act. 21 (1). https://doi.org/10.1186/s12966-024-01633-3.

Foster, M., Scott, F., Udu, K., Woodcock, A., Tweed, E., 2024. Chapter Ten - How does the cost of public transport affect mental health and wellbeing? In: Mindell, J.S., Watkins, S.J. (Eds.), Advances in Transport Policy and Planning. Academic Press, pp. 343–377.

García, I., Albelson, M., Puczkowskyj, N., Maheruma Khan, S., Fagundo-Ojeda, K., 2022. Harassment of low-income women on transit: a photovoice project in Oregon and Utah. Transp. Res. D: Transp. Environ. 112. https://doi.org/10.1016/j.trd.2022.103466.

Garritty, C., Hamel, C., Trivella, M., Gartlehner, G., Nussbaumer-Streit, B., Devane, D., et al., 2024. Updated recommendations for the Cochrane rapid review methods guidance for rapid reviews of effectiveness. BMJ. https://doi.org/10.1136/bmj-2023-076335.

Gates, S., Gogescu, F., Grollman, C., Cooper, E., Khambhaita, P., 2019. Transport and Inequality: An Evidence Review for the Department for Transport. NatCen. Department of Transport Accessed: https://assets.publishing.service.gov.uk/media/60080f728fa8f50d8f210fbe/Transport_and_inequality_report_document.pdf.

Glazener, A., Sanchez, K., Ramani, T., Zietsman, J., Nieuwenhuijsen, M.J., Mindell, J.S., et al., 2021. Fourteen pathways between urban transportation and health: a conceptual model and literature review. JTH 21, 101070. https://doi.org/10.1016/j.jth.2021.101070.

Goodman, A., Jones, A., Roberts, H., Steinbach, R., Green, J., 2013. We can all just get on a bus and go: rethinking independent mobility in the context of the universal provision of free bus travel to young londoners. Mobilities. https://doi.org/10.1080/17450101.2013.782848.

Green, J., Steinbach, R., Jones, A., Edwards, P., Kelly, C., Nellthorp, J., et al., 2014. On the buses: a mixed-method evaluation of the impact of free bus travel for young people on the public health. Public. Health Res. 2 (1). https://doi.org/10.3310/phr02010.

Grisé, E., Wasfi, R., Ross, N.A., El-Geneidy, A., 2019. Evaluating methods for measuring daily walking to public transport: balancing accuracy and data availability. JTH 15. https://doi.org/10.1016/j.jth.2019.100638.

Hirsch, J.A., Moore, K.A., Clarke, P.J., Rodriguez, D.A., Evenson, K.R., Brines, S.J., et al., 2014. Changes in the built environment and changes in the amount of walking over time: longitudinal results from the multi-ethnic study of atherosclerosis. Am. J. Epidemiol. 180, 799–809. https://doi.org/10.1093/aje/kwu218.

Hopson, L.M., Lidbe, A.D., Jackson, M.S., Adanu, E., Li, X., Penmetsa, P., et al., 2022. Transportation to school and academic outcomes: a systematic review. Educ. Rev. 76, 648. https://doi.org/10.1080/00131911.2022.2034748.

Jackson, S.E., Firth, J.A., Firth, J., Veronese, N., Gorely, T., Grabovac, I., et al., 2019. Social isolation and physical activity mediate associations between free bus travel and wellbeing among older adults in England. JTH 13, 274. https://doi.org/10.1016/j.jth.2019.03.006.

Jahangir, S., Bailey, A., Hasan, M.U., Hossain, S., Helbich, M., Hyde, M., 2021. When I Need to Travel, I Feel Feverish: everyday experiences of transport inequalities among older adults in Dhaka, Bangladesh. Gerontologist 62, 493. https://doi.org/10.1093/geront/gnab103.

Jamei, E., Chan, M., Chau, H.W., Gaisie, E., Lättman, K., 2022. Perceived accessibility and key influencing factors in transportation. Sustainability 14 (17), 10806. https://doi.org/10.3390/su141710806.

Janatabadi, F., Ermagun, A., 2022. "Slim down" with a ticket to ride: a systematic literature review. JTH 24, 101327. https://doi.org/10.1016/j.jth.2021.101327.

Joseph, L., Neven, A., Martens, K., Kweka, O., Wets, G., Janssens, D., 2023. Exploring changes in mobility experiences and perceptions after implementation of the bus rapid transit system in Dar es Salaam. Case Stud. Transp. Policy 9, 930. https://doi.org/10.1016/j.cstp.2021.04.012.

Kim, S., Park, J.-S., Park, M., Kim, Y., Lim, S., Lee, H.-E., 2018. Female non-smokers' environmental tobacco smoking exposure by public transportation mode. Ann. Occup. Environ. Med. 19, 30, 24. https://doi.org/10.1186/s40557-018-0239-7.

Klerings, I., Robalino, S., Booth, A., Escobar-Liquitay, C.M., Sommer, I., Gartlehner, G., et al., 2023. Rapid reviews methods series: guidance on literature search. BMJ Evid-Based Med. 28, 412–417. https://doi.org/10.1136/bmjebm-2022-112079.

Kumari, S., Sharma, A., Ghosh, A.K., 2024. A comprehensive review of noise pollution monitoring studies at bus transit terminals. Noise Mapp. 11. https://doi.org/10.1515/noise-2022-0180.

La, Q.N., Duong, D.V., Lee, A.H., Meuleners, L.B., 2016. Factors underlying bus-related crashes in Hanoi, Vietnam. Transp. Res. F: Traffic Psychol. Behav. 46, 426. https://doi.org/10.1016/j.trf.2016.06.023.

Lachapelle, U., Boisjoly, G., 2023. Breaking down public transit travel time for more accurate transport equity policies: a trip component approach. Transp. Res. A: Policy Pract. 175, 103756. https://doi.org/10.1016/j.tra.2023.103756.

Laverty, A.A., Webb, E., Vamos, E.P., Millett, C., 2018. Associations of increases in public transport use with physical activity and adiposity in older adults. Int. J. Behav. Nutr. Phys. Act. 15. https://doi.org/10.1186/s12966-018-0660-x.

Lawin, H., Ayi Fanou, L., Hinson, A.V., Stolbrink, M., Houngbegnon, P., Kedote, N.M., et al., 2018. Health risks associated with occupational exposure to ambient air pollution in commercial drivers: a systematic review. Int. J. Environ. Res. Public. Health. https://doi.org/10.3390/ijerph15092039.

Lemoine, P.D., Sarmiento, O.L., Pinzón, J.D., Meisel, J.D., Montes, F., Hidalgo, D., et al., 2016. TransMilenio, a scalable bus rapid transit system for promoting physical activity. J. Urban. Health 93, 256. https://doi.org/10.1007/s11524-015-0019-4.

Lewinson, T., Maley, O., Esnard, A.-M., 2017. Accessing faith-based organizations using public transportation: a qualitative and GIS study. J. Appl. Gerontol. 38, 323. https://doi.org/10.1177/0733464816687220.

Liu, Y., Tao, L., Zhang, J., Liu, J., Li, H., Liu, X., et al., 2020. Impact of commuting mode on obesity among a working population in Beijing, China: adjusting for air pollution. Diabetes Metab. Syndr. Obes.: Targets Ther. 13, 3959–3968. https://doi.org/10.2147/dmso.s265537.

Lucas, K., 2018. Editorial for special issue of European transport research review: transport poverty and inequalities. Eur. Transp. Res. Rev. 10, 1–3. https://doi.org/10.1007/s12544-018-0288-6.

Mah, S., Mitra, R., 2017. The effects of a free bus program on travel behaviour of older adults: a case study of a Canadian suburban municipality. Presented 95th Annu. Meet. Transportation Res. 20 Board. 2016.

Miner, P., Smith, B.M., Jani, A., McNeill, G., Gathorne-Hardy, A., 2024. Car harm: a global review of automobility's harm to people and the environment. J. Transp. Geogr. 115, 103817. https://doi.org/10.1016/j.jtrangeo.2024.103817.

Morris, A., Barnes, J., Fildes, B., 2017. Challenges of using the bus as an older person. WIT Trans. Built Environ. 176, 539–544.

Musselwhite, C., 2017. In: Musselwhite, C. (Ed.), Transport, Travel and Later Life 10. Emerald Publishing Limited, pp. 117–128. https://doi.org/10.1108/S2044-994120170000010004.

Musselwhite, C., 2022. A research agenda on transport and health and public buses: more research on the buses please!. JTH 24, 101355. https://doi.org/10.1016/j.jth.2022.101355.

Musselwhite, C., 2023. Improving mobility in marginalised communities. Future Transp. 3, 1347–1359. https://doi.org/10.3390/futuretransp3040074.

Nævestad, T.-O., Elvik, R., Milch, V., Karlsen, K., Phillips, R., 2022. Traffic safety in bus transport: an analysis of Norway's largest transit authority's contract requirements to bus companies. Transp. Res. F: Traffic Psychol. Behav. 89, 317. https://doi.org/10.1016/j.trf.2022.07.004.

Neupane, G., Chesney-Lind, M., 2013. Violence against women on public transport in Nepal: sexual harassment and the spatial expression of male privilege. Int. J. Comp. Appl. Crim. Justice 38, 23. https://doi.org/10.1080/01924036.2013.794556.

Niboye, E.P., 2023. Universal or specific? - violence against women in public spaces in Tanzania: experiences from public bus stations in Dar es Salaam City. Soc. Sci. Humanit. Open. 7. https://doi.org/10.1016/j.ssaho.2023.100430.

Nieuwenhuijsen, M.J., Khreis, H., Verlinghieri, E., Rojas-Rueda, D., 2016. Transport and health: a marriage of convenience or an absolute necessity. Environ. Int. 88, 150–152. https://doi.org/10.1016/j.envint.2015.12.030.

Noor, H.M., Nor, A.R.M., Kemanusiaan, F., Warisan, S. dan, 2016. A case study of socioeconomic influence on the use of public transport in Kota Kinabalu urban area, Malaysia. J. Kinabalu. https://doi.org/10.51200/ejk.v19i0.507.

Patterson, R., Webb, E., Hone, T., Millett, C., Laverty, A.A., 2019. Associations of public transportation use with cardiometabolic health: a systematic review and meta-analysis. Am. J. Epidemiol. 188, 785–795. https://doi.org/10.1093/aje/kwz012.

Patterson, R., Webb, E., Millett, C., Laverty, A.A., 2018. Physical activity accrued as part of public transport use in England. J. Public. Health 41. https://doi.org/10.1093/pubmed/fdy099.

Patterson, R., Webb, E., Mindell, J.S., Millett, C., Laverty, A.A., 2018. Ethnic group differences in impacts of free bus passes in England: a national study. JTH 11, 1. https://doi.org/10.1016/j.jth.2018.09.005.

Perez-Barbosa, D., Zhang, J., 2017. Transport-based social exclusion in rural Japan: a case study on schooling trips of high school students. Soc. Incl. 5 (4), 235–250. https://doi.org/10.17645/si.v5i4.1079.

Premkumar, J.P., Sameem Banu, M.S., Meenal, J., 2024. Does Tamil Nadu's free bus travel policy impact women's lives? Humanit. Arts Soc. Sci. Stud. 24 (1). https://doi.org/10.69598/hasss.24.1.260791.

Public Health Scotland, 2024. Transport Poverty - A Public Health Issue. Public Health Scotland (Accessed 04.08.25). https://publichealthscotland.scot/media/24759/transport-poverty-briefing_jan2024.pdf.

Rambaldini Gooding, D., Molloy, L., Parrish, A., Strahilevitz, M., Clarke, R., Perez, P., 2022. Free public transport and older people: an ethnographic study of an Australian bus service. Australas. J. Ageing 42, 409. https://doi.org/10.1111/ajag.13158.

Ramel Delobel, M., Heydari, S., De Nazelle, A., Praud, D., Salizzoni, P., Fervers, B., et al., 2024. Air pollution exposure in active versus passive travel modes across five continents: a Bayesian random-effects meta-analysis. Environ. Res. 261. https://doi.org/10.1016/j.envres.2024.119666.

Reinhard, E., Courtin, E., Van Lenthe, F.J., Avendano, M., 2018. Public transport policy, social engagement and mental health in older age: a quasi-experimental evaluation of free bus passes in England. J. Epidemiol. Community Health 72 (5), 361–368. https://doi.org/10.1136/jech-2017-210038.

Reulen, R.C., Kellen, E., Buntinx, F., Brinkman, M.T., Zeegers, M.P., 2015. A meta-analysis on the association between bladder cancer and occupation. Scand. J. Urol. Nephrol. 42, 64. https://doi.org/10.1080/03008880802325192.

Rissel, C., Curac, N., Greenaway, M., Bauman, A., 2012. Physical activity associated with public transport use–a review and modelling of potential benefits. Int. J. Environ. Res. Public. Health 9, 2454–2478. https://doi.org/10.3390/ijerph9072454.

Santana Palacios, M., Cochran, A., Bell, C., Hernández Jiménez, U., Leshner, E., Trejo Morales, F., et al., 2020. Bus rapid transit arrives in Barranquilla, Colombia: understanding a changing landscape through residents' travel experiences. Travel. Behav. Soc. 21, 131. https://doi.org/10.1016/j.tbs.2020.06.003.

Sharman, M.J., Stanesby, O., Jose, K.A., Greaves, S., Cleland, V.J., 2024. Free bus fares, bus use and physical activity: an exploratory cross-sectional study. Health Promot. J. Aust. 36. https://doi.org/10.1002/hpja.881.

Singh, V., Meena, K.K., Agarwal, A., 2021. Travellers' exposure to air pollution: a systematic review and future directions. Urban. Clim. 38. https://doi.org/10.1016/j.uclim.2021.100901.

Stafford, L., Tye, I., 2023. I have mentally cancelled a lot of trips: trips not made by disabled people due to public transport inequity in Lutruwita/Tasmania. J. Transp. Geogr. 111. https://doi.org/10.1016/j.jtrangeo.2023.103668.

Starbird, L.E., Dimaina, C., Sun, C.-A., Han, H.-R., 2018. A systematic review of interventions to minimize transportation barriers among people with chronic diseases. J. Community Health 44, 400. https://doi.org/10.1007/s10900-018-0572-3.

Stern, C., Lizarondo, L., Carrier, J., Godfrey, C., Rieger, K., Salmond, S., et al., 2020. Methodological guidance for the conduct of mixed methods systematic reviews. JBI Evid. Synth. 18, 2108–2118. https://doi.org/10.11124/JBISRIR-D-19-00169.

Stjernborg, V., 2024. Triggers for feelings of insecurity and perceptions of safety in relation to public transport; the experiences of young and active travellers. Appl. Mobilities. 1. https://doi.org/10.1080/23800127.2024.2318095.

Tao, L., Li, X., Zhang, J., Liu, J., Liu, Y., Li, H., et al., 2019. Association of commuting mode with dyslipidemia and its components after accounting for air pollution in the working population of Beijing, China. BMC Public. Health. https://doi.org/10.1186/s12889-019-6887-x.

Transport Scotland, 2024. Fair Fares Review Supporting Paper 1: Public Transport System Analysis. Transport Scotland (Accessed 3.18.25). https://www.transport.gov.scot/publication/public-transport-system-analysis-supporting-paper-one-fair-fares-review/economy-and-budget-context/.

van Erpecum, C.-P.L., Bornioli, A., Cleland, C., Jones, S., Davis, A., den Braver, N.R., et al., 2024. Chapter Five - 20 mph speed limits: a meta-narrative evidence synthesis of the public health evidence. In: Mindell, J.S., Watkins, S.J. (Eds.), Advances in Transport Policy and Planning. Academic Press, pp. 167–195.

Webb, E., Laverty, A., Mindell, J., Millett, C., 2016. Free bus travel and physical activity, gait speed, and adiposity in the english longitudinal study of ageing. Am. J. Public. Health 106, 136. https://doi.org/10.2105/ajph.2015.302907.

Whitley, E., Craig, P., Popham, F., 2019. Impact of the statutory concessionary travel scheme on bus travel among older people: a natural experiment from England. Ageing Soc. 40, 2480. https://doi.org/10.1017/s0144686×19000692.

Williams, A.J., McHale, C., Chow, C., Van Ry, R., Cope, A., 2024. Chapter Nine - systematic review of the associations between transport and loneliness. In: Mindell, J.S., Watkins, S.J. (Eds.), Advances in Transport Policy and Planning. Academic Press, pp. 283–342.

Xiao, C., Goryakin, Y., Cecchini, M., 2019. Physical activity levels and new public transit: a systematic review and meta-analysis. Am. J. Prev. Med. 56, 464–473. https://doi.org/10.1016/j.amepre.2018.10.022.

Yendra, D., Haworth, N., Watson-Brown, N., 2024. A comparison of factors influencing the safety of pedestrians accessing bus stops in countries of differing income levels. Accid. Anal. Prev. 207. https://doi.org/10.1016/j.aap.2024.107725.

Yin, C., Chen, Y., Sun, B., 2024. Nonlinear relationships of commuting and built environments surrounding residences and workplaces with obesity. Humanit. Soc. Sci. Commun. 11. https://doi.org/10.1057/s41599-024-03964-9.

Zamudio, C., Krapp, F., Choi, H.W., Shah, L., Ciampi, A., Gotuzzo, E., et al., 2015. Public transportation and tuberculosis transmission in a high incidence setting. PLoS ONE 10. https://doi.org/10.1371/journal.pone.0115230.

CHAPTER THREE

Urban streets as places: Effect on street use and health-related outcomes

Paulo Anciaes*
Centre for Transport Studies, University College London, London, United Kingdom
*Corresponding author. e-mail address: p.anciaes@ucl.ac.uk

Contents

Abstract

Urban streets can become places where people spend time and to which they attach meaning. This chapter reviews research on the outcomes of interventions to increase or improve the use of streets as places and achieve health-related outcomes. A scoping review approach was used, given the fragmentation of the literature. Preliminary searches in reference material identified 19 relevant interventions and 15 outcomes. We then searched for studies published since 2005 that provide quantitative evidence on

Advances in Transport Policy and Planning, Volume 18
ISSN 2543-0009, https://doi.org/10.1016/bs.atpp.2026.07.002

the effectiveness of those interventions on the identified outcomes. 39 relevant studies were identified. This is a small body of evidence, considering the quantity and variety of street placemaking interventions that have been applied around the world. Even well-established interventions such as pedestrianisation lack sufficient evaluations. Most evidence is related to part-time interventions such as street closures. There are few studies using robust evaluation methods – most studies have used simple before-after comparisons or post-implementation user surveys. Despite the methodological limitations and the variety of data used and interventions and contexts studied, the literature points to a mainly positive effect of street placemaking on the intensity and perceived quality of the use of streets as places and an equally positive effect on some health-related outcomes such as physical activity, social interaction, and air quality.

1. Introduction

Debates in urban studies often distinguish between *space* and *place*. Urban spaces are physical entities (such as streets and squares) that can be defined by objective attributes such as location, size, and layout. In contrast, urban places are spaces that people actively use and to which they attach personal, social, or cultural meaning (Schneecloth and Shibley, 1995; Carmona, 2021). Placemaking is the process through which spaces gain this meaning and become places.

Placemaking is a fuzzy concept, used with different definitions by many disciplines, such as urban planning (Strydom et al., 2018), urban design (Thomas, 2016), architecture (Unwin, 2020), public health (Couper et al., 2023), psychology (Toolis, 2017), sociology (Chica, 2021), economics (Kelly et al., 2017), environmental science (Nouri and Costa, 2017), tourism studies (Dupre, 2019), and art (Courage, 2020). The approaches of these disciplines differ in the type of outcomes they associate with placemaking. As an example, sociology is interested in how places contribute to social interaction or reduce crime. The approaches also differ in the relative importance they give to the outcomes and processes of placemaking. These processes can be personal, namely, how users attach meaning to a place, often referred to as "sense of place" (Relph, 1976; Canter, 1977). They can also involve physical changes to spaces, enabling them to be perceived as places by their users. These changes may stem from public policies or from initiatives led by communities, universities, and non-governmental organisations (Akbar and Edelenbos, 2021).

From an urban planning and design perspective, placemaking is concerned with how urban spaces can be planned and designed to bring about social change. Jane Jacobs was a pioneer in this type of thinking, advocating for density and diversity in land use as strategies to promote outcomes such as economic vitality, social cohesion, and crime reduction (Jacobs, 1961). Similarly, William Whyte showed that opportunities for social interaction are a key factor in attracting people to urban public spaces such as parks, plazas, and playgrounds, and that these interactions are facilitated by elements like street furniture, resting areas, greenery, and food vending (Whyte, 1980).

These ideas were later applied to urban streets, which are the primary form of public space in cities. It was recognised that urban streets are places where people spend time for work, shopping, leisure, or social activities. Jan Gehl focused on how streets can be designed to attract more people and more activities, emphasising, like Jane Jacobs, the importance of diversity of street uses (Gehl, 1971). Allan Jacobs's *Great Streets* then examined the role of each design element in the performance of streets as places, including street furniture and public art (Jacobs, 1993), while Donald Appleyard showed that streets cannot be used as social spaces unless motorised traffic is reduced (Appleyard, 1981). The idea of a "city of places" has been gaining ground (Jones et al., 2018; Von Schönfeld and Bertolini, 2017) and has been incorporated into the strategies of many city governments, pushing for streets that are "complete" (CoL, 2018), "healthy" (TfL, 2017), and "liveable" (PBOT, 2017). This idea has grown stronger during and after the Covid-19 pandemic, when the role of streets was re-questioned, and cities extended their efforts to create better streets for people (Oluyede et al., 2024).

The current understanding is that streets can become places through interventions that improve the experience of people spending time in them. Better experiences can then contribute to an increase in the use of the place, that is, in the number of people using the place and the time they spend there (Gehl, 1971, 2010). Both factors can act as catalysts for broader social changes. For example, public health can improve via an increase in physical activity. Other possible outcomes are strengthening the local economy, reducing crime and fear of crime, enhancing social interaction and community cohesion, and reducing local and global pollution (Carmona, 2019, 2021). All these outcomes contribute indirectly to public health improvements.

Research on the outcomes of placemaking in urban streets is much needed. This research can provide evidence on the effectiveness of different types of interventions, assisting planners in the selection of the most suitable interventions and the geographic areas that should be targeted. Research can also assist in the design (or redesign) of streets, by identifying appropriate design elements and their placement within the street layout. Research evidence can also support the allocation of funding and help to build public support for the interventions.

However, research on the outcomes of designing urban streets as places is scattered:

- Some studies are not published in academic journal articles but in reports issued by transport and urban planning agencies
- The literature is growing fast, especially since the growth of place-based interventions applied during and in the aftermath of Covid
- The literature has been produced by researchers from different disciplines, using their own concepts. The same intervention may be known by different terms
- The methods used are equally diverse, including before-after and cross-sectional approaches
- Given the diversity of interventions to improve urban streets as places, evidence on any one type of intervention is limited
- It is difficult to generalise results because interventions to improve the place dimension of a street are, by definition, specific to a given place

This chapter aims to integrate this scattered body of research. We use a scoping review approach to examine studies that measure the effects of interventions to increase or improve the use of streets as places. The focus is on outcomes related to street use and public health.

We consider:

- **Streets** only, not other public spaces such as parks – see a review on these other spaces in Hunter et al. (2019). We use a broad concept of streets, as linear or non-linear public spaces used for a variety of activities and bordered by buildings (thus including squares)
- **Place activities** only (i.e., stationary activities related to work, shopping, leisure, or social interaction), not movement, even by cycling or walking (for transport) – see review in Roaf et al. (2024)
- **People-based** place activities only, not vehicle-based, such as parking (including bicycle parking) – see review in Heinen and Buehler (2019)
- **Outcomes** only, not processes (e.g. the degree to which the public was involved in the interventions) – see review in Akbar and Edelenbos (2021)

We note that using a street as a place implies either no movement at all (for example, sitting in an outdoor café), slow movement without a specific destination (for example, strolling along a shopping street), or even fast movement for sport and leisure (e.g. jogging). However, we exclude from our review movement with a specific destination, even if this movement is on foot or by bicycle. While it is not usually possible to know who is walking for transport and who is strolling or window shopping, we review interventions aimed at walking when they are applied in a location where it is likely that walking is a place activity, such as a shopping street or a pedestrianised area where people engage in leisure or social activities.

We also note that even though place activities are not movement, they are still related to movement as both activities occur in the same space – streets. In most cases, place activities occur in streets where travelling is also happening. For example, people may be sitting or strolling while others are travelling (by car, bus, cycling, or walking) along the same street. In addition, the provision of space for place activities may be achieved by reallocating space previously allocated to movement, while the provision of *safe* space for place activities may be achieved by reducing traffic speeds or reducing or removing some travel modes from the traffic. As such, we consider in this review possible interventions on movement that have the objective of improving the place function of the street, but only when this is accompanied by additional measures to increase the attractiveness of the street for people.

In the next section, we explain why a scoping review is the most suitable approach to consolidate a diverse and fragmented body of evidence such as the one that is the focus of this study, and how we used this approach. Sections 3 and 4 then present and discuss the results.

2. Methods

2.1 Type of review

Scoping reviews are a less structured alternative to systematic reviews. The aim of a scoping review is to map a body of evidence and to identify knowledge gaps, rather than to produce detailed policy and practice implications based on a rigorous assessment of the strength of the evidence (Arksey and O'Malley, 2005; Munn et al., 2018). Scoping reviews are used to identify not only the answers provided by previous studies but also the types of questions that have been asked, the types of methods used to answer those questions, and the sources of evidence. A scoping review:

- collates and summarises information on broad problems or fuzzy concepts – in this chapter, the effect of street "placemaking" on "health"
- draws from different sources, both academic studies and grey literature
- includes studies with a variety of questions and methods – in this chapter, it is used to review a broad range of interventions aimed at different outcomes and applied in different types of streets, used by different groups
- has a structured process for searching studies and collecting information from them, but not for assessing the quality of that information

The review was conducted in five stages, following the framework outlined by Arksey and O'Malley (2005) and Levac et al. (2010) for scoping reviews: (1) Identifying the research question, (2) Identifying relevant studies, (3) Selecting studies, (4) Charting the data, and (5) Collating, summarizing, and reporting the results.

2.2 Identifying the research questions

The research questions are related to the effects of street placemaking interventions:

- What is the effect of those interventions on the intensity and quality of people-based place activities in those streets?
- What are the health-related outcomes of the interventions?

2.2.1 Types of interventions

We identified a set of suitable interventions for street placemaking drawn from the list of 210 interventions compiled by the author in *The Urban Streetspace Book* (Anciaes, 2022). This list was developed through discussions with street user group associations, as part of an EU-funded project (*Multimodal Optimisation of Roadspace in Europe*), and through a review of academic literature and policy documents. The sources used in that review were seven key works on urban design or street design: *Great Streets* (Jacobs, 1993), *Cities for People* (Gehl, 2010), *Public Places-Urban Spaces* (Carmona, 2021), *Street Design: The Secret to Great Cities and Towns* (Dover and Massengale, 2014), *Global Street Design Guide* (GDCI and NACTO, 2016), *Manual for Streets 2* (CIHT, 2010), and the *New York City Street Design Manual* (NYC DoT, 2020).

We selected 19 suitable interventions for the purposes of this review (Table 1), based on the criterion that they either provide additional space or improve existing space for people-based place activities on streets.

Table 1 Interventions to improve people-based place activities in urban streets.

Intervention	**Definition**	**Keywords**
Pedestrianisation	Space for the exclusive use of pedestrians at all times	Pedestriani* OR "pedestrian street" OR "pedestrian mall"
Shared space	Removal of barriers and formal demarcations between space used by different types of users	"shared space"
Wide spaces	Public (or pseudo-public) spaces on or next to streets, created by repurposing underused space or reallocating space from motorised users at intersections	Courtyard OR plaza OR square
Parklets	Small public spaces on the kerbside, replacing one or more car parking spaces	Parklet OR "pocket park"
Part-time or temporary spaces	Spaces for the exclusive use of pedestrians or place activities (sitting, playing, watching street performers) at certain times of day or days of week, or for a temporary period	"play street" OR "open street" OR car-free OR "market day" OR "night market" OR Ciclovia
Wider footways	Widening of street footways, or adding extra footways in the median strip, by reallocating space from motorised traffic.	"footway widen*" OR "sidewalk widen*" OR "wider footway" OR "wider sidewalk" OR "wider pedestrian"
Street vending	Space for structures on the footway for small shops and street vendors	kiosk OR stand OR vendor OR "food truck" OR stall
Storefront extensions	Space for stalls and other structures next to buildings with ground floor businesses	Storefront OR shopfront OR "shop display"
Outdoor cafés	Space for outdoor seating, with tables, operated by private businesses	Café OR restaurant OR dining OR bar

(continued)

Table 1 Interventions to improve people-based place activities in urban streets. (*cont'd*)

Intervention	Definition	Keywords
Rest points	Structures for people to sit on, such as benches or blocks	Rest OR bench OR seats
Shade and shelter	Structures to provide shade and shelter (excluding bus stop shelters)	Shade OR shelter OR cover
Public toilets	Provision of more or better public toilets	"public toilet" OR WC OR restroom
Street lights	Provision of more or better lighting	light OR lamp OR illumination OR lantern
Exercise equipment	On-street gym and fitness equipment	"fitness park" OR "outdoor gym"
Street greenery	Trees, planted areas, grass strips, or flower beds on the street footway, kerbside, or median strip	green* OR grass OR tree OR plant* OR flower OR garden OR hedge
Water	Artificial water-based features	blue OR water OR fountain OR "reflecting pool" OR splash OR mist
Public art	Murals, sculptures, or temporary street art	"public art" OR mural OR sculpture OR installation OR exhibit
Declutter	Reducing physical and visual clutter caused by street furniture and other structures on the footway	declutter
Inclusive design	Changes in street design to increase accessibility for all, uncluding people with mobility, sensory, or cognitive impairments	"inclusive design" OR "universal design" OR barrier-free OR accessibility OR tactile OR colour-contrast OR "dropped kerb" OR "dropped curb" OR ramps

From the seven works listed above, and preliminary searches, we also identified keywords to search for evaluation studies. Some keywords are specific to an intervention (third column of Table 1) and others are related to the general concept of placemaking (second row of Table 3).

2.2.2 Types of outcomes

We then identified a set of 15 suitable outcomes of street placemaking interventions (Table 2), drawn from the 28 street design policy objectives compiled by the author in Anciaes and Jones (2022), and supplemented with a search of the seven key works mentioned above. We assume that placemaking aims to increase the intensity of the use of streets as places (that is, the number of users) and the quality of that use. Following Gehl Institute (2016), we consider that quality to be reflected in three indicators: the time that users spend in the street and the diversity of street users (in terms of age and gender) and activities. We also considered a series of health outcomes and social and environmental outcomes indirectly related to health – hereafter we refer to these three outcomes as "health-related outcomes".

Table 2 Relevant outcomes of interventions to improve people-based place activities in urban streets.

Use of places	• Number of users (walking or engaged in stationary activities) • Time spent in the place • Diversity of users • Diversity of activities
Health	• Physical activity • Physical health (incidence of disease) • Mental health • Wellbeing • Collisions
Social	• Personal security (crime and fear of crime) • Social interaction • Social inclusion
Environmental	• Air quality • Noise • Local climate (e.g. urban heat island effect)

This list excludes:

- Outputs (rather than outcomes) of the interventions (e.g., amount of greenery, improvement of the visual environment)
- Outcomes related to movement (e.g., number of trips, travel time, trip quality, modal split, travel costs, access to local buildings)
- Outcomes related to vehicle-based place activities (e.g. ease of parking)
- Economic outcomes (e.g. effect on business revenue, property prices, and rents)

2.3 Identifying relevant studies

We then proceeded with the main stage of the search process. This was done in March 2025 and aimed at finding both peer-reviewed and non-peer-reviewed studies relevant to the research questions. The search covered titles and abstracts and used the keywords in Table 3, which combine four aspects:

- the "where" of the intervention (streets)
- "what" (placemaking) – including general terms for placemaking, common verbs used in relation to placemaking (such as synonyms of

Table 3 Search keywords.

Where	Street
What	AND: placemaking OR "place making" OR urbanism OR "public space" OR "urban space" OR "public place" OR "urban place" OR "street space" OR "streetspace" OR "street design" OR "urban design" OR "street quality" OR "place quality" OR "street environment" OR "built environment" OR "visual environment" OR streetscape OR townscape OR "public realm" OR "urban realm" OR livable OR liveable OR "sense of place" OR "healthy street" OR "complete street" OR improv* OR renew* OR regenerat* OR retrofit* OR reallocat* OR reclaim*
	OR [keywords from Table 1]
How	AND: intervention OR trial OR scheme OR experiment OR policy OR measure OR initiative OR program OR event OR project OR retrofit
For what	AND: effect* OR outcome OR impact OR evaluat* OR trial OR treatment OR "before-after" OR "before and after" OR "difference-in-differences" OR "time series" OR postintervention OR "post-intervention" OR contributed

"improvement"), and specific terms linked to the 19 specific types of interventions previously identified as relevant
- "how" (an intervention)
- "for what" (to achieve outcomes) – synonyms of "outcome" or possible methods used to evaluate those outcomes (e.g., "difference-in-differences")

We performed an initial search in Scopus (a general academic literature database) and then scanned the abstracts of the studies found in order to refine the search keywords. We then used these keywords in Scopus and two additional databases: PubMed (for health-related literature) and TRID (Transport Research International Documentation) (for transport-related literature). The search was restricted to studies in English published in the last 20 years (2005–2025), as previous studies are less likely to be relevant to contemporary transport policy paradigms for improving urban streets as places.

Duplicate entries were removed. We then reviewed all abstracts and then the full text of studies. At the abstract review stage, review studies were excluded but their reference lists were consulted to identify additional studies. We also identified studies that either cited or were cited by the selected ones. Finally, we performed a final search in Google Scholar searching specifically for grey literature. This search was similar to the one mentioned above but added the expression ("monitoring report" OR "evaluation report"), to identify relevant reports.

2.4 Study selection

Table 4 lists the selection criteria and examples of potential exclusions for each criterion.

- Interventions should have the main aim of physically changing urban streets to improve place activities (not movement)
- Studies should report effects on the use of streets as places or on health-related outcomes
- Studies should report a quantitative evaluation of user perceptions, behaviour, or effects of behaviour. "Evaluation" is understood as the comparison of values of indicators of the relevant outcomes before and after the intervention in a given street or area. The "before" values can be measured before the intervention or assessed retrospectively (e.g. self-assessed by the study participants based on their recollections). The comparison can refer to a control group or not.

Table 4 Inclusion criteria and examples of exclusions.

	Inclusion criteria	Examples of exclusions
Interventions	In cities	• Interventions in rural areas
	On streets, not other public spaces or spatial scales	• Interventions on off-street spaces such as public parks, vacant lots, parking lots, greenways (pedestrian paths along green or blue spaces), elevated walkways, and underground passages. • Interventions on tourist sites • City-wide interventions
	To improve streets as places, not streets for movement	• Interventions only aimed at improving movement (motorised traffic, cycling, micromobility, walking for transport, or pedestrian crossings) • Interventions only aimed at taming traffic (e.g., speed limits, point closures) without other measures to attract users, such as improving street design or creating opportunities for place activities • Interventions on roads (not streets) where movement by motorised travel modes is predominant even after the intervention • Interventions to improve vehicle-based stationary activities, such as car or cycle parking
	Interventions	• Street closures because of temporary works
	Physical interventions	• Financial or other incentives to walk • Community engagement • Lab-based experiments • Studies using virtual reality
Outcomes	Outcomes, not processes	• Governance • Public participation (e.g. co-design) • Public support

	Street use and health-related outcomes	• Studies only reporting changes in motorised traffic levels • Studies only reporting economic outcomes • Studies only reporting the effects of street improvements on gentrification
Evaluation	Evaluation	• Modelling, forecasting, and simulation studies • Cross-sectional studies • Stated preference/choice of hypothetical scenarios • Revealed preference studies of choices of locations to visit • Studies with only post-implementation statistics of street uses
	Quantitative evaluation	• Interviews or focus groups
	Evaluation of user perceptions, behaviour, or effects of behaviour	• Expert evaluations (e.g., street audits, Delphi methods) • Spatial analysis • Evaluation frameworks without an application

2.5 Charting the data and collating, summarising, and reporting the results

The following seven types of information were collected from each study: city and country, type of intervention, timing of intervention (full-time/part-time; permanent or temporary), data collected, evaluation method, effect on the use of streets (intensity and quality of place activities), and health-related outcomes.

We then summarise the results by describing patterns in each of the seven types of information collected, identifying research gaps and limitations.

3. Results

3.1 Search results and data extraction

The initial search yielded 7682, 1014, and 1007 results, from Scopus, Medline, and TRID, respectively. After 718 duplicates were removed,

8985 records remained. Following the abstract review, 47 records were retained, 41 of which could be retrieved. After full-text review, 23 records were retained.

An additional 16 studies were identified from the reference lists of the literature-review papers found in the initial search (3), documents that cited or were cited by the selected ones (8), and the search for non- peer-reviewed documents in Google Scholar (5). The final number of studies is 39. The table in the appendix shows the data extracted from these studies. The following sections summarise and analyse that data.

The most frequent reason for excluding studies was the sole focus on cycling or the improvement of pedestrian crossings. In particular, several excluded studies, especially from the USA, on "complete streets" were interventions on 4–6 lane roads (not streets) and the improvements were limited to adding cycle lanes. Other main reasons for exclusion were the sole focus on the effect of "pocket parks" in (off-street) vacant lots, the lack of an outcome evaluation of a real-world street intervention, and the analysis of economic outcomes only.

3.2 Type of study

Only five of the selected studies were 'grey literature' evaluation reports (Webster et al., 2006; Pratt, 2011; Loukaitou-Sideris et al., 2013; Gehl Studio and J. Max Bond Center, 2015; Happy City, 2019). All other studies were peer-reviewed journal or conference papers. Although the reference lists of peer-reviewed studies contained many references to evaluations, these mainly led to local or regional government websites that provided only descriptions of the schemes or usage statistics, with no outcome evaluation. In other cases, the references were to reports which are no longer publicly available.

Studies of interventions involving the redesign of streets were mostly published in transport and planning journals, while those of interventions involving regular street closures for place activities were published both in transport/planning and in health-related journals.

3.3 Cities and countries

Evidence comes from a variety of countries, but overwhelmingly from the USA (17 of the 39 studies). The other studies are from 16 different countries. Most are from the Global North, with only five from the Global South (India, Rwanda, Chile, Lebanon, and Mexico). Almost all studies concerned large cities. Some national-level reviews, such as those of "home zone" interventions in the UK, also includesmall towns.

3.4 Interventions

The street improvement schemes featured in the selected studies often combined various interventions from the list in Table 1. For example, the widening of footways was often part of major redesigns of streets, involving reallocation of space from motorised traffic and the addition or improvement of elements such as street vending areas, outdoor cafés, rest points, street lights, greenery, public art, and inclusive design. As such, these interventions were aggregated in the analysis that follows as "major design improvements". Schemes that added or improved some design elements but did not involve major reallocations of street space were aggregated as "minor design improvements".

There was a notable difference within the types of intervention we previously classified as "part-time or temporary spaces" in Table 1. Some of the interventions featured in the selected studies were 'pop-up spaces' that created a new public space using the entire street for a limited time. Others were regular closures of streets (and roads) to motorised traffic for events known as "Ciclovías", "open streets", or "play streets". During these events, the street is used for physical activity and leisure or for organised social and cultural activities. These types of events represent the largest evidence base among all the interventions included in this review. In the analysis that follows, we treat pop-up spaces and regular street closures as distinct categories.

Despite how common pedestrianised streets are in most countries, there has been little research evaluating the outcomes of pedestrianising a street in terms of its use and health-related outcomes. Our search found only four such studies, all of them using simple before-after comparisons or post-implementation user perceptions about the change, not robust evaluation methods. Most evaluation studies on pedestrianisation were excluded from our review because they focused only on the effect on local business revenue or on levels of support from local citizens and businesses.

Studies of shared space focused mainly on safety and on pedestrian interactions with vehicles (rather than other health-related outcomes), and on pedestrian satisfaction (rather than on the effect of the street transformation on the number of people using that street). Evidence on wide spaces (plazas) and parklets is scarce – only two studies were found for each of these interventions. These studies are non-peer-reviewed reports that did not use robust evaluation methods. No study was found that evaluated the outcomes of strategies to declutter footways or to add or improve storefront extensions, shade and shelter, public toilets, on-street exercise equipment, and water features.

Based on these results, the interventions were therefore regrouped in subsequent analyses into eight categories: pedestrianisation, shared space, wide spaces (plazas), parklets, pop-up spaces, regular street closures, major design improvements, and minor design improvements.

3.5 Timing

The majority of the reviewed studies focused on part-time street spaces, available for place activities only on weekends (and in several cases, only during the summer months). In some cases, the space was available only sporadically, during events organised a few days per year. Other interventions were temporary, implemented over a short period, as trials. Even pedestrianised streets were part-time or temporary, with only one exception (Nello-Deakin et al., 2024). However, shared spaces and design improvements were full-time and permanent.

3.6 Data

Many of the reviewed studies relied on survey data. Sample sizes varied, but in several cases were below 100. Two studies surveyed business owners, asking them to estimate the number of people entering their shops (Chaudhuri and Zieff, 2015; Winter et al., 2020). In several cases, surveys were conducted only at the post-implementation stage, asking street users about their perceptions of the changes resulting from the intervention. In other cases, users were asked about their alternative uses of time, had they not been in that street at that time. Non-users of the streets (e.g. residents in streets that were not improved) were rarely interviewed.

Other studies used on-site observations to count the number of people using a street and to classify the types of activity they engaged in (Pratt, 2011; Loukaitou-Sideris et al., 2013; Zieff et al., 2016; Carmona et al., 2018; Igel et al., 2020). Others used video recordings, which enabled more systematic pedestrian counts (Allirani et al., 2024) and more detailed analysis of pedestrian behaviour, such as conflicts with vehicles in shared spaces (Oh and Kent, 2017; Kaparias and Tsonev, 2023).

New methods of data collection, such as mobile phone tracking, are now common in transport studies. However, this data was used in only two of the reviewed studies to assess changes in numbers of people using a street (Rong and Freeman, 2024; Yoshimura et al., 2025). Other studies asked participants (children, in both cases) to wear devices (pedometers and accelerometers) over a few days, to compare physical activity during regular days and days when streets are closed to traffic (D'Haese et al., 2015; Cortinez-O'Ryan et al., 2017).

Some studies used secondary data, including pedestrian counts, motorised traffic counts, traffic speed, collisions, air pollution, and noise complaints. However, some of this data may not be suitable for evaluating interventions. For example, Carmona et al. (2018) observed that traffic and collision data were inconsistent and difficult to link with street interventions. Likewise, Webster et al. (2006) pointed out that the effect of an intervention on collisions may be inconclusive when the numbers of collisions are small.

Several studies used mixed methods (usually a survey complemented with observations or secondary data). However, these methods can produce inconsistent results. For example, in the study of Winter et al. (2020), 70% of businesses reported no increase in number of pedestrians, yet the authors recorded an increase in the number of pedestrians walking to the eight businesses surveyed. As such, it is difficult to draw solid conclusions about the effectiveness of the interventions.

Some studies collected data but did not report its analysis. For example, the study by Oh and Kent (2017) on shared space collected pedestrian volume data but did not report the results.

3.7 Methods

The reviewed studies employed a variety of methods. However, the identification and description of methods was often unclear in grey literature, and results were not always clearly presented (for example, only a chart was provided, without the underlying values).

In many cases, studies relied on simple comparisons of the values of a variable (e.g. pedestrian counts) before and after the implementation of the intervention or, in the case of part-time spaces, on days when the street was closed to motorised traffic and open to people, versus days when it was not. Some studies made simple comparisons with control sites, but only at the post-implementation stage (Carmona et al., 2018; Happy City, 2019).

The second most common method was simply asking users about their change in perceptions or behaviour following the interventions, or their behaviour if the intervention had not happened. In most cases, the analysis of the resulting data used simple descriptive statistics. The studies by Salvo et al. (2017) and Igel et al. (2020) improved on this approach by using logistic regression, while Semenza et al. (2007) applied analysis of variance to pre- and post-intervention data.

More robust evaluation methods compared improved streets with control streets. The methods used included difference-in-differences analysis (Rong and Freeman, 2024; Said et al., 2020; Jung et al., 2017), quasi-experimental before-after assessments with paired sample tests (Cambra and Moura, 2020), and *t*-tests of pre- and post-intervention data (Curl et al., 2015). Other studies considered control groups of participants, using pretest vs. post-test designs (Cortinez-O'Ryan et al., 2017; D'Haese et al., 2015), and propensity score matching to create a counterfactual group (Chang et al., 2017). A third approach was to aggregate data. For example, Benavides et al. (2023) used the fact that "open streets" were only active on certain days of the week to estimate the correlation, at an areal level, between the percentage of "open streets" and noise complaints in an area on a given day.

It is difficult to pinpoint the effect of an intervention, as the methods used to analyse it tend to restrict the temporal and spatial scope of the analysis. For example, Carmona et al. (2018) suggest that the increase in pedestrian volumes following the improvement of one street may be part of a long-term trend (which cannot be detected without a time series analysis over a long period). Interventions may also affect areas not targeted by the interventions, either positively or negatively (for example, if motorised traffic is displaced). In studies that considered those areas, they were used only as control sites, not to analyse the intervention's effects on those areas. For example, in the study by Nello-Deakin et al. (2024), people living on other streets had worse perceptions of pedestrianised streets than people living on these streets. This could be either because people living on other streets visited pedestrianised streets less often or because there was an increase in motorised traffic on other streets.

3.8 Outcomes

3.8.1 Overview

Table 5 synthesises the evidence of the effects of the eight types of intervention on the use of streets as places and on health-related outcomes. Full information is contained in the table in the appendix.

Several studies provided evidence on the effect on the number of pedestrians walking but fewer provided evidence on the effect on the number of people engaging in (stationary) place activities. No studies analysed changes in the diversity of users and activities. The few studies evaluating changes in time spent in places used self-reported, ordinal, and

Table 5 Summary of evidence on outcomes of interventions to improve place activities in urban streets.

Intervention	Effect on use of streets as places	Health-related outcomes
Pedestrianisation	More pedestrians (Allirani et al., 2024; Yoshimura et al., 2025)	• Less pollution (Allirani et al., 2024) • Higher quality of life (Allirani et al., 2024) and street liveability (Staricco et al., 2024) • Modest evidence of improvement in perceived noise, interaction with neighbourhoods, traffic, pollution, peacefulness, and traffic danger (Nello-Deakin et al., 2024) • Some perceptions of an increase in tumult and anti-social behaviour (Nello-Deakin et al., 2024)
Shared space	• More satisfaction with walking (Oh and Kent, 2017; Karndacharuk et al., 2015) and with place quality (Karndacharuk et al., 2015) • People walk less hastily and with more confidence (Kaparias and Tsonev, 2023)	• Traffic speeds: decrease (Oh and Kent, 2017) or increase (Karndacharuk et al., 2015) • Lower traffic volumes (Karndacharuk et al., 2015) • Fewer vehicle-pedestrian conflicts (Oh and Kent, 2017) and more satisfaction with safety and with lack of vehicle dominance (Karndacharuk et al., 2015)
Wide spaces (plazas)	More time spent in public spaces (Gehl Studio and J. Max Bond Center, 2015)	• Greater sense of inclusion, willingness to meet people (Happy City, 2019) • More social connectedness (Gehl Studio and J. Max Bond Center, 2015) • Greater perceived safety (Gehl Studio and J. Max Bond Center, 2015; Happy City, 2019)

(continued)

Table 5 Summary of evidence on outcomes of interventions to improve place activities in urban streets. (*cont'd*)

Intervention	Effect on use of streets as places	Health-related outcomes
Parklets	• More place activities (Pratt, 2011; Loukaitou-Sideris et al., 2013) • More pedestrians (Pratt, 2011; Loukaitou-Sideris et al., 2013)	Perception of ease of socialising: increase (Pratt, 2011; Loukaitou-Sideris et al., 2013) or decrease (Pratt, 2011)
Pop-up spaces	• More time spent in the area (Salvo et al., 2017) • Modest evidence of more users of the area (Winter et al., 2020)	More time spent outdoors or in a park and less time spent in sedentary activity (Salvo et al., 2017)
Regular street closures	• More use of streets among children (Adhikhari et al., 2021) • More outdoor playtime among children (Cortinez-O'Ryan et al., 2017) • More pedestrians (Rong and Freeman, 2024) • Modest increase in the number of people using local shops (Chaudhuri and Zieff, 2015)	• More physical activity (Wolf et al., 2015; Zieff et al., 2016; Cohen et al., 2016; Engelberg et al., 2014; Cortinez-O'Ryan et al., 2017; D'Haese et al., 2015) • More community cohesion (Zieff et al., 2016) • More social interaction (Adhikhari et al., 2021; D'Haese et al., 2015) • Less pollution (Kalisa et al., 2025; Shu et al., 2016; Whitlow et al., 2011) • More noise (Benavides et al., 2023)
Major design improvements (wider footways + other design elements)	• More place activities (Carmona et al., 2018) • Small increase in time spent outside (Webster et al., 2006) • Pedestrian volume: increase (Cambra and Moura, 2020; Chang et al., 2017; Shu et al., 2014), modest or no	• More physical activity (Curl et al., 2015) • Traffic volume: reduction (Webster et al., 2006) or little effect (Shu et al., 2014; Carmona et al., 2018) • Collisions: reduction (Biddulph, 2010) or no effect (Carmona et al., 2018; Webster et al., 2006).

	effect (Carmona et al., 2018; Said et al., 2020; Hagen and Tennøy, 2021; Jung et al., 2017) • Pedestrian satisfaction: increase (Said et al., 2020; Cambra and Moura, 2020; Jung et al., 2017; Curl et al., 2015; Webster et al., 2006) or small increase (Hagen and Tennøy, 2021) • Increase in pedestrian satisfaction in response to the wider sidewalk and rest point provision components of the scheme (Said et al., 2020) • Small increase in satisfaction with the area (Hagen and Tennøy, 2021)	• Fewer people walk on carriageway (Said et al., 2020) • Lower traffic speeds (Biddulph, 2010; Webster et al., 2006) • Increased perception that streets are safer for children (Biddulph, 2010) • Less crime and anti-social behaviour (Biddulph, 2010) • Reduction of most polluting vehicles and some pollutants (Shu et al., 2014) • Less noise and air pollution (Webster et al., 2006) • Small increase in commuting satisfaction (Hagen and Tennøy, 2021) • No significant effect on quality of life or community engagement (Curl et al., 2015) • No effect on social networks (Curl et al., 2015; Biddulph, 2010)
Minor design interventions (mix of public art, rest points, greenery)	No evidence	• More physical activity among children (Igel et al., 2020) • Better mental health (less depression) (Semenza et al., 2007) • More sense of community and social capital (Semenza et al., 2007) • More neighbourhood satisfaction, sense of place, and neighbourhood participation (Semenza and March, 2009) • More social interactions (Semenza et al., 2007; Semenza and March, 2009)

general indicators (e.g., the proportion of users who stated that they increased time spent in public spaces), not direct measurements of actual time people spent in a specific place.

The most frequent health outcomes studied were physical activity, collisions (or indicators of collision risk), and indicators of subjective wellbeing (e.g., perceived quality of life, satisfaction with the neighbourhood and with travel). Only one study analysed mental health outcomes (depression) (Semenza et al., 2007) and none analysed physical health outcomes. Health-related social and environmental outcomes were well covered (particularly social interaction, assessed by a variety of self-reported indicators). The only exception was the effect on local climate, which was not covered by any study.

3.8.2 Outcomes of each intervention

As shown in Table 5, pedestrianisation was associated with an increase in the number of pedestrians and with positive health-related outcomes such as reduced pollution, increased quality of life, and street liveability. However, a study in Barcelona (Nello-Deakin et al., 2024) found less optimistic results, with only modest evidence of improvement in residents' perceptions of social and environmental aspects and with some perceptions of negative social aspects such as tumult and anti-social behaviour.

Shared space was associated with greater satisfaction with walking and with place quality. It was also associated with better quality of the walking experience, as pedestrians walk less hastily and with more confidence. There is conflicting evidence regarding the effect of the intervention on traffic speeds. However, studies have found that shared spaces decrease traffic volumes and vehicle-pedestrian conflicts, increase perceived safety, and decrease perceived dominance of motorised vehicles.

Wide spaces (plazas) were associated with more time spent in public spaces and several positive social outcomes, including sense of inclusion, willingness to meet people, social connectedness, and perceived safety.

Parklets were associated with an increase in the number of pedestrians and place activities. There is inconclusive evidence regarding the effect on the perception of ease of socialising.

Pop-up spaces were associated with an increase in the time spent in the area but there was only modest evidence of an effect on the number of users of the area. The intervention was also linked to an increase in time spent outdoors or in a park and a decrease in time spent in sedentary activities.

Regular street closures were associated with an increase in the use of streets and outdoor playtime among children and with an increase in pedestrian volumes (although one study found only a modest increase in the number of people coming to local shops). Positive health-related outcomes include more physical activity, community cohesion, and social interaction. Three studies found a decrease in air pollution, but one study found that the intervention was associated with an increase in noise complaints.

Major design improvements were associated with an increase in the number of place activities and in satisfaction with the area. There was inconclusive evidence on the effect on pedestrian volumes and pedestrian satisfaction. Other documented positive outcomes include an increase in physical activity, lower traffic speeds, fewer people walking on the carriageway, increased perception that streets are safer for children, reduced crime and anti-social behaviour, reduced noise and air pollution, and increased commuting satisfaction. The reviewed studies found no significant effect on quality of life, community engagement, and social networks. There is inconclusive evidence on the effect on motorised traffic volumes and collisions. While major design improvements include a variety of changes in the street design, one study found that a scheme increased pedestrian satisfaction both in general and specifically linked to two changes: wider sidewalks and provision of rest points (Said et al., 2020).

There is no evidence on the effect of minor design improvements on the use of streets as places. However, these improvements were associated with several positive health-related outcomes such as more physical activity among children, improvement in mental health (depression), sense of community, social capital, neighbourhood satisfaction, sense of place, neighbourhood participation, and social interactions.

4. Discussion

4.1 Synthesis

There is increased interest in interventions that improve the use of urban streets as places, especially in the aftermath of the Covid-19 pandemic.

However, this review found that there is still insufficient evidence on the effectiveness of these interventions, especially considering the quantity and variety of interventions that have been implemented in cities around the world. Most evidence concerns part-time and temporary interventions such as regular street closures. Evidence on full-time, permanent changes to street design is limited. It is also difficult to isolate effects, as street improvement schemes usually include more than one intervention. Studies have also used a variety of different data sources and methods, sometimes resulting in inconsistent findings.

Despite the scarcity and fragmentation of relevant literature, the results suggest that interventions to improve the use of streets as places tend to have positive effects on the number and perceived quality of place activities. These interventions also tend to have positive health and health-related outcomes. In particular, the evidence of improvement in outcomes such as physical activity, social interaction, and air quality tends to be consistent. However, generalisation is difficult, because of the wide variety of countries where the evidence was obtained.

4.2 Research gaps

There is insufficient evidence on individual types of intervention to improve streets as places. Even well-established interventions such as pedestrianisation lack sufficient evaluation studies. There is also little evidence regarding interventions that have been common in many cities in recent years, such as new plazas replacing underused space at junctions and parklets replacing car parking spaces. Likewise, there is little evidence on the role of improvements in specific components of major street redesign schemes, such as wider footways, and the provision of more space for street vending, outdoor cafés, rest points, street lights, greenery, public art, and inclusive design elements. In addition, there is no evidence concerning the effect of other street design elements such as storefront extensions, shade and shelter, public toilets, on-street exercise equipment, and artificial water features. Another research gap is the effect of providing less, rather than more, street furniture, as part of strategies to declutter footways.

While studies covered a range of indicators of the use of streets as places and of health-related outcomes, there are still considerable gaps regarding aspects of both intensity and quality of street uses other than walking, as well as aspects of diversity of street users and activities.

There are also gaps regarding both physical and mental health outcomes. In addition, while the review found separate evidence on effects on the use of places and on some health-related outcomes, little is known about the pathways between the two types of effects, i.e., how the increase in the intensity and quality of the use of streets as places contributes to better health among users.

Finally, this review found few studies of interventions in cities in the Global South, especially interventions involving full-time, permanent changes to street design. This might be because the review was limited to studies in English – relevant studies may exist in other languages.

4.3 Methodological limitations

This review found few examples of robust evaluation methods applied to assess the effects of the interventions. Simple before-after comparisons, the most commonly used method, have limitations. If the 'before' and 'after' are specific moments in time, then the choice of these moments can affect the results, as they depend on the season (which influences weather conditions and holiday periods) and other contextual factors. The use of averages over a period does not solve the problem, as differences in the outcome variables do not necessarily indicate a direct effect, since there is no control for long-term trends and exogenous factors affecting the streets and their users during the periods considered.

Post-implementation surveys, the second most frequently used method, also have limitations. Non-users of the streets are seldom interviewed in these surveys. This can create self-selection bias, as users are more likely to report positive outcomes. The method also relies on people's recollections of the situation before the change or on their stated behaviour in a hypothetical scenario (i.e., if the space was not available).

There is also a need to use richer datasets, to produce more robust results. Observational methods have long been used in several studies to examine time spent in place activities at a given moment, but as shown in this review, they have not been widely applied to study changes in the use of streets following improvements. New technologies can support this by extracting more meaningful data from video footage. Data can also be collected from sensors installed on street furniture (to capture, for example, the number of people using a place, and how the space is used). The use of data from mobile phone tracking, already used regularly to study aspects of urban movement, could be extended to study place activities.

The temporal and spatial scope of evaluation studies also needs to be broadened. The effect of improvements in street quality may only be discernible in the medium and long term. Effects detected immediately following the intervention may be temporary. A longer period of monitoring and evaluation is needed to capture the full impact. In addition, effects may occur only when there is a general improvement in the street environments experienced by each individual in their daily life, which means that a wider spatial scale may be needed for evaluation studies, capturing all improvements made in an area. The effects of improvements in a single street may also be felt in a wider area, not only because the street may attract people living in other parts of the city (or outside the city) but also because improvements in one street may negatively affect other streets (for example, if motorised traffic is diverted).

4.4 Reflections on this scoping review

This review brought together a scattered body of literature containing studies from journals mostly read by transport and urban planning experts, and others mostly read by public health experts. The review also brought together evidence on a range of interventions that are diverse in nature but share the objective of improving streets as places, either through changes to street design or by providing regular events for place activities by closing the street to motorised traffic.

Reviewing a large number of interventions required the imposition of restrictions on the types of studies selected. This led to the exclusion of some types of interventions that could plausibly be considered as improving streets as places, such as speed limits and point closures. It also led to the exclusion of studies that could provide relevant evidence on possible effects but are not based on real-world interventions, such as virtual reality or stated preference methods.

Finally, while the aim was to review diverse sources of information, in practice it was difficult to locate relevant grey literature. Information on transport agency websites often lacks the required detail and full evaluation reports are not always made publicly available.

Appendix – Data extracted from reviewed studies.

Study	City	Intervention	Timing	Data	Method	Effect on street use	Health-related outcomes
Pedestrianisation							
Allirani et al. (2024)	Bengaluru, India	Pedestrianisation	Part-time (weekends), temporary (4 months)	• Pedestrian counts extracted from video data • Measurement of air pollution (PM2.5, PM10) • Survey (n = 656)	• Simple before-after comparison • Correlation between satisfaction with air quality and footfall and with quality of life	66% increase in number of pedestrians	• Decrease in pollution • Increase in perceived quality of life
Nello-Deakin et al. (2024)	Barcelona, Spain	Pedestrianisation	Full-time, permanent	Survey (n = 1211) of residents in pedestrianised and non-pedestrianised streets	User perceptions about change	N/A	• Less noise (18%), more interaction with neighbourhoods (9%), less traffic (9%), less pollution (8%), more peaceful (6%), less traffic danger (5%) • Lower values among residents of non-pedestrianised streets • Negative: too much tumult (23%) and anti-social behaviour (11%)
Staricco et al. (2024)	Turin, Italy	Pedestrianisation of four areas	Full-time, temporary (4 months)	Surveys (unknown sample size)	User perception about change	N/A	25–40% stated that the project improved the liveability of the streets

Yoshimura et al. (2025)	Osaka, Japan	Pedestrianisation, benches, tables	Full-time, temporary (1 month, every year)	Mobile phone tracking data	Simple comparison of pedestrian density during experiment vs. regular day	Increased number of pedestrians in the area	N/A
Shared space							
Karndacharuk et al. (2015)	Auckland, New Zealand	Shared space, benches, trees, outdoor dining	Full-time, permanent	• Motorised traffic data • Survey (n = 40 pre-implementation and 227 post-implementation)	• Simple comparison of before-after traffic data • User perception about change	• Higher satisfaction with place quality and pedestrian movement	• Lower traffic volume but higher traffic speed • Higher satisfaction with safety and with lack of vehicle dominance
Oh and Kent (2017)	Two streets in Seoul, South Korea	Shared space	Full-time, permanent	• Pre- and post-implementation video observation of pedestrians and motorised traffic • Post-implementation surveys (n = 320 and n = 112) in the two streets	• Simple before-after comparison of pedestrian and traffic data and interactions • User perception about change	• Increased pedestrian satisfaction • Pedestrian volume data collected but not reported in the study	• Motorised traffic speeds slightly decreased. • Reduced number of pedestrians in risky proximity to vehicles
Kaparias and Tsonev (2023)	London, UK	Shared space	Full-time, permanent	Pre- and post-implementation video observation of pedestrians and motorised traffic	Logistic regression	People walk less hastily and with more confidence	N/A

Plazas							
Gehl Studio and J. M-ax Bond Center (2015)	New York, USA	Seven plazas	Full-time, permanent	Survey of users (n = 489)	User perception about change	35–75% of users increased the time spent in public spaces	• 25–80% of users recognise or know more people in the neighbourhood since the plaza opened • 60–80% feel safer in the area
Happy City (2019)	Vancouver, Canada	Three new plazas	Full-time, permanent	Survey of users (n = 703)	Simple comparison with 3 control sites (in post-implementation stage)	N/A	Higher willingness to meet people, sense of inclusion, and safety, compared with control sites
Parklets							
Pratt (2011)	San Francisco, USA	Three parklets	Full-time, permanent	• Pedestrian counts • Observation of stationary activities • Post-implementation surveys of user perceptions (unknown sample sizes)	• Simple before-after comparison of pedestrian counts and stationary activities • User perception about change	• Number of people engaging in stationary activities increased in all three sites • Pedestrian volumes increased in only one of the three sites	Perception of area as a good place to socialise increased in one site and decreased in another
Loukaitou-Sideris	Los Angeles, USA	Two parklets	Full-time, permanent	• Pedestrian counts • Observation of	• Simple before-after comparison of pedestrian	• Increase in number of people sitting	Increase in perception of ease of socialising with others

et al. (2013)				stationary activities • Surveys of user perceptions (pre-implementation: n = 55; post-implementation: in the block: n = 122, in the parklet: n = 43)	counts and stationary activities • User perception about change	• Increase in pedestrian volumes	
Pop-up spaces							
Salvo et al. (2017)	Los Altos, USA	Pop-up park in whole street, with green area, seating, tables, shade, and skate park	Full-time, temporary (6 weeks+3.5 weeks thefollowing year)	Survey of users about alternative time use (n = 147)	Logistic regression	Pop-up park associated with higher odds of spending ≥30 min/week in the area	• Pop-up park associated with higher odds of spending ≥30 min/week outdoors or at a park and with lower odds of spending ≥30 min/week in front of a screen. • Only 15% would be at another park, if this pop-up park were unavailable

Winter et al. (2020)	Los Altos, USA	Pop-up parks in whole streets, with green area, seating, tables, shade, cultural/social/sport events	Full-time, temporary (2.5–6 weeks)	• Survey of local businesses about the number of pedestrians (n = 95) • Direct observation of number of pedestrians walking to specific businesses (n = 8)	• User perceptions about change • Simple before-after comparison of pedestrian counts	• 70% of businesses reported no increase in number of pedestrians • Increase in observed number of pedestrians walking to the 8 businesses surveyed	N/A
Regular street closures							
Whitlow et al. (2011)	New York, USA	Summer streets (closure of street to motorised traffic for citizens to engage in physical activity)	Part-time (Saturday morning), temporary (3 Saturdays)	Air pollution data	Simple comparison with times when traffic was allowed	N/A	• Reduced ultrafine concentrations • PM2.5 concentration remained high.
Engelberg et al. (2014)	San Diego, USA	Ciclovia (closure of streets to motorised traffic, for sports and recreation)	Part-time (1 day) (1 day)	Survey of users (n = 713)	Descriptive statistics	N/A	Without the event, 27% of attendees would have been inactive

D'Haese et al. (2015)	Ghent, Belgium	19 play streets (closure of streets to motorised traffic, for *recreational* activities)	Part-time (at least 7 consecutive days), temporary (2 months)	• Data from accelerometers used by 126 children for a week • Before-after survey of parents (n = 126)	Pretest vs. post-test design with control group	N/A	• Significant increase in moderate-to-vigorous physical activity and reduction in sedentary time in intervention but *not in control* group • 59% of parents in intervention area thought there was more social contact with neighbours
Wolf et al. (2015)	New York, USA	Summer streets (closure of street to motorised traffic for citizens to engage in physical activity)	Part-time (Saturday morning), temporary (3 Saturdays)	Survey (n = 274) of users	Descriptive statistics	N/A	Average of 26–68 min of moderate physical activity during the initiative among users who do not regularly engage in such activity
Chaudhuri and Zieff (2015)	San Francisco, USA	Open streets (street closure, events)	Part-time (Sundays), temporary (3 months)	Survey of business owners (n = 317)	Simple comparison of stated number of people coming to the shop during the Sunday event and on a usual Sunday	Modest increase in number of people coming to local shops	N/A
Cohen et al. (2016)	Los Angeles, USA	Ciclovia (closure of streets to motorised traffic, for sports and recreation)	Part-time (4 times a year), permanent	Survey of users (n = 1085)	Descriptive statistics	N/A	Without the event, 45% would have been sedentary, 40% would have been physically active elsewhere

Zieff et al. (2016)	San Francisco, USA	Play streets (closure of streets to motorised traffic, for recreational activities)	Part-time (Sundays), temporary (2 months)	• Observation of physical activity • Survey of users (n = 75)	• Simple comparison of physical activity before and after the intervention, on the same street • User perception about change	N/A	• Vigorous physical activity increased from 12% to 35%. • 93% of participants agreed that the initiative strengthens the community • 96% would seek more opportunities to engage in physical activity
Shu et al. (2016)	Los Angeles, USA	Ciclovia (closure of streets to motorised traffic, for sports and recreation)	Part-time (Sundays, a few times a year), permanent	Air pollution data (PM2.5)	Comparison of expected and measured PM2.5	N/A	49% reduction in on-road PM2.5 and 12% reduction in community-wide PM2.5
Cortinez-O'-Ryan et al. (2017)	Santiago, Chile	Play streets (closure streets to motorised traffic, for recreational activities)	Part-time (two evenings/week), temporary (3 months)	• Data from pedometers used by 100 children for a week • Before-after survey of parents (n = 100)	Pretest vs. post-test design with control group	Significant increase in after-school outdoor playtime	• Significant increase in daily number of steps, and % of children who meet recommended number of steps in intervention but not in control group • The event replaced screen-based activities for 62% of children
Kalisa et al. (2025)	Kigali, Rwanda	Car-free days (motorised traffic restriction on some major roads)	Part-time (Sunday morning, every 2 weeks), permanent	Air pollution data	Simple comparison with other days	N/A	15% reduction in PM2.5 on car-free days

Adhikhari et al. (2021)	Columbus, USA	Closure of street to traffic, play and sports activities aimed at children	Part-time (every other week), temporary (2 months)	Survey of children's caregivers (n = 69)	User perception about change	55% of children would be inside without the event	55% of caregivers had more contact with their neighbours because of the event.
Benavides et al. (2023)	New York, USA	Open streets (street closure for physical activity and recreation)	Part-time (period varies from street to street), permanent	Noise complaints	Correlation between % of open streets and noise complaints on an area in a given day	N/A	Open streets associated with more noise complaints
Rong and Freeman (2024)	New York, USA	Open streets (street closure for physical activity and recreation)	Part-time (period varies from street to street), permanent	Anonymised pedestrian movement data from mobile phone tracking	Difference-in-differences comparison with control streets	Increase in pedestrian activity	N/A
Major design improvements							
Said et al., (2020)	Beirut, Lebanon	Wider footway, removal of parking lane, seating, trees, lighting, colourful mural, tactile paving	Full-time, permanent	• Pedestrian counts • Survey (n = 279)	Difference-in-differences comparison with a control street in the same area	• Little evidence of impact on number of pedestrians • Increase in pedestrian satisfaction (overall and in response to wider sidewalk and provision of seating)	More pedestrians walking on footway, not carriageway

Carmona et al. (2018)	London, UK	Improvements in five streets and surrounding areas, including wider footways, new pavement, greenery, lighting, seating, other street furniture (bins), small square	Full-time, permanent	• Pedestrian counts (on one street only) • Observation of place activities (walking, formal/informal/café sitting, waiting, standing) • Motorised traffic data • Serious/fatal collision data	• Simple before-after comparison of number of pedestrians, motorised traffic, and collisions • Comparison of place activities with control streets (in the post-implementation stage)	• 5% change in number of pedestrians, but maybe part of long-term trend • More place activities than in control streets	Little evidence of changes in motorised traffic volumes and collisions, but data was poor and inconsistent
Hagen and Tennøy (2021)	Oslo, Norway	Improvements in city centre (wider footways, parklets, art installation, flowers, lighting, other street furniture, pedestrianisation events, removal of parking spaces)	Full-time, permanent	Yearly survey of city centre users over 3 years (n = 5457–6018) and commuters over 5 years (n = 548–1611)	Simple year-to-year comparisons	Small increase in satisfaction with walking experience, satisfaction with the area, and frequency of visits to the area, by walking	Small increase in commuting satisfaction

Cambra and Moura (2020)	Lisbon, Portugal	Improvements in two streets (wider footways, greenery, new plazas, kiosks, *cafés* with outdoor seating, improved pavement, tactile pavement)	Full-time, permanent	• Post-implementation survey (n = 802) • Pedestrian counts	Quasi-experimental before-after assessment with paired samples test	Improved walking satisfaction and pedestrian volumes	N/A
Jung et al. (2017)	Seoul, South Korea	Improvement of footways and public spaces in 28 streets	Full-time, permanent	• Pedestrian counts • Survey (n = 72 in each street) (secondary data)	Difference-in-differences comparison with a set of 218 control streets	• Increase in pedestrian satisfaction • No evidence of impact on number of pedestrians	N/A
Shu et al. (2014)	Santa Monica, USA	Wider footways, new street furniture, trees, light poles, stormwater management (plus measures for walking/cycling)	Full-time, permanent	• Pedestrian counts • Motorised traffic data • Air pollution data	Simple before-after comparisons	37% increase in number of pedestrians	• No change in motorised traffic volumes, but reduction in proportion of most polluting vehicles • Reduction in PM2.5 but not ultrafine particle concentrations

Chang et al. (2017)	Mexico City, Mexico	Wider footways, more public space, and greenery (as part of Bus Rapid Transit project)	Full-time, permanent	Survey (n = 1067 pre-implementation and 1420 post-implementation)	Propensity score matching	Increase in self-reported walking for recreation	N/A
Curl et al. (2015)	Seven streets (and surrounding areas) in the UK	Home zones (mix of interventions in the 7 sites, including shared spaces, footway widening, pavement markings, planters, traffic calming)	Full-time, permanent	Survey (n = 96 pre-implementation, n = 61 post-implementation), aged 65+	• *t*-tests in treatment and comparison sites • Correlated component regression	Improvement in perceptions of how easy it is to walk locally	• Higher likelihood of being more active post-intervention in treatment sites • No significant impact on quality of life, social networks, community engagement
Biddulph (2010)	Ten streets (and surrounding areas) in UK	Home zones (mix of interventions in the 10 sites, including shared spaces, footway widening, pavement markings, trees, planters, traffic calming, benches, play areas)	Full-time, permanent	• Speed and collisions data • Surveys	• Simple before-after comparison of speed and collision data • User perception about change		• Lower traffic speeds and fewer collisions • Increased perception that streets are safer for children. • In some cases, reduced crime and anti-social behaviour • No evidence of change in socialising

Webster et al. (2006)	Nine streets (and surrounding areas) in UK	Home zones (mix of interventions in the 9 sites, including shared spaces, footway widening, trees, planters, lighting, benches, public art, other street furniture, community areas, traffic calming)	Full-time, permanent	• Traffic counts, speed measurements • Collision data • Surveys (average of 96 responses per site pre-implementation and 74 post-implementation)	• Simple comparison before-after of traffic data • User perception about change	• 44% thought walking became more pleasant • Slight increase in time spent outside	• Reduced motorised traffic volumes and speeds • No conclusion about traffic collisions due to small numbers • In one site, reduced perception of noise and air pollution
Minor design improvements							
Igel et al. (2020)	Leipzig, Germany	Coloured pavement markings (hopscotch, labyrinths, "mirror me")	Full-time, permanent	Observation of physical activity	• Simple before-after comparison • Logistic regression	N/A	• Vigorous activity increased from 3% to 6% among children • Probability of vigorous activity significantly associated with coloured pavement

Semenza and March (2009)	Portland, USA	Street painting, information kiosks, benches, trellises for hanging gardens, planters, art wall	Full-time, permanent	Survey (n = 359)	User perception about change	N/A	Increased neighbourhood satisfaction (53%), social interactions (30%), sense of place (13%), and neighbourhood participation (43%)
Semenza et al. (2007)	Portland, USA	Murals, benches, information kiosks, trellises for hanging gardens, planters	Full-time, permanent	Surveys before (n = 325) and after (n = 349)	Analysis of variance (before-after survey data)	N/A	Significant improvements in mental health (depression), sense of community, social capital, and social interaction

References

Adhikhari, D., Henderson, T., Dolce, M., Banks, A.R., Zaim, H., Onwuka, A., Jones, N., 2021. An evaluation of PlayStreets in the South side neighborhood of Columbus, Ohio. Perspect. Public. Health 141, 97–101.

Akbar, P.N.G., Edelenbos, J., 2021. Positioning place-making as a social process: a systematic literature review. Cogent Soc. Sci. 7. https://doi.org/10.1080/23311886.2021.1905920.

Allirani, H., Dumka, A., Verma, A., 2024. A framework for assessment of pedestrianization impacts on quality of life: combining subjective and objective measures. Cities 145, 104688.

Anciaes, P., 2022. The Urban Streetspace Book - 210 Solutions to Redesign, Reallocate, or Regulate StreetspaceUniversity College London, London. https://discovery.ucl.ac.uk/id/eprint/10144332.

Anciaes, P., Jones, P., 2022. Pedestrian priority in street design – how can it improve sustainable mobility? Transportation Res. Procedia 60, 220–227.

Appleyard, D., 1981. Livable Streets. University of California Press, Berkeley, CA.

Arksey, H., O'Malley, L., 2005. Scoping studies: towards a methodological framework. Int. J. Soc. Res. Methodol. 8, 19–32.

Benavides, J., Rowland, S.T., Do, V., Goldsmith, J., Kioumourtzoglou, M.A., 2023. Unintended impacts of the open streets program on noise complaints in New York City. Environ. Res. 224, 115501.

Biddulph, M., 2010. Evaluating the English home zone initiatives. J. Am. Plan. Assoc. 76, 199–218.

Cambra, P., Moura, F., 2020. How does walkability change relate to walking behavior change? Effects of a street improvement in pedestrian volumes and walking experience. J. Transp. Health 16, 100797.

Canter, D., 1977. The Psychology of Place. The Architectural Press, London.

Carmona, M., 2019. Place value: place quality and its impact on health, social, economic and environmental outcomes. J. Urban. Des. 24, 1–48.

Carmona, M., 2021. Public Places Urban Spaces: The Dimensions of Urban Design (3rd ed). Routledge, New York.

Carmona, M., Gabrieli, T., Hickman, R., Laopoulou, T., Livingstone, N., 2018. Street appeal: the value of street improvements. Prog. Plan. 126, 1–51.

Chang, A., Miranda-Moreno, L., Cao, J., Welle, B., 2017. The effect of BRT implementation and streetscape redesign on physical activity: a case study of Mexico City. Transportation Res. Part. A: Policy Pract. 100, 337–347.

Chaudhuri, A., Zieff, S.G., 2015. Do open streets initiatives impact local businesses? The case of Sunday streets in San Francisco, California. J. Transp. Health 2, 529–539.

Chica, C.M., 2021. Toward a sociology of global comparative placemaking. Sociol. Compass 15, e12911.

CIHT (Chartered Institution of Highways and Transportation), 2010. Manual for Streets 2: Wider Application of the PrinciplesCIHT. https://www.ciht.org.uk/media/9351/manual-for-streets-2.pdf.

Cohen, D., Han, B., Derose, K.P., Williamson, S., Paley, A., Batteate, C., 2016. CicLAvia: evaluation of participation, physical activity and cost of an open streets event in Los Angeles. Preventive Med. 90, 26–33.

CoL (City of London, Canada), 2018. London complete streets design manual, https://london.ca/sites/default/files/2020-09/Complete%20Streets%20Design%20Manual.pdf.

Cortinez-O'Ryan, A., Albagli, A., Sadarangani, K.P., Aguilar-Farias, N., 2017. Reclaiming streets for outdoor play: a process and impact evaluation of "Juega en tu Barrio" (play in your neighborhood), an intervention to increase physical activity and opportunities for play. PLoS One 12, e0180172.

Couper, I., Jaques, K., Reid, A., Harris, P., 2023. Placemaking and infrastructure through the lens of levelling up for health equity: a scoping review. Health Place 80, 102975.

Courage, C., 2020. The art of placemaking: a typology of art practices in placemaking. In: Madanipour, A. (Ed.), The Routledge Handbook of Place. Routledge, London, pp. 11–55.

Curl, A., Thompson, C.W., Aspinall, P., 2015. The effectiveness of 'shared space' residential street interventions on self-reported activity levels and quality of life for older people. Landsc. Urban. Plan. 139, 117–125.

D'Haese, S., Van Dyck, D., De Bourdeaudhuij, I., Deforche, B., Cardon, G., 2015. Organizing "Play Streets" during school vacations can increase physical activity and decrease sedentary time in children. Int. J. Behav. Nutr. Phys. Act. 12, 1–9.

Dover, V., Massengale, J., 2014. Street Design: The Secret to Great Cities and Towns. Wiley, Hoboken.

Dupre, K., 2019. Trends and gaps in place-making in the context of urban development and tourism – 25 years of literature review. J. Place. Manag. Dev. 12, 102–120.

Engelberg, J.K., Carlson, J.A., Black, M.L., Ryan, S., Sallis, J.F., 2014. Ciclovía participation and impacts in San Diego, CA: The first CicloSDias. Preventive Med. 69, S66–S73.

GDCI (Global Designing Cities Initiative) and NACTO (National Association of City Transportation Officials), 2016. Global Street Design GuideIsland Press, Washington, DC. https://globaldesigningcities.org/publication/global-street-design-guide.

Gehl, J., 1971. Livet Mellem Husene [Life Between Buildings]. Arkitektens Forlag, København.

Gehl, J., 2010. Cities for People. Island Press, Washington.

Gehl Institute, 2016. The public life diversity toolkit, https://issuu.com/gehlarchitects/docs/public_life_diversity_toolkit_v2_fo.

Gehl Studio and J. Max Bond Center, 2015. Public Life and Urban Justice in NYC's Plazas, https://issuu.com/gehlarchitects/docs/nycplazastudy.

Hagen, O.H., Tennøy, A., 2021. Street-space reallocation in the Oslo city center: adaptations, effects, and consequences. Transportation Res. Part. D: Transp. Environ. 97, 102944.

Happy City, 2019. Well-being assessment: pavement-to-plaza program, https://vancouver.ca/files/cov/viva-vancouver-research-happy-city-well-being-assessment.pdf.

Heinen, E., Buehler, R., 2019. Bicycle parking: a systematic review of scientific literature on parking behaviour, parking preferences, and their influence on cycling and travel behaviour. Transp. Rev. 39, 630–656.

Hunter, R.F., Cleland, C., Cleary, A., Droomers, M., Wheeler, B.W., Sinnett, D., Nieuwenhuijsen, M.J., Braubach, M., 2019. Environmental, health, wellbeing, social and equity effects of urban green space interventions: a meta-narrative evidence synthesis. Environ. Int. 130, 104923.

Igel, U., Gausche, R., Krapf, A., Lück, M., Kiess, W., Grande, G., 2020. "Movement-enhancing footpaths" - a natural experiment on street design and physical activity in children in a deprived district of Leipzig, Germany. Preventive Med. Rep. 20, 101197.

Jacobs, J., 1961. The Death and Life of Great American Cities. Random House, New York.

Jacobs, A.B., 1993. Great Streets. MIT Press, Cambridge, MA.

Jones, P., Anciaes, P., Buckingham, C., Cavoli, C., Cohen, T., Cristea, L., Gerike, R. Halpern, C., Pickup, L, 2018. Urban mobility: preparing for the future, learning from the past - CREATE project summary and recommendations, https://discovery.ucl.ac.uk/id/eprint/10058850/.

Jung, H., Lee, S.Y., Kim, H.S., Lee, J.S., 2017. Does improving the physical street environment create satisfactory and active streets? Evidence from Seoul's design street project. Transportation Res. Part. D: Transp. Environ. 50, 269–279.

Kalisa, E., Sudmant, A., Ruberambuga, R., Bower, J., 2025. Natural experiments in urban air quality: lessons from car-free days and COVID-19 lockdowns in Kigali, Rwanda. Cities Health. https://doi.org/10.1080/23748834.2025.2468017.

Kaparias, I., Tsonev, I., 2023. Pedestrian behaviour in integrated street designs: a mesoscopic analysis. Trans. Res. Part. F: Traffic Psychol. Behav. 99, 113–126.

Karndacharuk, A., Vasisht, P., Prasad, M., 2015. Shared space evaluation: O'Connell street, Auckland. Australasian transport research forum 2015 Proceedings, https://australasiantransportresearchforum.org.au/wp-content/uploads/2022/03/ATRF2015_Resubmission_102.pdf.

Kelly, J., Ruther, M., Ehresman, S., Nickerson, B., 2017. Placemaking as an economic development strategy for small and midsized cities. Urban. Aff. Rev. 53, 435–462.

Levac, D., Colquhoun, H., O'Brien, K.K., 2010. Scoping studies: advancing the methodology. Implement. Sci. 5, 69.

Loukaitou-Sideris, A., Brozen, M., Abad Ocubillo, R., Ocubillo, K., 2013. Reclaiming the right-of-way evaluation report: an assessment of the spring street parklets. UCLA Luskin School of Public Affairs, https://www.lewis.ucla.edu/research/reclaiming-right-of-way-spring-street-parklets.

Munn, Z., Peters, M.D., Stern, C., Tufanaru, C., McArthur, A., Aromataris, E., 2018. Systematic review or scoping review? Guidance for authors when choosing between a systematic or scoping review approach. BMC Med. Res. Methodol. 18, 1–7.

Nello-Deakin, S., Vallvé, C.S., Akinci, Z.S., 2024. Who's afraid of pedestrianisation? Residents' perceptions and preferences on street transformation. Habitat Int. 150, 103117.

Nouri, A.S., Costa, J.P., 2017. Placemaking and climate change adaptation: new qualitative and quantitative considerations for the "place diagram". J. Urbanism: Int. Res. Placemaking Urban. Sustain. 10, 356–382.

NYC DoT (New York City Department of Transportation), 2020. Street Design Manual,3rd ed. NYC DOT. https://www.nycstreetdesign.info/about/download-manual.

Oh, S., Kent, J.L., 2017. Retrofitting traditional streets for shared uses: the 'Pedestrian Priority Street' in Seoul. In: Mulley, C., Gebel, K., Ding, D. (Eds.), Walking: Connecting Sustainable Transport with Health. Emerald Publishing Limited, Bingley, pp. 365–383.

Oluyede, L., Combs, T.S., Pardo, C.F., 2024. The why and how of COVID streets: a city-level review of research into motivations and approaches during a crisis. Transp. Rev. 44, 345–367.

PBOT (Portland Bureau of Transportation), 2017. PBOT livable streets strategy - best practices report, https://www.portland.gov/transportation/permitting/livable-streets.

Pratt, L., 2011. Parklet impact study: the influence of parklets on pedestrian traffic, behavior, and perception in San Francisco. San Francisco great streets project, https://groundplaysf.org/wp-content/uploads/LP_Parklet-Impact-Study_Report_2011.pdf.

Relph, E., 1976. Place and Placelessness. Pion, London.

Roaf, E., Larrington-Spencer, H., Lawlor, E.R., 2024. Interventions to increase active travel: a systematic review. J. Transp. Health 38, 101860.

Rong, H.H., Freeman, L., 2024. The impact of the built environment on human mobility patterns during Covid-19: a study of New York City's open streets program. Appl. Geogr. 172, 103429.

Said, M., Geha, G., Abou-Zeid, M., 2020. Natural experiment to assess the impacts of street-level urban design interventions on walkability and business activity. Transportation Res. Rec. 2674, 258–271.

Salvo, D., Banda, J.A., Sheats, J.L., Winter, S.J., Santos, D., King, A.C., 2017. Impacts of a temporary urban pop-up park on physical activity and other individual- and community-level outcomes. J. Urban. Health 94, 470–481.

Schneecloth, L., Shibley, S.R., 1995. Place-Making: The Art and Practice of Building Communities. John Wiley, New York.
Semenza, J.C., March, T.L., Bontempo, B.D., 2007. Community-initiated urban development: an ecological intervention. J. Urban. Health 84, 8–20.
Semenza, J.C., March, T.L., 2009. An urban community-based intervention to advance social interactions. Environ. Behav. 41, 22–42.
Shu, S., Batteate, C., Cole, B., Froines, J., Zhu, Y., 2016. Air quality impacts of a CicLAvia event in downtown Los Angeles, CA. Environ. Pollut. 208, 170–176.
Shu, S., Quiros, D.C., Wang, R., Zhu, Y., 2014. Changes of street use and on-road air quality before and after complete street retrofit: an exploratory case study in Santa Monica, California. Transportation Res. Part. D: Transp. Environ. 32, 387–396.
Staricco, L., Verlinghieri, E., Brovarone, E.V., 2024. Permanently temporary. Street experiments in the Torino Mobility Lab project. TeMA - J. Land. Use, Mobil. Environ. 3, 159–167.
Strydom, W., Puren, K., Drewes, E., 2018. Exploring theoretical trends in placemaking: towards new perspectives in spatial planning. J. Place. Manag. Dev. 11, 165–180.
TfL (Transport for London), 2017. Healthy streets for London. https://tfl.gov.uk/cdn/static/cms/documents/healthy-streets-for-london.pdf.
Thomas, D., 2016. Placemaking: An Urban Design Methodology. Routledge, New York.
Toolis, E.E., 2017. Theorizing critical placemaking as a tool for reclaiming public space. Am. J. Community Psychol. 59, 184–199.
Unwin, S., 2020. Analysing Architecture: The Universal Language of Place-making. Routledge, London.
Von Schönfeld, K.C., Bertolini, L., 2017. Urban streets: epitomes of planning challenges and opportunities at the interface of public space and mobility. Cities 68, 48–55.
Webster, D., Tilly, A., Wheeler, A., Nicholls, D., Buttr, S., 2006. Pilot home zone schemes: summary of the schemes. Transport Research Laboratory Report TRL 654, https://www.trl.co.uk/publications/trl654.
Whitlow, T.H., Hall, A., Zhang, K.M., Anguita, J., 2011. Impact of local traffic exclusion on near-road air quality: findings from the New York City "Summer Streets" campaign. Environ. Pollut. 159, 2016–2027.
Whyte, W.H., 1980. The Social Life of Small Urban Spaces. Conservation Foundation, Washington DC.
Winter, S.J., Sheats, J.L., Salvo, D., Banda, J.A., Quinn, J., Rivera, B.R., King, A.C., 2020. A mixed method study to inform the implementation and expansion of pop-up parks for economic, behavioral, and social benefits. J. Urban. Health 97, 529–542.
Wolf, S.A., Grimshaw, V.E., Sacks, R., Maguire, T., Matera, C., Lee, K.K., 2015. The impact of a temporary recurrent street closure on physical activity in New York City. J. Urban. Health 92, 230–241.
Yoshimura, Y., Yamaoka, K., Santi, P., 2025. Quantifying tactical urbanism: economic impact of short-term pedestrianization on retail establishments. Cities 160, 105803.
Zieff, S.G., Chaudhuri, A., Musselman, E., 2016. Creating neighborhood recreational space for youth and children in the urban environment: play (ing in the) Streets in San Francisco. Child. Youth Serv. Rev. 70, 95–101.

CHAPTER FOUR

Pedestrianisation in cities: A systematic review

Zanna Buckland[a,*], Emily Wall[a], Dena Kasraian[b], Audrey de Nazelle[a], and Ahmadreza Faghih Imani[a]

[a]Centre for Environmental Policy, Imperial College London, London, United Kingdom
[b]Faculty of Architecture and the Built Environment, Department of the Built Environment, TU Eindhoven, Eindhoven, Netherlands
*Corresponding author. e-mail address: zanna.buckland20@imperial.ac.uk

Contents

Abstract

Pedestrianisation – the transformation of streets into people-centric zones free of motor vehicles – has been a key urban revitalisation technique for decades, but only became more widespread, particularly in the UK and Europe, following the COVID-19 pandemic and resultant lockdown periods. This saw many cities promote active transport modes of walking and cycling, facilitate social distancing, and support outdoor dining by turning streets into traffic-free zones. However, only some of these pandemic measures progressed into permanently pedestrianised areas. This is due to the complex nature of such schemes, having to balance the needs of a variety of stakeholders with practical implementation considerations and design features. This research aims to identify the main benefits and barriers to implementing pedestrianisation schemes. A literature review was conducted to explore the types of pedestrian schemes that have been implemented worldwide and their impacts, across a wide range of studies. We also investigated the challenges in implementing

Advances in Transport Policy and Planning, Volume 18
ISSN 2543-0009, https://doi.org/10.1016/bs.atpp.2026.07.004

these schemes and identified researchers' recommendations for overcoming challenges, as well as areas for further work. The review found pedestrianisation offers a range of environmental, public health, and economic benefits, while local support and opposition, dominating car culture, and concerns around equity and accessibility are the main implementation barriers to overcome. Clear and transparent communication of the benefits and motivations behind pedestrianisation projects – through participatory planning processes and considered design – is found to be crucial for their ultimate success.

1. Intro and background

As cultural and financial hubs, cities are essential organisms in the ecosystem of humanity. Their dense populations also position them as key drivers for sustainable development and transitions (Wong, 2020); indeed, the 11th sustainable development goal is 'Sustainable Cities and Communities' (Scruggs, 2022). However, many cities still favour personal motorised vehicles over pedestrians, with roads often being central features of cities' infrastructure (Antupit et al., 1996; Brownrigg-Gleeson et al., 2023; Villani and Talamini, 2023). As city councils and urban planners seek to tackle problems such as reducing greenhouse gas emissions, improving citizens' quality of life, and addressing population increases, there is an increasing need to employ creative solutions (te Boveldt et al., 2023). Tactical urban revitalisation measures are necessary to initiate an 'urban paradigm shift' towards more sustainable living in cities (Chen, 2025; Villani and Talamini, 2023; Yassin, 2019).

One such approach is pedestrianisation: this is not a new concept (see e.g., Taylor and Newton, 1985), but has gained popularity in recent years, particularly during the COVID-19 pandemic (Bauer et al., 2023; Gregg, 2023; Yildizhan and Bilgic, 2023). Pedestrianisation can be defined as transformation of areas to be inaccessible to motorised traffic, excluding delivery and emergency vehicles, either all the time or during particular time periods. This usually involves redeveloping stretches of road or junctions into traffic-free zones that serve only pedestrians and cyclists, with the aim of creating areas that better serve local citizens and the wider urban community (Brownrigg-Gleeson et al., 2023; Uzunoĝlu and Uzunoĝlu, 2020).

Pedestrianisation can be a means of repurposing in-between spaces to better suit people rather than vehicles, particularly in dense urban areas (Sim, 2019). As stated in Sim (2019), "life between buildings' is more important than ever'. For the purpose of this review, we focus on pedestrianisation rather than including temporary road or lane closures, to avoid studies that investigate road closures for reasons other than to create more walkable streets.

Pedestrianisation offers benefits that include improvements to public health and urban environments through improving local air quality and reducing emissions (Lebrusán and Toutouh, 2020a), increasing active mobility – walking and cycling (Brownrigg-Gleeson et al., 2023), and making streets safer (Diaz and Koh, 2022). It can also lead to creation of more ergonomic, people-friendly streets and greener urban spaces, as well as contributing to climate change mitigation and reducing local greenhouse effects (Pousa-Unanue et al., 2025). Additionally, businesses could benefit from greater pedestrian footfall and residents from having a quieter, more walkable neighbourhood on their doorstep (von Schneidemesser and Betzien, 2021; Klemmer et al., 2018).

However, these positives are not always immediately apparent, and there are several challenges that might prevent policymakers from going ahead with implementation. For example, it is necessary for planners to consult with a range of stakeholders – such as local residents, business owners, and politicians – and to consider the potential social and economic impacts of these projects (Nello-Deakin, 2024; Nieuwenhuijsen and Khreis, 2016).

Many pedestrianisation projects have been implemented around the world in the last five years (2020–2025), though research into this urban transformation technique stretches back to the late 80's. Barcelona's superblock model is a prime example, utilising its grid structure to create people-centric 'green axes' streets and Ciclovia cycleways (Nello-Deakin, 2024; Nieuwenhuijsen et al., 2024), and Budapest is following suit, looking to create its own superblocks. Similarly, Paris boasts a network of around 100 pedestrianised streets in its city centre and hosts pedestrianisation days on the 1st Sunday of every month (Clean Cities Campaign, 2025; Paris je t'aime and Tourist Office, 2025). Brussels, Lisbon, and Zagreb have dedicated large, centralised areas and shopping streets to becoming pedestrianised zones (City of Brussels, 2025; Harris, 2025; Lisbon Portugal Tourism Guide, 2025; Pfanner, 2025). In London, the schemes have typically been implemented on short retail streets like South Kensington's Bute Street and Balham's Hildreth Street (Kensington and Chelsea London Borough Council, 2021; Wandsworth Borough Council, 2023). However, new pedestrianisation schemes, such as the one proposed for Oxford Street in London (Mayor of London, 2025), still face significant opposition (WSP, 2024).

While an increasing number of studies are investigating different aspects of pedestrianisation, a systematic review of the implemented schemes worldwide, the investigated impacts of pedestrianisation and the challenges and enablers of implementing pedestrianisation schemes is lacking. A literature review by Nieuwenhuijsen and Khreis (2016) collated research on schemes to remove traffic from cities, of which pedestrianisation is a common example, focusing largely on practicality and health impacts, and to some extent on environmental and social equity. Other examples of holistic, overarching research on the subject are literature reviews on economic impacts of pedestrian infrastructure (Volker and Handy, 2021), stakeholders in the governance process (Vitale Brovarone et al., 2023), and a study on barriers to pedestrianisation (Parajuli and Pojani, 2018), but none of these performed a literature review as broad as this one. This review addresses the gap by providing a pedestrianisation-focused review, exploring the literature on pedestrianisation schemes specifically and identifying their impacts, implementation challenges, and enablers. We address the following research questions:

- What kinds of pedestrianisation schemes have been implemented worldwide?
- Which impacts of pedestrianisation have been investigated, and what are the findings?
- What are the challenges of implementing pedestrianisation schemes, and what recommendations are there for addressing these challenges?

We examine these questions through a systematic literature review, which synthesises state-of-the-art findings on pedestrianisation schemes and their impacts worldwide, as well as the challenges and enablers of pedestrianisation. Finally, we identify gaps in the pedestrianisation research landscape and avenues for future research. Our findings are relevant for urban and transport researchers, planners and policy makers who are interested in pedestrianisation as a mechanism for achieving healthier, more sustainable urban areas.

2. Methodology

Addressing the research questions above, this systematic literature review aims to map the pedestrianisation schemes implemented worldwide and identify their various impacts, as well as the common barriers and enablers encountered.

Table 1 Inclusion and exclusion criteria for the literature review.

Inclusion	Exclusion
• Specifically explains pedestrianisation schemes and/or discusses the benefits and/or challenges of implementing them • Has at least 1 citation if published before 2020	• Not in English • Published before 2020 and has 0 citations • Not accessible via our academic institution • Irrelevant to the research questions, e.g., discusses pedestrian flows or tools for collecting pedestrian data rather than pedestrianisation schemes

The search was conducted in Web of Science and Scopus databases and was registered in PROSPERO (PROSPERO CRD420251137099) with the following search string:

('Pedestrianis*' OR 'Pedestrianis* area*') AND ('Barrier*' OR 'Challenge*' OR 'Support' OR 'Benefit*' OR 'Impact*' OR 'Enabler*' OR 'Motivator*').

Spreadsheets of the search metadata were retrieved and duplicates removed. Two researchers independently reviewed the titles and abstracts, excluding studies that did not meet the eligibility criteria (Table 1). They then carried out full-text screening and removed additional studies not aligned with eligibility criteria. A few supplementary papers were also included from an initial rapid search using terms such as 'pedestrianisation', 'implementation', and 'benefits' in Google Scholar.

Data extraction was carried out by two researchers. We charted the authors, title, journal, publication year, study design, geographic locations, intervention types, identified impacts of pedestrianisation, and identified challenges and enablers. We categorised findings based on 4 themes corresponding with the research questions: (1) pedestrianisation schemes and their typology; (2) pedestrianisation impacts; (3) challenges of pedestrianisation; and (4) enablers of pedestrianisation.

Given the high inclusion rate and the low rates of studies found in the Americas and Oceania, we wonder in retrospect whether 'pedestrianisation' might have been too specific a term. It is unclear what bias (if any) this might have introduced.

3. Results

The systematic searches in Web of Science and Scopus found 69 and 93 studies, respectively (PRISMA diagram in Fig. 1). Of these 162, 30 articles were found to be duplicates and removed before screening. 30 studies were eliminated after the title and abstract screening as they did not meet the eligibility criteria. A further 28 studies were excluded during full-text screening and access checks. Finally, 13 studies from our initial rapid search of Google Scholar that met the eligibility criteria were also included, bringing the total number of reviewed studies to 87.

3.1 Study characteristics

The reviewed articles span about four decades and most of the world, though some trends are evident. The majority of studies investigate cities in Europe (39) and the UK (12), with Spain, Greece, Türkiye, England, and Belgium being some of the most common countries (Fig. 2). Cities in Asian countries such as India and China also make up a significant proportion (32). Few articles examine cities in the Americas (8), Oceania (3), or Africa (2).

There is a sharp increase in pedestrianisation research over the last couple of decades, suggesting that it has recently gained more interest and popularity as a study topic (Fig. 3). This aligns with its application as a

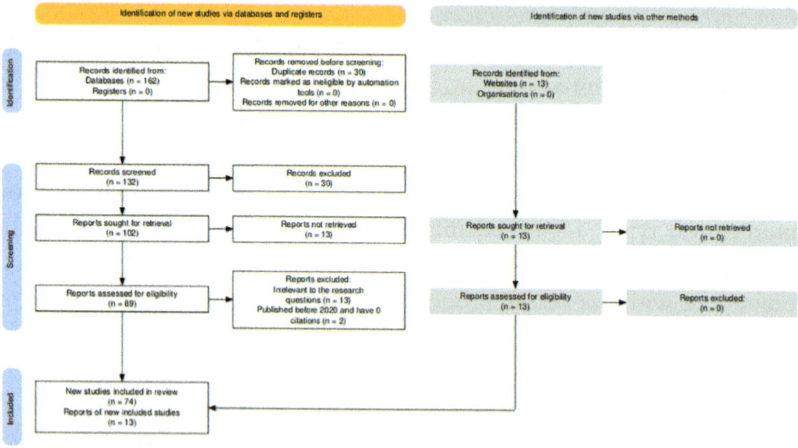

Fig. 1 PRISMA diagram outlining the systematic literature selection process for the review. Database searches yielded 162 articles, and 13 others from initial reading were also included. At the initial screening stage, records were assessed based on title and abstract, while reports assessed at the eligibility stage were based on the full texts. Our inclusion and exclusion criteria led the articles to be narrowed down to 87 (74 + 13) in total (Haddaway et al., 2022).

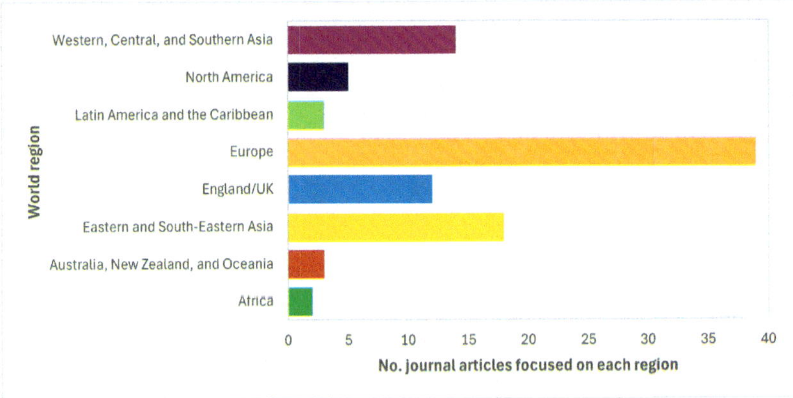

Fig. 2 Bar graph disaggregating literature review articles by world region. Some articles cover multiple regions and so are accounted for multiple times.

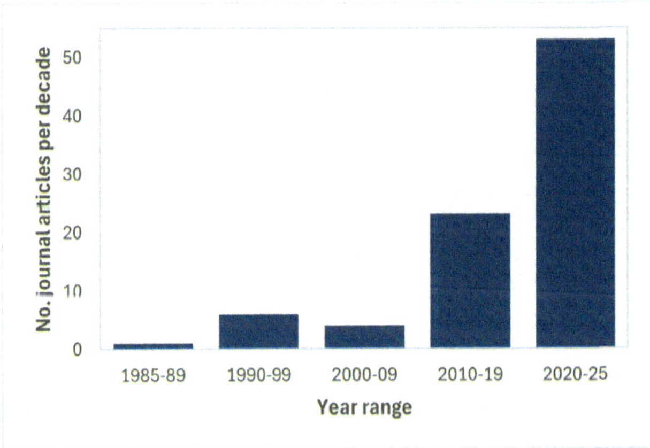

Fig. 3 Bar graph categorising papers by decade, with an overwhelming number published within the last 15 years.

policy aimed at reducing car use, addressing environmental issues, and improving public health.

Fig. 4 shows the distribution of the studies across the investigated themes. As they explored multiple aspects of pedestrianisation schemes, many papers were pertinent to more than one section of the results. Public health impacts were most frequently mentioned across most of the regions, apart from studies on Western, Central, and Southern Asia, which mentioned access and equity more often. Economic impacts were also frequently investigated, particularly in research from Europe and Asia. Studies

Africa	Australia, New Zealand, and Oceania	Eastern and South-Eastern Asia	England/UK	Europe	Latin America and the Caribbean	North America	Western, Central, and Southern Asia	REGION THEME
0	0	6	4	6	0	1	2	Environment impacts
1	0	12	8	17	3	1	6	Public health impacts
0	0	6	1	10	1	1	5	Economic impacts
0	0	3	3	14	2	0	3	Support of local residents
0	2	1	2	13	0	1	3	Mitigating opposition
0	1	2	4	15	2	0	3	Navigating existing cultures
1	2	6	1	12	1	0	9	Accessibility and equitability

Fig. 4 A summary of the literature reviewed, indicating the number of articles we included under each of the key themes identified. Articles are separated according to world region, while those spanning multiple themes or regions are counted each time they appear in the review results.

in Europe were relatively well distributed across the sub-themes, though a smaller proportion of these mention environmental impacts, which is noticeably low across the other regions too. Studies on schemes in Australia focus more on navigating car-dominating culture as well as access and equity concerns.

3.2 Typology of existing pedestrianisation schemes

This systematic literature review identified 87 academic papers on pedestrianisation, their impacts, challenges, and enablers (Table 2). Most (67)

Table 2 Summary of reviewed study characteristics, specifying the year published, intervention type, study type, cities studied, and review sections they are included in. Interventions: P = permanent pedestrianisation; T = temporary; C = traffic calming; PP = pedestrian priority. Study type: E = empirical; M = modelling/simulation; LR = literature review.

Author/s	Year	Intervention type	Study design	Cities, Countries	Section/s
Aceves-Gonzalez et al.	2020	P	E	Guadalajara, Mexico	3.2, 4.1
Allirani et al.	2024	P/T	E	Bengaluru, India	3.1, 3.2, 3.3, 4.1, 4.4
Allirani and Verma	2025	P	E	Bengaluru, India	4.1
Amistad	2010	PP	E	Vigan City, Philippines	3.2, 4.1, 4.3, 4.4
Annunziata and Pisano	2018	P	E	Cagliari, Italy	N/A
Antupit et al.	1996	PP	E	Seattle, Washington, USA	3.2
Aşilioğlu and Çay	2020	P	E	Ankara, Turkiye	4.4
Aydın and Ayataç	2015	P	E	Istanbul, Turkiye	4.4
Basbas	2007	P/C	M	Thessaloniki and Komotini, Greece	3.2
Brownrigg-Gleeson et al.	2023	P/T	E	Madrid, Spain	3.2, 4.1, 4.2, 4.3
Brugière et al.	2021	P	M	Hanoi, Vietnam	3.2, 4.1

(continued)

Table 2 Summary of reviewed study characteristics, specifying the year published, intervention type, study type, cities studied, and review sections they are included in. Interventions: P = permanent pedestrianisation; T = temporary; C = traffic calming; PP = pedestrian priority. Study type: E = empirical; M = modelling/simulation; LR = literature review. (*cont'd*)

Author/s	Year	Intervention type	Study design	Cities, Countries	Section/s
Brunner et al.	2025	P	E	Copenhagen, Denmark	3.2, 4.4
Buffoli et al.	2022	P	E	Saint German en Laye, France	3.2, 4.3, 4.4
Campisi et al.	2018	P	E	Palermo, Italy	3.2, 4.3
Castillo-Manzano et al.	2014	P/T	E	Seville, Spain	3.3, 4.1, 4.2
Chen	2025	PP	E	Hong Kong	4.1
Chiquetto	1996	P	M	Chester, England	3.2
Chiquetto and Mackett	1995	P/C	M	Chester, England	3.1, 3.2
Crabbe and Elsom	1998	P/C	E	Various cities, UK and Europe	3.1, 3.2
Diaz and Koh	2022	P	E	Cebu City, Philippines	3.1, 3.2, 3.3, 4.4
Douglas et al.	2022	P	E	London, England	3.2
Fournier	2021	PP	M	Various cities	N/A
Giannakos et al.	2016	C	M	Thessaloniki, Greece	3.2

Iliopoulou et al.	2020	P	M	Alexandroupoli, Greece	3.2
James et al.	2022	T	E	Newcastle, England	4.3
Jiménez-Espada et al.	2023	C	E	Barcelona, Spain	4.1
Kärrholm	2008	P	E	Malmo, Sweden	3.3, 4.4
Kębłowski et al.	2019	P	E	Brussels, Belgium	4.1, 4.4
Kepaptsoglou et al.	2015	P/C	E/M	Athens, Greece	3.2, 4.3
Kim et al.	2021	P	E	Seoul, South Korea	3.2
Kiminami and Dunn	2025	P	E	London, England	4.4
Kırmızı	2022	P	E	Samsun, Turkiye	3.3, 4.2, 4.3, 4.4
Klaever and Verlinghieri	2025	P	E	Berlin, Germany	4.1, 4.3, 4.4
Kubat et al.	2015	P	E	Istanbul, Turkiye	4.4
Kyriakidis et al.	2023	P/T	E	Athens, Greece	3.2, 4.1, 4.2, 4.3
Lambe et al.	2017	T	E	Various cities, Ireland	3.2, 3.3, 4.1, 4.2, 4.3
Lebrusán and Toutouh	2020 (a)	P/C	E	Madrid, Spain	3.1, 3.2
Lebrusán and Toutouh	2020 (b)	C	E	Madrid, Spain	3.1, 3.2

(continued)

Table 2 Summary of reviewed study characteristics, specifying the year published, intervention type, study type, cities studied, and review sections they are included in. Interventions: P = permanent pedestrianisation; T = temporary; C = traffic calming; PP = pedestrian priority. Study type: E = empirical; M = modelling/simulation; LR = literature review. (*cont'd*)

Author/s	Year	Intervention type	Study design	Cities, Countries	Section/s
Ma et al.	2019 (a)	P	M/E	Fo Shan, China	3.1, 3.2
Ma et al.	2019 (b)	P	E/M	Fo Shan, China	3.2, 3.3, 4.4
Ma et al.	2020	P	M	Tai Zhou, China	3.1, 3.2
Mahajan and Voßkämper	2025	C	E	Montevideo, Uruguay	3.2, 4.1, 4.3
Melia and Shergold	2018	P/C	E	Brighton, England	4.1, 4.2, 4.3
Mohajer Milani and Assarzadeh	2024	P	E	Tehran, Iran	3.2, 4.4
Murakami et al.	2021	P	E	Hong Kong	3.3
Nello-Deakin	2024	P/T/C	E	Barcelona, Spain	3.2, 4.1, 4.2, 4.4
Nello-Deakin et al.	2024	P/T/C	E	Barcelona, Spain	3.3, 4.1, 4.2
Nieuwenhuijsen and Khreis	2016	P/T/C	LR	Various cities, Europe, Asia	3.1, 3.2, 4.2, 4.3, 4.4
Nugroho et al.	2018	P	E	Various cities, Indonesia	3.2, 4.4

O'Regan et al.	2024	P	M	Cork, Ireland	3.1, 3.2
Panagopoulos et al.	2018	P	E	Kalamaria, Greece	3.1, 3.2, 3.3, 4.3, 4.4
Parajuli and Pojani	2018	P	E	Brisbane, Australia; Kathmandu, Nepal	4.2, 4.3, 4.4
Pedilarco et al.	2024	P	M	Cagliari, Italy	3.3, 4.4
Pitsiava-Latinopoulou and Basbas	2000	P/T	M	Katerini and Rhodes, Greece	3.1, 3.2, 4.4
Pousa-Unanue et al.	2025	C	E	Various cities, Spain	3.3
Rahaman et al.	2012	P	E	Guimarães, Portugal	3.3, 4.1, 4.2, 4.3
Rahul & Verma	2013	P	E	Bangalore, India	3.2, 3.3, 4.2, 4.3
Salleh et al.	2021	P/C	M	Penang, Malaysia	3.2, 3.3
Sandahl & Lindh	1995	P	E	Various cities, Sweden	3.3, 4.3
Sandoval Alfaro et al.	2024	P	E	San Jose, Costa Rica	3.2, 3.3, 4.3, 4.4
Semple & Fountas	2023	P	E	Edinburgh, Scotland	3.2, 4.1, 4.3
Shahmoradi & Guimarães	2024	P	E	Isfahan, Iran	3.1, 3.2, 3.3, 4.1, 4.4

(continued)

Table 2 Summary of reviewed study characteristics, specifying the year published, intervention type, study type, cities studied, and review sections they are included in. Interventions: P = permanent pedestrianisation; T = temporary; C = traffic calming; PP = pedestrian priority. Study type: E = empirical; M = modelling/simulation; LR = literature review. (*cont'd*)

Author/s	Year	Intervention type	Study design	Cities, Countries	Section/s
Shahmoradi et al.	2023	P	E	Isfahan, Iran	3.3, 4.2, 4.4
Sider et al.	2014	P/T	E	Montreal, Canada	3.1
Soares & Tosato	2024	P	M	Various cities	4.1, 4.2
Sylliris et al.	2023	P	E	Thessaloniki, Greece	3.1, 3.2, 4.3, 4.4
Tarriño-Ortiz et al.	2021	C	E	Madrid, Spain	3.2, 4.1, 4.2, 4.3
Taxiltaris et al.	2002	P/C	M	Komotini, Greece	N/A
Taylor & Newton	1985	P	E	Various cities, Australia	4.2, 4.4
te Boveldt et al.	2023	P	E	Brussels, Belgium	4.1, 4.2, 4.3
Treija et al.	2023	P	E	Riga, Latvia	4.1
Uzunoĝlu & Uzunoĝlu	2020	P	E	Nicosia Walled City, Cyprus	4.1, 4.2, 4.4
van Soesbergen & Mulligan	2024	P	E	London, England	3.1, 3.2

Villani & Talamini	2023	P/T	E	Hong Kong	4.3, 4.4
Villar-Abeijon et al.	2025	P	E	Barcelona, Spain	3.3, 4.3
Vitale Brovarone et al.	2023	P	LR/E	Turin, Italy	4.2, 4.3
Volker & Handy	2021	P/C	LR	Cities in US and Canada	3.3, 4.2
von Schneidemesser & Betzien	2021	P/C	E	Berlin, Germany	3.3, 4.2
Wahba et al.	2020	P	E	Cairo, Egypt	3.2
Wang et al.	2021	P	M	Tai Zhou, China	3.1, 3.2
Whelan	1994	P/T/C	E	Various cities	N/A
Wong	2020	C	E	Hong Kong	3.1, 3.2, 4.4
Yassin	2019	P	E	Various cities	4.4
Yıldırım & Çelik	2023	P/T	M	Istanbul, Turkiye	3.2, 4.4
Yildizhan & Bilgic	2023	C	E	Eskişehir, Turkiye	3.2, 4.3
Yiu	2011	P/T	E	Hong Kong	3.3, 4.2
Zhang et al.	2019	P	M	Fo Shan, China	3.1, 3.2, 3.3

were empirical studies of real-world pedestrianisation cases, some (21) were modelling or simulation scenarios, and a few used both techniques, while only three were literature reviews – the last result confirms the need for this systematic literature review. An overwhelming 84 % of the studies also focused on or mentioned permanent pedestrianisation schemes, although some also discussed temporary, traffic calming, or pedestrian priority measures. Eight articles only researched calming measures such as low-emissions zones, while four studied only pedestrian priority and two temporary pedestrianisation.

Through exploring the literature, it became clear that the types of pedestrianisation schemes could be classified in several different ways. This included temporal and spatial scales, as well as by their purpose or function, delineated by specific design features, as shown in Table 3 below.

3.3 Impacts of pedestrianisation

3.3.1 Environmental and climate impacts

3.3.1.1 Decreasing greenhouse gas emissions

Greenhouse gas (GHG) emissions – a driver of climate change, and primarily referring to carbon monoxide (CO), carbon dioxide (CO_2), and nitrous oxides (NO_x) – can be decreased locally by employing pedestrianisation for traffic reduction (Nieuwenhuijsen and Khreis, 2016). Numerous studies examining pedestrianisation's impact on GHG emissions from vehicles have found reductions in local emissions, but mixed results regarding the effects on non-local emissions (Chiquetto and Mackett, 1995; Crabbe and Elsom, 1998).

Through in-situ measurements or traffic simulations, several studies conclude that GHG emissions – particularly CO and NO_2 – are reduced following pedestrianisation, although this is typically contained to the redeveloped areas (Pitsiava-Latinopoulou and Basbas, 2000; Sylliris et al., 2023). This emissions reduction is not found to necessarily extend to neighbouring regions, and can even have detrimental effects on surrounding areas (Crabbe and Elsom, 1998; O'Regan et al., 2024; Wang et al., 2021). Mesoscopic and microscopic traffic and emissions simulations carried out by Sider et al. (2014) dispute these results, finding that pedestrianisation alone does not decrease GHG emissions in the wider neighbourhood.

However, Lebrusán & Toutouh conducted two studies that measured the effects of Madrid Central low-emissions zones (LEZs) on GHG emissions – particularly SO_2, NO_2, and O_3, finding that NO_2 was reduced

Table 3 Different classifications of pedestrianisation schemes.

Type	Definition
Temporal	
Permanent	Closed to all motor traffic, at all times of the day and week **Design features:** repaved roads, street furniture, greenery, public facilities, play or outdoor gym equipment, outdoor seating for hospitality establishments, cycle lanes
Temporary	Closed to motor traffic during certain times of the day or week **Design features:** roadblocks such as bollards or planters, signposting, traffic sensors
Seasonal	Closed during certain parts of the year, such as during the summer months or holiday periods **Design features:** banners and signposting, roadblocks, planters, market stalls
Short-term	Permanently or temporarily closed for a particular window of time **Design features:** Festival or market stalls, roadblocks, banners/signs
Spatial	
One street or road	All or part of a side street/road being closed
Main traffic artery	All or part of a major road being closed
City or town centre	Transformation of a central block of roads into a pedestrian-only zone
Zoned areas	A system of pedestrianised zones interlaced or surrounded by roads for traffic, such as superblocks
Neighbourhood or city-wide schemes	A network of pedestrianised areas that are designed in a cohesive way or feed into each other
Areas next to or surrounding public transport links	Pedestrianised streets or squares leading into metro/train/bus stations, or complemented by cycle lanes

(continued)

Table 3 Different classifications of pedestrianisation schemes. (*cont'd*)

Type	Definition
Purpose or function	
Residential or school streets	Closing these streets to vehicles or restricting vehicle access only to residents or school drop-offs
Tourism	Improving walkability around cultural landmarks or supporting the preservation of heritage sites to account for greater numbers of pedestrians
Commercial or retail streets	Closing these streets to vehicles or restricting vehicle access only to local shop owners or customers, for economic benefits
Traffic calming	Closing streets or roads to reduce traffic in the surrounding road network
Environmental and climate benefits	Improving the local environment by reducing local vehicle emissions and introducing more greenery, shade, or high-albedo paving
Public health benefits	Improving public health by reducing local air pollution, enhancing walkability, and promoting active travel
For events or recreation	Street closures to allow for one-off events such as festivals or market days, or sports such as marathons or cycling

following these traffic calming schemes being implemented (Lebrusán and Toutouh, 2020a; Lebrusán and Toutouh, 2020b). The potential for pedestrianisation to reduce NO_x emissions is corroborated by van Soesbergen and Mulligan (2024).

3.3.1.2 Mitigating the urban heat island effect

A benefit of pedestrianising roads is mitigation of the urban heat island (UHI) effect – higher temperatures in urban areas compared to rural areas. Two studies researched pedestrianisation's impact on microclimates and the UHI effect, finding positive impacts from urban design choices such as replacing tarmac with high-albedo materials and addition of vegetation (Sylliris et al., 2023; Wong, 2020). Although these features are not exclusive to pedestrianisation projects, the schemes open up opportunities to redesign streets to mitigate the UHI effect.

Sylliris et al. (2023) explore climate resilience properties of pedestrianised street designs in Thessaloniki, Greece by simulating various interventions. Their 'total pedestrianisation scenario' – prohibiting traffic and upgrading the environment with reflective or photocatalytic pavements and more vegetation (e.g., with trees and green roofs) – had the greatest cooling properties, helping to mitigate the UHI effect. Another microclimate study found similar results by investigating part-time pedestrianisation as a traffic calming measure in Hong Kong (Wong, 2020; Wong, 2020) performed in-situ temperature sampling at various locations along a pedestrianised street, finding limited cooling effects from reducing traffic flow alone. They also found higher levels of pedestrian activity resulted in warmer local air temperatures, and recommended more vegetation for mitigating the UHI effect.

A series of studies carried out on Chinese cities in 2019 and 2020 used the simulation tool ENVI-met to calculate humans' physiological equivalent temperatures (PETs) under different pedestrianisation scenarios (Ma et al., 2019a; Ma et al., 2020). Although primarily aimed at understanding pedestrianisation's effect on thermal comfort, their results showing the cooling potential of pedestrianisation measures also imply benefits for mitigating the UHI effect.

3.3.1.3 Environmental benefits from urban greenery

Inclusion of green spaces and shrubbery is not an inherent or essential element of pedestrianisation, but several studies have found greenery to have a positive impact on effectiveness and public acceptance of these projects (Allirani et al., 2024; Shahmoradi and Guimarães, 2024). Not only does urban greenery provide practical benefits for cooling and air quality management, it also improves the visual appeal of pedestrianised zones (Ma et al., 2020; Panagopoulos et al., 2018; Zhang et al., 2019). It has been less well-studied how useful car-free areas are for encouraging the return of wildlife, flood risk management, or as green corridors, although Diaz and Koh (2022) and Panagopoulos et al. (2018) have touched on some of these factors.

3.3.2 Public health impacts

3.3.2.1 Air quality improvements

PM10 and PM2.5 measurements (concentration of particles smaller than 10 μm and 2.5 μm respectively) are used for calculating air quality indexes (AQIs), which can provide insight into pedestrianisations' health benefits

(Douglas et al., 2022). The decrease in local air pollution as a result of vehicle reductions is one of the most widely studied topics in the literature and links to decreased GHG emissions (Allirani et al., 2024). Studies exploring pedestrianisation's impact on GHG emissions tend to also discuss particulate matter (PM) reductions, while others only discuss PM reductions, as they have implications for public health (Chiquetto and Mackett, 1995).

Several studies simulate different traffic interventions and compare the effect on air pollutant levels, concluding that there is a marked improvement in local air quality following pedestrianisation (Iliopoulou et al., 2020; Pitsiava-Latinopoulou and Basbas, 2000; Sylliris et al., 2023). Iliopoulou et al. (2020) applied a bi-level network model to Alexandroupoli, Greece, comparing partial (one-directional) and complete (two-directional) pedestrianisation scenarios to find pollution reductions in both cases. Pitsiava-Latinopoulou and Basbas (2000) utilised traffic network simulator TRAF-NETSIM combined with Signalized Intersection Design and Research Aid (SIDRA) to model traffic interventions in Katerini and Rhodes, also in Greece. They found NO2, CO, and hydrocarbon (HC) emissions were reduced following implementation of the proposed pedestrianisation scheme (Pitsiava-Latinopoulou and Basbas, 2000). Sylliris et al. (2023) explored the impact on microclimate from simulating 'conservative' and 'radical' car-free interventions, finding the radical scenario mildly reduces PM levels and significantly reduces NO2 in the simulation regions compared to existing conditions (Sylliris et al., 2023). Using EPISODE dispersion modelling, O'Regan et al. (2024) compared a baseline simulation with a pedestrianisation scenario in Cork, Ireland, finding that this improved air quality and reduced NO_2 exposure in the pedestrianised streets.

Two studies by Lebrusán & Toutouh use a smart city sensor network to monitor the real air pollution impacts of LEZs in Madrid (Lebrusán and Toutouh, 2020a; Lebrusán and Toutouh, 2020b). Though limited by the number of available sensors to monitor PM2.5 and PM10, Lebrusán and Toutouh (2020a) demonstrated how traffic reductions from pedestrianisation could reduce pollutant levels in the city, while Lebrusán and Toutouh (2020b) showed the same effect for NO_2 emissions. This longitudinal study, which collected data using smart city sensor networks across two periods of 30 months, evaluated the three pollutants with most cause for public health concerns (SO_2, NO_2, and O_3). A significant decrease was found in NO_2 levels across the studied periods, while slight increases in O_3 and SO_2 were attributed to differences in reactions with lower NO emissions in the area (Lebrusán and Toutouh, 2020b). Another study found significant reductions in NO_x emissions in the Strand-Aldwych project over the two years after it was implemented (van Soesbergen and Mulligan, 2024). However, the same study found that, while PM2.5 was reduced at street level in the pedestrianised zone, it increased in surrounding streets (van Soesbergen and Mulligan, 2024).

The air quality improvement potential of pedestrianisation schemes is supported by Nieuwenhuijsen and Khreis (2016), a literature review on car-free policies and their public health benefits. The review identified that research generally observes negative impacts on air quality from traffic rather than positive impacts from removing traffic, but concluded that this implies benefits from implementing traffic-restricting policies like pedestrianisation (Nieuwenhuijsen and Khreis, 2016). In a study of Bengaluru, India, by Allirani et al. (2024), measured PM levels – recorded using low-cost sensors – are used to calculate an objective indicator for quality of life (QOL). This research found temporary weekend pedestrianisation measures led to lower pollution levels, which contributed to a higher QOL for local citizens (Allirani et al., 2024).

To investigate pedestrianisation's effect on perceptions of air quality, Kim et al. (2021) surveyed users of pedestrianised zones in Seoul. This revealed that positive perceptions of air quality rely on several factors, including visibility of fine particles and dust, surrounding greenery, and proximity to traffic, which are all improved by pedestrianisation (Kim et al., 2021). A study in Bangalore, India on the economic benefits of pedestrianisation quotes air quality improvements can save cities money, estimating savings at 1611 rupees per day (Rahul and Verma, 2013).

Several papers contest pedestrianisation's positive effects on air quality (Brugière et al., 2021; Chiquetto, 1996). This is primarily due to traffic being redistributed to other roads, resulting in overall PM emission increases. Brugière et al. (2021) modelled emissions and distribution of air pollutants in a pedestrianisation case near Hoan Kiem lake in Hanoi, Vietnam. Employing an Operational Street Pollution Model (OSPM) in GAMA simulation software, the researchers found detrimental effects on the average air quality index (AQI) in the regions neighbouring pedestrianisation measures (Brugière et al., 2021), Chiquetto (1996) used Simulation and Assignment of Traffic in Urban Road Networks (SATURN) for emissions and dispersion modelling of a pedestrianisation scheme in Chester, finding that, despite the project's overall environmental benefits, traffic displacement to alternative routes would cause a slight increase in PM emissions.

Unfortunately, stabilisation of air pollution at decreased levels can take some time, so pollutant levels can appear to increase in the short-term following pedestrianisation, despite it having proven long-term air quality benefits (Giannakos et al., 2016; Kepaptsoglou et al., 2015). This is associated with short-term traffic displacement, which can cause increased congestion and vehicle emissions in surrounding streets (Chiquetto and Mackett, 1995; Wang et al., 2021). Urban canyon simulations in Hong Kong found that traffic reductions resulted in limited local air quality improvements, and no direct benefits from traffic calming, even demonstrating potential negative effects on neighbouring streets (Wang et al., 2021), and Crabbe and Elsom (1998) corroborates this result.

3.3.2.2 Traffic displacement and distal air quality effects

Reduced air pollution has been shown to be a major health benefit offered by pedestrianisation. However, several studies question whether this extends to neighbouring non-pedestrianised areas, finding negative air quality impacts from displacing traffic away from pedestrianised zones into neighbouring roads (Chiquetto and Mackett, 1995; Giannakos et al., 2016).

Two studies describe positive distal effects from reduced traffic in one area (Iliopoulou et al., 2020; Nieuwenhuijsen and Khreis, 2016), Nieuwenhuijsen and Khreis (2016) identify in their literature review that city-wide rollouts of pedestrianisation can ultimately cause traffic evaporation and decrease PM pollutants and GHG emissions in the long term.

However, (Wang et al., 2021) contests these positive effects, finding many other factors – including random particulate dispersion, wind speed, and traffic displacement – influence pedestrianisation's effectiveness for reducing air pollution in surrounding areas. Crabbe and Elsom (1998) also support this conclusion, finding that traffic flow redistribution via pedestrianisation is effective for local traffic management, but results in high PM levels due to increases in idling vehicles in neighbouring roads (Crabbe and Elsom, 1998; O'Regan et al., 2024) finds a similar result, as their simulated scenario shows improvements in targeted pedestrianised streets but no change to the total emissions in the studied region.

Rather than deterring pedestrianisation projects, these potential negative impacts signal the importance of ensuring alternative routes and modes of travel are sufficient to handle traffic displacement and evaporation effects. Traffic modelling software such as SATURN, geographic information systems (GIS), and Visum are useful for determining traffic rerouting options (Basbas, 2007; Giannakos et al., 2016; Salleh et al., 2021), Basbas (2007) employed SATURN to investigate pedestrianisation's impacts on fuel consumption, while Giannakos et al. (2016) uses static and dynamic traffic simulations in Visum for a similar investigation. Both studies determined there would also be an increase in fuel consumption where alternative routes or transport modes are insufficient (Basbas, 2007; Giannakos et al., 2016; Salleh et al., 2021) demonstrated how to develop GIS-based traffic models for exploring pedestrianisation's impact on traffic volume in neighbouring streets.

3.3.2.3 Promoting active mobility

Besides improving local air quality, pedestrianisation can encourage local residents to switch from private cars to alternative modes of transport (walking, cycling, and public transport) (Brownrigg-Gleeson et al., 2023; Mahajan and Voßkämper, 2025; Yildizhan and Bilgic, 2023). Collectively, these are termed 'active transportation' modes, as they encourage people to use their bodies for travel, instead of the more sedentary action of driving from A to B.

Promoting walkability is a recurring theme in pedestrianisation research (Kyriakidis et al., 2023; Nugroho et al., 2018; Yıldırım and Çelik, 2023; Yıldırım and Çelik, 2023) analysed citizens' behaviour following implementation of a pedestrianisation scheme in Istanbul, Türkiye. They found space reconfiguration had a direct impact on pedestrian behaviour, encouraging people to walk and socialise more – a finding supported by Mohajer Milani and Assarzadeh (2024). Brunner et al. (2025) and Sandoval Alfaro et al. (2024) also identified that urban design features and people-oriented spaces are important for prioritising pedestrians and improving walkability. Nugroho et al. (2018) found schemes in the Indonesian cities of Bandung and Bogor increased active travel and walking, particularly in younger and healthier citizens.

Kyriakidis et al. (2023) conducted an online survey about the Great Walk of Athens project in Greece, identifying an uptick in active travel and decrease in motor vehicle use, but some opposition due to a lack of public participation in the development process. However, these findings might not be generalisable due to the project being implemented during the pandemic. Regardless, the researchers observed higher levels of support from cyclists and pedestrians, as did (Panagopoulos et al., 2018) in their study of usage and perception of pedestrian and cycling streets in Kalamaria, also in Greece (Kyriakidis et al., 2023; Panagopoulos et al., 2018). Pedestrianisation's benefits for walkability are advantageous for cyclists as well, sometimes even going hand-in-hand with cycle lane improvements (Lambe et al., 2017; Mahajan and Voßkämper, 2025; Semple and Fountas, 2023). In Edinburgh, Scotland, Semple and Fountas (2023) found high support from active travellers in their active travel survey, explaining how these schemes can be useful for reducing collisions too.

A survey by Tarriño-Ortiz et al. (2021) on the introduction of an LEZ in Madrid showed that active travellers support traffic-reduction policies (Tarriño-Ortiz et al., 2021). The researchers found a similar sentiment among public transport users, as well as pedestrians and cyclists, and that the LEZ's success was reinforced by robust public transit networks. Yildizhan and Bilgic (2023) even found active travel policy investments could raise significant revenue for local municipalities, in their cost-benefit analysis on sustainable transportation infrastructure in Eskişehir, Türkiye.

No studies found significant negative impacts on active mobility. However, if the public perceives pedestrianisation as a measure for reducing car use or forcing a travel mode shift, this can be detrimental to its reception and acceptance, particularly among older adults (Brownrigg-Gleeson et al., 2023; Kyriakidis et al., 2023; Nieuwenhuijsen and Khreis, 2016).

3.3.2.4 Pedestrian safety benefits

Pedestrianisation's ability to lower morbidity and mortality comes not just from active travel and air quality benefits but also pedestrian safety enhancements, creating walkable areas with decreased risk of traffic accidents (Antupit et al., 1996; Yıldırım and Çelik, 2023). Vulnerable parties such as children and older citizens (Amiour et al., 2022), could stand to benefit the most from the provision of safer and more walkable streets that are separated from traffic-filled roads (Amistad, 2010; Pitsiava-Latinopoulou and Basbas, 2000).

Physical safety improvements are a natural benefit of removing cars and making streets more walkable (Amistad, 2010; Antupit et al., 1996; Campisi et al., 2018; Yıldırım and Çelik, 2023). A case study of creating walkable streets in Seattle, Washington stated that the city is responsible for incorporating pedestrian safety into urban design (Antupit et al., 1996). A SWOT analysis by Campisi et al. (2018) highlighted safety and security as strengths of a pedestrianised area in Palermo, Italy, which is supported by Yıldırım and Çelik, 2023; Pitsiava-Latinopoulou and Basbas (2000) found reduced road collisions due to pedestrianisation, but argued that safety provisions are reliant on features such as traffic signals and additional signage, which are important to have installed on the boundaries of pedestrianised zones. However, Wahba et al. (2020) point out in their study of

Cairo that some pedestrian safety features, such as bollards, can actually hinder pedestrian movement, so a balance must be struck in these cases.

Aceves-González et al. (2020) performed a road audit and user survey exploring physical and perceived pedestrian safety features in Guadalajara, Mexico. The study found that the organisation of pedestrian infrastructure is important for both actual and perceived safety, and that presence of obstacles, kerbside parking, and lack of traffic signals are major detrimental factors (Aceves-González et al., 2020). Successful pedestrianisation measures should also foster a sense of safety – interviews and surveys carried out for pedestrianised zones in Cebu City, Philippines and Indonesian cities Bandung and Bogor revealed this as the most important driver for increased footfall (Diaz and Koh, 2022; Nugroho et al., 2018). Perceived road safety benefits from pedestrianisation are shown to be as important as physical safety improvements for gaining public support in case studies of Saint German en Laye, France and Isfahan, Iran (Buffoli et al., 2022; Shahmoradi and Guimarães, 2024).

3.3.2.5 Improved thermal comfort

The rise in average surface temperature around the world – particularly rapid in urban regions – puts citizens at risk of heat-related afflictions, especially in warmer months (Liu et al., 2022). For people more vulnerable to heat effects (children and older adults) this is especially concerning, and pedestrianisation's ability to improve thermal comfort will be useful for future urban developments. Some of the studies that demonstrated pedestrianisation's role in UHI mitigation also researched its thermal comfort benefits (Ma et al., 2019a; Ma et al., 2020; Sylliris et al., 2023; Zhang et al., 2019).

Through exploring pedestrian zones' climate resilience, Sylliris et al. (2023) found shaded areas, environmentally-friendly paving materials, and vegetation contributed to thermal comfort improvements. A series of studies on pedestrianised areas in China confirmed that pedestrianisation can have a positive impact on thermal comfort (Ma et al., 2019a; Ma et al., 2020; Zhang et al., 2019). Wong (2020) performed temperature sampling on different regions of a pedestrian street in Hong Kong, finding less correlation between pedestrianised areas and improved thermal comfort (Wong, 2020). However, this disregarded urban design features that target cooling like those identified in the other studies; with the right design measures, improved thermal comfort could be a useful benefit of pedestrianisation (Ma et al., 2019a; Sylliris et al., 2023; Zhang et al., 2019).

3.3.2.6 Decreased noise pollution

Noise pollution from living near roads, especially those with heavy traffic, can cause health problems such as increased blood pressure and increased stress hormones due to disturbed sleep (Brogan, 2017; Cai et al., 2017). Pedestrianisation measures can mitigate this, but while some studies mention its potential for reducing noise pollution (Amistad, 2010; Chiquetto, 1996; Panagopoulos et al., 2018; Pitsiava-Latinopoulou and Basbas, 2000), only a few study it in detail (Lebrusán and Toutouh, 2020b; Nello-Deakin, 2024; van Soesbergen and Mulligan, 2024).

Lebrusán and Toutouh (2020b) examined equivalent sound pressure, percentile noise, and noise pollution by measuring and calculating monthly mean values for each metric. Limited road traffic flows due to the Madrid Central LEZ was found to reduce all three metrics over the studied period (Lebrusán and Toutouh, 2020b). According to local sound pressure level measurements, the Strand-Aldwych pedestrianisation project in central London was shown to result in a similar environmental noise reduction (van Soesbergen and Mulligan, 2024). Both studies indicate that traffic-reduction schemes such as pedestrianisation can positively influence noise pollution (Lebrusán and Toutouh, 2020b; van Soesbergen and Mulligan, 2024; Nello-Deakin, 2024) points out that pedestrianisation could introduce more noise pollution from pedestrians and cyclists later into the night that might disturb local residents, but this is arguably less harmful than noise from road traffic (Brogan, 2017; Nello-Deakin, 2024).

3.3.2.7 Creating greener public spaces

Green spaces are beneficial for the physical and mental health of city-dwellers, and urban regeneration projects like pedestrianisation provide natural opportunities to reintroduce greenery into the concrete jungle (Antupit et al., 1996). Besides the microclimate improvements vegetation provides – including UHI mitigation, local cooling, and air pollution reduction (Allirani et al., 2024; Ma et al., 2019b) – greener urban spaces offer more attractive areas. These can promote mental wellbeing, enhance social interaction, and encourage local residents to spend time outside (Shahmoradi and Guimarães, 2024).

Several studies have compared pedestrianisation's success with and without greenery. Ma et al. (2020) found incorporating more trees in these schemes has a significant cooling effect when compared to the baseline scenario, while grass had some cooling effects, but not as significant as tree cover. Surveys of pedestrians revealed their preference is for greener spaces, and that this is an important factor in their decision to use newly pedestrianised areas (Panagopoulos et al., 2018). Incorporating greenery into street designs also increases the air quality improvement potential of pedestrianisation (Allirani et al., 2024; Shahmoradi and Guimarães, 2024). Greenery has also been shown to promote emotional well-being and relaxation, and encourage people to spend more time walking through pedestrianised spaces, which has the dual benefits of increasing happiness and active travel (Brunner et al., 2025; Yang et al., 2024).

3.3.3 Economic impacts

3.3.3.1 Effects on pedestrians' spending habits

Contrary to the perception of many local businesses, studies on the local economic impact of pedestrianisation have typically found that active travellers' spending is significantly higher than that of people who drive to shops (Lambe et al., 2017; von Schneidemesser and Betzien, 2021; Volker and Handy, 2021; von Schneidemesser and Betzien, 2021) surveyed shoppers and traders on two intersecting retail streets in Berlin. Although they found active travellers spent less on average than car drivers in the area, the volume of pedestrians and cyclists was higher than drivers at any given time, and they visited more frequently, resulting in higher total revenue from active travellers. Over half of the customers surveyed also lived under one kilometre away, contradicting traders' beliefs that the majority had travelled in from further afield. A literature review on cost-benefit analyses of switching from cars to active travel modes also found that active travellers spent more at most shops – except supermarkets – than drivers (Volker and Handy, 2021).

Several studies have estimated the revenue increases that higher volumes of pedestrian shoppers can bring to retail areas post-pedestrianisation; one on Bangalore, India and another for Cebu, Philippines (Diaz and Koh, 2022; Rahul and Verma, 2013). Businesses tend to underappreciate the economic value of local residents, who are more likely to walk to their establishments, and of cyclists, who are likely to be attracted to car-free zones (Castillo-Manzano et al., 2014; Lambe et al., 2017). A comparative study of partially pedestrianised retail streets in Hong Kong similarly finds that increased pedestrian flows bring in greater revenue for local shops (Yiu, 2011; Pedilarco et al., 2024) support this finding, showing how commercial attractors (such as shopping markets and landmarks) and increased economic activity can be useful incentives for pedestrianisation.

3.3.3.2 Increased visitor footfall and tourism

The increased visitor footfall in areas following pedestrianisation translates into a higher amount of spending by pedestrians, and greater tourism revenue, particularly for areas with existing historical or cultural value (Castillo-Manzano et al., 2014; Sandahl and Lindh, 1995; Shahmoradi and Guimarães, 2024). Pedestrianised areas have been found to encourage a higher frequency of existing customer visits as well as increasing overall visitor numbers, which can bring in more money for local businesses (Panagopoulos et al., 2018; Yiu, 2011). This is especially the case where pedestrianisation incorporates people-friendly design features like ergonomic furniture, children's play areas, wider and clearer pavements, and public toilets or drinking water facilities (Allirani et al., 2024; Castillo-Manzano et al., 2014; Diaz and Koh, 2022; Rahaman et al., 2012; Sandoval Alfaro et al., 2024; Shahmoradi and Guimarães, 2024). It is important to note that redeveloped areas risk attracting too many new visitors and tourists, which could disturb existing residents, as explained in a study on perceptions of street transformation (Nello-Deakin et al., 2024).

A couple of studies explore the usefulness of pedestrianisation for improving tourists' experience of an area, through improving thermal comfort or walkability – which can provide further economic benefits (Sandoval Alfaro et al., 2024). 'Thermal calendars' developed in two studies of pedestrianisation in China were based on pedestrians' perceptions of temperature at regular intervals on the hottest days of the year (Ma et al., 2019b; Zhang et al., 2019). Increased shading, vegetation, and improved paving materials were recommended to reduce heat stress. Another study on a UNESCO heritage site in Penang showcased how GIS spatial analysis can identify where pedestrianised streets would be most effective for easing tourist crowds and travel in a particular area (Salleh et al., 2021). Pousa-Unanue et al. (2025) supports this with statistical and geographical analyses of LEZs in Spanish cities, which finds that these areas can induce touristification and cause shifts in tourists' and residents' movements.

3.3.3.3 Changes in business demographics and potential gentrification

Pousa-Unanue et al. (2025) highlights how increased tourism from traffic-reduction measures like LEZs and pedestrianisation can promote gentrification and amplify socioeconomic impacts for local residents. A major economic impact of pedestrianisation is that it can induce business district transformations (Sandahl and Lindh, 1995; Shahmoradi et al., 2023). This can be altering the demographic of local establishments, commercial gentrification, or changes to retail rent prices.

A prime example is in a study by Shahmoradi et al. (2023), who carried out observations and GIS spatial analyses on a pedestrianised street in Isfahan, Iran (Shahmoradi et al., 2023). They found that the area transitioned to house more hospitality establishments – like cafes and restaurants – in place of retail outlets selling clothes for example, despite the area being historically clothing- and textiles-oriented. This could be a positive change for people living in and visiting the area, but detrimental to businesses that had previously existed there, although retail stores that survive could benefit from increased footfall with people visiting nearby cafes or restaurants. A study of Malmö, a retail district in Sweden, explored pedestrianisation's use for 'territorialising' and designating commercial areas (Kärrholm, 2008), Kärrholm (2008) postulated that material design and social perceptions of an area are key factors in territorialisation. By mapping sociodemographic changes, another study found that local populations shifted towards younger and Global North residents following pedestrianisation in Barcelona, which also falls within the definition of gentrification (Villar-Abeijon et al., 2025).

It is important that policymakers sufficiently consider the risk of pedestrianisation coinciding with or inducing gentrification in a given area, as this can introduce inequities following implementation. A study in Samsun, Türkiye found that where pedestrianisation is enacted in a top-down manner, without appreciation for the existing physical and cultural landscape, streets can be stripped of their character, removing local citizens' sense of identity and affiliation with them (Kırmızı, 2022). Pedestrianisation in itself is not the problem here, as confirmed by a study of Hong Kong commercial districts, which found that preserving long-standing establishments can negate potential gentrification effects (Murakami et al., 2021).

The same study exposed a related consideration; the potential for urban revitalisation to increase retail rents in a given area (Murakami et al., 2021), which is backed up by Sandahl and Lindh (1995). According to a comparison of equivalent pedestrianised and non-pedestrianised shopping streets in Hong Kong, pedestrianisation can cause rental values to increase by as much as 17 % (Yiu, 2011); Rahul and Verma (2013) also found a significant increase in average rental prices following pedestrianisation, they noted this as a benefit rather than a drawback, explaining that the associated increase in revenue could alleviate the burden of potential rent increases (Rahul and Verma, 2013).

3.4 Challenges and enablers of pedestrianisation

3.4.1 Local residents and public participation

3.4.1.1 Challenge: Gaining support from residents and other citizens

Support from pedestrians and local residents is essential to the success of pedestrianisation schemes, as they are the primary beneficiaries of these measures' positive effects. Local residents are also most affected by related renovation works and changes made during implementation, so it's important they understand and agree with the motivations for pedestrianisation in their neighbourhoods (Soares and Tosato, 2024).

Allirani et al. (2024) demonstrated how support can be garnered for pedestrianisation, while Allirani and Verma (2025) used a qualitative pedestrian level of service (PLOS) evaluation criteria to determine that a pedestrianised street in Bengaluru, India appealed to local residents, especially when associated cultural activities were offered in the space. Amistad (2010) finds high levels of acceptability from local citizens in Vigan City, Philippines, as well as an understanding of the necessity for pedestrianisation schemes, particularly for improving pedestrian safety, as long as they align with the existing culture of the city.

Local residents, active travellers, and shoppers are typically supportive of these schemes, more so than casual visitors, business owners, or those forced to use alternative transportation modes (Brownrigg-Gleeson et al., 2023; Rahaman et al., 2012; Semple and Fountas, 2023; Tarriño-Ortiz et al., 2021; Rahaman et al., 2012) found pedestrians were supportive of pedestrianisation in Guimarães, Portugal, though this was dependent on perceived safety and a lack of hindrances. Semple and Fountas (2023) found preferred travel modes before and after pedestrianisation were one of the most significant factors in dictating support levels among residents; active travellers have more to gain from pedestrianised zones, therefore being more likely to appreciate them.

Public support is also affected by distance from pedestrianised areas, as local residents stand to gain more from these schemes than visitors. This can cause locals to be more positive and welcoming of redevelopment (Castillo-Manzano et al., 2014; Melia and Shergold, 2018; te Boveldt et al., 2023). A study in Brussels, Belgium found citizens living further away from a given pedestrianised area tended to show more opposition to it, which could be attributed to removal of parking availability (te Boveldt et al., 2023), Shahmoradi and Guimarães (2024) showed that pedestrianisation enhances socialisation and even creates a better sense of belonging for locals and non-locals alike.

Though many studies found high residential support, several researchers raised concerns about potential nuisance or disruption to locals due to increased human activity, noise pollution, more visitors and tourists, or renovation works (Kyriakidis et al., 2023; Melia and Shergold, 2018; Nello-Deakin, 2024; Semple and Fountas, 2023). A couple of these studies discovered that residents' opposition often stems from traffic rearrangement or accessibility issues (Melia and Shergold, 2018), particularly among older people (Brownrigg-Gleeson et al., 2023).

Nello-Deakin (2024) and Nello-Deakin et al. (2024) provide good overviews of residential perceptions towards Barcelona's 'green axes' pedestrianisation scheme. Surveys and interviews of local citizens found they perceive 'excessive street life' and 'property price increases' as negative impacts of pedestrianisation, though these can be counteracted by community and traffic-reduction benefits (Nello-Deakin, 2024; Nello-Deakin et al., 2024). 3D maps and visualisations can be useful for convincing residents of pedestrianisation's benefits (Brugière et al., 2021).

3.4.1.2 Recommendations: Need for public participation and consultation

The importance of carrying out appropriate engagement practices with local residents, pedestrians, and business owners – the users of revitalised spaces – is a common theme throughout the literature surrounding stakeholder support of pedestrianisation. Many studies recommend participatory exercises and public consultations as key mechanisms for successful pedestrianisation (Aceves-González et al., 2020, Jiménez Espada et al., 2023).

Aceves-González et al. (2020) highlighted how pedestrians' opinions of which street features benefit their safety align with results of a physical audit, and how this can inform the public space design. This is corroborated by Jiménez-Espada et al. (2023), whose SWOT analysis of an LEZ in Madrid aligns with the perceptions of citizens. (Jiménez-Espada et al., 2023) also mentioned the need for participatory planning processes, stating that lack of consultation threatens successful implementation. Survey responses for the Great Walk of Athens project implemented during COVID-19 showed citizens were dissatisfied by the lack of public consultation and clarity surrounding the project's aims (Kyriakidis et al., 2023).

Lambe et al. (2017) cite the 'silent majority' as a barrier to car-restrictive active travel policies in Ireland, explaining how opposing parties are often the most vocal, which can lead policymakers to believe they lack public support (Lambe et al., 2017; Nello-Deakin, 2024). These results show that a lack of clear incentives might not in itself be an issue, but miscommunication can be (Uzunoĝlu and Uzunoĝlu, 2020). A solution to this was laid out by Uzunoĝlu and Uzunoĝlu (2020), who recommended using active engagement platforms to communicate with local stakeholders with regards to pedestrianised streets in the Walled City of Nicosia, Cyprus.

A lack of participatory practices was found to foster distrust within the local community in the case of Chaharbagh Abbasi, a pedestrian street in Iran (Shahmoradi and Guimarães, 2024). This can be harmful for a range of demographics, and small sample size is noted as a limitation for a pedestrianisation study in Edinburgh (Semple and Fountas, 2023). Tarriño-Ortiz et al. (2021) showed how participatory planning processes are benefitted by the ability to select particular groups of citizens, particularly under-represented ones. Older adult citizens are an example of a group that might be disproportionately excluded from web-based surveys, but need to be considered when implementing pedestrianisation (Nello-Deakin, 2024; Tarriño-Ortiz et al., 2021), Kębłowski et al. (2019) highlight that a lack of participatory practices, or too narrow a focus – such as transport policies specifically for sustainability – can exclude or negatively impact working-class residents.

Treija et al. (2023) show the importance of community engagement for creating more liveable and greener spaces that will actually be used by citizens in their analysis of urban experiments in Riga, Latvia. Similarly, Chen (2025) discusses how a range of stakeholders and community participation are necessary to develop sustainable pedestrianised environments, as evidenced by the case of Des Voeux Road Central in Hong Kong. By analysing participatory design processes and tactical urbanism they found that, while involving the local community in the decision-making for pedestrianisation is imperative (Chen, 2025; Mahajan and Voßkämper, 2025; Treija et al., 2023), it is important to balance this with input from knowledgeable professionals, including spatial design experts, architects, environmentalists, and policymakers (Chen, 2025).

Klaever and Verlinghieri (2025) examined participatory processes in the pedestrianisation of Lausitzer Platz in Berlin, exploring the reasons why local residents might not join consultations. The study found that, although all their interviewees did participate, pre-existing social inequalities such as differences in life experiences and prior involvement in local politics or consultations influenced how actively they participated, which could affect the outcome of such consultation processes.

3.4.2 Mitigating stakeholder opposition and distrust

3.4.2.1 Challenge: Opposition and distrust from local businesses and stakeholders

Local business owners often hold negative perceptions of proposed pedestrianisation projects, despite studies showing transitions to active travel typically increase spending in local establishments (Nello-Deakin, 2024; Volker and Handy, 2021; Nello-Deakin, 2024) explores the risk of creating winners and losers, and the trade-offs made between local businesses, claiming that inequities between streets can be more harmful to businesses than residents.

Commercial gentrification and increases in retail rent are some of the most prominent pedestrianisation impacts (Rahul and Verma, 2013; Yiu, 2011). Business district transformation due to pedestrianisation can cause traders who lose business or feel they no longer fit in to vacate these areas (Kırmızı, 2022; Shahmoradi et al., 2023; Kırmızı, 2022) speculates this is due to design and implementation rather than pedestrianisation schemes themselves.

Perceived impacts can feed into opposition from local businesses, as explored in several studies that surveyed or interviewed business owners about their local pedestrianisation projects (Brownrigg-Gleeson et al., 2023; von Schneidemesser and Betzien, 2021; Volker and Handy, 2021). Multiple studies found that retailers often associate cars and parking with revenue, but that concerns about traffic reduction are unfounded, as increases in pedestrian and cyclist visitors tend to cancel out negative economic effects (Lambe et al., 2017; von Schneidemesser and Betzien, 2021; Volker and Handy, 2021; Brownrigg-Gleeson et al., 2023) corroborate this, finding more concern among small independent retailers than from shoppers or larger businesses.

Despite concerns around reduced revenue, economic returns for car-free streets are shown to be better than those with car traffic, and pedestrianisation has been shown to increase retail income (Nieuwenhuijsen and Khreis, 2016; Rahul and Verma, 2013; von Schneidemesser and Betzien, 2021; Parajuli and Pojani (2018) contested business owners' opposition, finding support from merchants in both Brisbane and Kathmandu, and that deliveries and unloading were not significant concerns for their interviewees. This study, and another on pedestrianisation in Australia, found development of pedestrian malls was beneficial to commercial retailers, although skewed towards hospitality establishments and 'daily need' stores (Parajuli and Pojani, 2018; Taylor and Newton, 1985). This potentially leads to changes in the business demographic for pedestrianised areas, which should be mitigated by defined aims and engagement (Taylor and Newton, 1985).

In the case of Guimarães city centre in Portugal, shopkeepers were supportive of pedestrianisation measures on the pavements outside their stores, as most shoppers were arriving on foot, although they recommended that their requests for concentrated parking offerings and pavement shades, for example, be considered by local policymakers (Rahaman et al., 2012). Pedestrianisation projects require input from many different parties, with varied interests. A lack of political and institutional support was found to be one of the biggest barriers to pedestrianisation (Parajuli and Pojani, 2018). This can lead to a vicious cycle of lower public support discouraging political will and vice versa.

3.4.2.2 Recommendations: Need for political stability and trust among collaborators

Vitale Brovarone et al. (2023) highlighted conflicts between different actors on the Torino Mobility Lab project in Turin, dividing these into substantive, procedural, and relational conflicts. The researchers identified that differing opinions between political actors and a lack of skills and resources in local government can lead to unsuccessful or disjointed implementation (Vitale Brovarone et al., 2023; Lambe et al., 2017) and Kyriakidis et al. (2023) both identified the need for harmony and technical expertise among political collaborators, strong community engagement, and clear communication of purpose (Kyriakidis et al., 2023; Lambe et al., 2017).

For Asuncion Street in Seville, Spain, a lack of communication with local business owners triggered anti-pedestrianisation sentiment and debate in the community (Castillo-Manzano et al., 2014). Several researchers recommend better engagement with local traders and stakeholders – and more research of pedestrianisation's impacts on businesses – to overcome strong opposition, especially given business owners' influence on their communities and potential to sway other stakeholders' opinions (Castillo-Manzano et al., 2014; Lambe et al., 2017; te Boveldt et al., 2023).

Taylor and Newton (1985) also discussed the importance of state-level interest for pedestrianisation, on top of local engagement. They found federal interest was necessary for gaining funding (Taylor and Newton, 1985), while Uzunoĝlu and Uzunoĝlu (2020) recommends transferring more funding and power to local governments to enact these projects, as they have a better understanding of the complexity for their specific cases. To avoid stakeholder dissatisfaction, policymakers should aim to align their vision with locals' expectations for a given project (Kırmızı, 2022).

Melia and Shergold (2018) claim political will and careful consideration of visual improvements are needed to overcome logistical obstacles and promote pedestrianisation's benefits. This is helpful for improving public acceptance, especially when coupled with environmental awareness and supportive political ideology (Tarriño-Ortiz et al., 2021). Soares and Tosato (2024) presented a model for determining the degree to which an area can be pedestrianised while maintaining public favour and positive attitudes. Nello-Deakin et al. (2024) outlined how a formal governance framework of different actors' responsibilities could improve dialogue and stakeholder collaboration for 'green axes' pedestrianisation measures in Barcelona (Nello-Deakin et al., 2024).

3.4.3 Navigating existing cultures and planning decisions

3.4.3.1 Challenge: Dominating car culture as a barrier to implementation

'Dominating car culture' is one of the most significant barriers to pedestrianisation, particularly when proposed as a traffic management measure rather than community or sustainability enhancement (Klaever and Verlinghieri, 2025; Parajuli and Pojani, 2018). This can be a challenging landscape to navigate, as transforming this culture relies on city-wide introductions of car-free zones and concrete examples of how the benefits outweigh the costs (Brownrigg-Gleeson et al., 2023; Villani and Talamini, 2023).

Motor vehicle dominance is strongly intertwined with local businesses' and residents' opposition to pedestrianisation (te Boveldt et al., 2023; Vitale Brovarone et al., 2023). Te Boveldt et al. (2023) found car dominance and ownership is the biggest cause of opposition, but saw potential for societal transformation. Vitale Brovarone et al. (2023) revealed a strongly car-centric local culture in Turin, Italy, finding opposition is linked to pedestrianisation's 'incompatibility with scenic value'. Loss of car mobility and parking availability on pedestrian streets, and traffic displacement were also identified as perceived disadvantages of pedestrianisation (Panagopoulos et al., 2018).

These findings are backed up by Mahajan and Voßkämper (2025), who find car-centric culture and lack of active travel focus in Montevideo, Uruguay poses a significant barrier to pedestrian-friendly urban design schemes. However, this study found awareness campaigns and citizen-led action could surmount these attitudes, drive change, and incentivise a shift to active travel modes (Mahajan and Voßkämper, 2025; Nieuwenhuijsen and Khreis (2016) observe that shifting to car-free neighbourhoods can provide multitudes of benefits, a major one being better use of public space – though these benefits must be demonstrated to local communities to gain support. Public space is inefficiently used by vehicle traffic and parking spots, and removing roads can free up vast amounts of space for public use, which can ultimately influence the social and mobility behaviour of citizens (Brownrigg-Gleeson et al., 2023).

The unpopularity of pedestrianisation for traffic management can also be mitigated by advocating for its community benefits, as well as placing it within incremental rollouts of car-restrictive policies (Lambe et al., 2017; Vitale Brovarone et al., 2023; Vitale Brovarone et al. (2023) found access and parking restrictions were tolerated more when there is a clear, purposeful vision, while Kepaptsoglou et al. (2015) and Nieuwenhuijsen and Khreis (2016) also advocate for phase-based implementation of pedestrianised zones.

Other measures to reduce opposition include acknowledging the need for some car access and parking in proximity to pedestrianisation schemes (Campisi et al., 2018; Rahaman et al., 2012), particularly to cater for older and disabled people (Sandoval Alfaro et al., 2024; Semple and Fountas, 2023). Although Melia and Shergold (2018) and Parajuli and Pojani (2018) both find limited opposition from motorists and residents due to reduced parking availability, incorporating these provisions can help ease negative perceptions about pedestrianisation measures (Brownrigg-Gleeson et al., 2023; Lambe et al., 2017; Semple and Fountas, 2023; te Boveldt et al., 2023).

3.4.3.2 Recommendations: Need for complementary and supplementary policies

The success of pedestrianisation projects relies heavily on their placement within wider urban revitalisation or community development schemes, as well as adjacent local transport and economic policies to support their implementation (Lambe et al., 2017; Rahul and Verma, 2013; Lambe et al. (2017) showed how transportation policies must be multi-level and transcend simple infrastructure change to avoid failure due to a lack of public acceptance.

Local stakeholders interviewed by Tarriño-Ortiz et al. (2021) suggested complementary policies for pedestrianisation such as increased public transport services and funding, and promotion of mobility sharing, claiming these might improve acceptability from a broader demographic of citizens. Other studies agree with this, with further recommendations for improving projects' success including parking and traffic-access restrictions and increased housing and facilities nearby (Amistad, 2010; Kepaptsoglou et al., 2015; Nieuwenhuijsen and Khreis, 2016; Sandahl and Lindh, 1995).

Nieuwenhuijsen and Khreis (2016) explain how these intertwined policies can promote sustainable economic growth, attract citizens to live closer to pedestrianised areas, and mitigate traffic displacement effects. Villar-Abeijon et al. (2025) also points out the importance of complementary policies such as rent controls, public housing investments, and stricter business regulations to prevent vulnerable populations and local business owners from being displaced, supported by Kırmızı, (2022). Rollout of multi-level policies can be supported by data-collection instruments such as smart-city sensors (James et al., 2022) or decision-support tools for assessing multi-criteria schemes (Buffoli et al., 2022; Nieuwenhuijsen and Khreis, 2016).

Pedestrianisation is often part of a wider climate adaptation strategy, and several studies advocate for the benefits of holistic approaches to climate and transport (Kyriakidis et al., 2023; Sylliris et al., 2023; Yildizhan and Bilgic, 2023). Other examples are 'compact city' and '15-minute city' strategies, described by Kyriakidis et al., (2023), who recommend urban design schemes are accompanied by supplementary interventions. Finally, holistic approaches are crucial for public favourability, as community-wide visions, if communicated well, can help appease some criticisms of these schemes (Melia and Shergold, 2018).

3.4.4 Considering accessibility and equitability

3.4.4.1 Challenge: Concerns about equity and ease of access

Equity is a key consideration for any transport policy change; particularly public space transformations like pedestrianisation (Nieuwenhuijsen and Khreis, 2016). Public acceptance – and subsequent success – is heavily reliant on equitability and accessibility to the full range of citizens who wish to use pedestrianised areas (Nello-Deakin, 2024). Pedestrianisation projects which haven't sufficiently addressed mobility and accessibility considerations can alienate certain groups of people and make them feel unwelcome (Panagopoulos et al., 2018).

This is particularly a concern where pedestrianisation has led to gentrification and consequential rent increase or invasion from retail chains, such as for İstiklal Street in Samsun, Türkiye, where shopkeepers were found to be unhappy with the way in which the street had been pedestrianised (Kırmızı, 2022). The failures of this and similar cases can be attributed to top-down planning and a lack of customised policies for the region, a conclusion supported by a multi-embedded study of planning in Asian cities by Villani and Talamini (2023), Kırmızı (2022) also showed that preserving cultural and historical landscapes is important for encouraging local and non-local citizens to continue using pedestrianised areas, as did Amistad (2010). Another major trade-off can be unplanned transformation of commercial districts and the demographic of their tenants, which can be inequitable for local residents (Kırmızı, 2022; Shahmoradi et al., 2023).

A study of a pedestrianisation project in Brussels shows how even seemingly progressive schemes that challenge existing mobility paradigms can lack equitable and participative methods (Kębłowski et al., 2019; Kębłowski et al. (2019) emphasises how pedestrianisation policies can put pressure on working-class neighbourhoods and urges policymakers to improve the equitability and messaging of these kinds of sustainability policies. This is especially important because, as shown in Klaever and Verlinghieri (2025), societal inequalities can influence how involved local residents are in participatory consultations and thereby the equity of resulting schemes.

Failed pedestrianisation schemes are often linked to urban design faults as well. Panagopoulos et al. (2018) stated that, while pedestrianisation offers opportunities for biophilic design and street improvement is one of its most important functions, a case in Kalamaria and Thessaloniki, Greece didn't deliver on this. Kırmızı (2022) expressed that dulled streetscapes and lack of glass roofing reduced the cultural atmosphere in their study of street revitalisation in Samsun, Türkiye, (Kırmızı, 2022); Aydın and Ayataç (2015) found pedestrianised spaces were used as transitionary routes instead of the intended sociable spaces due to ineffective design features.

3.4.4.2 Recommendations: Need for ergonomic and accessible design

The design and layout of pedestrianised streets are major factors in their ultimate success or failure. This includes arrangement of redeveloped spaces around existing establishments (Yıldırım and Çelik, 2023), introducing ergonomic furniture or public facilities, for example (Aşilioğlu and Çay, 2020), and use of environmentally-friendly construction materials (Sylliris et al., 2023).

Allirani et al. (2024) developed a composite subjective and objective QOL indicator for a pedestrianisation case in Bengaluru, showing these schemes' potential to improve QOL for not just local residents but also the wider community. This is supported by several other papers, including one that isolated quality criteria for pedestrianised streets in Ankara, Türkiye, thereby explaining how well-designed, user-friendly pedestrian areas can improve QOL for the public (Aşilioğlu and Çay, 2020; Pitsiava-Latinopoulou and Basbas, 2000; Aşilioğlu and Çay, 2020) defined several quality criteria of pedestrianisation schemes, including functional features, cultural preservation, and aesthetic value, while Buffoli et al. (2022) showed pedestrianised streets could improve perceptions of urban areas. Several studies also highlight the sociability and cultural benefits provided by pedestrianised spaces (Aydın and Ayataç, 2015; Mohajer Milani and Assarzadeh, 2024; Nieuwenhuijsen and Khreis, 2016; Shahmoradi and Guimarães, 2024, Yassin, 2019).

Aydın and Ayataç (2015) showed that citizen participation in the planning process was necessary to enhance sociability in pedestrianised spaces in a historical neighbourhood in Istanbul. In their study of Haft-e Tir Square in Tehran, Iran, Mohajer Milani and Assarzadeh (2024) highlighted how urban squares with pedestrian-friendly design elements are more conducive to walking and socialising. Shahmoradi and Guimarães (2024) also identified social interaction as a key benefit of a pedestrianisation scheme in Isfahan. The same study advocated for improving social equity through accessibility upgrades such as better public facilities (toilets and seating areas) and more walkable streets (Shahmoradi and Guimarães, 2024). This is particularly useful for disabled citizens and disadvantaged groups, as confirmed by a user survey on a street renovation in Saint German en Laye, France, which was implemented during COVID-19 (Buffoli et al., 2022).

Pedestrianisation is also useful for defining the purpose of public spaces, especially for directing social interactions and behaviour changes (Kärrholm, 2008; Mohajer Milani and Assarzadeh, 2024; Taylor and Newton, 1985; Yıldırım and Çelik, 2023), Kärrholm (2008) highlighted how pedestrianisation can be used to differentiate shopping zones from other parts of the city in a process called territorialisation. Pedilarco et al. (2024) attempt to determine quantitative criteria for identifying streets to pedestrianise in Cagliari, Italy, but find that tactical urbanisation and pedestrianisation schemes are largely case-specific and must be designed based on their purpose. This is best done through functional and spatial modifications, including clear physical designations such as traffic-restricting bollards and repaved roads (Kubat et al., 2015; Parajuli and Pojani, 2018).

The cooling capacity of pedestrianisation is reliant on repaving of these areas, as recommended in studies of thermal comfort (Ma et al., 2019b; Sylliris et al., 2023; Wong, 2020). These studies highlight the need to incorporate vegetation and climate-friendly materials into pedestrianised streets, which can improve their visual quality and attract more visitors (Nugroho et al., 2018; Shahmoradi and Guimarães, 2024). Ergonomic furniture and retexturing of surfaces can also improve accessibility and inclusivity – particularly for disadvantaged groups – but designers should consider hiding technical features such as air conditioners and electrical wiring (Shahmoradi and Guimarães, 2024; Uzunoĝlu and Uzunoĝlu, 2020).

Brunner et al. (2025) demonstrates the importance of features that encourage pedestrians to engage with their surroundings to evoke positive emotions and well-being, as well as increase favourability. The study analysed pedestrians' emotions towards urban design features within pedestrianised areas in Copenhagen, Denmark, showing that high-quality open spaces featuring greenery and human-oriented architecture, coupled with low traffic, create pedestrian-friendly environments, promote relaxation, and reduce boredom when walking (Brunner et al., 2025).

Thoughtful street design is important to build public support for these projects and enhance historical and cultural activity (Allirani et al., 2024). Considered design features can help improve users' sense of security (Diaz and Koh, 2022) and align pedestrianised streets with surrounding areas (Nello-Deakin, 2024), Kiminami and Dunn (2025) analysed pedestrian movements through the pedestrianised Strand-Aldwych area in London, finding deep mapping with GIS a useful method to assess the effectiveness of such schemes and highlight how pedestrians engage with street furniture and other urban design elements. Improved facilities and features, such as wider pavements or public toilets, encourage more positive attitudes towards pedestrianisation by creating a better QOL for local citizens (Allirani et al., 2024; Sandoval Alfaro et al., 2024).

4. Discussion

This literature review highlighted the main avenues for pedestrianisation research and where gaps persist, divided into four sub-sections: pedestrianisation schemes and their typology, impacts, challenges, and enablers of pedestrianisation.

4.1 Impacts of pedestrianisation

4.1.1 Environmental and climate benefits

Studies explicitly exploring environmental benefits and impacts of pedestrianisation projects comprised a surprisingly small proportion of the literature. Many papers referenced the purported climate mitigation and emissions reductions from removing traffic, and the potential for reducing the UHI effect and increasing green spaces. However, few papers focused solely on using pedestrianisation for solving climate change and environmental issues.

The few studies that did focus on using pedestrianisation to solve issues like thermal comfort and environmental air pollution found that specific urban design measures were necessary for this (Sylliris et al., 2023; Wong, 2020). Recommendations included implementing full traffic restrictions over larger areas, repaving pedestrianised sections of roads, and incorporating lots of vegetation (Ma et al., 2020; Zhang et al., 2019). There is some evidence of GHG emissions reductions from these projects (Lebrusán and Toutouh, 2020a; Pitsiava-Latinopoulou and Basbas, 2000), but it is less clear, as pedestrianisation's direct impact on emissions can be difficult to isolate, however, other studies have shown the potential for GHG emissions reductions from switching to active travel modes (Guo et al., 2025; Negev et al., 2022).

More research on environmental impacts would be helpful, and particularly on how climate resilience and wildlife corridors in urban environments can be improved by leveraging the revitalisation opportunities presented by pedestrianisation schemes.

4.1.2 Public health benefits

The public health benefits of walking as an active travel mode are numerous, and are drivers for pedestrianisation, among other traffic-reduction policies (Gascon et al., 2019). This study has categorised these benefits into air quality, traffic displacement, active mobility, pedestrian safety, thermal comfort, and greener spaces.

This was the largest section of the review, because demonstrating health benefits is a good way to justify and garner public support for major public revitalisation works like pedestrianisation. Pedestrianisation has been proven to reduce air pollution (Iliopoulou et al., 2020; O'Regan et al., 2024), encourage switches to active travel modes (Yıldırım and Çelik, 2023), enhance pedestrian safety and thermal comfort (Campisi et al., 2018; Ma et al., 2019a), and reduce noise pollution from traffic (van Soesbergen and Mulligan, 2024). Creation of greener spaces is not an inherent feature of pedestrianised zones, but revitalising spaces creates an opportunity to introduce more greenery back into urban areas. Studies using simulated scenarios tended to dispute pedestrianisation's air pollution reduction potential (Brugière et al., 2021), while empirical research instead showed improvements in air quality (Lebrusán and Toutouh, 2020b; Pitsiava-

Latinopoulou and Basbas, 2000), which might indicate that peripheral benefits, such as changes to travel behaviour, in real pedestrianisation cases also help to reduce air pollution.

Potential traffic displacement is a concern of implementing pedestrianisation projects, but some studies showed traffic evaporation is possible post-implementation in the longer term. The traffic displacement and transport mode-switching phenomena and their impacts on cities' air pollution would benefit from further research, which could take the form of longitudinal before-and-after case studies. Some relevant examples are Thomas and Aldred (2024), Tarriño-Ortiz et al. (2021), and van Soesbergen and Mulligan (2024).

An article for Citylab, Bloomberg News even mentioned decreased terrorism risk as a benefit of pedestrianisation (Quilty-Harper, 2024), which is supported by a case study of New York City that describes ramming attacks using motor vehicles as weapons (Hess and Mandhan, 2023), though this assumes pedestrianised zones are fully closed off from motor vehicles.

Although socialisation improvements and increased human activity in pedestrianised areas were discussed in the literature, research on mental health benefits is scarce – besides research by Brunner et al. (2025) showing improved walking experiences – so this could be another area for further study.

4.1.3 Economic benefits

Potential effects on local economies are a key consideration for decision-makers implementing pedestrianisation. Through transaction tracking and pedestrian counts, researchers have been able to show that pedestrianisation brings economic uplifts. However, this evidence base is still somewhat limited, and discussions with business owners might benefit from combining precedential cases with area-specific data.

The risk of gentrification and pushing traders out of pedestrianised areas is a significant concern, particularly since several studies have shown these areas favour hospitality establishments and convenience stores over other kinds of businesses (Shahmoradi et al., 2023). Pedestrianisation schemes can also increase tourist activity, and tourism is sometimes a driver for these projects (Sandoval Alfaro et al., 2024). While this might be beneficial to local retailers, it could be disruptive to local residents (Nello-Deakin, 2024). Utilisation of cost-benefit and SWOT analyses, as well as more studies performing transaction and visitor tracking, are helpful for building stronger economic cases for pedestrianisation.

4.2 Challenges and recommendations

4.2.1 Challenges of pedestrianisation

Gaining support from various stakeholders is vital to pedestrianisation schemes' success, and research gives particular attention to local residents and business owners. This was one of the biggest discussion points in the literature. The majority of these studies used interviews, surveys, and consultations to collect feedback from these stakeholders.

Residents were found to be mostly supportive, with their main concerns relating to potential inconveniences to their daily lives (Soares and Tosato, 2024). These could be due to short-term redevelopment works, or an influx of pedestrian activity and noise pollution post-implementation (Nello-Deakin et al., 2024). However, the benefits of reduced traffic-related noise pollution in residential streets are likely to outweigh the noise from temporary construction works or increased human activity.

Businesses, on the other hand, are found to generally oppose changes, due to perceived disruption of regular operations or an anticipated drop in revenue. However, lots of studies provide evidence to the contrary, so this is not an unscalable barrier (Parajuli and Pojani, 2018; Taylor and Newton, 1985; von Schneidemesser and Betzien, 2021). Although business owners are often found to be sceptical, they tend to be open to negotiation and compromises, which occasionally means having to make trade-offs. In stakeholder interactions, promoting open dialogue is the most important factor in gaining trust and support and encouraging positive opinions of projects (Castillo-Manzano et al., 2014).

Dominating car culture and equity considerations are other core factors that determine the degree of public support. Pedestrianisation is often partially or wholly used as a means of reducing motor traffic and car dominance, which can aggravate people who rely on driving for work, essential shopping trips, or disability purposes – many studies found this was one of the most significant barriers to implementing pedestrianisation (Klaever and Verlinghieri, 2025; Nieuwenhuijsen and Khreis, 2016; Parajuli and Pojani, 2018). It is also important to ensure these projects result in areas that are equitable and accessible to all and avoid significantly differentiating between one street and the next (Kębłowski et al., 2019; Panagopoulos et al., 2018). Although the literature disagrees over the inherent equity of pedestrianisation projects, they must at least aim to promote equity and inclusivity to gain popularity.

Though these aspects can be difficult to gauge and quantify, urban design features like ergonomic seating and textured surfaces can help ease disparities (Aşilioğlu and Çay, 2020; Yıldırım and Çelik, 2023). Pitching pedestrianisation as community revitalisation instead of car-reduction measures and making provisions or compromises for those who need to use cars are other ways to ease opposition (Nieuwenhuijsen and Khreis, 2016). Future research on the efficacy of these measures for improving the popularity and acceptance of pedestrianisation projects would be insightful.

4.2.2 Enablers of pedestrianisation

Communication of pedestrianisation schemes and use of supporting policies were revealed to be crucial to success and acceptance. A lack of these was frequently cited as a major trigger for failure.

In this context, communication encompasses both delivery of project proposals and functionality of their designs. Many researchers identified this in their conclusions, highlighting the need to keep stakeholders informed and satisfied through participatory processes and public engagement (Klaever and Verlinghieri, 2025; Shahmoradi and Guimarães, 2024), recommending use of online and in-person consultation platforms, less technical language, and conversational, narrative approaches (Tjandradewi et al., 2006). A mixture of one-to-one and group meetings are also useful, and researchers advise consulting with as diverse a range of stakeholders as possible (Chen, 2025; Treija et al., 2023).

Complementary policies in pedestrianisation scenarios are usually transport- or economy-related, to ensure projects don't interfere too much with the operation of transport links or retailers in the vicinity (Lambe et al., 2017; Tarriño-Ortiz et al., 2021). Simultaneous accessibility and safety improvements to walkability of neighbouring streets and public transport availability can help encourage citizens to continue visiting pedestrianised regions (Amiour et al., 2022). Lots of studies discuss this, but only a few effective solutions are proposed; more specific guidance in this area could be useful for policymakers.

By virtue of situating pedestrianisation within broader, overarching community improvement schemes, they will be working in tandem with other transport and sustainability policies. A few studies have worked on developing criteria for selecting streets to pedestrianise and assess them (Allirani et al., 2024; Campisi et al., 2018; Pedilarco et al., 2024; Wahba et al., 2020), but more review-style research would be valuable for informing these kinds of identification criteria and the implementation of future schemes.

5. Conclusion

This research seeks to answer what kinds of pedestrianisation schemes have been implemented worldwide; which of their impacts have been investigated and what the findings are; and the challenges and recommendations for implementing these schemes. This was achieved by performing a systematic literature review to identify relevant articles and synthesise their results – the results of this paper address a gap in the literature for a review of the state-of-the-art on pedestrianisation schemes. Our conclusions can inform future research and implementation of these schemes by highlighting key benefits, challenges, and drivers.

A significant portion of the literature comprises empirical studies on real pedestrianisation cases, with a much smaller portion being modelling or simulation-based, and only a few literature reviews. While some of these look at traffic calming or pedestrian priority schemes, the majority of studies included focus on permanent pedestrianisation interventions. These interventions typically involve a redesign of the targeted street space that includes blocking off and repaving roads with new paving materials, incorporating more street furniture and greenery, and improving accessibility and walkability.

Pedestrianisation schemes have been shown to have impacts and benefits in the realms of environment and climate change mitigation, public health, and economic effects. In some cases, they can reduce GHG emissions, mitigate the UHI effect, and provide opportunities for urban greening, all of which contribute to improved climate resilience in urban environments. There is some crossover here with public health benefits, such as reducing localised air and noise pollution, enhancing thermal comfort and pedestrian safety, incentivising active mobility, and improving walking experiences for better mental health. These benefits, on top of the potential for supporting local retailers and increasing spending by pedestrians, are useful drivers of pedestrianisation. This is provided increases in tourism and the spread of gentrification – which often accompanies pedestrianisation – are well managed.

Implementation of successful pedestrianisation measures requires involvement from the local community – local residents and active travellers have been shown to broadly support these schemes, although there remains some opposition from local businesses, elected officials, and dominating car culture in cities. These challenges can be mediated through clear, direct communication and compromises to ease concerns around potential inconveniences, inequity and accessibility issues, or loss of revenue. It is necessary to engage businesses and other stakeholders by highlighting the evidence for short- and long-term benefits of pedestrianisation, and this underlines the need for further supporting research.

To enable more effective and successful pedestrianisation, researchers recommend clear communication and community engagement such as consultations and participatory planning processes. To encourage public acceptance, it is also useful to implement these interventions within wider neighbourhood revitalisation schemes and alongside other policies such as public transport improvements, subsidies for local retailers, and traffic-calming measures.

While this research was able to capture a vast number of articles in the systematic review, in reading through these studies, some articles that were referenced often and seemed relevant did not appear in our systematic search (Buzasi et al., 2021; Hass-Klau, 1993; Özdemir and Selçuk, 2017; Soni and Soni, 2016). Further iterations of the search string or more time spent on snowball sampling might have allowed more of these to be picked up. A more extensive review might provide further insight into the key themes identified or expose other characteristics of pedestrianisation, while more focused reviews could explore one of these themes in greater depth. As around 90 % of the literature focuses on cities in Europe, the UK, and Asia (Fig. 3), the generalisability of this study could be limited as it overlooks schemes in other parts of the world.

5.1 Areas for further research

In going through the literature on pedestrianisation, we were able to identify areas that remain under-researched and need further work.

In terms of environmental and health impacts, there is little mention of short-term local air and noise pollution, as well as public costs, from pedestrianisation construction works and the trade-off of embodied carbon in materials used. There also aren't many studies that consider pedestrianisation's potential to be implemented within or alongside wildlife rejuvenation projects and urban green corridors for enhancing biodiversity. Further studies on these schemes' mental health and wellbeing benefits, as well as their distal impacts on emissions, would be useful.

Pedestrianisation's impacts are best studied through longitudinal studies that measure pre- and post-implementation. These can be used to investigate air pollution impacts, but also effects on gentrification, social responsibility and behaviour, such as how people treat public space.

Another factor that was outside the scope of this review was gender differences in acceptance of pedestrianisation schemes, and a more detailed analysis might research this.

Cost-benefit analyses could help explore the economic trade-offs of pedestrianisation and create a stronger evidence base in support of these schemes. Finally, it would be interesting to investigate the need for adequate connectivity with public transport modes, as well as access for delivery and emergency vehicles, by comparing real-world cases that have implemented these elements.

References

Aceves-González, C., Ekambaram, K., Rey-Galindo, J., Rizo-Corona, L., 2020. The role of perceived pedestrian safety on designing safer built environments. Traffic Injury Prev. 21, S84–S89.

Allirani, H., Dumka, A., Verma, A., 2024. A framework for assessment of pedestrianization impacts on quality of life: combining subjective and objective measures. Cities 145, 1–13.

Allirani, H., Verma, A., 2025. Development of level of service criteria for pedestrianized urban street: a quantitative and qualitative approach. J. Transp. Eng. Part. A: Syst. 151 (3), 1–13.

Amiour, Y., Waygood, E.O.D., van den Berg, P.E.W., 2022. Objective and perceived traffic safety for children: a systematic literature review of traffic and built environment characteristics related to safe travel. Int. J. Environ. Res. Public. Health 19 (5), 1–29.

Amistad, F.T., 2010. Assessment of the pedestrianization policy in Vigan City: UNESCO world heritage site. J. Urban. Plan. Dev. 136 (1), 11–22.

Antupit, S., Gray, B., Woods, S., 1996. Steps ahead: making streets that work in Seattle, Washington. Landsc. Urban. Plan. 35, 107–122.

Aşilioğlu, F., Çay, R.D., 2020. Determination of quality criteria of urban pedestrian spaces. ACE: Architecture, City Environ. 15 (44), 1–25.

Aydın, M.Ç., Ayataç, H., 2015. A pedesterianization case in the context of public interest: a pedesterianization project in Eminönü historical peninsula (Hobyar neighborhood and surroundings). A/Z ITU J. Fac. Archit. 12 (1), 3–13.

Basbas, S., 2007. Transport demand management and energy consumption in urban areas. WIT Trans. Ecol. Environ. 105, 3–12.

Bauer, J., Funk, K., Rochford, P., 2023. Pedestrian zones are here to stay. National League of Cities [Internet]. 2023 Sep 13 [cited 2024 Jul 28]; [about 2 screens]. Available from: https://www.nlc.org/article/2023/09/13/pedestrian-zones-are-here-to-stay/.

Brogan, C., 2017. Noise from busy roads might increase heart disease risk, finds new study. Imperial College London News [Internet]. 2017 May 31 [cited 2025 Aug 28]; [about 4 screens]. Available from: https://www.imperial.ac.uk/news/179722/noise-from-busy-roads-might-increase/.

Brownrigg-Gleeson, M.L., Monzon, A., Cortez, A., 2023. Reasons to pedestrianise urban centres: impact analysis on mobility habits, liveability and economic activities. Sustainability. 15, 1–25.

Brugière, A., Pham, M.D., Chapuis, K., Drogoul, A., Gaudou, B., Grignard, A., et al., 2021. Experimenting the impact of pedestrianisation on urban pollution using tangible agent-based simulations: application to Hoan Kiem District, Hanoi, Vietnam. Modelling, Simulation and Applications of Complex Systems: Springer Proceedings in Mathematics & Statistics. Springer Nature Singapore Pte Ltd, pp. 43–77.

Brunner, L.M., Basaran, G.G., Haustein, S., Klockner, C.A., Ingvardson, J.B., Nielsen, O.A., et al., 2025. Emotional experiences of urban walking environments: an application of the circumplex model of affect. J. Transp. & Health 42, 1–18.

Buffoli, M., Mangili, S., Capolongo, S., Brambilla, A., 2022. Explorative study on urban public space renovation during COVID-19: test of a visual web-based survey about the City of Saint German en Laye, France. Sustainability 14, 1–17.

Buzasi, A., Palvolgyi, T., Csete, M.S., 2021. Assessment of climate change performance of urban development projects – Case of Budapest, Hungary. Cities 114, 1–11.

Cai, Y., Hansell, A.L., Blangiardo, M., Burton, P.R., Hoogh, K. d, Doiron, D., et al., 2017. Long-term exposure to road traffic noise, ambient air pollution, and cardiovascular risk factors in the HUNT and lifelines cohorts. Eur. Heart J. 38, 2290–2296.

Campisi, T., Canale, A., Tesoriere, G., 2018. SWOT analysis for the implementation of spaces and pedestrian paths at the street markets of Palermo. AIP Conf. Proc. 2040, 140003.

Castillo-Manzano, J.I., Lopez-Valpuesta, L., Asencio-Flores, J.P., 2014. Extending pedestrianization processes outside the old city center; conflict and benefits in the case of the city of Seville. Habitat. Int. 44, 194–201.

Chen, F., 2025. Spatial design professional-led multi-stakeholders and community participation in co-creating a walkable and inclusive public space. J. Asian Archit. Build. Eng. 1–17.

Chiquetto, S., 1996. The environmental impacts from the implementation of a pedestrianisation scheme. Transp. Res. Part. D. 2 (2), 133–146.

Chiquetto, S., Mackett, R., 1995. Modelling the effects of transport policies on air pollution. Sci. Total. Environ. 169, 265–271.

City of Brussels, 2025. Pedestrian zone. https://www.brussels.be/pedestrian-zone; 2025 (accessed 17 June 2025).

Clean Cities Campaign, 2025. Parisians say yes to more green and pedestrian friendly streets. Clean Cities Campaign [Internet]. 2025 Mar 24 [cited 2025 Aug 31]; [about 1 screen]. Available from: https://cleancitiescampaign.org/parisians-say-yes-to-more-green-and-pedestrian-friendly-streets/.

Crabbe, H., Elsom, D.M., 1998. Air quality effectiveness of traffic management schemes: U.K. and European case studies. Environ. Monit. Assess. 52, 173–183.

Diaz, C.E., Koh, K., 2022. Estimating the potential retail impact of improving the pedestrian environment in the Downtown Cebu City. Asian Transp. Stud. 8, 1–9.

Douglas, C.M.S., Mulligan, M., Soesbergen, A.V., Burke, S., 2022. Guidance on applying environmental intelligence to inform green investment, In: Proceedings of the 2022 ACM Conference on Information Technology for Social Good (GoodIT '22), September 07–09, Limassol, Cyprus, Association for Computing Machinery.

Gascon, M., Götschi, T., de Nazelle, A., Gracia, E., Ambròs, A., Márquez, S., et al., 2019. Correlates of walking for travel in seven european cities: the PASTA project. Environ. Health Perspect. 127 (9), 1–13.

Giannakos, L., Mintsis, E., Basbas, S., Mintsis, G., Taxiltaris, C., 2016. Simulating traffic and environmental effects of pedestrianization and traffic management. A comparison between static and dynamic traffic assignment. 3rd Conference on Sustainable Urban Mobility, May 26–27, Volos, Greece, Elsevier. pp. 313–320.

Gregg, K., 2023. Victor Gruen versus Jan Gehl – and the contemporary model of pedestrianization. J. Urban. Des. 28 (5), 471–488.

Guo, Y., Bigazzi, A.Y., Chen, X., 2025. Potential greenhouse gas emission reduction from active transportation: Comparing travel behavior patterns. Transportation Res. Part. D: Transp. Environ. 145, 1–14.

Haddaway, N.R., Page, M.J., Pritchard, C.C., McGuinness, L.A., 2022. PRISMA2020: an R package and Shiny app for producing PRISMA 2020-compliant flow diagrams, with interactivity for optimised digital transparency and Open Synthesis. Campbell Syst. Rev. 18, e1230. https://doi.org/10.1002/cl2.1230.

Harris, A., 2025. Budapest reclaims streets for the next generation. Eurocities [Internet]. 2025 Jan 31 [cited 2025 Jun 17]; [about 5 screens]. Available from: https://eurocities.eu/stories/budapest-reclaims-streets-for-the-next-generation/.

Hass-Klau, C., 1993. Impact of pedestrianization and traffic calming on retailing: a review of the evidence from Germany and the UK. Transp. Policy 1 (1), 21–31.

Hess, P., Mandhan, S., 2023. Ramming attacks, pedestrians, and the securitization of streets and urban public space: a case study of New York City. Urban. Des. Int. 28, 19–34.

Iliopoulou, C., Tseliou, M., Kepaptsoglou, K., Papadimitriou, S., 2020. Demonstrative case of a pedestrian network design model considering effects on motorized traffic. Transp. Res. Rec. 2674 (7), 373–384.

James, P., Jonczyk, J., Smith, L., Harris, N., Komar, T., Bell, D., et al., 2022. Realizing smart city infrastructure at scale, in the wild: a case study. Front. Sustain. Cities 4, 1–12.

Jiménez Espada, M., García, F.M.M., González-Escobar, R., 2023. Citizen perception and Ex Ante acceptance of a low-emission zone implementation in a medium-sized Spanish City. Buildings 13 (249), 1–23.

Kärrholm, M., 2008. The territorialisation of a pedestrian precinct in Malmö: materialities in the commercialisation of public space. Urban. Stud. 45 (9), 1903–1924.

Kębłowski, W., Criekingen, M.V., Bassens, D., 2019. Moving past the sustainable perspectives on transport: an attempt to mobilise critical urban transport studies with the right to the city. Transp. Policy 81, 24–34.

Kensington and Chelsea London Borough Council, 2021. Bute Street - Proposed Improvements, https://consult.rbkc.gov.uk/communities/bute-street-proposed-improvements/; 2021 (accessed17 June 2025).

Kepaptsoglou, K., Karlaftis, M.G., Gkotsis, I., Vlahogianni, E., Stathopoulos, A., 2015. Urban regeneration in historic downtown areas: an ex-ante evaluation of traffic impacts in Athens, Greece. Int. J. Sustain. Transp. 9 (7), 478–489.

Kim, U., Lee, J., He, S.Y., 2021. Pedestrianization impacts on air quality perceptions and environment satisfaction: the case of regenerated streets in downtown seoul. Int. J. Environ. Res. Public. Health 18, 1–16.

Kiminami, C.A.G., Dunn, S., 2025. London's strand: from pedestrianisation to humanisation. Eur. J. Geogr. 16 (1), 18–29.

Kırmızı, M., 2022. Local shopkeepers' perspectives on an attempt for municipally-led commercial gentrification via pedestrianization. Planlama 32 (3), 345–360.

Klaever, A., Verlinghieri, E., 2025. Who is (not) in the room? An epistemic justice perspective on low-carbon transport transitions. J. Environ. Policy Plan. 27 (2), 79–94.

Klemmer, K., Brandt, T., Jarvis, S., 2018. Isolating the effect of cycling on local business environments in London. PLoS ONE 13 (12), 1–13.

Kubat, A.S., Ozer, O., Gumru, F.B., Argin, G., 2015. Evaluating the impacts of an urban design project: multi-phase analyses of taksim square and Gezi Park, Istanbul. Proceedings of the 10th International Space Syntax Symposium.

Kyriakidis, C., Chatziioannou, I., Iliadis, F., Nikitas, A., Bakogiannis, E., 2023. Evaluating the public acceptance of sustainable mobility interventions responding to Covid-19: the case of the Great Walk of Athens and the importance of citizen engagement. Cities 132, 1–15.

Lambe, B., Murphy, N., Bauman, A., 2017. Smarter travel, car restriction and reticence: understanding the process in Ireland's active travel towns. Case Stud. Transp. Policy 5, 208–214.

Lebrusán, I., Toutouh, J., 2020a. Using smart city tools to evaluate the effectiveness of a low emissions zone in Spain: Madrid Central. Smart Cities 3 (25), 1–23.

Lebrusán, I., Toutouh, J., 2020b. Assessing the environmental impact of car restrictions policies: Madrid Central Case. Smart Cities: ICSC-Cities 2019. Springer Publishing, Soria, Spain, pp. 9–24.

Liu, Z., Zhan, W., Bechtel, B., Voogt, J., Lai, J., Chakraborty, T., et al., 2022. Surface warming in global cities is substantially more rapid than in rural background areas. Commun. Earth & Environ. 3 (219), 1–9.
Ma, X., Fukuda, H., Zhou, D., Wang, M., 2019a. The evaluation of outdoor thermal sensation and outdoor energy efficiency of a commercial pedestrianized zone. Energies 12, 1–19.
Ma, X., Fukuda, H., Zhou, D., Wang, M., 2019b. A study of the pedestrianized zone for tourists: urban design effects on humans' thermal comfort in Fo Shan City, Southern China. Sustainability 11, 1–20.
Ma, X., Wang, M., Zhao, J., Zhang, L., Liu, W., 2020. Performance of different urban design parameters in improving outdoor thermal comfort and health in a pedestrianized zone. Int. J. Environ. Res. Public. Health 17, 1–19.
Mahajan, R., Voßkämper, T., 2025. 'This won't work in Uruguay!' Taking on Montevideo's car-centric culture. Cities & Health 1–7.
Mayor of London, 2025. Overwhelming support from Londoners and businesses for Mayor's bold plans to pedestrianise Oxford Street. Greater London Authority [Internet]. 2025 Jun 17 [cited 2025 Aug 31]; [about 3 screens]. Available from: https://www.london.gov.uk/overwhelming-support-for-mayors-oxford-street-plans.
Melia, S., Shergold, I., 2018. Pedestrianisation and politics: a case study. Transport Proceedings of the Institution of Civil Engineers. ICE Publishing.
Mohajer Milani, A.M., Assarzadeh, H., 2024. An inquiry into sociability through spatial configuration of urban environment a case study of haft-Tir square. J. Environ. Stud. 50 (3), 325–347.
Murakami, J., Villani, C., Talamini, G., 2021. The capital value of pedestrianization in Asia's commercial cityscape: evidence from office towers and retail streets. Transp. Policy 107, 72–86.
Negev, M., Zea-Reyes, L., Caputo, L., Weinmayr, G., Potter, C., de Nazelle, A., 2022. Barriers and enablers for integrating public health cobenefits in urban climate policy. Annu. Rev. Public. Health 43, 255–270.
Nello-Deakin, S., 2024. Winner" versus "loser" streets? Pedestrianisation and intra-neighbourhood equity. J. Urban. Mobil. 5, 1–10.
Nello-Deakin, S., Vallve, C.S., Akinci, Z.S., 2024. Who's afraid of pedestrianisation? Residents' perceptions and preferences on street transformation. Habitat. Int. 150, 1–12.
Nieuwenhuijsen, M.J., Khreis, H., 2016. Car free cities: pathway to healthy urban living. Environ. Int. 94, 251–262.
Nieuwenhuijsen, M., de Nazelle, A., Cirach Pradas, M., Daher, C., Dzhambov, A.M., Echave, C., et al., 2024. The superblock model: a review of an innovative urban model for sustainability, liveability, health and well-being. Environ. Res. 251, 1–11.
Lisbon Portugal Tourism Guide, 2025. Rua Augusta: visitor's guide to Lisbon's main pedestrian shopping street, https://www.lisbonportugaltourism.com/guide/rua-augusta.html; 2025 (accessed 17 June 2025).
Nugroho, S.B., Zusman, E., Nakano, R., 2018. Pedestrianisation programs and its impacts on the willingness to increase walking distance in Indonesian cities: The case of Bandung City and Bogor City, Indonesia, Transportation Systems in the Connected Era: Proceedings of the 23rd International Conference of Hong Kong Society for Transportation Studies 2018, Hong Kong, Hong Kong Society for Transportation Studies Limited.
O'Regan, A.C., Grythe, H., Sousa-Santos, G., Nyhan, M.M., 2024. Modeling the impact of pedestrianization on urban air quality, 10th IEEE International Smart Cities Conference: Smart Cities: Revolution for Mankind, ISC2 2024 - Proceedings, 1-6.
Özdemir, D., Selçuk, İ., 2017. From pedestrianisation to commercial gentrification: the case of Kadıköy in Istanbul. Cities 65, 10–23.

Panagopoulos, T., Tampakis, S., Karanikola, P., Karipidou-Kanari, A., Kantartzis, A., 2018. The usage and perception of pedestrian and cycling streets on residents' well-being in kalamaria. Greece. Land. 7 (100), 1–17.

Parajuli, A., Pojani, D., 2018. Barriers to the pedestrianization of city centres: perspectives from the Global North and the Global South. J. Urban. Des. 23 (1), 142–160.

Paris je t'aime – Tourist Office, 2025. Pedestrianized areas of Paris. https://parisjetaime.com/eng/article/pedestrianized-areas-of-paris-a002; 2025 (Accessed 31 August 2025).

Pedilarco, G., Caselli, B., Coni, M., Garau, C., Zazzi, M., 2024. Criteria to identify streets to be pedestrianised near major commercial attractors: the case study of the san benedetto market in Cagliari (Italy). Computational Science and its Applications: ICCSA 2024 Workshops Part XI, Hanoi, Vietnam pp. 3–19.

Pfanner, N., 2025. More streets in Zagreb city centre to be pedestrianised. TimeOut [Internet]. 2023 Sep 15 [cited 2025 Jun 17]; [about 1 screen]. Available from: https://www.timeout.com/croatia/news/more-streets-in-zagreb-city-centre-to-be-pedestrianised-091523.

Pitsiava-Latinopoulou, M., Basbas, S., 2000. The impact of pedestrianization schemes on the environmental quality at central areas. Urban. Transp. Environ. 21st Century 1, 503–512.

Pousa-Unanue, A., Femenia-Serra, F., Alzua-Sorzabal, A., 2025. Examining low-emission zones in urban destinations: climate change action or further touristification? Boletin 104, 1–44.

Rahaman, K.R., Lourenço, J.M., Viegas, J.M., 2012. Perceptions of pedestrians and shopkeepers in european medium-sized cities: study of Guimarães, Portugal. J. Urban. Plan. Dev. 138 (1), 26–34.

Rahul, T.M., Verma, A., 2013. Economic impact of non-motorized transportation in Indian cities. Res. Transp. Econ. 38, 22–34.

Quilty-Harper, C., 2024. The radical changes coming to the City of London. Bloomberg [Internet]. 2024 Jan 22 [cited 2024 Aug 8]; [about 4 screens]. Available from: https://www.bloomberg.com/news/features/2024-01-22/in-the-city-of-london-radical-changes-encourage-more-cyclists-pedestrians.

Salleh, A.H., Naharudin, N., Halim, M.A., Ruslan, N., 2021. Feasibility study on walkable City through implementation of car-free zones and its effect on traffic movement in georgetown, Penang using GIS Network Analysis. IOP Conference Series: Earth and Environmental Science, IOP Publishing. pp. 1–8.

Sandahl, J., Lindh, C., 1995. Impact of improving the attractiveness of town centres. Transp. Policy 2 (1), 51–56.

Sandoval Alfaro, C., Leon Ortiz, A., Tarquino Torres, F., 2024. Pedestrianization around the San José market determining the walkability index, Proceedings of the 22nd LACCEI international Multi-conference for Engineering, Education and Technology, San Jose, Costa Rica, Latin American and Caribbean Consortium of Engineering Institutions.

Scruggs, G., 2022. Integrating the SDGs in Urban Project Design: Recommendations from the Global Future Cities Programme. UN-Habitat, Nairobi.

Semple, T., Fountas, G., 2023. Demographic and behavioural factors affecting public support for pedestrianisation in city centres: the case of Edinburgh, UK. Int. J. Transp. Sci. Technol. 12, 103–118.

Shahmoradi, S., Abtahi, S.M., Guimarães, P., 2023. Pedestrian street and its effect on economic sustainability of a historical Middle Eastern city: the case of Chaharbagh Abbasi in Isfahan, Iran. Geogr. Sustain. 4, 188–199.

Shahmoradi, S., Guimarães, P., 2024. Toward social sustainability: evidence from the Chaharbagh Abbasi Pedestrian Street in a historical Middle Eastern city, Iran. Sustain.: Sci., Pract. Policy 20 (1), 1–16.

Sider, T.M.N., Alam, A., Farrell, W., Hatzopoulou, M., Eluru, N., 2014. Evaluating vehicular emissions with an integrated mesoscopic and microscopic traffic simulation. Can. J. Civ. Eng. 41 (10), 856–868.

Sim, D., 2019. Soft City: Building Density for Everyday Life. Island Press, Washington, USA, Island.

Soares, A.J., Tosato, G., 2024. An urban system mathematical approach with human factor: the case of pedestrianization in a consolidated area. Ecol. Model. 489, 1–7.

Soni, N., Soni, N., 2016. Benefits of pedestrianization and warrants to pedestrianize an area. Land. Use Policy 57, 139–150.

Sylliris, N., Papagiannakis, A., Vartholomaios, A., 2023. Improving the climate resilience of urban road networks: a simulation of microclimate and air quality interventions in a typology of streets in thessaloniki historic centre. Land 12 (414), 1–24.

Tarriño-Ortiz, J., Soria-Lara, J.A., Gómez, J., Vassallo, J.M., 2021. Public acceptability of low emission zones: the case of "Madrid Central". Sustainability 13, 1–17.

Taylor, M.A.P., Newton, P.W., 1985. Urban design and revitalisation – an Australian perspective. Urban. Ecol. 9, 1–23.

te Boveldt, G., Wilde, L.D., Keseru, I., Macharis, C., 2023. Pedestrianisation as a step in a societal transformation? An analysis of support and opposition in Brussels. Cities 143, 1–12.

Thomas, A., Aldred, R., 2024. Changes in motor traffic in London's low traffic neighbourhoods and boundary roads. Case Stud. Transp. Policy 15, 1–14.

Tjandradewi, B.I., Marcotullio, P.J., Kidokoro, T., 2006. Evaluating city-to-city cooperation: a case study of the Penang and Yokohama experience. Habitat. Int. 30, 357–376.

Treija, S., Stauskis, G., Koroļova, A., Bratuškins, U., 2023. Community engagement in urban experiments: joint effort for sustainable urban transformation. Landsc. Architecture Art. 22 (22), 89–97.

Uzunoĝlu, K., Uzunoĝlu, S.S., 2020. The importance of pedestrianization in cities - assessment of pedestrianized streets in Nicosia Walled City. Eur. J. Sustain. Dev. 9 (2), 589–614.

van Soesbergen, A., Mulligan, M., 2024. Net impact of London Strand-Aldwych pedestrianisation project on air quality and noise. Urban. Clim. 58, 1–13.

Villani, C., Talamini, G., 2023. Failed pedestrian street experiments in high-density urban Asia: a matter of policies? J. Urban. Mobil. 4, 1–11.

Villar-Abeijon, P., Miralles-Guasch, C., Marquet, O., 2025. Can pedestrianization trigger gentrification? Analysis of Barcelona's sociodemographic changes following pedestrianization schemes. Transp. Res. Part. D: Transp. Environ. 142, 1–17.

Vitale Brovarone, E., Staricco, L., Verlinghieri, E., 2023. Whose is this street? Actors and conflicts in the governance of pedestrianisation processes. J. Transp. Geogr. 107, 1–11.

Volker, J.M.B., Handy, S., 2021. Economic impacts on local businesses of investments in bicycle and pedestrian infrastructure: a review of the evidence. Transp. Rev. 41 (4), 401–431.

von Schneidemesser, D., Betzien, J., 2021. Local business perception vs. Mobility behavior of shoppers: a survey from Berlin. Transp. Find. 1–6.

Wahba, S., Kamel, B., Kandil, A., Fadda, N., 2020. Pedestrian mall as an enabler to enhance street life and promote walkability in downtown Cairo. J. Eng. Appl. Sci. 67 (3), 565–584.

Wandsworth Borough Council, 2023. Wandsworth Local Plan 2023–2038: adopted July 2023 [Internet]. London: Wandsworth Design & Print; 2023. [cited 2025 Jun 17]. Available from: https://www.wandsworth.gov.uk/media/large/adopted_local_plan.pdf.

Wang, H., Brimblecombe, P., Ngan, K., 2021. A numerical study of local traffic volume and air quality within urban street canyons. Sci. Total. Environ. 791, 1–11.

Wong, P.P.Y., 2020. A microclimate study of traffic and pedestrianization scenarios in a densely populated Urban City. Adv. Meteorol. 2020, 1–8.

WSP, 2024. Oxford Street Programme: Consultation Report 2023. Westminster City Council, London.

Yang, L., Yang, H., Yu, Y., Lu, Y., Cui, J., Lin, D., 2024. Exploring non-linear and synergistic effects of green spaces on active travel using crowdsourced data and interpretable machine learning. Travel. Behav. Soc. 34, 1–13.

Yassin, H.H., 2019. Livable city: An approach to pedestrianization through tactical urbanism. Alex. Eng. J. 58, 251–259.

Yıldırım, Ö.C., Çelik, E., 2023. Understanding pedestrian behavior and spatial relations: a pedestrianized area in Besiktas, Istanbul. Front. Architectural Res. 12, 67–84.

Yildizhan, F., Bilgic, S., 2023. The financial impact of the COVID-19 pandemic on public transportation and sustainable policy recommendations: a case study of Eskişehir. Gazi Univ. J. Sci. 36 (2), 573–590.

Yiu, C.Y., 2011. Impact of a pedestrianisation scheme on retail rent – an empirical study in Hong Kong. J. Place. Manag. Dev. 4 (3), 231–242.

Zhang, L., Ma, X., Zhao, J., Wang, M., 2019. Tourists' thermal experience and health in a commercial pedestrianized block: a case study in a hot and humid region of Southern China. Int. J. Environ. Res. Public. Health 16, 1–15.

Further reading

Annunziata, A., Pisano, C., 2018. An analytical tool to support the pedestrianisation process: the case of Via Roma, Cagliari. J. Land. Use, Mobil. Environ. 11 (1), 119–132.

Buckland, Z., Kasraian, D., Faghih Imani, A., Wall, E., no.date. Pedestrianisation in cities: a systematic review. PROSPERO 2025 CRD420251137099. Available from https://www.crd.york.ac.uk/PROSPERO/view/CRD420251137099.

Fournier, N., 2021. Hybrid pedestrian and transit priority zoning policies in an urban street network: evaluating network traffic flow impacts with analytical approximation. Transp. Res. Part. A 152, 254–274.

Shekarrizfard, M., Faghih-Imani, A., Tétreault, L.-F., Yasmin, S., Reynaud, F., Morency, P., et al., 2017. Regional assessment of exposure to traffic-related air pollution: Impacts of individual mobility and transit investment scenarios. Sustain. Cities Soc. 29, 68–76.

Taxiltaris, C., Basbas, S., Nikolaou, K., Tzevelekis, I., 2002. Environmental impact assessment of major pedestrianization schemes through the use of modelling techniques. Fresenius Environ. Bull. 11 (10a), 800–805.

Tétreault, L.-F., Eluru, N., Hatzopoulou, M., Morency, P., Plante, C., Morency, C., et al., 2018. Estimating the health benefits of planned public transit investments in Montreal. Environ. Res. 160, 412–419.

Whelan, J., 1994. Assessing urban planning schemes by means of multi-criteria evaluation techniques: the case of pedestrianisation. Urban. Stud. 31 (2), 309–328.

CHAPTER FIVE

Health and equity outcomes of ciclovías in latin America: A scoping review

Eleanor Lyons[a,*] and Daniele Carrieri[b]
[a]South West Public Health Training Programme, Exeter, United Kingdom
[b]Department of Public Health and Sport Sciences, Faculty of Health and Life Sciences, University of Exeter, Exeter, United Kingdom
*Corresponding author. e-mail address: eleanor.lyons100@gmail.com

Contents

Abstract

This scoping review aimed to synthesise evidence on the health and physical activity impacts of Ciclovías in Latin America, with particular attention to equity in access and participation. Eligible studies included English, Spanish, or Portuguese language papers examining adult participation in Ciclovías, while single 'closed street' events (e.g., annual car-free days, marathons, or cycling events) were excluded. The review followed the framework and incorporated a consultation exercise to inform the study design. Seven databases (PubMed, CINAHL, SciELO, LILACS, Google Scholar, Human Kinetics Journal, and MEDLINE) were searched, supplemented by forward and backward citation tracking and hand searching. Data from included studies were extracted and coded

Advances in Transport Policy and Planning, Volume 18
ISSN 2543-0009, https://doi.org/10.1016/bs.atpp.2026.07.006

using NVivo, and thematic analysis identified key themes. Thirteen studies met the inclusion criteria, the majority of which were cross-sectional (n = 11). Four overarching themes emerged: physical activity outcomes, demographic patterns of participation, spatial distribution of infrastructure, and wider social benefits. Findings suggest that Ciclovías can provide accessible opportunities for physical activity and represent a cost-effective public health intervention. However, participation was predominantly among males, individuals with moderate education levels, and those from middle socio-economic groups, while routes were more frequently located in affluent areas, limiting access for disadvantaged populations. The evidence base remains limited by its predominantly cross-sectional design and focus on established programmes, particularly in Bogotá, Colombia. Future research should prioritise longitudinal and multi-city evaluations and incorporate equity-focused frameworks, such as minimum standards approaches, to better address inequalities in access and participation.

1. Introduction

Physical inactivity is a significant burden to health and mortality (Rezende et al., 2016; Stingl-Zúñiga et al., 2023; Xu et al., 2022). Internationally, 7 % of all-cause deaths can be attributed to inactivity (Katzmarzyk et al., 2022). World Health Organization (2024) recommends >150 min of moderate, or 75 min of vigorous physical activity per week. However, 31 % of the global population (World Health Organization, 2024), and 35 % of Latin America's population are physically inactive (OECD and The World Bank, 2020). Countries within Latin America (LA) have the greatest absolute mortality burden related to inactivity (Guthold et al., 2018; Katzmarzyk et al., 2022). It is projected that, if the 2010–22 trends of physical inactivity continue within LA, 40 % of the population will demonstrate insufficient physical activity by 2030 (Strain et al., 2024).

Physical inactivity presents an additional financial burden on health services. Ding et al. (2016) conservatively estimated that, in 2013, international health-care systems spent INT$53.8 billion as a result of physical inactivity. By 2030, 499.2 million cases of preventable non-communicable disease are projected if activity levels remain static (Santos et al., 2023). The Global Action Plan therefore seeks for a 15 % reduction in physical inactivity by 2030 (World Health Organization, 2018).

International governments have many challenges in increasing physical activity levels. Urban environments can present a barrier to engaging in physical activity (Bauman et al., 2012; Cain et al., 2014; Giles-Corti et al., 2016; Sallis et al., 2012; Sallis et al., 2016). The rapid urbanisation of LA has resulted in 81 % of citizens living within urban areas (Ritchie et al., 2024).

Recreational space for physical activity is therefore in high demand. Barreno et al. (2021) outlined that only 14.5 % of their Latin American study population considered their neighbourhood to be designed for walking or cycling. Furthermore, only 39.75 % perceived their neighbourhood to be safe (Barreno et al., 2021). LA therefore has many additional barriers preventing populations from achieving adequate exercise levels.

Many cities within LA are seeking to reduce these barriers by providing increased recreational space on a weekly basis, through Ciclovías (open streets). Ciclovía programs are typically a weekly event, closing roads to motor vehicles, providing expansive space for pedestrians, runners, cyclists and others to undertake physical activity. LA holds the largest number of Ciclovías globally (Kuhlberg et al., 2013; Meisel et al., 2014; Pratt et al., 2014) with the most famous being in Bogotá, Colombia (Bird et al., 2017) where 121 km of streets are closed to motorised traffic every Sunday, and bank holiday between 7 am and 2 pm.

Despite many Ciclovías being embedded within LA cities since the 1970s (Bird et al., 2017), a preliminary literature search suggested that, as of July 2024, no systematic literature review has been published, reviewing the health impacts of Ciclovías within LA, despite calls for more extensive research (Becerra et al., 2013; Bird et al., 2017; Glazener et al., 2022; Hernández et al., 2022). This scoping review, therefore, aims to identify the breadth and depth of current studies regarding the health impacts of Ciclovías in LA.

Secondly, this paper seeks to review the existing research surrounding the access to and participation in Ciclovías regarding gender, age, and socioeconomic status. LA presents significant inequalities, with the 10 % highest earners making 12 times more than the poorest 10 % (Bachelet, 2024; United Nations in the Caribbean, 2021). Participation in physical activity follows a social gradient: those more economically advantaged are more likely to be physically active than those less advantaged (Ball et al., 2015). Werneck et al. (2022a) warn that policies focused on promoting leisure-time physical activity risks sustaining or increasing inequalities for women and people of lower socioeconomic status, who typically display the lowest levels of activity. Ciclovías however are frequently credited as having the potential to provide socially inclusive space to complete physical activity (Ball et al., 2015; Cortinez-O'Ryan et al., 2020; Werneck et al., 2022b). This scoping review evaluates the literature available regarding the demographics and equity of Ciclovía participation.

2. Methodology

A scoping review approach was chosen for this research, following the five stages as outlined by (Arksey and O'Malley, 2005). This was undertaken in order to identify gaps in knowledge and research to build a greater body of literature (Munn et al., 2018) in relation to the health and inequality impacts of Ciclovías in LA. This paper provides a summary of these results and a synthesis of previously published research.

2.1 Stage 1: Identifying the research question and consultation exercise

A preliminary search was performed, which showed that, whilst there is some evidence on the impacts of Ciclovías, there is no recent singular research paper which collates the knowledge regarding health and equity. A consultation exercise was completed with members of Mobility and Health in Latin America (MoviSaL); an independent group made up of Latin American public health and transportation professionals and researchers. Additionally, members of the Faculty of Public Health Transport Specialist Interest Group, and an urban geographer and researcher were consulted. The consultation provided useful insight to further define the study question.

A SPIDER tool for qualitative evidence synthesis (Cooke et al., 2012) was used to define the search strategy (Fig. 1).

2.2 Stage 2: Identifying relevant studies

Between May and June 2024, a comprehensive literature search was conducted using seven databases: PubMed, CINHAL, SCiELO, LILACS, Google Scholar, Human Kinetics Journal and Medline, with advice regarding search terms obtained from academic library support at the University of Exeter. Backward and forward reference searching of all included articles was completed and key journals were hand-searched for additional studies. These were: Health Promotion International, The

SPIDER: Sample, Phenomenon of Interest, Design, Evaluation, Research type (Cooke et al., 2012).
Sample: Adults (18+) living in LA.
Phenomenon of interest: Any study that looks at Ciclovías (or local variation of the name) as the primary focus within LA.
Design: all study designs to be accepted but will be evaluated for quality.
Evaluation: Improvement of health; physical activity levels, quality of life, social cohesion, safety or air pollution and/or demographics and access to Ciclovías.
Research type: all empirical research types accepted.

Fig. 1 SPIDER tool.

Search terms:
(Ciclovía-Recreativa* OR closed street* OR Ciclovía* OR Sunday Streets* OR Car free Sunday* OR Open Streets*)

AND

(physical activity* OR physical exercise* OR exercise* OR quality of life* OR air pollution* OR road safety* OR noise pollution* OR health* OR mental health* OR demographics*)

Fig. 2 Search terms.

Journal of Transport and Health, and the European Journal of Public Health. All articles from each database and search were imported to endnote. Duplicate research was then removed.

The following **exclusion** criteria were applied: *1.* articles not published in English, Spanish or Portuguese; *2.* articles where health or demographics and access to Ciclovías (as defined above) were not the primary or secondary outcomes; *3.* the research was not conducted in LA; *4.* the Ciclovía is not a regular event (i.e. only happens yearly such as marathons); *5.*the research considered evaluation of permanent cycleways, parks or pavements; and *6.* abstract-only papers without the full text being available.

The search terms can be seen in Fig. 2.

2.3 Stage 3: Study selection

A total of 359 studies were originally identified through electronic database searches and additional record searching. All articles were screened via title and abstract by a single reviewer against the inclusion/exclusion criteria. A random 10% sample of titles and abstracts was then reviewed independently by a second reviewer. A third reviewer was available to discuss disagreements. No disagreements occurred. Full text screening was then completed by a single reviewer. Full texts meeting the criteria were then included within this review. A Preferred Reporting Items for Systematic Reviews and Meta-Analyses (PRISMA) flow chart is shown in Fig. 3 and visually demonstrates the study selection process.

2.4 Stage 4: Charting the data

13 full text studies were uploaded onto NVivo 14 (a qualitative data management software). All papers were read multiple times. During this process, each paper was coded into relevant categories relating to the papers outcomes and aims. Coding of papers was completed intuitively, with themes developing through the coding process. Coding included quotes, results, and discussions and recommendations. Patterns within subthemes

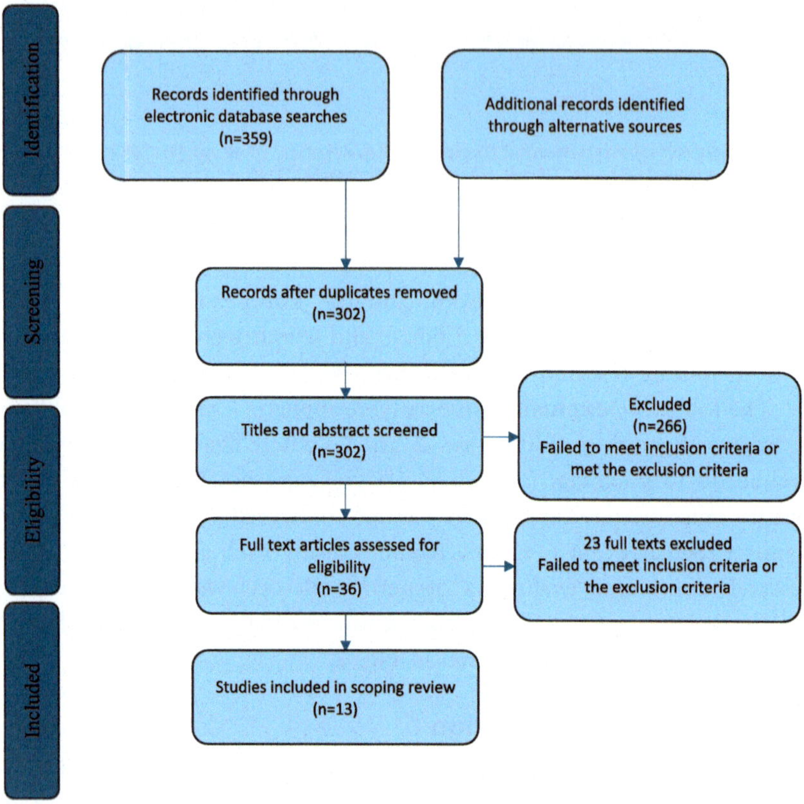

Fig. 3 Preferred reporting items for systematic reviews and —meta-analyses.

were then identified to form the overarching themes. The overarching themes have then been displayed within the results section and key findings synthesised using a qualitative thematic analysis. Within the literature gender has been classified by self-identification, and not biological sex. Therefore, its discussion refers to the socially constructed roles and identities associated with gender.

Quality assessment.

The 2018 Mixed Methods Appraisal Tool was used to evaluate the quality of primary research (Hong et al., 2018). Quality assessment of all included articles was completed by a single reviewer. No articles were excluded due to quality but consideration regarding quality was observed during analyses of the data.

Ethics:

This scoping review solely uses previously published data, with no public involvement. Therefore, ethical approval was not required for this study.

Results.

Descriptive summary.

13 papers were included within this scoping review. The main points of each paper are summarised below (Table 1). The most prevalent study designs were cross-sectional (n = 10), a case study (n = 1), a health impact assessment (n = 1) and an economic assessment (n = 1). The majority of papers used validated questionnaires and surveys. Publication date spanned from 2004 to 2023. Within cross-sectional studies, sample size ranged from 235 to 3282. Ten papers assessed the Ciclovía in Bogotá, Colombia, in addition to other cities, with six of these looking exclusively at Bogotá.

Quality assessment:

A significant limitation of the available research is the cross-sectional nature of the studies which frequently relied upon self-reported measures. No study used an objective measure for physical activity levels. Across the studies, there was a significant risk of non-response bias and observation bias. Whilst some studies outlined the use of probabilistic sampling to select participants, few discussed the impact of non-responders. A significant proportion of studies used opportunistic sampling. Several studies did not use validated questionnaires to obtain data. Power analysis for sample size was not always obtained, and small response rates in some studies resulted in underpowered studies. Direct causation cannot be assumed from the research given its observatory nature and high risk of bias and confounders. A more detailed analysis of the quality of each study can be found in Table 1.

Thematic synthesis:

From the included literature four broad themes were identified: (1) Ciclovías and physical activity, (2) demographic differences in attendance, (3) spatial differences in Ciclovía infrastructure and (4) social and societal benefits. These key themes are discussed within the remainder of this section.

The themes were developed iteratively throughout the coding process. Sub-themes were also identified under each of the categories, where applicable. Table 2 gives example quotations to support the findings. Several sub-themes had just one paper supporting them and were therefore excluded from the main body of this paper. A full table of quotation for each sub-theme can be found in Appendix 1.

Table 1 Summary of included papers.

Identification number #	Papers	Focus	Main findings	Location	Quality assessment using mixed methods appraisal tool (MMAT) version 2018 (Hong et al., 2018).
#1	Mejía-Arbeláez et al. (2021)	A cross-sectional study reviewing the trajectories of Ciclovía participants. Assessing urban segregation according to socioeconomic characteristics, physical activity levels and sociodemographic status.	The greatest mobility between socioeconomic neighbourhoods was in Bogotá. Physical activity levels did not differ for sex or SES.	Bogotá, Colombia, Mexico City, Mexico, Santiago de Cali, Colombia, Santiago de Chile, Chile	Sampling strategy: Study notes systematic sampling but no further detail. Representative sample: 3282 participants across 4 Ciclovías. Appropriate measures: Surveys were developed using surveys the SALURBAL (Salud Urbana en America Latina/ Urban Health in Latin America) protocol. Risk of non-response bias: Significant risk of non-response bias within this study as well as risk of response bias from participants. Statistical analysis: Pearson $\chi 2$ has been used as well as a multi-level logistic regression.

#2	Parra et al. (2020)	An ecological cross-sectional study exploring the geographic distribution of Ciclovías, and access based on social economic status (SES).	The most disadvantaged neighbourhoods were, based on the median distance 6 times further from Ciclovías than the least deprived neighbourhoods.	Bogotá, Colombia	Representative sample: Residential blocks included representation of 74 % of the city. Appropriate measures: Secondary data obtained from the Cadastre Office of Bogota. SES categories pre-established using the socioeconomic stratification system implemented in Colombia in 1980s. Risk of non-response bias: Aggregated data used therefore no risk of non-response bias. Statistical analysis: Kruskal-Wallis equality-of-populations rank test to determine statistically significant differences in the distances between the different categories of SES.

(continued)

Table 1 Summary of included papers. *(cont'd)*

Identification number #	Papers	Focus	Main findings	Location	Quality assessment using mixed methods appraisal tool (MMAT) version 2018 (Hong et al., 2018).
#3	Sarmiento et al. (2010a)	Data collection through interviews, consultations and a literature search.	The study estimated that each Ciclovía provides the opportunity of an average of 360 min of exercise to participants. Whilst providing environmental, and social benefits to participants and the host cities.	Ottawa, Cambridge, San Francisco, El Paso, Chihuahua Zapopan, Guadalajara, Ciudad de Mexico, Ciudad de Guatemala, San Salvador, Caracas, Armenia, Cucuta, Medellin, Antioquia Municipalities, Pereira, Bogotá, Pasto, Quito, Guayaquil, Cuenca, Lima, Salvador, Brasilia, Belo Horizonte, Rio de Janeiro, Sao Paulo, Curitiba, Santiago.	Representative sample: A systematic search of literature and interviews of experts to review 38 Ciclovías across 11 countries. Appropriate measures: Descriptive display of the characteristics and health benifits of the Ciclovía programmes, kilometres of Ciclovías, and estimated average yearly minutes per week of physical activity for the Ciclovías. Risk of non-response bias: Unclear as study is a synthesis of existing research and data. Therefore, this was not addressed within the study. Statistical analysis: Estimations of physical activity levels and comparisons with WHO guidelines are appropriate and transparently calculated.

#4	Torres et al. (2013)	A cross-sectional study, assessing the demographics of participants from the Ciclovía (closed streets) and the Cicloruta (bike lanes) within Bogotá, Colombia.	The majority of participants met the physical activity recommendations during their leisure time (LTPA). Ciclovía users had a greater perception of social capital and safety. Most Ciclovía participants lived in middle socioeconomic zones and had low to middle educational levels.	Bogotá, Colombia	Sampling strategy: Opportunistic non-probability sampling was carried out at two interception points on the Ciclovía. Researchers sampled every 3rd adult. Representative sample: Whilst the sample may be representative to Ciclovía users at the survey times and location it is not representative of the broader population. Appropriate measures: The study used adapted validated international questionnaires to complete the surveys. It is not stated if adapted questionnaires were piloted. There is a risk of response bias from participants. Additionally, observer bias may be present during the classification of exercise intensity. Risk of non-response bias: Due to the opportunistic sampling method, as well as

(continued)

Table 1 Summary of included papers. (*cont'd*)

Identification number #	Papers	Focus	Main findings	Location	Quality assessment using mixed methods appraisal tool (MMAT) version 2018 (Hong et al., 2018).
					the study not addressing non-response bias there is likely a high degree of non-response bias. Statistical analysis: 95 % confidence intervals, and P values have been used, as well as logistic regression analysis when examining LTPA and characteristics of participants. However, there is no power analysis, therefore it is unclear if this sample size is large enough to obtain statistical significance.
#5	Sarmiento et al. (2010b)	A cross-sectional study assessing health-related quality of life (HR-QOL), physical activity and the built	Adults who met PA recommendations and participated in the Ciclovía had a higher mean (HR-QOL) score and perceived	Bogotá, Colombia	Sampling strategy: Probability sampling, in the form of random block sampling was completed. Representative sample: The study has chosen to exclude

	environment in Bogotá, Colombia.	their health as good/ excellent.		the wealthiest neighbourhoods due to previous low response rates, and the poorest neighbourhoods due to extreme poverty. Appropriate measures: adapted version of the WHOQOL-BREF, which is internationally validated. CDC HRLQL-4 scale as well as the International Physical Activity Questionnaire. (IPAQ) for physical activity. Some adaptations were made to ensure the questionnaires were situationally appropriate for Bogotá, Colombia. However, it is not clear if the adapt questionnaires were piloted. Risk of non-response bias: The response rate was 66.7 %. Statistical analysis: Logistic regression has been used within this study to adjust for confounders along side P values.

(continued)

Table 1 Summary of included papers. (*cont'd*)

Identification number #	Papers	Focus	Main findings	Location	Quality assessment using mixed methods appraisal tool (MMAT) version 2018 (Hong et al., 2018).
#6	Gómez et al. (2010)	A cross-sectional study looking at residents over 60 years, to evaluate the impact of built environment on walking patterns.	The presence of a Ciclovía within neighbourhoods was marginally associated with walking >150 min.	Bogotá, Colombia	Sampling strategy: Probabilistic selection of 58 neighbourhoods followed by the random selection of individuals that met the inclusion criteria. Representative sample: Only generalisable to Bogotá, Colombia population over the age of 60. Appropriate measures: Object measures using GIS to review the built environment. Face to face interviews by trained interviewers used an adapted version of International Physical Activity Questionnaire. Unclear if the adapted questionnaire was piloted. Risk of non-response bias:

					High risk, paper does not identify non-response rate of selected individuals. Statistical analysis: Multilevel adjusted models and odds ratios completed.
#7	Gómez et al. (2015)	A cross-sectional study reviewing the urban environment, and social conditions associated with Ciclovía participation.	Being male and educated was positively associated with Ciclovía participation. As was living in the neighbourhood Ciclovías ran. Only 7 % of participants reported attending frequently. Perceived safety issues and traffic fatalities in neighbourhoods reduced attendance.	Cali, Colombia	Sampling strategy: Probabilistic sampling design without replacement. 67 neighbourhoods were probabilistically selected from a sampling frame of 860. At random two blocks in each neighbourhood were selected with an average of 12 houses within each block. 1 adult (18–44) were chosen to complete the survey. Representative sample: Small age range of 18–44. Not representative of older populations. Appropriate measures: The questionnaire and protocol

(continued)

Table 1 Summary of included papers. *(cont'd)*

Identification number #	Papers	Focus	Main findings	Location	Quality assessment using mixed methods appraisal tool (MMAT) version 2018 (Hong et al., 2018).
					were approved via ethics, but it is not an internationally validated tool. The researchers have used geographic information to map out the built environment within neighbourhoods. Socioeconomic status was obtained using the spatial stratification used by the municipality of Cali and is therefore at an aggregated and not individual level. Risk of non-response bias: The response rate of this study was 66.9 %. This rate was lower in upper-middle class neighbourhoods (48 %). Statistical analysis: A multilevel logistic regression was used for the analysis. The model was adjusted for all individual and

					geographic variables. T analysis assumed a random intercept form, and regression coefficients were taken as fixed.
#8	Velázquez-Cortés et al. (2023)	A quantitative health impact assessment to review the impact of Ciclovías on diseases and additional premature deaths.	Ciclovías were shown to reduce an estimated 363 annual premature deaths, saving US$194 million and 1036 Disability-Adjusted Life Years (DALYs) across 15 Ciclovías.	Rosario, Argentina, El Alto Bolivia, São Paulo Brazil, Santiago de Chile Bogota, Cali, and Medellin Colombia, Cuenca and Quito Ecuador, Guatemala City Guatemala, Guadalajara, Mexico City, and Puebla Mexico, Panama City Panama, Lima Peru	Sampling strategy: Data collected via local data therefore sampling strategy is not applicable. Representative: demographic data was included for all participants of each of the included Ciclovías across 15 Latin American cities. The data was collected at a local level by city authorities. Ethnicity data was however not collected due to open street reports not containing this data. Appropriate measures: Physical activity was quantified in minutes, and health impacts were estimated using WHO

(continued)

Table 1 Summary of included papers. (*cont'd*)

Identification number #	Papers	Focus	Main findings	Location	Quality assessment using mixed methods appraisal tool (MMAT) version 2018 (Hong et al., 2018).
					recommendations and DALYS. Risk of non-response bias: The study doesn't report nonresponse rates as it uses existing data. Statistical analysis: The use of scenario modelling, 95 % confidence levels and stratification by activity and disease is both robust and appropriate.
#9	Rodrigues et al. (2022)	A cross-sectional study, to review the use of the Ciclovía in São Paulo, Brazil. Examining differences in leisure time physical activity according to proximity to the Ciclovía,	A higher prevalence of leisure time physical activity in non-users than users of the Ciclovía.	São Paulo, Brazil	Sampling strategy: The paper selected households, at random, that lived within 1500 m of the Ciclovía. Cluster sampling was conducted using a 2-stage selection and probability sampling. Address and then associated telephone numbers were randomly selected within

	demographics. As well as exploring the barriers to use.		each cluster. Representative sample: Only included people that lived within 1500 m of the Ciclovia within São Paulo, Brazil. Appropriate measures: International Physical Activity Questionnaire was used to collect information regarding engagement. Risk of non-response bias: There is a very high non-response rate within the study. With only 235 residents responding to the survey, the power analysis suggested that 616 participants were needed for statistical significance. There is a risk therefore of self-selection bias that the study does acknowledge. Additionally, there was a requirement of having a computer which may have prevented lower SES groups from accessing the survey. Statistical analysis: Underpowered study.

(continued)

Table 1 Summary of included papers. *(cont'd)*

Identification number #	Papers	Focus	Main findings	Location	Quality assessment using mixed methods appraisal tool (MMAT) version 2018 (Hong et al., 2018).
#10	Medina et al. (2019)	A cross-sectional study to explore the demographic, program use and exercise intensity of participants.	The average participant spent 221 min completing moderate-to-vigorous physical activity. Men, those ages 40–64, and classified themselves as very or sufficiently active were more likely to attend.	Mexico City, Mexico	Sampling strategy: 16 observation points along the route spaced 2.5 km apart. Participation was estimated by counting every 15 min and multiplying this number by 4 and comparing to previous participation numbers. Participants were asked at random. However, how this was conducted is not clear, as there is likely observer bias when selecting participants. Representative sample: Risk of observer bias when selecting participants, in addition to non-response bias. Appropriate measures: The participation count is estimated. The questionnaire uses a validated questionnaire; the global physical activity

					questionnaire (GPAQ). Risk of non-response bias: 17.2 % of the 871 people asked declined and 4.8 % gave incomplete data, resulting in 679 participants. There is a risk of non-response bias and observer bias regarding selection of participants at 'random'. Statistical analysis: Descriptive statistics as well as logarithmically analysis were conducted to combat confounders such as sociodemographic.
#11	Montes et al. (2012)	A Cost benefit analysis of Ciclovías and their health benefits.	Ciclovías in all 4 cities demonstrated a significant cost-benefit ratio. With Bogotá demonstrating the greatest at 3.23–4.26 per 1 USD spent.	Bogotá and Medellín, Colombia, Guadalajara, México, San Francisco, USA.	Sampling strategy: The study obtained data on the characteristics of each program from the directors and managers of each Ciclovía. Therefore, it is unclear of the quality and accuracy of the data. Representative sample: Representative of Bogotá and

(continued)

Table 1 Summary of included papers. (*cont'd*)

Identification number #	Papers	Focus	Main findings	Location	Quality assessment using mixed methods appraisal tool (MMAT) version 2018 (Hong et al., 2018).
					Medellín, Colombia, Guadalajara, México, and San Francisco Ciclovía users. Appropriate measures: Using regular participation counts and Ciclovía use based on previous surveys conducted in 2005 and 2010. Health Economic Assessment Tool (HEAT) a recognised and international validated model as well as a Direct Health Benefit analysis. Risk of non-response bias: Not applicable. Statistical analysis: A cost-benefit ratio completed using the with sensitivity analysis and linear regression to predict the 5-year cost-benefit ratio pattern for Bogotá.

#12	Gómez et al. (2004)	Cross-sectional study measuring the prevalence of leisure time activity in women 18–69.	Physical inactivity was associated with not participating in activities such as Ciclovías.	Bogotá, Colombia	Sampling strategy: A multistage probability survey was conducted. 1045 completed the survey with selected people then completing a structured interview. The study does not identify a sampling frame. Representative sample: Only reviews women 18–69 in the Santa Fe locality of Bogota. Appropriate measures: The paper used existing data from a previous study seeking to determine the prevalence of cardiovascular risk factors. Data was collected using International Physical Activity Questionnaire and CELAFICS consensus to classify levels of physical activity. Risk of non-response bias: 97 % participation, however unclear sampling strategy increases risk of selection bias. Statistical analysis: Descriptive statistics alongside logistic regression.

(continued)

Table 1 Summary of included papers. (*cont'd*)

Identification number #	Papers	Focus	Main findings	Location	Quality assessment using mixed methods appraisal tool (MMAT) version 2018 (Hong et al., 2018).
#13	Teunissen et al. (2015)	A cross-sectional study mapping the access to sustainable transport, including Ciclovías.	Higher socioeconomic neighbourhoods have greater spatial access to Ciclovías when compared to lower SES neighbourhoods.	Bogotá, Colombia	Sampling strategy: Geographic Information System (GIS) Spatial information on the TransMilenio, Cicloruta and Ciclovías. Aggregated data to code SES categories. Representative sample: Aggregated level data for only Bogota, Colombia. Appropriate measures: GIS data and SES using DANE national census 2005. Risk of non-response bias: Not applicable. Statistical analysis: Mapping spatial access for descriptive data

Table 2 Examples of quotations to support findings.

Theme	**Example of supporting quotations**
Theme 1: Ciclovías and physical activity	
Meeting exercise recommendations:	"61.7 % of participants accumulated enough physical activity during the program alone to meet the criteria for sufficiently active and 26.7 %...meet the criteria for very active" (Medina et al., 2019).
Additional exercise from the Ciclovía:	"...11.8 % of [participants] reported that they would exercise or do other sports in other settings [if not at the Ciclovía]" (Montes et al., 2012).
Theme 2: Demographic differences in attendance	
Gender differences:	"female users ranged from 25 % (750; El Alto) to 45 % 22,500; Guatemala" (Velázquez-Cortés et al., 2023).
Educational level:	[participants] "who had completed high school were more likely to participate in this program than those with incomplete high school or less (POR = 2.28; 95 %CI: 1.03–5.09)" (Gómez et al., 2015).
Socioeconomic status:	"67.6 %, are from middle socioeconomic strata and that a significant portion of participants, 24.2 %, are from the low SES" (Teunissen et al., 2015).
Self-perceived quality of life (QoL) and Health:	[Ciclovía participants who met physical activity recommendations] "were more likely to perceive their health status as good/excellent [prevalence = 78.63] vs. not meeting recommendations [prevalence = 60.53]" (Sarmiento et al., 2010b).
Theme 3: Spatial differences in Ciclovía infrastructure	
	"median distance to the Ciclovía according to SES ranges from 2930 m for SES 1 (most disadvantaged) to 482 m for

(continued)

Table 2 Examples of quotations to support findings. (*cont'd*)

Theme	Example of supporting quotations
	SES 6 (wealthiest)" (Parra et al., 2020). "Mexico City and Santiago Chile, where the majority of Ciclovía routes are located in geographic units belonging to high SES categories (90.22 % and 77.85 %, respectively)" (Mejía-Arbeláez et al., 2021).
Theme 4: Social and societal benefits	
Safety:	"...participants reported a higher perception of safety 51.2 % regarding traffic and 42.4 % about crime" (Torres et al., 2013).
Social Cohesion:	"... promotes social cohesion through interaction between different SES" (Teunissen et al., 2015).
Economic impact:	"Guadalajara's program showed that the mean annual benefit for mortality prevention ranged from US $664,727 to US $10,146,740" (Montes et al., 2012).

3. Theme 1: Ciclovías and physical activity

Meeting exercise recommendations: #1, #3–5, #8, #9, #10–12. Ciclovías aid residents to meet the World Health Organization (2020) recommended >150 min of physical activity per week, or leisure time physical activity (LTPA) recommendations. There was a significant variation of participants reporting to have met the WHO recommendations; 27.18 % (Mejía-Arbeláez et al., 2021) to 88.5 % (Medina et al., 2019). The percentage of participants meeting LTPA recommendations only ranged from 59.5 % (Torres et al., 2013) to 60.1 % (Mejía-Arbeláez et al., 2021). All considered studies with physical activity as an outcome identified that a significant proportion of Ciclovía participants reached recommended activity levels.

Additional exercise from the Ciclovía: #10 and #12. Few studies assessed if the Ciclovías were adding exercise into residents' lives, or if Ciclovía participants would have been completing the exercise regardless. Medina et al. (2019) demonstrated that 45.2 % of their study population would be completing moderate to vigorous intensity exercise if they weren't already at the Ciclovía. Whereas Montes et al., (2012) suggested that only 11.8 % of their surveyed participants would be completing alternative exercise.

Frequency of use: #3, #4 #7, #10. Four studies described the frequency of Ciclovía attendance within their results. Frequency of attendance varied across the studies. Gómez et al. (2015) outlined that 92.7 % of their participants had never attended the Ciclovía. The other three papers surveyed participants already at the Ciclovía, with each paper using different criteria to define frequent attendance. Medina et al. (2019) suggested that 39.6 % of their participants attend twice a month, whereas Sarmiento et al. (2010b) showed just 10.1 % attending within the last 4 weeks.

4. Theme 2: Demographic differences in attendance

Gender: #7, #8, #10, #4, #2, #1, #11. All seven studies that examined the gender of participants identified that being male was strongly associated with attending the Ciclovía, or in time spent at the Ciclovía. Medina et al. (2019) was the only study which identified that women made up a greater proportion of Ciclovía participants (at 51.3 %), but outlined that men spent more time there and were more likely to attend frequently. One study (Mejía-Arbeláez et al., 2021) suggested that meeting PA recommendations did not differ by gender whilst participating at the Ciclovía.

Educational level: #1, #4, #7, #10. Across the studies there was no agreed consensus to which education level may have been positively associated with Ciclovía attendance. Two studies (Medina et al., 2019; Mejía-Arbeláez et al., 2021) demonstrated that college- or masters-level education was present in a significant proportion of attendees. Gómez et al. (2015) identified that completing high school education was associated with Ciclovía attendance, compared to those who did not complete high school. A further study identified educational levels, high school or lower made up 51.1 % of attendees (Torres et al., 2013).

Socioeconomic status (SES): #1, #4, #7, #10, #13. Many of the studies combined low- and middle-income neighbourhoods together. However, middle-income groups formed most participants in a large proportion of the research. Three of the studies (Mejía-Arbeláez et al., 2021; Teunissen et al., 2015; Torres et al., 2013) reported that the majority of participants are of middle socioeconomic status ranging from 51.74 % (Mejía-Arbeláez et al., 2021) to 67.6 % (Teunissen et al., 2015) and 24.2 % from low SES (Teunissen et al., 2015). One study identified that the largest proportion of participants were from high-income neighbourhoods (Medina et al., 2019). However, in many studies, the highest income groups made the smallest percentage of the participants.

Self-perceived quality of life (QoL) and Health: #1 and #5. Two studies, that collectively reviewed 38 Ciclovías, concluded that the majority of participants deemed their health to be good or excellent. Additionally, those meeting physical activity recommendations scored higher on QoL, and on their perceived health status (Sarmiento et al., 2010b).

5. Theme 3: Spatial differences in Ciclovía infrastructure

Spatial difference in Ciclovía location: #1, #2, #5, #7, #9, #13. All the studies suggested that the majority of Ciclovías were situated within high socioeconomic areas, however the specific proportion differs between cities. Parra et al. (2020) identified that there is a sixfold difference in the distance to Ciclovías from the lowest and highest SES areas in Bogota, Colombia. Two of the studies (Rodrigues et al., 2022; Teunissen et al., 2015) suggested that there is no statistical difference between distance from Ciclovía and participation. Contrary to this, Gómez et al. (2015) and Sarmiento et al. (2010b) suggested that greater access, i.e. living within a Ciclovía corridor, was positively associated with attendance. Two studies (Mejía-Arbeláez et al., 2021; Teunissen et al., 2015) suggested that Ciclovías were typically situated within historical centres and near tourist attractions and therefore not within lower SES areas. Teunissen et al. (2015) suggested that mountainous areas, where low SES populations typically reside, are negatively associated with Ciclovía use.

6. Theme 4: Social and societal benefits

Safety: #1, #4, #6, #7. The reviewed papers suggested that the majority of Ciclovía participants deemed the intervention to be a safe environment. However, one study (Gómez et al., 2015) identified a negative association between Ciclovía use in neighbourhoods where there were reported traffic fatalities. Gómez et al. (2010) identified that increased perceived safety from traffic was positively associated with walking.

Social Cohesion: #1, #4, #13. Studies suggested that the Ciclovía brought increased social cohesion within cities due to increased mobility between areas, and that this increased social cohesion, reduced conflict, and promoted interactions. Torres et al. (2013) identified that Ciclovía participants were more likely to help each other than the general population. Mejía-Arbeláez et al. (2021) suggested that the level of social cohesion is not uniform across Ciclovías and varries between cities. Bogotá and Santiago de Cali demonstrated the highest percentage of residents moving between socioeconomic areas compared to Mexico City and Santiago de Chile, were participants were more likely to stay in a similar SES neighbourhood to that of their own.

Economic impact: #8, #11. The studies demonstrated that Ciclovías provided significant cost ratios, via the health benefits provided by additional exercise. Both studies demonstrated that even if relatively small proportions of the participants achieved the recommended physical activity during the Ciclovía, there was significant economic and health benefits.

7. Discussion

This scoping review collated 13 sources to synthesise the health impacts of Ciclovías in LA. The findings demonstrate that Ciclovías have the potential to significantly impact and improve physical activity levels, and health within Latin American cities, whilst ensuring a substantial cost-benefit ratio. Even if only 5 % of users replaced sedentary behaviour with physical activity, the savings from the reduction in premature deaths is estimated at US$25.1 million (Velázquez-Cortés et al., 2023). Research conducted by O'Donovan et al. (2017, 2024) identified that 'weekend warriors', participating in ≥ 150 min of exercise per week but within 1–2 sessions each week, may be sufficient to reduce the risk of both chronic vascular disease and cancer. Therefore, initiatives such as the Ciclovía may provide urban residence, the space and safety to complete physical activity. O'Donovan et al. (2024) also highlights an issue in the data collection regarding physical activity in many Latin American countries, with data frequently being estimated, meaning caution must be taken when reviewing physical activity data. The health impacts and physical activity within these countries may be being underestimated, and the impact of Ciclovías upon physical activity may not be being fully recognised.

Ciclovías transgress beyond improving physical activity and provide residents with valuable protected space within densely populated cities to create social cohesion and improve QoL. Jamie Ortiz Marino, one of the founding architects of Bogotá's Ciclovía, writes: 'Ciclovía is the world's largest outdoor classroom' (University of California and Institute of Transportation Studies, 2024). Ciclovías provide a mechanism for social integration across socioeconomic groups on a weekly basis. This is of particular importance due to high levels of social segregation and safety fears within many Latin American cities (Semets and Salman, 2016). It is important to recognise that the successful social cohesion fostered within Bogotá, and Santiago de Cali cannot always be replicated within different locations without consideration of the spatial distribution. However, the Ciclovía undoubtably provides a mechanism for social integration across socioeconomic groups on a weekly basis.

LA demonstrates persistent health inequalities with vast disparities in life expectancies and health (Bilal et al., 2019; Dávila-Cervantes and Agudelo-Botero, 2019). Ciclovías are free at the point of access, however there is a significant discrepancy within the demographics of those attending. Gender is the biggest imbalance in regards to participation. The included studies reflect global trends, suggesting that women are more likely to be inactive than men, where, in LA 41.2% (CI 34.3–48.5) of women are physically inactive (Cohen et al., 2016; Strain et al., 2024). There are many social, cultural, economic, and environmental factors contributing to lower female activity levels globally (Edwards and Sackett, 2016; Larsen et al., 2013; Peng et al., 2023; Scharff et al., 1999). Therefore, despite Ciclovía programs being available for all, they do not address the inequalities within exercise and gender but may sustain them. Further exploration is needed regarding what factors shape women's participation in Ciclovías. Gómez et al. (2015) identify that Ciclovía programs need to work towards increasing the social participation of women to reduce gender disparity.

Urban segregation and spatial differences occur across LA cities, resulting in further social segregation; reduced access to public spaces, parks and public transport contributes to urban inequalities (Borsdorf et al., 2016; Giles-Corti et al., 2016; Gutman and Patel, 2018). Equitable access to Ciclovías is therefore crucial to ensure the most deprived areas within cities can access the intervention without the additional cost of time and finances. Whilst some papers (Rodrigues et al., 2022; Teunissen et al., 2015) suggest that geographical positioning for Ciclovías does not impact participation; lower income neighbourhoods live up to six times further from Ciclovías than the most affluent areas (Parra et al., 2020). Middle income households are the majority of attendees (Mejía-Arbeláez et al., 2021; Teunissen et al., 2015). Individuals with lower socioeconomic status are more likely to be physically inactive, contributing to further health inequalities (Werneck et al., 2022b). Velázquez-Cortés et al. (2023), identifies that there would be greater benefits achieved if organisers sought to promote equity, prioritising those within lower economic groups.

8. Gaps in the literature

Air pollution is a significant risk to health in LA (Bell et al., 2006; Nelson et al., 2024; World Health Organization, 2019). Ninety-five percent of the residents in Latin Americas mega-cities inhabit areas with a particulate matter greater than the WHO's air quality recommendations (Gouveia et al., 2021). Additionally, poor and peripheral neighbourhoods are more likely to experience higher air pollution (Gouveia et al., 2022; Guzmán et al., 2023). Yet there is minimal research evaluating the impact of Ciclovías on air pollution, reflected by Glazener et al. (2022). Kigali, Rwanda hosts car-free Sundays, research suggests that during these events particulate matter (PM_{10}) decreases by approximately 15 %, reducing the annual output by 3.7 % across the city (Kalisa et al., 2021; Sarmiento et al., 2010a) demonstrated that PM_{10} along the Ciclovía routes are 13 times higher on a regular day compared to when the Ciclovía is running. Ciclovías therefore have the potential to improve air quality within large cities, and more research surrounding the impacts would be deeply beneficial. Furthermore, research should explore how this potential improvement in air quality impacts lower socioeconomic groups, given that in many cities the Ciclovías do not pass through these neighbourhoods at the same volume as more affluent areas. This potentially further increases the imbalance of air quality, and the associated health impacts.

UNICEF (2021) identifies that 'exclusion is often the consequence of invisibility'. This invisibility is apparent through a gap in research looking at the impact and access to Ciclovías to those with disabilities. Mora et al. (2021) suggest that one in five households in LA living in extreme poverty includes a person with disabilities. Bassett-Gunter et al. (2019) identify that people with physical disabilities typically participate in less leisure time physical activity, with very few meeting the recommended amount to obtain the health benefits. This is reflected by Mejía-Arbeláez et al. (2021) and Sarmiento et al. (2010b) demonstrating that the majority of participants attending the Ciclovía deemed themselves to have good or excellent health. Causation between Ciclovía and perceived health-status cannot be assumed through the available research, due to its cross-sectional nature, these results may likely demonstrate a lack of inclusivity of those with physical disabilities.

9. Study strengths and limitations

This review has combined all the available literature in English, Spanish and Portuguese to examine the health benefits and equity access of Ciclovías. The consultation with individuals and organisation situated in both England and Latin America prior to the study provided vital insight to shape the direction of this research.

This study is not without its limitations. Whilst LILACS and SciELO index English translations to ensure the inclusion of Spanish and Portuguese papers, it cannot be conclusively assumed that Spanish and Portuguese studies have not been missed. Additionally, this study looked solely at published research and did not take grey literature into account, therefore potentially forgoing relevant evidence. Thirdly, this research reviews Ciclovías independently from their sister program, Recreativas. Sarmiento et al. (2017) suggest that Recreativas may be more inclusive of women. Parra et al. (2020) identify that the urban distribution of Recreovía sites in Bogota has less inequalities. Including Recreativas in the scoping review may have given a deeper understanding of the interaction and parallel benefits of both simultaneous interventions. The main body of research examined was cross-sectional in nature, meaning any associations demonstrated within the papers cannot prove causation. The complex setting of these papers makes isolating variables difficult, with many confounders at play. There is significant risk of selection and non-participant bias within the participant cohort across the studies. Finally, most of the studies reviewed Bogota, Colombia. Whilst this is likely due to Bogota's Ciclovía being the largest and most established, it is difficult to generalise the results to other cities and countries due to the vast heterogeneity of Ciclovía structure, policy, and design.

10. Recommendations

Evaluation should move beyond participation counts and cross-sectional studies, to look at the longitudinal benefits across multiple cities. Research should seek to evaluate the additional minutes of exercise added through the participation of Ciclovías, whilst assessing the equitable access of Ciclovías. The work by Thomas et al. (2022) provides a robust guide to assessing equity using a minimum standard approach. Thomas et al. (2022) explain that the minimum standard approach is based upon Rawls' theory of egalitarianism to ensure distributive justice. Therefore, policy efforts should be prioritised for those defined as the most in need. By using the minimum standards approach within research it can highlight the extent to which Ciclovia's serve those most in need. By evaluating Ciclovías through the equity minimum standards the focus may be placed on gender, age, sexual orientation, ethnicity, socio-economic deprivation, disability status, the availability and cost of transport to reach Ciclovías, spatial location and air quality impacts of Ciclovías. Improving the research around equity can allow policymakers to develop Ciclovías to support the specific needs of their community.

Policymakers should seek to improve access within their local communities particularly for women and individuals within the lowest socioeconomic groups. Ongoing co-production and development should seek to include these demographics. New Ciclovía developments should include the time and resources to evaluate their impact upon the population's health.

11. Conclusion

Ciclovías are an important part of many Latin American cities' culture and history. Whilst never intended as a mass public health intervention, there is huge potential to improve the health of millions. This paper has synthesised the results of 13 studies to identify the current knowledge and gaps in research. Ciclovías offer densely populated urban areas with a myriad of benefits, however they require further robust and extensive research, to ensure they continue to meet the needs of residents and to address issues around equity.

Appendix 1: Quotations

Theme 1: Ciclovías and physical activity.

Meeting exercise recommendations:	"PA recommendations during the program (51.13 %), ranging from 27.18 % (Santiago de Chile) to 87.24 % (Mexico City)" (Mejía-Arbeláez et al., 2021). "The mean physical activity duration in each visit ranged from 11 min (Medellin) to 113 min (Santiago de Chile)" (Velázquez-Cortés et al., 2023). "61.7 % of participants accumulated enough physical activity during the program alone to meet the criteria for sufficiently active and 26.7 %…meet the criteria for very active" (Medina et al., 2019). "The presence of Ciclovía (recreational program) was marginally associated with having walked at least 150 minutes in a usual week (POR//1.29, 95 % CI//0.97, 1.73" (Gómez et al., 2010). "14.1 % of program participants were physically inactive, 15.6 % were sufficiently active, and 70.3 % were very active based on WHO guidelines" (Medina et al., 2019). "[participants who] rode a bicycle reported spending significantly more time at the MEB program compared to those who performed other activities ($p < 0.01$)" (Medina et al., 2019). "88.4 % of the [Ciclovía] users accumulated enough MVPA during the event to meet the weekly physical activity recommendations proposed by the WHO" (Mejía-Arbeláez et al., 2021). "Bogotá and Mexico City….85.61 % and 60.19 %, respectively [met the LTPA] and more than 80 % of users in both cities reported meeting overall PA recommendations (85.61 % in Bogotá, 83.36 % in Mexico City)" (Mejía-Arbeláez et al., 2021). "Most Ciclovía participants met the physical activity recommendation in leisure time (59.5 %)" (Torres et al., 2013). "…regular participation…had increased odds of meeting the LTPA recommendation (odds ratio [OR] = 1.7; 95 % confidence interval [CI] = 1.1, 2.4)" (Torres et al., 2013). "[regular participation increased the odds of] performing vigorous (OR = 4.9; 95 % CI = 2.5, 9.2) and moderate (OR = 1.9; 95 % CI = 1.2, 3.0) activity during the Ciclovía" (Torres et al., 2013). "Walking or jogging (OR = 1.3; 95 % CI = 0.8, 1.9) and using other wheels during the Ciclovía (OR = 1.7; 95 % CI = 0.7, 3.5) were also positively associated with meeting the LTPA recommendation; however, the association was

	not significant." (Torres et al., 2013). "... currently only 18 % [of Bogotá's inhabitants] meet the recommendation in leisure time" (Torres et al., 2013). "Higher prevalence of individuals engaging in at least 150 min per week of LTPA among users than non-users (Prevalence Ratio = 2.19, IC95 % 1.66 to 2.90)" (Rodrigues et al., 2022). "... adjusted odds ratio (OR) of being physically inactive in leisure time.... participation in Ciclovía; usually; 1.00, occasionally; 3.55, never; 7.41" (Gómez et al., 2010). "41.6 % of adult users reported moderate to vigorous activities for at least 3 hours" (Montes et al., 2012). ...prevalence of physically active adult users was estimated to be 35.7 % [for the Bogotá Ciclovía] ... 34.3 % of adult users in the Vía RecreActiva, 62.6 % in the Ciclovía of Medellín (Montes et al., 2012). "On average participants accumulated 221 min of MVPA [moderate to vigorous physical activity) at the program on the days they participated" (Medina et al., 2019). "Minhocão usage was positively associated with walking, moderate, and vigorous LTPA...vigorous exercise 55.9 % (95 % CI 43.0-68.1), moderate 86.7 95 % CI 75.6-93.2) $p < 0.0001$" (Rodrigues et al., 2022). "Bogotá, 20 % of those who reported program participation during the last month reported doing 30 minutes of PA during leisure time per day on at least 5 days" (Sarmiento et al., 2010a).
Additional exercise from the Ciclovía:	"...11.8 % of [participants] reported that they would exercise or do other sports in other settings [if not at the Ciclovía]" (Montes et al., 2012). "54.8 % reported that they would be engaged in sedentary or light intensity activities if they were not at the MEB program" (Medina et al., 2019). "Activities if participants do not attend the program; Active and very active 45.2 (CI 41.4, 49.0)" (Medina et al., 2019). "39.6 % indicated that they participated in the program at least twice per month" (Medina et al., 2019). "92.7 % of the study population (n = 729) had not participated within the Cali Ciclovía" (Gómez et al., 2015). "[participants] that came alone and every Sunday reported a higher number of minutes in the MEB compared to those that came with someone and less frequent users ($p < 0.05$)" (Medina et al., 2019). "10.1 % [of participants used the Ciclovía] during the last 4 weeks" (Sarmiento et al., 2010b). "...55.2 % of Ciclovía [users surveyed] ... were regular participants of the program" (Torres et al., 2013). "... average use times of 2 hours or more potentially contributes substantially to meeting overall population requirements for weekly physical activity" (Sarmiento et al., 2010a).

Theme 2: Demographic difference in attendance

Gender	"The model showed that male gender was positively associated with participation in the CP (POR = 1.85; 95 % CI: 1.013.41)" (Gómez et al., 2015). "… female users ranged from 25 % (750; El Alto) to 45 % (22 500; Guatemala" (Velázquez-Cortés et al., 2023). "… men spent more time participating in the MEB than women did ($p < 0.05$)" (Medina et al., 2019). "We estimated that 51.3 % were women [of the 679 participants]" (Medina et al., 2019). "… programs were primarily men 70.1 % in Ciclovía" (Torres et al., 2013). "Colombian women from low SES populations are more at risk for physical inactivity" (Parra et al., 2020). "Meeting PA recommendations did not differ by sex, SES and educational level" (Mejía-Arbeláez et al., 2021). "Based on the multivariate model, men…were more likely to attended the program more frequently compared to their counterparts" (Medina et al., 2019). "… men participated approximately three times more often than women" (Montes et al., 2012). "… the cost–benefit ratio for men ranged from 2.12 to 2.80 versus 1.11 to 1.46 for women" (Montes et al., 2012). "… the cost–benefit ratio for men ranged from 2.12 to 2.80 versus 1.11 to 1.46 for women" (Medina et al., 2019).
Educational level	"… 61.2 % had a Master's degree or higher" (Medina et al., 2019). "… had high educational attainment (at least College or technical studies) (49.21 %)" (Mejía-Arbeláez et al., 2021). [participants] "who had completed high school were more likely to participate in this program than those with incomplete high school or less (POR = 2.28; 95 % CI: 1.03-5.09)" (Gómez et al., 2015). "… low to middle educational attainment (51.1 % high school or below)" (Torres et al., 2013). "Master's degree or higher spent less time in the program than those with a high school or Bachelor's degree ($p < 0.001$)" (Medina et al., 2019).
Socioeconomic differences	"… lived in the middle SES (51.74 %) and had a car at home (50.33 %)" (Mejía-Arbeláez et al., 2021). "… living in neighbourhoods of middle socioeconomic status was negatively associated (POR = 0.40; 95 % CI: 0.17-0.97)" (Gómez et al., 2015). "Most Ciclovía participants reported living in low- and middle-SES categories of 1 to 4 (92 %)" (Torres et al., 2013). "66.1 % of the Ciclovía participants reported not having a car" (Torres et al., 2013). "67.6 %, are from middle socioeconomic strata and that a significant portion of participants, 24.2 %, are from the low SES" (Teunissen et al., 2015).

	"Ciclovía participants reported living in middle socioeconomic status categories (64 %)" (Torres et al., 2013). "Socioeconomic status...[high] 8 %" (Torres et al., 2013).
Age	"40.7 %... [were 30 to 49 years old attending the] Ciclovía who were regular participants" (Torres et al., 2013). "64.1 % were between 18 to 40 years of age" (Medina et al., 2019). "41–64-year-olds spent more time in the program than those aged 18–40 years ($p < 0.05$)" (Medina et al., 2019). "Based on the multivariate model, those within the 41–64-year-old group were more likely to attend the program more frequently compared to their counterparts" (Medina et al., 2019).
Self-perceived health and Quality of life	"Most of the participants in Bogotá (58.74 %) and Santiago de Cali (65.69 %) reported their health to be good, and in Santiago de Chile to be excellent (69.08 %)" (Mejía-Arbeláez et al., 2021). [Ciclovía participation who met PA recommendations] ... "were more likely to perceive their health status as good/excellent (meeting recommendations [prevalence = 78.63] vs. not meeting recommendations [prevalence = 60.53]; $P < .0001$)" (Sarmiento et al., 2010b). [participants perceiving their health as good/excellent was higher in] "Ciclovía participation [75.97] vs. nonparticipation [60.62]; $P = .001$)" (Sarmiento et al., 2010b). "Adults who reported engaging in leisure physical activities ... were more likely to have a higher mean score of HR-QOL...[mean = 95.82] vs. not meeting [exercise] recommendations [mean = 90.79]; $\beta = 4.7$; $P < .0001$" (Sarmiento et al., 2010b).
Outcome three: Spatial differences in Ciclovía infrastructure	
	"... the proximity between people's residences and the nearest access to the elevated avenue was not statically associated with LTPA" (Rodrigues et al., 2022). "... access to Ciclovía is greatest for high SES and lowest for low SES" (Teunissen et al., 2015). "[high middle- and low-income use] suggests that access to Ciclovía and participation are unrelated" (Teunissen et al., 2015). "Low SES generally reside in more mountainous areas... [which has] a negative influence on Ciclovía use" (Teunissen et al., 2015). "It is composed of seven routes primarily located in Santiago's affluent north-east area and the historical centre" (Mejía-Arbeláez et al., 2021). "Unlike Mexico City and Santiago Chile, where the majority of Ciclovía routes are located in geographic units belonging to high SES categories (90.22 % and 77.85 %, respectively), routes in Bogotá and Santiago de Cali are

	distributed more broadly throughout the city" (Mejía-Arbeláez et al., 2021). "Participation in the CP [Ciclovía programme] was positively associated with living in neighbourhoods with Ciclovía corridors (POR = 4.27; 95 % CI: 1.66-11.02)" (Gómez et al., 2015). "... median distance to the Ciclovía according to SES ranges from 2930 m for SES 1 (most disadvantaged) to 482 m for SES 6 (wealthiest)" (Parra et al., 2020). "... over a sixfold difference in distance to Ciclovía from the lowest to highest SES group" (Parra et al., 2020). "... perceived lack of access is one of the main reasons for not participating in the Ciclovía" (Sarmiento et al., 2010a). "... access to Ciclovía is greatest for high SES and lowest for low SES" (Teunissen et al., 2015). "... lower access in low SES areas is also partially explained by the fact that the streets that are closed ... [are] main avenues for touristic attractions" (Teunissen et al., 2015).
Outcome four: Social and societal benefits	
Safety	"...participants reported a higher perception of safety (51.2 % regarding traffic and 42.4 % about crime" (Torres et al., 2013). "Most [participants] reported feeling safe with respect to crime in the Ciclovía program (65.51 %)" (Mejía-Arbeláez et al., 2021). "Negative association...among those living in neighbourhoods with reported traffic fatalities in 2011 (POR = 0.45; 95 % CI: 0.22-0.92)" (Gómez et al., 2015). "Participants who reported feeling safe or very safe from traffic were more likely to report walking for at least 60 minutes (POR//1.50, 95 % CI//1.11, 2.03)" (Gómez et al., 2010).
Air Pollution	"[Particulate matter (PM_{10}) along the Ciclovía] showed the PM_{10} was 13 times higher on a regular day (65 µg/m3) than on a Sunday" (Sarmiento et al., 2010a).
Social Cohesion	"... the willingness of Ciclovía participants to help each other (62.4 %) ... helping another participant get up after a fall (73.2 %)" (Torres et al., 2013). "... regular Ciclovía participation were more likely to have higher [social cohesion] perception of the Ciclovía (OR = 2.0; 95 % CI = 1.4, 2.8) than infrequent participants" (Torres et al., 2013). [In Bogota and Santiago de Cali] ... "participants were more likely to visit higher or lower SES neighbourhoods than their average SES-of-neighbourhood origin" (Mejía-Arbeláez et al., 2021). "Mexico City and Santiago de Chile were more likely to stay in geographic units similar to their average SES-of-origin, having lower overall mobility" (Mejía-Arbeláez et al., 2021).

	"City statistics show that 41 % of Bogotá residents believed that most inhabitants are not willing to help each other" (Torres et al., 2013). "... promotes social cohesion through interaction between different SES" (Teunissen et al., 2015).
Economic impact of physical activity	... "if only about 17.5 % of the Ciclovía users meet PA recommendations, each would represent a cost that is approximately 16 % of the benefit produced" (Montes et al., 2012). ... "Guadalajara's program showed that the mean annual benefit for mortality prevention ranged from US $664,727 to US $10,146,740" (Montes et al., 2012). "Considering only bicyclists, the cost–benefit ratio ranged from 1.79 to 2.36. Considering only pedestrians, the cost–benefit ratio ranged from 1.26 to 1.66" (Montes et al., 2012). "... annual premature deaths would be prevented each year, corresponding to an economic value of US $25·1 million (18·7 million–34·2 million)" (Velázquez-Cortés et al., 2023). "363 (95 % CI 271–494) annual premature deaths could be prevented each year, corresponding to an economic value of US$194·1 million" (Velázquez-Cortés et al., 2023).

References

Arksey, H., O'Malley, L., 2005. Scoping studies: towards a methodological framework. Int. J. Soc. Res. Methodol. 8 (1), 19–32. https://doi.org/10.1080/1364557032000119616.

Bachelet, P.A., 2024. The Complexities of Inequality in Latin America and the Caribbean. Inter-American Development Bank.

Ball, K., Carver, A., Downing, K., Jackson, M., O'Rouke, K., 2015. Addressing the social determinants of inequities in physical activity and sedentary behaviours. Health Promotion Int. 30 (2), ii8–ii19. https://doi.org/10.1093/heapro/dav022.

Barreno, M., Sisa, I., Yépez García, M.C., Shen, H., Villar, M., Kovalskys, I., et al., 2021. Association between built environment and physical activity in Latin American countries: a multicentre cross-sectional study. BMJ Open. https://doi.org/10.1136/bmjopen-2020-046271.

Bassett-Gunter, R., Angevaare, K., Tomasone, J., Leo, J., Varughese, B., Langvee, J., et al., 2019. A systematic scoping review: resources targeting the training and education of health and recreation practitioners to support physical activity among people with physical disabilities. Disability Health J. 12 (4), 542–550. https://doi.org/10.1016/j.dhjo.2019.06.007.

Bauman, A.E., Reis, R.S., Sallis, J.F., Wells, J.C., Loos, R.J.F., Martin, B.W., 2012. Correlates of physical activity: why are some people physically active and others not? Lancet 380 (9838), 258–271. https://doi.org/10.1016/S0140-6736(12)60735-1.

Becerra, J.M., Reis, R.S., Frank, L.D., Ramirez-Marrero, F.A., Welle, B., 2013. Transport and health: a look at three Latin American cities. J. Transp. & Health 4 (4), 654–666. https://pdxscholar.library.pdx.edu/cgi/viewcontent.cgi?article=1017&context=commhealth_fac.

Bell, M.L., Davis, D.L., Gouveia, N., Borja-Aburto, V.H., Cifuentes, L.A., 2006. The avoidable health effects of air pollution in three Latin American cities: Santiago, São Paulo, and Mexico City. Environ. Res. 100 (3), 431–440. https://doi.org/10.1016/j.envres.2005.08.002.

Bilal, U., Alazraqui, M., Caiaffa, W.T., Lopez-Olmedo, N., Martinez-Folgar, K., Miranda, J.J., et al., 2019. Inequalities in life expectancy in six large Latin American cities from the SALURBAL study: an ecological analysis. Lancet Planet. Health 3 (12), e503–e510. https://doi.org/10.1016/S2542-5196(19)30235-9.

Bird, A., Díaz del Castillo, A., Hipp, J.A., Sarmiento, O.L., 2017. Open Streets Trends and Opportunities. Active Living Research. https://activelivingresearch.org/open-streets-trends-and-opportunities

Borsdorf, A., Hidalgo, R., Vidal-Koppmann, S., 2016. Social segregation and gated communities in Santiago de Chile and Buenos Aires: a comparison. Habitat. Int. 54, 18–27. https://doi.org/10.1016/j.habitatint.2015.11.033.

Cain, K.L., Millstein, R.A., Sallis, J.F., Conway, T.L., Gavand, K.A., Frank, L.D., et al., 2014. Contribution of streetscape audits to explanation of physical activity in four age groups based on the microscale audit of pedestrian streetscapes (MAPS). Soc. Sci. & Med. 116, 82–92. https://doi.org/10.1016/j.socscimed.2014.06.042.

Cohen, D.A., Han, B., Derose, K.P., Williamson, S., Paley, A., Batteate, C., 2016. CicLAvia: evaluation of participation, physical activity, and cost of an open streets event in Los Angeles. Preventive Med. 90, 26–33. https://doi.org/10.1016/j.ypmed.2016.06.009.

Cooke, A., Smith, D., Booth, A., 2012. Beyond PICO: The SPIDER tool for qualitative evidence synthesis. Qualitative Health Res. 22 (10), 1435–1443. https://doi.org/10.1177/1049732312452938.

Cortinez-O'Ryan, A., Moran, M.R., Rios, A.P., Anza-Ramirez, C., Slovic, A.D., 2020. Could severe mobility and park use restrictions during the COVID-19 pandemic aggravate health inequalities? Insights and challenges from Latin America. Cad. de. Saúde Pública 36 (9), e00185820. https://doi.org/10.1590/0102-311X00185820.

Dávila-Cervantes, C., Agudelo-Botero, M., 2019. Health inequalities in Latin America: persistent gaps in life expectancy. Lancet Planet. Health 3 (12), e492–e493. https://doi.org/10.1016/S2542-5196(19)30244-X.

Ding, D., Lawson, K.D., Kolbe-Alexander, T., Finkelstein, E.A., Katzmarzyk, P.T., van Mechelen, W., et al., 2016. The economic burden of physical inactivity: a global analysis of major non-communicable diseases. Lancet 388 (10051), 1311–1324. https://doi.org/10.1016/S0140-6736(16)30383-X.

Edwards, E.S., Sackett, S.C., 2016. Psychosocial variables related to why women are less active than men and related health implications. Clin. Med. Insights: Women's Health 9 (1), 47–56. https://doi.org/10.4137/CMWH.S34668.

Giles-Corti, B., Vernez-Moudon, A., Reis, R., Turrell, G., Dannenberg, A.L., Badland, H., et al., 2016. City planning and population health: a global challenge. Lancet 388 (10062), 2912–2924. https://doi.org/10.1016/S0140-6736(16)30066-6.

Glazener, A., Wylie, J., van Waas, W., Khreis, H., 2022. The impacts of car-free day and events on the environment and human health. Curr. Environ. Health Rep. 9 (2), 165–182. https://doi.org/10.1007/s40572-022-00342-y.

Gómez, L.F., Mateus, J.C., Cabrera, G., 2004. Leisure-time physical activity among women in a neighbourhood in Bogotá, Colombia: prevalence and socio-demographic correlates. Cad. de. Saúde Pública 20 (4), 1155–1165. https://doi.org/10.1590/s0102-311x2004000400026.

Gómez, L.F., Mosquera, J., Gómez, O.L., Moreno, J., Pinzón, J.D., Jacoby, E., et al., 2015. Social conditions and urban environment associated with participation in the Ciclovía program among adults from Cali, Colombia. Cad. de. Saúde Pública 31 (1), 257–266. https://doi.org/10.1590/0102-311X00086814.

Gómez, L.F., Parra, D.C., Buchner, D., Brownson, R.C., Sarmiento, O.L., Pinzón, J.D., et al., 2010. Built environment attributes and walking patterns among the elderly population in Bogotá. Am. J. Preventive Med. 38 (6), 592–599. https://doi.org/10.1016/j.amepre.2010.02.005.

Gouveia, N., Kephart, J.L., Dronova, I., McClure, L., Granados, J.T., Betancourt, R.M., et al., 2021. Ambient fine particulate matter in Latin American cities: levels, population exposure, and associated urban factors. Sci. Total. Environ. 772, 145035. https://doi.org/10.1016/j.scitotenv.2021.145035.

Gouveia, N., Slovic, A., Kanai, C.M., Soriano, L., 2022. Air pollution and environmental justice in Latin America: where are we and how can we move forward? Curr. Environ. Health Rep. 9 (2), 152–164. https://doi.org/10.1007/s40572-022-00341-z.

Guthold, R., Stevens, G.A., Riley, L.M., Bull, F.C., 2018. Worldwide trends in insufficient physical activity from 2001 to 2016: a pooled analysis of 358 population-based surveys with 1.9 million participants. Lancet Glob. Health 6 (10), e1077–e1086. https://doi.org/10.1016/S2214-109X(18)30357-7.

Gutman, J., Patel, N., 2018. Addressing spatial inequity in Latin American cities. Brookings Institution. https://www.brookings.edu/articles/addressing-spatial-inequity-in-latin-american-cities/.

Guzmán, L., Beltrán, C., Morales, R., Sarmiento, O., 2023. Inequality in personal exposure to air pollution in transport microenvironments for commuters in Bogotá. Case Stud. Transp. Policy 11 (2), 100963. https://doi.org/10.1016/j.cstp.2023.100963.

Hernández, E., Guzmán, C., Serón, P., 2022. Interventions based on environmental determinants for nutritional and physical activity behaviours in Colombia: a scoping review. BMJ Open. 12 (9), e060085. https://doi.org/10.1136/bmjopen-2021-060085.

Hong, Q.N., Pluye, P., Fàbregues, S., Bartlett, G., Boardman, F., Cargo, M. , et al., 2018. Mixed methods appraisal tool (MMAT), version 2018. Canadian Intellectual Property Office, Industry Canada.

Kalisa, E., Sudmant, A., Ruberambuga, R., Bower, J., 2021. From car-free days to pollution-free cities: reflections on clean urban transport in Rwanda. International Growth Centre. https://www.theigc.org/publications/car-free-days-pollution-free-cities-reflections-clean-urban-transport-rwanda#:~:text=Using%20high%2Dquality%20dat%2C%20this,and%20the%20COVID%2D19%20lockdown.

Katzmarzyk, P.T., Friedenreich, C., Shiroma, E., Lee, I.-M., 2022. Physical inactivity and non-communicable disease burden in low-, middle-, and high-income countries. J. Phys. Act. Health 56, 101–106. https://www.ncbi.nlm.nih.gov/pmc/articles/PMC8478970/.

Kuhlberg, J., Hipp, A., Eyler, A., 2013. Open streets initiatives in the U.S.: closed to traffic, open to physical activity. J. Phys. Act. Health 10 (1), 117–123. https://doi.org/10.1123/jpah.2012-0376.

Larsen, B.A., Pekmezi, D., Marquez, B., Benitez, T.J., Marcus, B.H., 2013. Physical activity in Latinas: social and environmental influences. Women's Health 9 (2), 201–210. https://doi.org/10.2217/whe.13.9.

Medina, C.R.-M., Bautista-Arredondo, M., Barquera, S., Janssen, I., 2019. Move on bikes program: a community-based physical activity initiative. Int. J. Environ. Res. Public. Health 16 (10), 1685. https://doi.org/10.3390/ijerph16101685. Article.

Meisel, J., Sarmiento, O., Montes, F., Martínez, E., Lemoine, P., Valdivia, J., et al., 2014. Network analysis of Bogotá's Ciclovía Recreativa, a self-organized multisectorial community program to promote physical activity in a middle-income country. Am. J. Health Promotion 28 (3), 127–136. https://doi.org/10.4278/ajhp.120912-QUAN-443.

Mejía-Arbeláez, C.T., Sarmiento, O.L., Vega, R.M., Martínez, L., Medina, C., Useche, A.F., et al., 2021. Social inclusion and physical activity in Ciclovía Recreativa programs in Latin America. Int. J. Environ. Res. Public. Health 18 (2), 655. https://doi.org/10.3390/ijerph18020655.

Montes, F., Sarmiento, O., Zarama, R., Pratt, M., Wang, G., Jacoby, E., et al., 2012. Do health benefits outweigh the costs of mass recreational programs? An economic analysis of four Ciclovía programs. J. Urban. Health 89 (1), 153–170. https://doi.org/10.1007/s11524-011-9628-8.

Mora, M.E.G., Orellanda, S.S., Freire, G., 2021. Disability inclusion in Latin America and the Caribbean: a path to sustainable development (Report No. P175383). World Bank. https://documents.worldbank.org/curated/en/099015112012126833/pdf/P17538305622600c00bf3f09659df1f2f79.pdf.

Munn, Z., Peters, M.D.J., Stern, C., Tufanaru, C., McArthur, A., Aromataris, E., 2018. Systematic review or scoping review? Guidance for authors when choosing between a systematic or scoping review approach. BMC Med. Res. Methodol. 18, *143*. https://doi.org/10.1186/s12874-018-0611-x. Article.

Nelson, G., Rodriguez-Hernandez, J., Kephart, J., Ortigoza, A., Morales Betancourt, R., Texcalac Sangrador, J., et al., 2024. Short-term associations between fine particulate air pollution and cardiovascular and respiratory mortality in 337 cities in Latin America. Sci. Total. Environ. 920, 171073. https://doi.org/10.1016/j.scitotenv.2024.171073. Article.

OECD & The World Bank, 2020. Health at a Glance: Latin America and the Caribbean 2020OECD Publishing. https://doi.org/10.1787/6089164f-en.

O'Donovan, G., Lee, I.-M., Hamer, M., Stamatakis, E., 2017. Association of "Weekend Warrior" and other leisure time physical activity patterns with risks for all-cause, cardiovascular disease, and cancer mortality. JAMA Intern. Med. 177 (3), 335–342. https://doi.org/10.1001/jamainternmed.2016.8014.

O'Donovan, G., Petermann-Rocha, F., Ferrari, G., Lee, I.-M., Hamer, M., Stamatakis, E., et al., 2024. Associations of the 'weekend warrior' physical activity pattern with all-cause, cardiovascular disease and cancer mortality: the Mexico City prospective study. Br. J. Sports Med. 58 (7), 359. https://doi.org/10.1136/bjsports-2023-107612.

Parra, D.A., Pinzon, D., Van Zandt, J., Brownson, A., Gomez, R.L., 2020. Geographic distribution of the Ciclovía and Recreovía programs by neighborhood SES in Bogotá: how unequal is the geographic access assessed via distance-based measures. J. Urban. Health 98 (1), 101–110. https://doi.org/10.1007/s11524-020-00496-w.

Peng, B., Ng, J., Ha, A., 2023. Barriers and facilitators to physical activity for young adult women: a systematic review and thematic synthesis of qualitative literature. Int. J. Behav. Nutr. Phys. Act. 20, 23. https://doi.org/10.1186/s12966-023-01411-7. Article.

Pratt, M., Orozco, A., Hernandez-A, O., Reis, R., Sarmiento, O., 2014. Obesity prevention lessons from Latin America. Preventive Med. 69, 120–122. https://doi.org/10.1016/j.ypmed.2014.09.021.

Rezende, L.F.M., Sá, T.H., Mielke, G.I., Rey-López, J.P., Lee, I.-M., 2016. All-cause mortality attributable to sitting time: analysis of 54 countries worldwide. Am. J. Preventive Med. 51 (2), 253–263. https://doi.org/10.1016/j.amepre.2016.01.022.

Ritchie, H., Samborska, V., Roser, M., 2024. Urbanization. Our World in Data. https://ourworldindata.org/urbanization.

Rodrigues, E.Q., Lopes, G., Ribeiro, E.H.C., Barrozo, L.V., Bernal, R.T.I., Andrade, D.R., et al., 2022. Use of an elevated avenue for leisure-time physical activity by adults from downtown São Paulo, Brazil. Int. J. Environ. Res. Public. Health 19 (9), 5581. https://doi.org/10.3390/ijerph19095581.

Sallis, J.F., Conway, T.L., Adams, M.A., Frank, L.D., Pratt, M., Salvo, D., et al., 2016. Physical activity in relation to urban environments in 14 cities worldwide: a cross-sectional study. Lancet 388 (10034), 2207–2217. https://doi.org/10.1016/S0140-6736(15)01284-2.

Sallis, J.F., Floyd, M., Rodríguez, D., Saelens, B., 2012. Role of built environments in physical activity, obesity, and cardiovascular disease. Circulation 125 (5), 729–737. https://doi.org/10.1161/CIRCULATIONAHA.110.969022.

Santos, A., Willumsen, J., Meheus, F., Ilbawi, A., Bull, F., 2023. The cost of inaction on physical inactivity to public health-care systems: a population-attributable fraction analysis. Lancet Glob. Health 11, 32–39. https://doi.org/10.1016/S2214-109X(22)00464-8.

Sarmiento, O.L., Rios, A., Paez, D.C., Quijano, K., Fermino, R., 2017. The Recreovía of Bogotá, a community-based physical activity program to promote physical activity among women: baseline results of the natural experiment *Al Ritmo de las Comunidades*. J. Phys. Act. Health 14 (6). https://pubmed.ncbi.nlm.nih.gov/28608844/.

Sarmiento, O.L., Schmid, T.L., Parra, D.C., Díaz-del-Castillo, A., Gómez, L.F., Pratt, M., et al., 2010b. Quality of life, physical activity, and built environment characteristics among Colombian adults. J. Phys. Act. Health 7 (2), S181–S195. https://pubmed.ncbi.nlm.nih.gov/20702906/.

Sarmiento, O.L., Torres, A., Jacoby, E., Pratt, M., Schmid, T.L., Stierling, G., 2010a. The Ciclovía-Recreativa: a mass-recreational program with public health potential. J. Phys. Act. Health 7 (2), S163–S180. https://doi.org/10.1123/jpah.7.s2.s163.

Scharff, D.P., Homan, S., Kreuter, M., Brennan, L., 1999. Factors associated with physical activity in women across the life span: implications for program development. Women & Health 29 (2), 115–134. https://pubmed.ncbi.nlm.nih.gov/10427652/.

Semets, P., Salman, T., 2016. The multi-layered-ness of urban segregation: on the simultaneous inclusion and exclusion in Latin American cities. Habitat. Int. 54, 80–87. https://doi.org/10.1016/j.habitatint.2015.08.013.

Stingl-Zúñiga, I., Farías-Valenzuela, C., Ferrero-Hernández, P., Marques, A., Rezende, L.F.M., Castillo-Paredes, A., et al., 2023. All-cause mortality attributable to sitting time and physical inactivity in Chilean adults. BMC Public. Health 23, 1234. https://doi.org/10.1186/s12889-023-16467-0. Article.

Strain, T., Flaxman, S., Guthold, R., Semenova, E., Cowan, M., 2024. National, regional and global trends in insufficient physical activity among adults from 2000 to 2022: a pooled analysis of 507 population-based surveys with 5.7 million participants. Lancet Glob. Health 12 (9), 1232–1243. https://doi.org/10.1016/S2214-109X(24)00150-5.

Teunissen, T., Sarmiento, O., Zuidgeest, M., Brussel, M., 2015. Mapping equality in access: the case of Bogotá's sustainable transportation initiatives. Case Stud. Transp. Policy 3 (4), 457–467. https://doi.org/10.1080/15568318.2013.808388.

Thomas, A., Furlong, J., Aldred, R., 2022. Equity in temporary street closures: the case of London's Covid-19 'School Streets' schemes. Transportation Res. Part. D: Transp. Environ. 110, 103402. https://doi.org/10.1016/j.trd.2022.103402. Article.

Torres, A., Sarmiento, O.L., Stauber, C., Zarama, R., 2013. The Ciclovía and Cicloruta programs: promising interventions to promote physical activity and social capital in Bogotá, Colombia. Am. J. Public. Health 103 (1), 23–30. https://doi.org/10.2105/AJPH.2012.301142.

UNICEF, 2021. *There are nearly 19.1 million children with disabilities in Latin America and the Caribbean, UNICEF's most comprehensive statistical analysis finds*. https://www.unicef.org/lac/en/press-releases/there-are-nearly-19-million-children-disabilities-latin-america-and-caribbean.

United Nations in the Caribbean, 2021. *Regional human development report: Trapped? Inequality and economic growth in Latin America and the Caribbean. United Nations*. https://caribbean.un.org/en/149807-regional-human-development-report-2021-trapped-high-inequality-and-low-growth-latin-america.

University of California & Institute of Transportation Studies, 2024. *Ciclovía at 50: Changing street cultures across the world*. UCLA Institute of Transportation Studies. https://www.its.ucla.edu/tribe-event/ciclovia-at-50/.

Velázquez-Cortés, D., Nieuwenhuijsen, M., Jerrett, M., Rojas-Rueda, D., 2023. Health benefits of open streets programmes in Latin America: a quantitative health impact assessment. Lancet Planet. Health 7 (8), 590–599. https://doi.org/10.1016/S2542-5196(23)00109-2.

Werneck, A.O., Aguilar-Farias, N., Ferrari, G., Brazo-Sayavera, J., García-Witulski, C., Dourado, V.Z., et al., 2022a. Time trends and inequalities of physical activity domains and sitting time in South America. J. Glob. Health 12, 04027. https://doi.org/10.7189/jogh.12.04027.

Werneck, A.O., Barbosa, L., Silva, E.C.M., Araujo, R.H.O., 2022b. Sociodemographic inequalities in physical activity in Latin America: time for policies targeted at groups that need it the most. Int. J. Public. Health 67, 1605125. https://doi.org/10.3389/ijph.2022.1605125. Article.

World Health Organization, 2018. *Seventy-first World Health Assembly: Provisional agenda item 12.2 – Physical activity for health.* https://apps.who.int/gb/ebwha/pdf_files/WHA71-REC1/A71_2018_REC1-en.pdf.

World Health Organization, 2019. *Ambient (outdoor) air quality and health.* https://www.who.int/news-room/fact-sheets/detail/ambient-(outdoor)-air-quality-and-health.

World Health Organization, 2024. *Physical activity.* https://www.who.int/news-room/fact-sheets/detail/physical-activity.

World Health Organization, 2020. *WHO guidelines on physical activity and sedentary behaviour* (ISBN 9789240015128). World Health Organization. https://iris.who.int/bitstream/handle/10665/336656/9789240015128-eng.pdf?sequence=1.

Xu, Y.-Y., Xie, J., Yin, H., Yang, F.-F., Ma, C.-M., Yang, B.-Y., et al., 2022. Burden of disease attributable to low physical activity and its trends from 1990 to 2019: an analysis of the Global Burden of Disease study. Front. Public. Health 10, 1018866. https://doi.org/10.3389/fpubh.2022.1018866.

CHAPTER SIX

Health impacts of fare-free transportation initiatives around the world: A scoping review

Jacob Albin Korem Alhassan*, **Chima Casmir Ibeh, and Daniel Fuller**
Community Health and Epidemiology, University of Saskatchewan, Saskatoon, SK, Canada
*Corresponding author. e-mail address: jacob.alhassan@usask.ca

Contents

Abstract

This scoping review examined the health and equity impacts of fare-free transportation initiatives, which aim to improve access to services and social participation. A comprehensive search of MEDLINE, PubMed, PsycINFO, and Web of Science identified 8745 articles; after screening and full-text review, 27 studies were included. These studies were conducted across eight countries predominantly in Europe and north America. Overall, findings suggest that fare-free transportation initiatives have positive health effects. They improve access to healthcare services, reduce social isolation and improve social engagement/participation. They also improve mental health outcomes and support physical activity in some contexts, thereby contributing to better overall health outcomes, including reductions in obesity, depression, and cardiovascular disease. The sense of entitlement to fare-free transportation also enhances wellbeing, particularly among socially excluded populations. The review highlights significant equity benefits, with the greatest improvements seen among vulnerable groups such as older adults, youth, ethnic minorities, and racialized communities. By reducing financial and mobility barriers, these programs broaden access to health-promoting resources. However, some unintended consequences were noted. Increased reliance on fare-free transportation for short journeys may reduce physical activity, potentially offsetting some health gains. In conclusion, fare-free transportation initiatives demonstrate strong potential to improve population health and reduce inequities, particularly for

Advances in Transport Policy and Planning, Volume 18
ISSN 2543-0009, https://doi.org/10.1016/bs.atpp.2026.07.009

disadvantaged groups. Future research and policy should focus on enhancing accessibility and maximizing benefits while minimizing drawbacks such as reduced physical activity.

1. Introduction

Public transportation is a significant social determinant of health given its ability to facilitate access to people, places and resources necessary for maintaining wellbeing (McCarthy, 2006). Transportation research over the last three decades has consistently shown that transportation systems are a major public health concern and that the ways transportation systems are organized can influence population health outcomes (Godlee, 1992).

A recent review identified fourteen pathways through which urban transportation systems can either improve or deplete health (Glazener et al., 2021). Transportation systems influence health by facilitating/denying people's ability to access resources that influence health; by increasing people's direct exposure to health promoting or depleting factors; or determines people's behaviours in ways that might either promote or worsen health.

First, transportation systems determine access to healthcare services (Corcoran et al., 2012). Where public transportation systems are absent or inadequate, extra barriers emerge for those seeking to access healthcare and these barriers can be particularly acute for those in rural areas (Alhassan et al., 2021; Yadav et al., 2025), people experiencing other forms of marginalization such as vulnerable youth (Johnston et al., 2015), historically marginalized groups such as Indigenous peoples (Hanson et al., 2021) or people peripheralized due to disabilities (Bezyak et al., 2020). Access to other key resources such as food (Rajasooriar and Soma, 2022), employment (Blumenberg and Ong, 2001; Dobbs, 2007) and the ability to participate in social life (Lucas, 2004) all depend on transportation systems. Transportation systems can also determine if people will participate in physical activity and by how much (Langlois et al., 2016); their exposure to noise (Brown and van Kamp, 2017) and environmental toxins (Kennedy, 2004) as well as their risk of injury (Ahmed et al., 2023). These patterns hold in high- and low-income countries (Jones et al., 2016) although those most at risk of transportation related externalities are often equity deserving groups (Alhassan et al., 2023; Linovski et al., 2021).

The benefits of public transportation access on population health have led many organizations and societies to create fare-free transportation initiatives of varied comprehensiveness (Kirschen et al., 2023). A recent review of fare-free transportation initiatives identified wide variations from fully fare-free systems to initiatives that are partially fare-free (Kębłowski, 2020). Fare-free transportation initiatives can be small initiatives aimed at promoting mobility of specific demographic groups such as older adults and vulnerable communities (Alhassan et al., 2025; Rambaldini-Gooding et al., 2023). Larger scale initiatives also exist. For example, Tallin, Estonia has a municipal level fare-free transportation initiative (Gabaldón-Estevan et al., 2019). Although much less common, fare-free transportation can exist at the national level such as Luxembourg's current fare-free national transportation initiative. Nonetheless, countries like Luxembourg have much smaller populations- similar to the size of some cities (Ruud, 2023).

Many public transportation systems have experienced budget cuts leading to inaccessibility. Evidence from countries such as Poland, Greece, Portugal and Canada show that these budget cuts have negative health impacts (Alhassan et al., 2021; Anciães, 2013; Taylor, 2006). Although some public transportation schemes have experienced budget cuts, others have witnessed increased investments including the initiation of fare-free transportation services. According to a recent scoping review, major investments in public transportation such as the creation of new high speed rail can boost economic development and promote access (Alhassan and Anciaes, 2025). Less research evidence exists on the socio-economic impacts of investments in fare-free transportation initiatives.

This chapter sought to close gaps in the academic literature by providing an up-to-date synthesis of existing literature on the impacts of fare-free transportation initiatives around the world. It aimed to describe initiatives at different scales and from different parts of the world. Adopting a broad scope, it explored different types of initiatives including concessionary bus passes aimed at specific target population groups and also included fare-free transportation initiatives that cover the entire population. The chapter will describe the methodology used in identifying literature and the final set of studies that were reviewed. The findings section describes the different types of fare-free transportation initiatives identified in the literature and highlights the major impacts of these initiatives on health in the locales where they have been implemented. Finally, we describe how the impacts of the identified initiatives vary for different sociodemographic groups before discussing the implications of these findings for future research and policy action.

2. Methodology

A scoping review methodology was utilized to identify primary empirical studies on health impacts of fare-free transportation initiatives. There are several approaches for reviewing literature ranging from unsystematic narrative reviews to traditional systematic reviews that may even culminate in a meta-analysis. Scoping reviews are an appropriate methodology for systematically retrieving literature on a given subject where an insufficient number of studies exist, and the primary focus of the research is identifying these studies rather than necessarily evaluating the quality of the studies. This approach is also appropriate when the expected literature comes from a variety of disciplines and for pragmatic reasons such as limited researcher resources.

We utilized the five key steps for conducting scoping reviews as described by Arksey and O 'malley (2005). First, a research question was identified – we sought to answer the following questions: 1. What are the health impacts of fare-free transportation initiatives? 2. How do these impacts vary across the population? Second, we identified studies that are relevant for answering the research question through a systematic search of the literature using major databases. Third, we screened identified studies and the most relevant ones were reviewed and included in the final review. Fourth, specific information pertinent to the research question were extracted from the included studies and analysed. Finally, we summarized, synthesized and presented the included studies.

We conducted a systematic search in February 2024 of four key health and social science databases that index journals focused on transportation policy and health. The specific databases searched were Web of Science, PubMEd, PsychInfo and Medline. These searches were conducted in consultation with a health science librarian who helped identify the appropriate databases. Two key concepts guided the search. The first was different variations of *fare-free transportation* and the second concept was *health impacts*. The specific search terms that were used to execute the search were as follows.: "Transportation/ or free transportation," OR "Transportation/ or free bus," OR "Transportation/ or bus pass," OR "free transit," OR "concessionary transportation," OR "subsidy transportation" AND "Quality of Life"/or Health Impact*," OR "Health Outcome*," OR "Health Policy" OR "Health Services Accessibility/or Health Access," OR "Health Services Accessibility/or Healthcare Access," OR "Social Determinants of Health"/or Health Inequities/or Health

Inequit*". The keyword combination was appropriate and resulted in a total of 8745 identified records which were all screened by two authors (JAKA and ICC) for inclusion.

All identified records were imported into the Rayyan software specifically designed to aid in scoping and systematic reviews (Ouzzani et al., 2016). For each database, a Research Information System (RIS) file was downloaded containing bibliometric information of the included records. Once imported into the Rayyan software reviewers could see the titles and abstracts of each record in an interface that allowed each reviewer to click to either "include", "exclude" or tag as "maybe". We conducted a systematic de-duplication of records. Once papers were identified as appropriate for the review, we also hand searched the internet and searched included studies' reference lists to identify other relevant studies not included in the systematic search process. Both reviewers agreed on each study before it was included. The specific data extracted on each study included methodological information, contextual data such as the location of the study as well as the major health impacts of the fare-free transportation initiative.

Specific criteria were used to decide which studies would be included in the final list of studies. First, we only included studies published in peer reviewed academic journals and did not include grey literature such as technical reports or media publications. Second, we only included studies that were published in the English language. Third, we only included records for which we could find the full text. Fourth, we only included studies that were published after the year 2000. Finally, we only included primary empirical studies (qualitative, quantitative, controlled trials and observational) that were directly relevant to the primary research question: studies on the health impacts of fare-free transportation initiatives. We excluded any systematic reviews, meta syntheses and metanalyses or any other study type that did not present empirical findings. Once data charting was completed, we synthesised results by identifying the commonly described types of fare-free transportation initiatives and their health impacts. For example, among included studies, we grouped together studies that described initiatives embedded in public transportation systems and those outside it. We also grouped together study findings on health impacts of fare-free transportation initiatives by focusing on physical, mental and healthcare access. We then synthesised these studies based on similarity.

3. Findings

We identified 8745 records from the four databases (see Fig. 1) – 1235 were duplicates and therefore removed without review and 7510 titles and abstracts were screened by two reviewers. In total, 7456 irrelevant records were removed, and 54 full text articles were read. A total of 29 records were excluded at this stage (6 conference abstracts without full texts and 23 studies not specifically focused on the health impacts of fare-free transportation initiatives). A total of 25 articles out of the 54 full texts read met all criteria

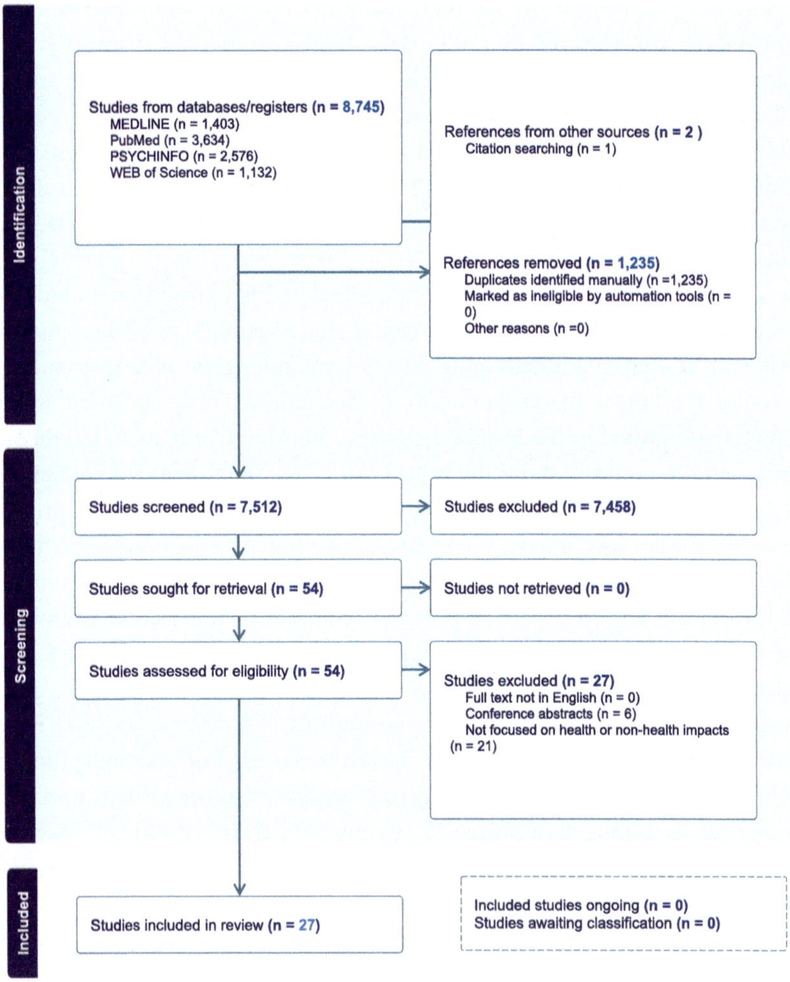

Fig. 1 PRISMA-ScR diagram of included studies.

and two (2) more articles were identified through hand searching and search of reference lists of the included studies. This led to a total of 27 included studies as shown in Fig. 1.

The included studies were from 8 countries – predominantly in Europe and North America. The included studies were from Australia (1), Canada (4), Estonia (1), Ethiopia (1), Finland (1), South Korea (1), United Kingdom (14) and the United States of America (4). Although most studies were focused on urban areas a few studies drew on rural areas (Alhassan et al., 2025; Gabaldón-Estevan et al., 2019; Whitley et al., 2020). The studies were predominantly quantitative studies although a few others exclusively used qualitative methodologies to reveal participant perspectives of the impacts of fare-free transportation initiatives (Goodman et al., 2018; Jones at al., 2013; Jones et al., 2012; Rambaldini-Gooding et al., 2023). Except for five studies where the fare-free transportation initiatives were community driven bus services, all initiatives reported on in this chapter were embedded in public transportation systems.

3.1 Types of fare-free transportation initiatives

The studies included in this review encompass a broad range of fare-free transportation initiatives. These include universally fare-free transportation initiatives provided by governments or community based organizations (Alhassan et al., 2025; Gabaldón-Estevan et al., 2019; Holland et al., 2024), fare-free initiatives targeted at specific sociodemographic groups (Shin, 2021; Webb et al., 2016, 2012; Whitley et al., 2020) and initiatives embedded in existing social/health programs (Holland et al., 2024; Izumi et al., 2023). We group fare-free transportation initiatives into two broad categories. Whereas the first group of fare-free transportation initiatives are typically provided and funded by governments (municipal, regional or national) as part of the public transportation system, the second type of fare-free transportation initiatives are not embedded in the public transportation system.

3.1.1 Fare-free transportation initiatives embedded in public transportation systems

Most fare-free transportation initiatives are usually provided by governments at different levels either to the whole population or to specific groups. The distinguishing element of these initiatives is that they are embedded in the traditional public transportation system. Over half of the included studies were from England and reported on concessionary bus pass programs and fare-free travel options where the public transportation system operates as is but is delivered free of charge to specific demographic groups (Coronini-Cronberg et al., 2012; Edwards et al., 2013; Green et al., 2014; Whitley et al., 2020). The free bus pass program in England is a national program with some local add-ons. It is only off-peak and accounts for most of the off-peak bus usage in some areas. Operators receive a reduced reimbursement which, in principle, pays them only for the journeys that would have been made without the scheme. England's fare-free transportation program for older adults was started in 2006. Although embedded in the traditional public transportation system which was itself not fare-free, the free bus pass program allowed for people aged 60 years and above to travel fare-free all day on weekends/public holidays and from 9:30 am on weekdays (Coronini-Cronberg et al., 2012). Like the national program, another program from England is the fare-free travel initiative offered to youth in London aged 18 years and under. This initiative, created in 2005 initially covered those under 17 but was eventually extended to those aged 18 and under (Goodman et al., 2014). Here, again the fare-free transportation initiative was embedded within the public transportation system in London, which itself was not fare-free but allowed a specific group (youth) to travel for free. In Kingston, Canada, Holland et al. (2024) described a fare-free transportation initiative for people on income assistance embedded in the traditional public transportation system provided by the municipal government. Another Canadian example is an initiative described by Mah and Mitra (2017) where the town of Oakville provided a fare-free transportation program for older adults. In some cases these initiatives are means tested as in the case of a Washington based study in the United States where low income individuals received up to 6 months of fare-free travel (Brough et al., 2022). Tallin, Estonia provides an example not simply of the embedding of fare-free transportation into an existing transportation system but transforming the entire public transportation system to make it fare-free (Gabaldón-Estevan et al., 2019).

3.1.2 Fare-free transportation initiatives not embedded in public transportation systems

Less common (five studies) but also existing in the included studies are fare-free transportation initiatives and programs that are not embedded in the traditional public transportation system. These initiatives although sometimes created using government funds operate independently of public transportation systems and either set out to fill a specific gap (provide transportation access where it is unavailable), provide fare-free transportation to specific groups such as school children or provide means tested fare-free transportation as part of social inclusion and economic empowerment programs. In Australia, Rambaldini-Gooding et al. (2023) describe the Gong shuttle which provides fare-free transportation parallel to the traditional public transportation system – the Wollongong public transport network. The fare-free service mainly caters to the needs of older adults, is operated by a local company that prioritizes accessible transportation and is funded through a collaboration between the University of Wollongong and the Wollongong city council. A USA based study also described a fare-free transportation initiative aimed at promoting travel and recreation among children where the initiative was not directly embedded in traditional public transportation system (Patel et al., 2021). In this study, the department of parks, recreation and open spaces in Miami-Dade County, Florida provided fare-free transportation to an after-school health and wellbeing program – the Fit2Play program (Patel et al., 2021). The fare-free transportation in this case was provided using a van dedicated to the program. In some other studies, fare-free transportation was provided in the form of cash transfers to specific groups such as low-income populations or unemployed people who then used the cash resources to access either public or private transportation options. In an Ethiopia based study, Franklin (2018) described the use of a cash transfer to support job searches. People experiencing unemployment were given cash which they subsequently used to access public and private transportation to aid in their job search. Similarly, unlike fare-free transportation interventions that are embedded in the public transportation system, Izumi et al. (2023) describe a fare-free transportation initiative involving the transfer of rideshare (Uber) credits to patients in selected community clinics to reduce transportation barriers and food insecurity challenges. Finally, in a rural Canadian community predominantly inhabited by Indigenous peoples, Alhassan et al. (2025) describe the creation of a fare-free intercommunity transportation initiative to support travel between two communities 2.5 h apart. Here, due to the absence of a public transportation system, the fare-free transportation initiative operated on its own and was maintained by a community organization although funding had been provided by the Federal government. This second set of fare-free transportation initiatives were different from the first in that while they sometimes received government funding or provided resources that might lead beneficiaries to use public transportation systems, they operated separately from public transportation systems and were not (necessarily built to be) embedded in existing public transportation systems Table 1.

Table 1 List of included studies.

Author (s) /year	Country	Type of free transportation service	Methodology			Health impacts				Equity
			Qual	*Quant*	*Mixed*	Healthcare Access	*Social isolation,* engagement and participation	Mental health	Physical activity/ obesity	
Jackson et al. (2019)	United Kingdom	Concessionary bus pass (CBP)		x			x	x	x	x
Reinhard et al. (2018)	United Kingdom	Free bus passes		x				x		
Green et al. (2014)	United Kingdom	Free bus travel			x				x	x
Green et al. (2014)	United Kingdom	Free transportation			x	x				x
Jones et al. (2012)	United Kingdom	Concessionary fares for public transport	x					x	x	x
Reinhard et al. (2019)	United Kingdom	Free bus pass		x			x	x	x	
Izumi et al. (2023)	United States	Free rideshare-based transportation services			x	x				x

Franklin (2018)	Ethiopia	Transport subsidies		x				x		x
Alhassan et al. (2025)	Canada	Free bus service			x	x	x	x		x
Whitley et al. (2020)	United Kingdom	Statutory concessionary travel scheme			x	x				x
Goodman et al. (2014)	United Kingdom	Free bus travel	x						x	x
Rambaldini-Gooding et al. (2023)	Australia	Free bus service	x				x	x	x	x
Pesola et al. (2022)	Finland	Free public transit		x					x	x
Patel et al. (2021)	United States	Free transportation		x				x		x
	Canada	Free bus transit,			x		x	x	x	x

(continued)

Table 1 List of included studies. (*cont'd*)

Author (s) /year	Country	Type of free transportation service	Methodology			Health impacts				Equity
			Qual	Quant	Mixed	Healthcare Access	Social isolation, engagement and participation	Mental health	Physical activity/ obesity	
Mah and Mitra (2017)										
Holland et al. (2024)	Canada	Transit pass			x	x				x
Webb et al. (2012)	United Kingdom	Free bus transportation		x					x	x
Brough et al. (2022)	United States	Subsidy		x		x				x
Coronini-Cronberg et al. (2012)	United Kingdom	Free bus travel		x			x	x	x	x
Patterson et al. (2018)	United Kingdom	Free bus travel		x			x		x	x
Webb et al. (2016)	United Kingdom	Bus pass		x					x	x

Gabaldón-Estevan et al. (2019)	Estonia	Fare-free transportation			x		x		x
Stepaniuk et al. (2008)	Canada	Free bus pass and Group transit training		x		x	x		
Shin (2021)	South Korea	Transit subsidies		x				x	x
Gase et al. (2014)	United States	Free bus and rail transit passes			x		x	x	x
Edwards et al. (2013)	United Kingdom	Free bus travel		x			x		x
Jones et al. (2013)	United Kingdom	Free bus travel	x			x		x	x

3.2 Health impacts of fare-free transportation initiatives

3.2.1 Impacts on healthcare access

One of the main impacts of fare-free transportation initiatives relates to their impact on access to healthcare and other services necessary for maintaining health. Interestingly not many included studies specifically described fare-free transportation initiatives as improving health via the healthcare access pathway. For the few that did, they highlighted the role of fare-free transportation in supporting access to medical treatment and the ability to pick up prescriptions on time. According to Izumi et al. (2023), the use of a fare-free transportation initiative to improve healthcare access and food security was highly effective because it supported patients to seamlessly pick up prescriptions. This was often coordinated with food produce pick up as well. A Canadian study by Alhassan et al. (2025) similarly showed that a fare-free transportation initiative operating between two communities (2.5 h apart) promoted access to healthcare services. In this study an estimated 22 % of trips by the fare-free bus was for medical appointments and participants indicated that the fare-free bus allowed them to consistently attend recurrent medical appointments. An English study also revealed that concessionary bus passes improved access to services including medical services for older adults and that these improvements began to be reversed when age requirements for eligibility began to be more restrictive (Whitley et al., 2020). Finally, in a USA based study, Brough et al. (2022) showed that the provision of free transit passes improved access to services including health. Combining access to healthcare with other essential trips under "essential travel", they found that people were more likely to use fare-free travel for essential trips including healthcare when compared to controls. Although access to healthcare services was reported in studies it was often subsumed under other travel categories or combined with access to other services.

3.2.2 Impacts on social isolation, social engagement and participation

Many of the included studies explored the role of fare-free transportation initiatives in promoting social engagement and participation often with a special focus on older adults. Most of these studies revealed that access to fare-free transportation significantly increases the number of trips taken by older adults to participate in social activities, allowing them to feel engaged while doing so (Jackson et al., 2019; Mah and Mitra, 2017; Rambaldini-Gooding et al., 2023; Reinhard et al., 2019). Using social isolation as part of a mediation analysis, Jackson et al. (2019) have shown that the use of concessionary bus passes among older adults in England improved social participation and engagement. By measuring social isolation on an index that quantifies frequency of visits with friends, living status and membership to social organizations, Jackson et al. (2019) showed that reduced social isolation is one of the primary mechanisms by which ownership of concessionary bus passes improved quality of life. A Canadian study also showed that the use of fare-free bus passes increased the number of trips undertaken by older adults thus suggesting better social engagement and opportunities to participate in activities (Stepaniuk et al., 2008). For many older adults, the benefits of fare-free transportation move beyond the simple instrumental ability to travel elsewhere to participate in social activities and extends to their sense of self and belonging. In a qualitative study by Jones et al. (2013), research participants indicated that the very idea of being entitled to a concessionary bus pass did not only make them feel socially worthy but equipped them to exercise their mobility rights. These feelings combat feelings of isolation given that access to the bus became a broader metaphor and practical experience of participants' 'right to the city'. In other contexts such as Canada, Alhassan et al. (2025) have shown that older adults using fare-free transportation are better able to participate socially because they consider transportation to be a safety issue due to harsh winters. Many older adults would rather miss out on social activities than risk their physical and psychological safety while winter-driving. Given increasing morbidity with age, the ability to continue to travel due to fare-free transportation for older adults improves participation but also enhances greater mobility. There is evidence of a dose response effect such that the withdrawal of concessionary fare systems or the tightening of eligibility criteria is associated with reversal in social engagement and participation gains. The evidence on the ability of fare-free transportation systems to reduce social isolation and improve social engagement and participation is significant but not unanimous. In a South Korean study, Shin (2021) showed that while the total number of trips taken by older adults compared to younger people significantly increased due to transit fare exemptions, increases in travel by older adults for social activities and leisure were insignificant.

3.2.3 Impacts on mental health outcomes and wellbeing

Like studies measuring the impacts of fare-free transportation systems on social engagement, participation and isolation, several other studies have focused on mental health outcomes such as depressive symptoms and indicators of overall wellbeing. Unlike the studies focused on social engagement that tended to be focused on older adults, the studies on mental health outcomes often focused on the overall population, older adults, youth or a combination (Gabaldón-Estevan et al., 2019; Gase et al., 2014; Jones et al., 2012). Most of the existing literature has revealed that access to fare-free transportation reduces stress and promotes mental health. In a quantitative study of 17,953 older adults in England, Reinhard et al. (2019) revealed that changes in travel behavior (increased transportation use) among older adults due to fare-free transportation was associated with increased total cognitive function and memory. In a prior study, Reinhard et al. (2018) showed that the availability of fare-free transportation was associated with an 8 % increase in travel for older adults and that this change in travel behaviour reduced depressive symptoms (by 0.952 points on the Center for Epidemiologic Studies Depression Scale). In this study it was found that while among older adults who used the fare-free bus pass 22.6 % reported being depressed, this number rose to 27.3 % among older adults who did not use the fare-free bus passes. Jackson et al. (2019) have shown similarly that ownership of concessionary bus passes in the English context was associated with lower odds of depressive symptoms, a better quality of life and higher reported life satisfaction. Studies focused on youth also reveal that fare-free transportation has mental health benefits because of increased sociability, expanded freedoms and a sense of easing some of the stresses associated with transitioning from childhood to adulthood. Goodman et al. (2014) have described how young adults in London report improved wellbeing because of their newly gained freedom provided by fare-free transportation. This allows them to travel without having to rely on parents.

3.2.4 Impacts on physical activity and active travel

Arguably the most common health impact of fare-free transportation initiatives reported in the literature has been the impact on physical activity levels, active travel and in some cases obesity rates. Several studies have highlighted that the provision of fare-free transportation significantly influences active travel patterns both for children and youth (Edwards et al., 2013; Pesola et al., 2022) as well as older adults (Coronini-Cronberg et al., 2012; Webb et al., 2016). In some studies these changes in active travel and physical activity levels translate to reductions in obesity (Webb et al., 2012; Webb et al., 2016). According to Webb et al. (2016) who drew on a sample of 4650 fare-free bus pass eligible people (those aged 62 and above) in England, fare-free transportation plays a critical role in public transportation use and active travel. In this sample, the authors showed that fare-free bus pass holders were ten times more likely to use public transportation which is one of the main methods of active travel. Additionally, those who utilized fare-free bus passes were 40 % more likely to be physically active than those who did not use a free bus pass. Their analyses of interrelated outcomes also showed that female fare-free bus pass holders had lower Body Mass Indices (BMI) and smaller waist circumferences than counterparts who did not have free bus passes (Webb et al., 2016).

In some studies, however, the relationship between access to fare-free transportation and active travel and related outcomes was more complex. In a comparison of the effect of a fare-free bus on active travel among children in two Finnish towns (one with fare-free travel and one without), Pesola et al. (2022) showed that the children in the town with fare-free bus travel achieved more active travel via walking to use the buses. Contrastingly, the children in the town without fare-free travel gained more active travel from cycling. There was no statistically significant difference in total amount of time spent on active travel for children with access to fare-free transportation compared to children without access. In an English study by Edwards et al. (2013), it was found that the introduction of a fare-free transportation intervention had mixed effects on active travel patterns, and these varied when comparing youth with adults. Overall, youth made more average trips per day by bus and travelled longer distances however there was an increase in the number of bus rides for short distances (travel for 1 KM or less). These travel patterns by youth were similar for adults although adults did not frequently use the fare-free bus for short distance travel. Additionally, while youth saw a reduction in cycling and walking rates as measured by average trips per day, there was an increase in cycling and walking rates for adults as measured by average trips per day. The distanced walked remained the same before and after the introduction of the fare-free transportation system for both youth and adults. The total distance cycled rose substantially for adults after the introduction of fare-free transportation even though it fell for youth (Edwards et al., 2013). In their study of the impacts of fare-free transportation on active travel for older adults, Coronini-Cronberg et al. (2012) found that fare-free bus pass ownership was consistently associated with use of active travel measured as walking 3 or more times per week. Finally, Shin (2021) similarly found that fare-free transportation improves active travel (measured in terms of active travel time) for older adults although this increase tends to be higher among older adults from high income households.

3.3 Health equity dimensions of fare-free transportation initiatives

Although the included studies were not consistently framed to explore health equity dimensions of fare-free transportation initiatives, they included data and methods that allowed for descriptions of how health impacts of fare-free transportation initiatives might vary by socioeconomic position. Age was one of the most common variables used by authors to reveal differential health impacts of fare-fare-free transportation initiatives although other variables such as gender, race/ethnicity and income status were featured in several studies.

3.3.1 Age related health equity impacts of fare-free transportation initiatives

Several of the included studies directly or indirectly compared how fare-free transportation initiatives differently impact health outcomes across age groups. Although a number of studies either focused specifically on youth (Gase et al., 2014; Franklin, 2018; Patel et al., 2021) or older adults (Reinhard et al., 2018; Jackson et al., 2019; Whitley et al., 2020) some set out to compare outcomes across age categories (Edwards et al., 2013; Jones et al., 2013). Included studies often revealed that older adults were more likely to be eligible for fare-free transportation under existing initiatives and were often those most likely to benefit from health improvements. According to Whitley et al. (2020) older adults (aged 65–74) who were consistently eligible for fare-free bus passes were more likely to use fare-free transportation than 50–59 year olds who were consistently ineligible. Additionally, beyond differential patterns of usage tied directly to age-related eligibility criteria, particular benefits and disbenefits of fare-free transportation initiatives can vary significantly across age. In their analysis of the impacts of fare-free transportation targeted at youth (12–17 years) in London, Edwards et al. (2013) showed that the initiative was beneficial for youth who had a higher average number of trips per day and covered longer distances than adults (25–59 years) who were not eligible for fare-free transportation. Nevertheless, there was a higher number of short trips (trips 1KM or less) by youth likely signalling reduced physical activity. Another common age-related differential impact of fare-free transportation initiatives relates to trip purpose. In a Canadian study of a non-age restricted fare-free transportation initiative, it was found that while adults and children were more likely to use a fare-free bus for visits, older adults were consistently more likely to use the fare-free bus to attend medical appointments (Alhassan et al., 2025). The most obvious age-related differential impact of fare-free transportation initiatives is that beneficiary ages often enjoy the health benefits associated with public transportation. However, it is possible to see a decline in physical activity among younger populations related to increased use of fare-free transportation for very short trips.

3.3.2 Gender related health equity impacts of fare-free transportation initiatives

Fare-free transportation initiatives also often have differential impacts by gender. In several of the included studies, females were often more likely to use fare-free transportation services and health impacts sometimes disproportionately benefitted them. Although many studies did not reveal the total proportion of fare-free transportation initiative beneficiaries who were female, respondents to surveys were often female. For example, Mah and Mitra (2017) indicated that 77 % of the respondents to a survey on impacts of a fare-free transportation initiative in Oakville, Canada were female. Similarly, data from Webb et al. (2016) based on an English sample revealed that fare-free bus pass holders were often more likely to be female (1.67 odds ratio). In a study from a rural community in Canada, Alhassan et al. (2025) also indicated that out of a total of 1185 bus rides as part of a fare-free transportation program, 53 % of the trips were made by females. These data indicate that females appear to be more likely to benefit from fare-free transportation initiatives. Given higher usage by females, the positive health impacts of fare-free transportation initiatives also appear to benefit females more. Apart from Reinhard et al. (2018) whose gender stratified analysis did not find major differences in the health benefits of fare-free transportation initiatives, some studies showed that fare-free transportation initiatives have greater health benefits for females. For example, according to Webb et al. (2016) positive physical health outcomes such as reduced body mass index, improved gait and reduced waist circumference were more pronounced in female bus pass holders compared to their peers who did not have fare-free bus passes although these differences were not found when comparing male fare-free bus pass holders with males without bus passes. Finally, Alhassan et al. (2025) also showed that among beneficiaries of a fare-free bus service, females were more likely to use the bus to travel for visits and medical appointments while males were more likely to use the fare-free bus to travel for work. These differences also help explain why females may be more likely to receive the positive health benefits of fare-free transportation initiatives.

3.3.3 Racial/ethnicity related health equity impacts of fare-free transportation initiatives

Although several included studies routinely reported on sociodemographic characteristics of survey and interview respondents and often described the racial/ethnic makeup of respondents, very few studies specifically explored racial/ethnic differences in impacts of fare-free transportation initiatives. Racialized groups such as Black populations appear to be more likely than White majorities and other racialized groups to utilize fare-free transportation initiatives. According to Patterson et al. (2018), Black people eligible for fare-free bus passes were more likely (84 %) than White (74 %) and South Asian (75 %) counterparts to hold passes. A USA based study similarly found that Black people were more likely to use fare-free transportation as part of an experimental initiative and that Hispanics had lower utilization rates (Brough et al., 2022). Much less research evidence has been dedicated to explore how these differential patterns of usage translate to health outcomes. Edwards et al. (2013) showed that although more Black people utilized a fare-free transportation initiative in London, they were also at the highest risk of assault on public transportation (Odds Ratio = 1.53). Finally, use of fare-free transportation by ethnic minorities has important health implications. Use of fare-free bus passes serves as a key source of physical activity for ethnic minorities and Patterson et al. (2018) estimate that whereas white populations accumulated 29 % of their active travel through use of a fare-free bus service, this number was 44 % for South Asians and 56 % for Black people.

3.3.4 Income related health equity impacts of fare-free transportation initiatives

Finally, fare-free transportation initiatives tend to have the highest effect on people on low incomes. In a Canadian study, Mah and Mitra (2017) estimated that people on low incomes were 5.34 times likely to be negatively impacted by the cessation of the fare-free transportation initiative than others. People on low incomes are more likely to utilize fare-free transportation initiatives and one of the primary mechanisms of improved health is via increased access to resources and increase in disposable income (Alhassan et al., 2025; Brough et al., 2022; Holland et al., 2024). Although most studies showed improved outcomes for low income populations due to fare-free transportation initiatives, Shin (2021) showed that specific benefits of fare-free transportation initiatives such as improved physical activity tend to benefit people on high incomes more than those on low incomes.

4. Discussion

Fare-free transportation initiatives have existed in different shapes around the world over the last half century and a recent estimate indicates that these initiatives exist in over 100 locations worldwide (Kębłowski, 2020). Although these initiatives often have a clear political meaning, seeking to open up the commons and ensure fair access to resources and opportunities for all, in the context of Henri Lefebvre's 'right to the city', they also have practical implications for health and equity (Dellheim, 2018). This review set out to describe the academic literature on health impacts of fare-free transportation initiatives and to highlight the implications and impacts of these initiatives on health equity.

We acknowledge some limitations of the review. First, although the review was comprehensive it focused on peer-review sources and therefore did not identify initiatives that exist but have not been written about in the peer review literature such as the fare-free bus travel for 5–21-year-olds across Scotland (Transport Scotland, 2022) or the City of Miami's fare-free bus transportation program (City of Miami, 2025). We also acknowledge that most of the included studies were from Western countries and may not represent experiences in other parts of the world.

Fare-free transportation initiatives encompass a plethora of interventions ranging from those targeted at specific key populations such as youth and/or older adults to those implemented more broadly (Gabaldón-Estevan et al., 2019); indeed a third of all included studies here were focused on youth and older adults in the United Kingdom (Coronini-Cronberg et al., 2012; Patterson et al., 2018; Reinhard et al., 2019; Whitley et al., 2020). While this body of research is important, context matters and the insights from these studies are not always applicable elsewhere. More research is needed to confirm/deny the health and equity impacts described here. Despite the context specific nature of many of the included studies, much of the research evidence shows that health impacts of fare-free transportation initiatives typically follow anticipated pathways connecting public transportation and health such as through changes in physical activity levels, social interactions and access to resources (Glazener et al., 2021). Nonetheless, some of the existing literature reveals that some characteristics that are intrinsic to fare-free transportation initiatives such as *the idea of being entitled to transportation* conferred by fare-free transportation initiatives can promote health on its own (Jones et al., 2013). Most of the included studies utilized quantitative methodologies allowing for measuring the direction and effect sizes of fare-free transportation initiatives however, qualitative methods might allow for further exploring the mechanisms by which fare-free transportation initiatives influence health.

Fare-free transportation initiatives are sometimes critiqued and seen as unsustainable yet not many of the included studies necessarily utilized cost-benefit analyses to provide monetary valuations of the salutogenic impacts of these initiatives. While studies such as the one by Franklin (2018) show the economic implications and social return on investment of fare-free transportation initiatives by directly connecting fare-free transportation to employment outcomes, much more evidence might be useful for policy makers to better understand the economic benefits of fare-free transportation initiatives. Improvements in the mental health and social participation of older adults as well as reductions in obesity and other noncommunicable diseases attributable to public transportation justify further investments in public transportation (Alhassan and Anciaes, 2025). Given the wealth of evidence connecting fare-free transportation initiatives to improved physical and mental health (Coronini-Cronberg et al., 2012; Webb et al., 2016), social return on investment analyses on the value of health improvements related to public transportation investments would further support policy action on fare-free transportation.

Moreover, fare-free transportation initiatives promote equity and health equity by increasing the travel options of many who would otherwise not be able to travel. Much of the existing evidence has revealed equity implications of fare-free transportation drawing on different axes of social location such as age, income, race/ethnicity and gender (Patterson et al., 2018; Reinhard et al., 2018; Whitley et al., 2020). These studies show greater participation in social life by young and older adults due to fare-free transportation initiatives but would be further strengthened by exploring other axes of social location such as disability status and the specific impacts of these initiatives on sexual minorities. Such analysis would help better calibrate fare-free transportation initiatives to be responsive to the needs of those who are often not well served by existing transportation systems.

Finally, more evidence is needed to better understand the sustainability of fare-free transportation initiatives and the extent to which the health benefits described are maintained over time. In some of the included studies (Alhassan et al., 2025), the fare-free transportation initiatives existed only over a defined period or had ceased. Further research evidence on the contexts and mechanisms that ensure sustainability of these initiatives would be useful. Similarly, many studies did not explore long term impacts of fare-free transportation initiatives. Many of the studies included here were structured as pre-post analyses, revealing how specific health outcomes improved after the creation of the fare-free transportation initiatives under study. Except for studies such as the one by Pesola et al. (2022) that included both an intervention city and a non-intervention city, most studies utilized pre-post analyses that did not allow for a clear sense of if and how long the described benefits lasted. More evidence is therefore needed to answer not simply the question of whether fare-free transportation initiatives might be beneficial for health but whether these impacts last even after the initiatives cease and for how long.

Fare-free transportation initiatives are a valuable tool for increasing disposable income for low-income populations and ensuring inclusion for routinely excluded populations. They promote physical health, social interaction and mental health via traditional pathways by which use of public transportation is salutogenic. Nonetheless these initiatives may improve health intrinsically, and research focused on showing the economic value of these health improvements might appeal to policy makers interested in pursuing fare-free transportation initiatives.

References

Ahmed, S.K., et al., 2023. Road traffic accidental injuries and deaths: a neglected global health issue. Health Sci. Rep. 6 (5), 1–6. https://doi.org/10.1002/hsr2.1240.

Alhassan, J.A.K., Anciaes, P., 2025. Public transport investments as generators of economic and social activity. J. Transp. Health 41 (May 2024), 101989. https://doi.org/10.1016/j.jth.2025.101989. Elsevier Ltd.

Alhassan, J.A.K., et al., 2021. "It feels like somebody cut my legs off": austerity, transportation and the "web of dispossession" in Saskatchewan, Canada. Soc. Sci. Med. 282, 114147. https://doi.org/10.1016/j.socscimed.2021.114147.

Alhassan, J.A.K., et al., 2023. Producing vulnerability: a qualitative analysis of health equity impacts of budget cuts to intercity public transportation - evidence from saskatchewan, Canada. J. Transp. Health 33, 101715. https://doi.org/10.1016/j.jth.2023.101715. Elsevier Ltd.

Alhassan, J.A.K., Fuller, D., Woytowich, R., 2025. The promises and perils of a free rural inter - city transportation scheme: a mixed - methods study from Northern Saskatchewan. Can. J. Public Health. https://doi.org/10.17269/s41997-024-00986-3. Springer International Publishing, (0123456789).

Alhassan, J.A.K., Smith, C., Hanson, L., 2021. Politics, transportation, and the people's health: a socio-political autopsy of the demise of a 70-year-old bus company. Crit. Public Health 32 (4), 1–12. https://doi.org/10.1080/09581596.2021.1905152. Taylor & Francis.

Anciães, P.R., 2013. 'Rethinking the Death of Railways in the Portuguese Countryside', 1st EURUFU (European Rural Futures) Conference - Transport and Mobility in Rural Areas, pp. 45–57.

Arksey, H., O 'malley, L., 2005. Scoping studies: towards a methodological framework. Int. J. Soc. Res. Methodol. 8 (1), 19–32. https://doi.org/10.1080/1364557032000119616.

Bezyak, J.L., et al., 2020. Community participation and public transportation barriers experienced by people with disabilities. Disabil. Rehabil. 42 (23), 3275–3283. https://doi.org/10.1080/09638288.2019.1590469. Taylor & Francis.

Blumenberg, E., Ong, P., 2001. Cars, buses and jobs: welfare participants and employment access in Los Angeles. Transp. Res. Rec. 1756 (1), 22–31.

Brough, R., Freedman, M., Phillips, D.C., 2022. Experimental evidence on the effects of means-tested public transportation subsidies on travel behavior. Reg. Sci. Urban Econ. 96 (May), 103803. https://doi.org/10.1016/j.regsciurbeco.2022.103803. (The Authors).

Brown, A.L., van Kamp, I., 2017. WHO environmental noise guidelines for the European region: a systematic review of transport noise interventions and their impacts on health. Int. J. Environ. Res. Public Health 14 (8), 1–44. https://doi.org/10.3390/ijerph14080873.

City of Miami, 2025 Request on-demand transportation, transportation & roadways. Available at: https://www.miami.gov/Transportation-Roadways/Request-On-Demand-Transportation (Accessed: 7 July 2025).

Corcoran, K., McNab, J., Girgis, S., 2012. Is transport a barrier to healthcare for older people with chronic diseases? Asia Pac. J. Health Manag. 7 (1), 49–56.

Coronini-Cronberg, S., et al., 2012. The impact of a free older persons' bus pass on active travel and regular walking in England. Am. J. Public Health 102 (11), 2141–2148. https://doi.org/10.2105/AJPH.2012.300946.

Dellheim, J., 2018. The political economy of transport. In: Dellheim, J., Prince, J. (Eds.), Free Public Transit and Why We Don't Pay to Ride Elevators. Black Rose Books, Montreal, pp. 17–27.

Dobbs, L., 2007. Stuck in the slow lane: reconceptualizing the links between gender, transport and employment. Gend, Work Organ. 14 (2), 85–108.

Edwards, P., et al., 2013. Health impacts of free bus travel for young people: evaluation of a natural experiment in London. J. Epidemiol. Commun. Health 67 (8), 641–647. https://doi.org/10.1136/jech-2012-202156.

Franklin, S., 2018. Location, search costs and youth unemployment: experimental evidence from transport subsidies. Econ. J. 128 (614), 2353–2379. https://doi.org/10.1111/ecoj.12509.

Gabaldón-Estevan, D., et al., 2019. Broader impacts of the fare-free public transportation system in Tallinn. Int. J. Urban Sustain. Dev. 11 (3), 332–345. https://doi.org/10.1080/19463138.2019.1596114. Taylor & Francis.

Gase, L.N., et al., 2014. Estimating the costs and benefits of providing free public transit passes to students in Los Angeles County: Lessons learned in applying a health lens to decision-making. Int. J. Environ. Res. Public Health 11 (11), 11384–11397. https://doi.org/10.3390/ijerph111111384.

Glazener, A., et al., 2021. Fourteen pathways between urban transportation and health: a conceptual model and literature review. J. Transp. Health 21 (April), 101070. https://doi.org/10.1016/j.jth.2021.101070. Elsevier Ltd.

Godlee, F., 1992. Transport: a public health issue. Br. Med. J. 304 (January), 48–50.

Goodman, A., et al., 2014. "We Can All Just Get on a Bus and Go": rethinking independent mobility in the context of the universal provision of free bus travel to young londoners. Mobilities 9 (2), 275–293. https://doi.org/10.1080/17450101.2013.782848.

Goodman, A., et al., 2018. "We've been researched to death": exploring the research experiences of urban indigenous peoples in Vancouver, Canada. Int. Indig Policy J. 9 (2). https://doi.org/10.18584/iipj.2018.9.2.3.

Green, J., et al., 2014. On the buses: a mixed-method evaluation of the impact of free bus travel for young people on the public health. Public Health Res. 2 (1), 1–206. https://doi.org/10.3310/phr02010.

Hanson, C., et al., 2021. Here today, gone tomorrow: public transportation and vulnerabilities in rural and remote Canada. https://www.criaw-icref.ca/wp-content/uploads/2022/02/Here-Today-Gone-Tomorrow-Final-Report.pdf.

Holland, M.R., et al., 2024. Moving on income as a social determinant of health: free transit for social assistance recipients in Kingston, Ontario. Can. J. Public Health 115. Springer International Publishing, pp. 111–116. https://doi.org/10.17269/s41997-023-00816-y.

Izumi, B.T., et al., 2023. Feasibility of using rideshare transportation to reduce barriers to participating in a clinic-based food insecurity intervention. Prog. Community Health Partnersh: Res. Educ. Action 17 (2), 287–294. https://doi.org/10.1353/cpr.2023.a900209.

Jackson, S.E., et al., 2019. Social isolation and physical activity mediate associations between free bus travel and wellbeing among older adults in England. J. Transp. Health 13 (January), 274–284. https://doi.org/10.1016/j.jth.2019.03.006. Elsevier Ltd.

Johnston, K., et al., 2015. Increasing access to sexual health care for rural and regional young people: similarities and differences in the views of young people and service providers. Aust. J. Rural Health 23 (5), 257–264. https://doi.org/10.1111/ajr.12186.

Jones, A., et al., 2012. Rethinking passive transport: bus fare exemptions and young people's wellbeing. Health Place 18 (3), 605–612. https://doi.org/10.1016/j.healthplace.2012.01.003. Elsevier.

Jones, A., et al., 2013. Entitlement to concessionary public transport and wellbeing: a qualitative study of young people and older citizens in London, UK. Soc. Sci. Med. 91, 202–209. https://doi.org/10.1016/j.socscimed.2012.11.040. Elsevier Ltd.

Jones, S., et al., 2016. Public transport and health outcomes in rural sub-Saharan Africa – A synthesis of professional opinion. J. Transp. Health 3, 211–219. https://doi.org/10.1016/j.jth.2015.12.005.

Kębłowski, W., 2020. Why (not) abolish fares? Exploring the global geography of fare free public transport. Transportation 47 (6), 2807–2835. https://doi.org/10.1007/s11116-019-09986-6. Springer US.

Kennedy, L.G., 2004. Transportation and environmental justice. In: Lucas, K. (Ed.), Running on Empty: Transport, Social Exclusion and Environmental Justice. The Policy Press, Bristol, pp. 155–179. https://doi.org/10.4324/9781315678986-32.

Kirschen, M., et al., 2023. Fare-Free Transit Evaluation Framework, Fare-Free Transit Evaluation Framework. The National Academies Press, Washington, DC doi: 10.17226/26732.

Langlois, M., et al., 2016. Can transit-oriented developments help achieve the recommended weekly level of physical activity? J. Transp. Health 3 (2016), 181–190. https://doi.org/10.1016/j.jth.2016.02.006.

Linovski, O., Dorries, H., Simpson, S.-A., 2021. Public Transit and Equity-Deserving Groups: Understanding Lived Experiences. Winnepeg.

Lucas, K., 2004. Transport and social exclusion. In: Lucas, K. (Ed.), Running on Empty: Transport, Social Exclusion and Environmental Justice. The Policy Press, Bristol, pp. 39–53.

Mah, S., Mitra, R., 2017. The effects of a free bus program on older adults travel behaviour: a case study of a Canadian suburban municipality. Case Stud. Transp. Policy 5 (3), 460–466. https://doi.org/10.1016/j.cstp.2017.05.003. Elsevier.

McCarthy, M., 2006. Transport and health. In: Marmot, M., Wilkinson, R. (Eds.), Social Determinants of Health, 2nd ed. Oxford University Press, Oxford, pp. 131–146.

Ouzzani, M., et al., 2016. Rayyan-a web and mobile app for systematic reviews. Syst. Rev. 5 (1), 1–10. https://doi.org/10.1186/s13643-016-0384-4. Systematic Reviews.

Patel, H.H., et al., 2021. The relationship between transportation vulnerability, school attendance, and free transportation to an afterschool program for youth. Transportation 48 (5), 2315–2333. https://doi.org/10.1007/s11116-020-10131-x. Springer US.

Patterson, R., et al., 2018. Ethnic group differences in impacts of free bus passes in England: a national study. J. Transp. Health 11 (January), 1–14. https://doi.org/10.1016/j.jth.2018.09.005. Elsevier Ltd.

Pesola, A.J., et al., 2022. The effects of free-fare public transportation on the total active travel in children: a cross-sectional comparison between two Finnish towns. J. Transp. Health 27 (May), 101506. https://doi.org/10.1016/j.jth.2022.101506. Elsevier Ltd.

Rajasooriar, D., Soma, T., 2022. Food access, mobility, and transportation: a survey and key informant interviews of users of non-profit food hubs in the City of Vancouver before and during the COVID-19 crisis. BMC Public Health 22 (1), 1–18. https://doi.org/10.1186/s12889-021-12434-9. BioMed Central.

Rambaldini-Gooding, D., et al., 2023. Free public transport and older people: an ethnographic study of an Australian bus service. Australas. J. Ageing 42 (2), 409–416. https://doi.org/10.1111/ajag.13158.

Reinhard, E., et al., 2018. Public transport policy, social engagement and mental health in older age: a quasi-experimental evaluation of free bus passes in England. J. Epidemiol. Commun. Health 72 (5), 361–368. https://doi.org/10.1136/jech-2017-210038.

Reinhard, E., et al., 2019. Public transportation use and cognitive function in older age: a quasiexperimental evaluation of the free bus pass policy in the United Kingdom. Am. J. Epidemiol. 188 (10), 1774–1783. https://doi.org/10.1093/aje/kwz149.

Ruud, S.F., 2023. Giving up control: devaluation of railway work in Luxembourg's fare-free public transportation system? Anthropol. Work Rev. 44 (2), 94–104. https://doi.org/10.1111/awr.12259.

Shin, E.J., 2021. Exploring the causal impact of transit fare exemptions on older adults' travel behavior: evidence from the Seoul metropolitan area. Transp. Res. Part A: Policy Practice 149 (May), 319–338. https://doi.org/10.1016/j.tra.2021.05.007. Elsevier Ltd.

Stepaniuk, J.A., et al., 2008. Impact of transit training and free bus pass on public transportation use by older drivers. Prev. Med. 47 (3), 335–337. https://doi.org/10.1016/j.ypmed.2008.03.002.

Taylor, Z., 2006. Railway closures to passenger traffic in Poland and their social consequences. J. Transp. Geogr. 14 (2), 135–151. https://doi.org/10.1016/j.jtrangeo.2005.05.003.

Transport Scotland, 2022. Young Persons' (Under 22s) Free Bus Travel. Press Release.

Webb, E., et al., 2016. Free bus travel and physical activity, gait speed, and adiposity in the english longitudinal study of ageing. Am. J. Public Health 106 (1), 136–142. https://doi.org/10.2105/AJPH.2015.302907.

Webb, E., Netuveli, G., Millett, C., 2012. Free bus passes, use of public transport and obesity among older people in England. J. Epidemiol. Commun. Health 66 (2), 176–180. https://doi.org/10.1136/jech.2011.133165.

Whitley, E., Craig, P., Popham, F., 2020. Impact of the statutory concessionary travel scheme on bus travel among older people: a natural experiment from England. Ageing Soc. 40 (11), 2480–2494. https://doi.org/10.1017/S0144686×19000692.

Yadav, A., et al., 2025. "'With the free bus, you didn't have to worry": mental wellbeing impacts of a free intercity transportation service in Canada'. J. Transp. Healthpp. 1–10. Available at: https://www.sciencedirect.com/science/article/pii/S2214140525002233.

CHAPTER SEVEN

Impact of low emission zone on both physical and mental health: A systematic review

Kübra Çevrim[a,*] and Şeref Oruç[b]

[a]Department of Civil Engineering, Faculty of Engineering and Architecture, Batman University, Batman, Turkey

[b]Department of Civil Engineering, Faculty of Engineering, Karadeniz Technical University, Trabzon, Turkey

*Corresponding author. e-mail address: kubra.cevrim@batman.edu.tr

Contents

Abstract

Air pollution significantly impacts human health and social welfare, particularly in urban areas due to vehicle emissions. To address this issue, various transportation planning strategies have been implemented, including Low Emission Zones (LEZs). This policy is rapidly spreading worldwide, especially in Europe and the United Kingdom. This study systematically reviews the effects of LEZs on human health. Research indicates that $PM_{2.5}$ from vehicle emissions, which human lungs cannot filter, is linked to numerous respiratory and cardiovascular diseases, such as ischemic heart disease leading to heart attacks; strokes; chronic and acute lower respiratory diseases; and low birth weight among newborns. The study compiles evidence showing that air pollution decreases after LEZ implementation, leading to a reduction in these

Advances in Transport Policy and Planning, Volume 18
ISSN 2543-0009, https://doi.org/10.1016/bs.atpp.2026.07.007

diseases. LEZs involve restrictions such as prohibiting vehicles with inadequate emission standards or diesel fuel from entering the area, or imposing charges if they do so. These zones affect not only residents within the LEZ but also those outside it. Diesel vehicle owners may feel socially excluded and experience related anxiety when unable to enter the zone. Additionally, these vehicle owners may heavily use surrounding areas to avoid charges, causing air quality outside the LEZ to deteriorate. This negatively impacts the health of those living outside the LEZ and can similarly cause anxiety. The review concludes that when creating traffic regulation policies, it is essential to consider the effects on the entire zone, not just specific areas. While the literature confirms that LEZ implementation improves air quality by reducing vehicle emissions, it also highlights potential negative impacts on the physical and mental health of those living outside the zone and vehicle owners.

1. Introduction

Air pollution is the biggest environmental threat to human health worldwide. Traffic-related pollutants, in particular particulate matter (PM) and nitrogen oxides (NO_x), are a significant risk to human health (WHO, 2021). To mitigate these risks, measures are being implemented in urban areas, one of which is the implementation of Low Emission Zones (LEZs). LEZ can generally be defined as the exclusion of motor vehicles that do not meet emission standards in certain areas. The primary goal is to reduce vehicular emissions. While LEZs have been effective in reducing exhaust emissions, it is known that they have no impact on non-exhaust emissions such as clutch, tire and brake or road surface abrasion (Ezeah et al., 2015). It also aims to protect the environment and human health by promoting physically active forms of transportation in the LEZ.

1.1 History of low emission zones in Europe

The first LEZ implementation in Europe took place in 1996 in the Swedish cities of Stockholm, Goteborg, and Malmö. The policy initially banned the oldest heavy-duty vehicles and required middle-aged heavy-duty vehicles to be equipped with certified emission control devices or new engines. In 2002, entry criteria for these zones were revised to include restrictions on NO_x emissions. By 2006, the Swedish government established a national LEZ program. Under this program, vehicles complying with Euro 2 and Euro 3 emission standards were allowed to operate within LEZs for eight years from their initial registration; vehicles meeting Euro 4 standards could be used until 2016, and those meeting Euro 5 standards until 2020. Outside Sweden, the first LEZ-like measure was implemented in the Mont-Blanc tunnel between France and Italy, where heavy-duty vehicles not meeting at least Euro 3 emission standards were banned from using the tunnel (Göteborgs Stad, 2006; Holman et al., 2015). Some of the implementations in Europe are as follows:

In Rome, a restricted area prohibiting the entry of all vehicles during certain hours was established in 2001. The foundation of the LEZ was laid in the following years, with bans on older diesel vehicles introduced in 2002 and vehicles without catalytic converters in 2003. Within these zones, emissions of PM_{10} and nitrogen dioxide (NO_2) were monitored, revealing reductions of approximately 33 % and 58 % in PM_{10} and NO_2 concentrations, respectively (Cesaroni et al., 2011; Pasquier and André, 2016).

In Germany, the first LEZ implementation began in 2008 in the cities of Berlin, Cologne, and Hanover. In Munich, an additional ban on the entry of heavy-duty vehicles was introduced in February 2008 alongside the LEZ. A comparison between the LEZs in Berlin and Munich showed a significant reduction in NO_2 concentrations in the Munich zone, attributed to the additional heavy vehicle restriction (Morfeld et al., 2014; Gu et al., 2022).

The first LEZ in Rotterdam was implemented in 2016, following the air quality regulation introduced in 2015. A study examining the impact of the zone on traffic revealed that the use of polluting vehicles decreased by approximately 50 %. However, LEZ policies also aim to enhance mobility and promote sustainability. The study found that the number of vehicles operating within the LEZ was only 2 % below the targeted level, indicating that the desired level of sustainability had not been fully achieved (Attia et al., 2023).

The first LEZ in Madrid was implemented in 2018. A study investigating its short-term impact on traffic reduction found that the LEZ led to a 4 % decrease in weekday traffic within the zone. However, despite the reduction inside the LEZ, traffic increased in surrounding border areas. This rise was attributed to vehicle movement between the LEZ and adjacent zones, indicating that the measures taken to discourage car use were insufficient (Moral-Carcedo, 2022).

1.2 Ultra low emission zone: Case of London

In the United Kingdom, the first LEZ was implemented in May 2007, covering central London and much of its surrounding area. In early 2008, the scope of the LEZ was expanded to include diesel heavy goods vehicles (HGVs), buses, and intercity coaches. The first phase targeted heavy vehicles over 12 tonnes and trucks that did not meet the Euro 3 emission standard, while the second phase, introduced in July 2008, covered light commercial vehicles weighing between 3.5 and 12 tonnes that complied with at least the Euro 3 standard. By 2012, owners of vehicles failing to meet minimum requirements were required to pay a daily charge of £100–£200, depending on the vehicle type. In 2013, the LEZ was extended to encompass the entirety of Greater London, including Heathrow Airport, all local roads, and motorways (Ellison et al., 2013; Zhai and Wolff, 2021). On April 8, 2019, the Ultra Low Emission Zone (ULEZ), featuring the world's strictest LEZ restrictions, was introduced in central London. While the LEZ targeted heavy and light commercial vehicles, the ULEZ applied to all vehicle types. Additionally, due to the implementation of congestion pricing within this zone, vehicles failing to meet emission standards were subject to significantly higher charges. Although the ULEZ was confined to the city center, it was expected to reduce vehicle emissions across Greater London due to the inflow of vehicles from surrounding areas. In terms of its overall impact, the ULEZ led to approximately a 3 % reduction in NO_2 and NO_x concentrations across London; however, no significant change was observed in O_3 and $PM_{2.5}$ levels. These findings suggest that the ULEZ alone is insufficient and that a broader set of policies at the city, regional, and interregional levels is required to effectively reduce air pollution (Ma et al., 2021).

2. Method

Since the first LEZ implementation was made in 1996, the literature review was limited to publications released from 1996 onwards. The keywords used in the search were: "Low Emission Zone" AND ["health" OR "health effect" OR "public health"]. Four different eletronic databases of academic literature were searched in January 2025: Google Scholar, Web of Science (WoS), PubMed, and Transport Research International Documentation (TRID). The study selection, screening, and data extraction processes were conducted using Covidence (project ID: 543426). The process is illustrated in the PRISMA flow chart in Fig. 1. Of the 24 studies included in the review, three were identified as review articles (Chamberlain et al., 2023; Andriolli and Silva, 2024; Broster and Terzano, 2025). Upon analysis, it was found that some of the studies surveyed within these reviews were also among those included in our systematic review.

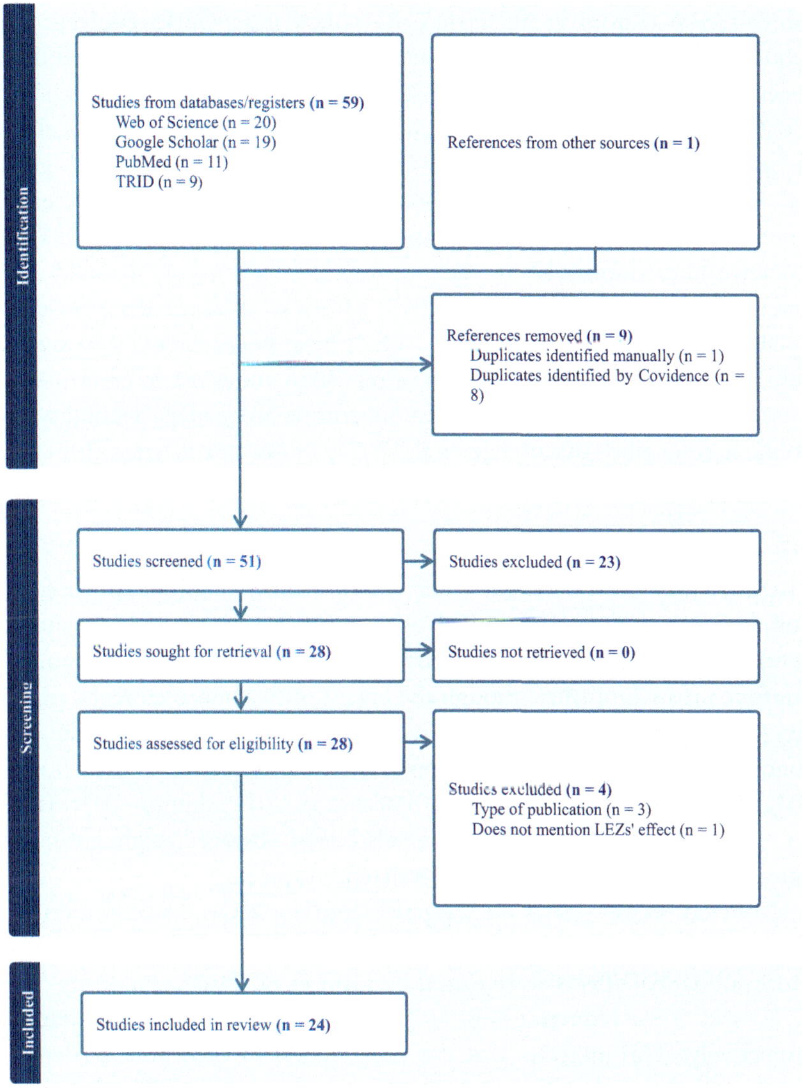

Fig. 1 PRISMA flow chart.

3. Results

3.1 Interventions

Low Emission Zone (LEZ) implementations are structured in alignment with the European Emission Standards framework. Initial interventions focused on banning older diesel vehicles or those without catalytic converters (Cesaroni et al., 2011). As policy frameworks evolved, subsequent interventions extended the restrictions to vehicles that did not meet the specified Euro emission standards (Malina and Scheffler, 2015; Gehrsitz, 2017; Vandenhole, 2025). In some implementations, vehicles were categorized using a color-coded labeling system (e.g., green, yellow, red) based on their Euro standard classification to facilitate enforcement and compliance monitoring (Poulhès and Proulhac, 2021). In stricter interventions, heavy-duty vehicles were entirely banned from entering the LEZ (Wood et al., 2015; Mudway et al., 2019; Xiao et al., 2024). In many metropolitan areas, LEZs have been deployed incrementally, wherein the spatial expansion of regulated zones are accompanied by a proportional relaxation of restriction criteria to manage feasibility and public acceptability (Knamiller et al., 2024; Pestel and Wozny, 2021).

3.2 Air pollution

The impact of Low Emission Zone (LEZ) implementations on air pollution has been extensively studied using both quantitative and qualitative assessments. Studies conducted across Europe indicate that LEZs generally improve urban air quality, though the extent of this improvement varies by city and pollutant (see Tables 1 and 2). Reported reductions in NO_2 concentrations range from approximately 5 % to 58 %, while reductions in PM_{10} concentrations vary between 3 % and 51 %. In addition, decreases in NO_x and $PM_{2.5}$ concentrations have also been observed, highlighting the potential of LEZs to reduce traffic-related emissions.

Mudway et al. (2019), a 7 $\mu g/m^3$ drop in NO_2 concentration was recorded, although no significant change was observed for PM_{10} and $PM_{2.5}$. More substantial effects were found by Host et al. (2020), reporting 51 %, 47 %, and 37 % reductions in NO_x, $PM_{2.5}$, and PM_{10} concentrations, respectively. This indicates that the effectiveness of LEZ policies depends largely on the scale of implementation and the stringency of vehicle restrictions.

In Germany, one study (Rohlf et al., 2020) reported a 6 % reduction in PM_{10}, another study (Pestel and Wozny, 2021) reported reductions of 5 % in NO_2 and 6 % in PM_{10}. In some German cities, including Berlin, Hanover, Cologne, and Munich, PM_{10} concentrations decreased by approximately 3 %, although no measurable improvement in NO_2 levels was observed (Margaryan, 2021).

Table 1 Summary of the physical health effects of LEZ.

Author, year and location	LEZ intervention	Air pollution outcomes	Health outcomes
(Cesaroni et al., 2011), Rome, Italy	Old diesel vehicles and vehicles without catalytic converters were forbidden	33 % and 58 % reduction in PM_{10} and NO_2 emissions from passenger cars	Average years of life gained (YLG) of 3.4 days per person
(Wood et al., 2015), London, UK	Heavy vehicles were forbidden	No reductions of practical importance in NO_2, PM_{10} and $PM_{2.5}$ concentration	No measurable improvement in respiratory/allergic symptoms in schoolchildren but only current symptoms of rhinitis (cold/allergic rhinitis) were significantly associated with air pollution levels
(Malina and Scheffler, 2015), Germany	Three different stages for diesel and gasoline vehicles	7.5 $\mu g/m^3$ reduction in PM_{10} concentration	Premature mortalities were decreased by ~840 at the mean, for a total of ~1219 incidents
(Gehrsitz, 2017), Germany	Different stages for all vehicles	6–8 % reduction in PM_{10} levels also reduction the number of days per year on which legal pollution limits are exceeded by three days	No substantial improvements in infant health outcomes, such as low-birth weight and stillbirths
(Mudway et al., 2019), London, UK	Heavy vehicles were forbidden	7 $\mu g/m^3$ reduction in NO_2 concentration but no reductions of practical importance in PM_{10} and $PM_{2.5}$ concentration	Forced vital capacity (FVC) values decreased in children, only a limited decrease in rhinitis symptoms was observed in terms of respiratory and allergic symptoms
(Griffin et al., 2020), West Yorkshire, UK	17 Different hypothetical strategies	Return the petrol-to-diesel fuel ratio to the year 2000 level within seven years	Significant improvements in quality adjusted life expectancy (QALE) across all population groups
(Host et al., 2020), Paris, France	Four different hypothetical scenarios for all vehicles	51 %, 47 % and 37 % reduction in NO_x, $PM_{2.5}$ and PM_{10} concentration	Prevented 340 deaths, 170 low-weight births, 130 ischemic heart disease cases, 2930 asthma cases/year

(continued)

Table 1 Summary of the physical health effects of LEZ. *(cont'd)*

Author, year and location	LEZ intervention	Air pollution outcomes	Health outcomes
(Rohlf et al., 2020), Germany	The most emission-intensive vehicles were banned from entering	6 % reduction in PM_{10} concentration	15.8 million EURO reduction in pharmaceutical spending for heart and respiratory diseases
(Pestel and Wozny, 2021), Germany	Three different stages	5 % and 6 % reduction in NO_2 and PM_{10} concentration	Reduced hospital diagnoses for ischemic heart disease and chronic respiratory conditions
(Margaryan, 2021), Germany	Three stages, with each stage excluding an additional emission class of vehicles	3 % reduction in PM_{10} concentration no reductions of practical importance in NO_2 concentration	2–3 % reduction in cardiovascular diseases, especially strong effects for 65 + age group and 7–13 % reduction in cerebrovascular diseases, including stroke
(Poulhès and Proulhac, 2021), Paris, France	Vehicles with a green sticker corresponding to electric or hydrogen vehicles are allowed to enter	13–43 % reduction in the number of residents exposed to $NO_2 > 40\ \mu g/m^3$	Health benefits were observed among the wealthiest and most mobile individuals (e.g., workers and students), while vulnerable groups such as the elderly, children, and the unemployed benefited the least
(Flanagan et al., 2022), Malmö, Sweden	Hypothetical scenario replacing Euro 5 or lower vehicles with Euro 6	13 % reduction in NO_2 concentration	Prevention of 9–26 deaths, 12 respiratory hospitalizations, 8 asthma cases, 9 hypertensive disorders of pregnancy per year
(Xiao et al., 2024), London, UK	Ultra-Low Emission Zone (ULEZ)	34 % reduction in non-compliant vehicle counts	Significant increase in active school travel; potential for long-term physical and mental health gains in children
(Nishitateno and Burke, 2024), Tokyo, Japan	Non-compliant diesel trucks and buses were banned	7 % reduction in PM_{10} concentration	0.2 % reduction in low-birthweight; estimated 1272 babies avoided low birthweight status

Table 2 Summary of the mental health effects of LEZ.

Author, year and location	LEZ intervention	Air pollution outcomes	Health equity and public acceptance outcomes
(Morton et al., 2021), Scotland	A hypothetical scenario in which diesel and petrol vehicles from specified vintages are banned	Not measured.	Public acceptance is most strongly determined by individuals' attitudes, which are positively influenced by feelings of pride and satisfaction, perceptions of fairness and policy effectiveness, and negatively influenced by discomfort, disappointment, and perceptions of high costs
(Verbeek and Hincks, 2022), London, UK and Brussels, Belgium	Non-compliant diesel and petrolium cars were banned in two cities	In Brussels, lower-income areas had higher exposure to NO_2. In London, higher-income areas often had more exposure to NO_2.	In Brussels, the LEZ appears to support environmental justice by including both highly polluted and low-income areas. In London, however, the LEZ provides less improvement in air quality, which is more evident in low-income areas.
(Jiménez-Espada et al., 2023), Cáceres, Spain	A hypothetical scenario	Not measured.	More than 50 % of citizens are open to walking, reducing the use of private cars and improving quality of life.
(Sarmiento et al., 2023), Germany	Vehicles not complying with predefined emission standards	4.1 $\mu g/m^3$ and 2.1 $\mu g/m^3$ reduction in NO_2 and PM_{10} concentrations	A short-term drop in life satisfaction especially for diesel car owners, working-age individuals, and those living near the zone, but this effect faded over time, and even those who commuted into the area experienced similar dissatisfaction without gaining health benefits.

(continued)

Table 2 Summary of the mental health effects of LEZ. (*cont'd*)

Author, year and location	LEZ intervation	Air pollution outcomes	Health equity and public acceptance outcomes
(Knamiller et al., 2024), Bradford, UK	Four types with different levels of restriction, which would charge vehicles that do not comply with Euro 4 (petrol cars) or Euro 6 (diesel cars) standards	Not measured.	Public health messages, especially those focused on children and supported by local health data helped increase public acceptance, while economic concerns, misinformation, and factors like the pandemic limited the perception and impact of the policy.
(Blandin et al., 2025), Grenoble, France	Two different scenarios with varying the ban time slot	Not measured.	Over 60 % of trips can be shifted to active or public transportation modes, but vulnerable and low-income groups face greater challenges in this transition; households unable to afford vehicle renewal are at increased economic and health risk.
(Vandenhole, 2025), Ghent, Belgium	Diesel vehicles below Euro 5 and petrol vehicles below Euro 2 standards are banned.	Not measured.	The air quality coalition saw LEZ as protecting vulnerable groups through cleaner air, while the anti-social coalition claimed LEZ harmed low-income people by limiting access; both used health to support their political views.

3.3 Health effects

3.3.1 Physical health

Air pollution is associated with many health conditions such as infant health, lung and respiratory diseases. Additionally, it affects important health metrics such as mortality rates and life expectancy. Vehicle emissions such as NO_2, $PM_{2.5}$ and PM_{10} pose particularly serious threats to public health. In order to prevent this, traffic policies are of great importance. In this respect, the impact of LEZ interventions on physical health was investigated. A summary of these studies is given in Table 1.

According to Cesaroni et al. (2011), in terms of life expectancy and mortality, the decline in NO_2 and PM_{10} levels led to substantial public health gains. An average increase of 3.4 days in life expectancy per person was estimated under the optimal scenario, amounting to 921 Years of Life Gained (YLG) per 100,000 individuals. In the area where all vehicles were restricted from Monday to Friday between 06:30–18:00 and on Saturdays between 14:30–18:00, a significantly higher gain of 19 days per person was recorded. However, these health benefits were predominantly concentrated in central urban areas with higher socioeconomic position (SEP); high SEP groups achieved 1387 YLG per 100,000 population, compared to only 340 YLG in low SEP groups. In contrast, no significant changes were detected in non-intervention areas, highlighting the potential risk of exacerbating existing socioeconomic inequalities.

Another study (Griffin et al., 2020), searching 17 hypothetical Low Emission Zone (LEZ) interventions aimed at reducing petrol-to-diesel fuel usage, identified Strategy 11 as the most effective and equitable option. Strategy 11 was to return the petrol-to-diesel fuel ratio to Year 2000 levels within 7 years. This strategy yielded 1278 Quality-Adjusted Life Years (QALYs) and 1391 Equally Distributed Equivalent QALYs (EDE QALYs). This strategy demonstrated the greatest reduction in health inequalities across all Index of Multiple Deprivation (IMD) groups and provided the highest contribution to social care benefits. In contrast, other strategies exhibited notable trade-offs between total health gains and equity. For instance, Strategy 6, which involved upgrading all private vans to Euro 4 within 2 years, was economically advantageous with a net production-consumption gain of £20 million but produced substantially fewer health benefits. Sensitivity analyses further supported the robustness of Strategy 11, indicating a 75% probability of it being the most effective and equitable intervention.

The reduction in air pollution also has significant impact on mortality. Under the strictest LEZ scenario in the Paris region, substantial decreases in pollutant levels were observed, particularly for NO_2 and $PM_{2.5}$, resulting in a 91 % reduction in the number of individuals exposed to NO_2 above the regulatory threshold. This prevented approximately 340 deaths annually and a gain of 114,300 (about 2028/100,000 year/person) life years (Host et al., 2020). The LEZ scenario in Malmö is estimated to result in a 13 % reduction in NO_2 concentrations, which could potentially prevent between 9 and 26 deaths (Flanagan et al., 2022).

LEZ interventions have been effective in preventing cardiovascular and respiratory diseases. Under the strictest LEZ scenario in the Paris region, a 2 % reduction in ischaemic heart disease (IHD) cases (130 cases) and a 3 % reduction in asthma cases in children (2930 cases) were estimated (Host et al., 2020). LEZ implementations in Germany have led to statistically significant reductions in hospital admissions due to ischaemic heart disease and chronic lower respiratory diseases, primarily within the designated intervention areas. The most pronounced effects were observed in cases presenting with acute symptoms and in hospitals located within LEZ boundaries, while no comparable benefits were identified in areas outside the LEZs (Pestel and Wozny, 2021).

According to another study conducted in Germany, LEZs led to improvements in air quality, particularly through an up to 3 % reduction in PM_{10} levels, which in turn resulted in significant health benefits, most notably among individuals aged 65 and older. These benefits included marked decreases in cardiovascular and especially cerebrovascular diseases, with reductions ranging from 7 % to 13 %. However, no reductions of practical importance were observed for chronic conditions such as respiratory diseases, diabetes, and dementia, a finding partially attributed to the structure of Germany's healthcare policies, including routine follow-up programs for chronic patients (Margaryan, 2021).

LEZ interventions have also shown effects in infant and children health. In Malmö, the average reduction in NO_2 concentration was 13 %, which corresponded to a 2 % decrease in childhood asthma cases, a 0.4 % decrease in hospital admissions for respiratory diseases and a 4.1 % decrease in hypertensive disorders during pregnancy (Flanagan et al., 2022).

During the first three years of the London's Low Emission Zone (LEZ), no reduction of practical importance was observed in the prevalence of respiratory and allergic diseases among children. This was attributed to the

LEZ's limited impact on air quality during that period. There were no notable changes in measured NO_x and NO_2 levels, while PM_{10} and $PM_{2.5}$ levels showed only modest reductions, and only at roadside monitoring stations. The main reason this reduction was not observed in the early phase of the LEZ implementation is that Euro 3 and 4 diesel engines failed to produce the predicted NO_x emissions under real-world driving conditions. A significant association was found solely between air pollution and current rhinitis symptoms, with no link identified for asthma, eczema, or other allergic conditions. These findings indicate that children's exposure levels remained unchanged over the three-year period. Additionally, symptoms were found to be more prevalent among boys, children with high body mass index (BMI), and certain ethnic groups (Wood et al., 2015). The London's LEZ led to a significant improvement in air quality, particularly with annual average reductions in NO_2 levels ranging from 1 to 1.35 $\mu g/m^3$. This improvement corresponded with a decline in the proportion of children living in highly polluted areas, decreasing from 99 % to 34 %. However, no clear reductions were observed in PM_{10} and $PM_{2.5}$ concentrations. In terms of lung function, reductions capable of being practically important were observed but did not achieve statistical signifance in forced vital capacity (FVC) measurements associated with both NO_2 and PM_{10} exposure, suggesting that long-term exposure to air pollution can exert chronic effects on children's lung development. Nonetheless, no reductions of practical importance were observed in respiratory symptoms such as asthma, cough, or wheeze. A slight decreasing trend was noted for rhinitis, though statistical significance was only reached when pilot year data were included. While ethnic differences appeared to influence lung function outcomes, socioeconomic status did not show a substantial effect (Mudway et al., 2019). London's Ultra Low Emission Zone (ULEZ) was found not only to reduce air pollution but also to induce positive health-related behavioral changes in children's transportation habits. A significant shift from passive transportation (e.g., private car use) to active transportation modes (e.g., walking, cycling) was observed, with 42 % of children transitioning to active commuting. This behavioral shift has the potential to enhance physical activity levels among children, thereby contributing to reductions in sedentary behavior and associated risks such as obesity, childhood diabetes, and asthma. Furthermore, such lifestyle changes may yield long-term benefits for children's lung development, cardiometabolic health, and psychological well-being. However, the study's reliance on a single-day transportation record and the absence of direct physical activity measurements limit the ability to draw definitive conclusions regarding health outcomes, necessitating cautious interpretation of the results (Xiao et al., 2024).

LEZ implementations in Germany resulted in significant reductions in daily average PM_{10} levels, particularly improving air quality in areas with high traffic density. However, the impact of these improvements on infant health has been limited; reductions capable of being practically important were observed but did not achieve statistical signifance in indicators such as birth weight, rates of low birth weight, or stillbirth (Gehrsitz, 2017).

The large-scale LEZ implemented in Japan in 2003 led to measurable improvements in air quality, particularly with up to a 7 % reduction in PM_{10} concentrations, yielding significant public health benefits. The rate of low birth weight (<2500 g) decreased by 0.2 %, while the incidence of very low birth weight (<1500 g) declined by 0.1 %; corresponding to approximately 1743 additional infants born at healthier weights. Moreover, the average birth weight increased by 6 g. These effects were more pronounced in prefectures with stricter emissions regulations, such as Tokyo and Saitama, whereas areas with more lenient standards, including Kanagawa and Chiba, experienced more limited improvements (Nishitateno and Burke, 2024).

3.3.2 Mental health effects and public opinion

One of the aims of LEZ implementations is to encourage residents in the area to increase their mobility by adopting active modes of transportation. However, when local residents do not embrace this policy, another problem emerges that poses a threat to public health. This problem is the psychological distress experienced by residents due to the LEZ implementation. As part of the restrictions, vehicles that do not meet the defined emission standards are banned from entering the zone. For residents who own such vehicles, this can lead to problems such as lack of parking or difficulties in accessing their homes or workplaces. Consequently, these circumstances may lead to anxiety among residents, and in the long term contribute to the development of mental health conditions such as depression and anxiety disorder. Studies examining the psychosocial public health impacts of LEZ interventions have particularly focused on the period after 2021. It is thought that the prominence given to societal responses during the COVID-19 pandemic has contributed to this focus. Although these studies do not extensively address the impact of LEZs on air pollution, they do assess public responses to LEZ policies and the expected improvement in air quality. A summary of these studies is given in Table 2.

The success of LEZ intervantions in terms of public health outcomes depends not only on their technical effectiveness but also directly on public attitudes, emotional responses, perceptions, and trust in government. The most influential factor in the public acceptance of LEZ implementations is individuals' attitudes toward the policy. These attitudes are strengthened by positive emotions, a sense of fairness, and belief in the policy's effectiveness, while perceptions of high cost and negative emotions weaken them. Trust in government has a significant indirect effect on these mediating factors and plays a crucial role in determining public acceptance. While personal norms have a strong influence, the impact of social norms appears to be more limited. Individuals with higher awareness tend to evaluate LEZs more positively; women and younger people are more supportive of the policy, whereas retirees and multi-vehicle owners are more likely to oppose it. Targeted communication strategies aimed at these specific groups could enhance public support (Morton et al., 2021). LEZ implementations should be evaluated also in terms of social justice and transportation equity. In Brussels, a strong negative correlation was found between income levels and NO_2 exposure, revealing that lower-income neighborhoods are disproportionately exposed to air pollution. The LEZ boundaries in Brussels include areas with both high exposure and low income, presenting a relatively equitable example of environmental policy. In contrast, London exhibited a weaker, slightly positive correlation, indicating a different distribution of air pollution exposure across income groups. However, the expansion of the Ultra Low Emission Zone has been associated with accessibility challenges and financial burdens for some low-income households. In both cities, older, non-compliant vehicles are more commonly owned by lower-income individuals, making these groups more economically vulnerable to LEZ policies. Public transportation is more accessible in low-income areas in Brussels, whereas in London, transit services are predominantly concentrated in higher-income regions. This disparity is particularly evident in Northeast London, where the convergence of low income, a high proportion of older vehicles, and poor public transportation access heightens the risk of social exclusion (Verbeek and Hincks, 2022).

Another study (Jiménez-Espada et al., 2023) was conducted in Spain to assess the potential public health impact of LEZ policies through public perceptions, attitudes and behavioural tendencies. According to the findings, 45 % of participants believed that LEZs would improve public health, while 31 % thought they would enhance quality of life. Additionally, positive inclinations toward walking (55 %) and willingness to reduce private car use (32 %) suggest that LEZ policies promoting active lifestyles may be well-supported by the public. Furthermore, a substantial majority (74 %) reported being informed about climate change, and awareness of environmental labeling and sustainable city initiatives was also high. However, punitive measures such as urban tolls were largely rejected by the public (61 %). In contrast, supportive and accessible strategies—such as public transportation subsidies, incentives for environmentally friendly vehicles, and the improvement of pedestrian infrastructure—were more widely accepted. Ultimately, the realization of LEZs' public health benefits depends not only on environmental regulations but also on incentive-based policy designs shaped by public engagement, awareness, and positive attitudes. Success lies not only in technical implementation but in participatory, informative, and socially inclusive approaches.

A study conducted in Germany measured the effects of LEZs on air quality and physical health and indicated that their mental health impact is likely to be short-term. LEZs in Germany have led to significant improvements in air quality, particularly in the levels of NO_2 and PM_{10}, contributing to a reduction in hypertension rates among individuals aged 60 and over. This indicates the potential of LEZ policies to mitigate cardiovascular disease risks. However, during the same period, a short-term decline in life satisfaction was observed, particularly among diesel vehicle owners, working-age individuals, and residents living near LEZ boundaries. This negative effect is temporary, typically dissipating within two to three years as individuals gradually adapt to the policy. An increase in ozone (O_3) concentrations during spring and summer months was also observed. Individuals residing outside LEZ boundaries but regularly commuting into them also experienced a drop in life satisfaction, without gaining the associated health benefits. To ensure the sustainable success of the policy, improvements in transportation alternatives such as public transit and cycling infrastructure are recommended, along with communication strategies to make health benefits more visible (Sarmiento et al., 2023).

In the case of Bradford, where a high burden of respiratory illness and social disadvantage is prominent, child-focused health messaging, especially when supported by local cohort data such as the "Born in Bradford" study, proved effective in overcoming public and administrative resistance to the LEZ policy. Statements such as "these data belong not to someone else's children, but to Bradford's children" were found to be more persuasive than abstract policy arguments, enhancing the emotional and political appeal of the intervention. Practitioners noted that while initial public reactions were driven by economic concerns, health-centered messaging helped to counterbalance these fears. Nonetheless, some groups continued to perceive the policy as an "additional tax" or as driven by "governmental interests," and the absence of a strong, centrally coordinated communication campaign contributed to the spread of misinformation. Additionally, the COVID-19 pandemic created limitations such as public distraction and data disruption. Overall, the findings demonstrate that anchoring environmental interventions like LEZs in local public health data can significantly enhance public acceptance and policy sustainability (Knamiller et al., 2024).

LEZs have the potential to improve public health and reduce transportation inequalities when accompanied by appropriate support mechanisms. It was found that 60 % of motorized trips could be replaced by alternative transportation methods (e.g., e-bikes, public transit, walking), though this rate drops to 53 % among high-vulnerability (HV) households. While 8 % of the general population is directly affected by LEZ policies, this figure rises to 10 % among vulnerable groups, and a small but exposed subgroup (0.4 %) is simultaneously low-income, vulnerable, and lacks access to transportation alternatives. The planned 2025 ban on Crit'Air 3 and older vehicles is expected to disproportionately affect low-income households in Grenoble Metropolis, France. The Crit'Air 3 label is assigned to Euro 2 and Euro 3 vehicles registered between 1997 and 2005, as well as Euro 4 vehicles registered between 2006 and 2010. Consequently, 295 families, representing 0.1 % of the study sample, are at risk due to the lack of viable alternatives. Under extended policy scenarios, the number of affected households increases by 43 %, while restricting LEZ operational hours to 08:00–20:00 yields only a marginal 2 % improvement in exposure reduction, highlighting the need to address nighttime pollution exposure. Profile analyses reveal that groups categorized by "financial hardship," "lack of alternatives," and "costly dependency" have low adaptive capacity and are at heightened health risk. As a result, policy recommendations include €1500 e-bike subsidies, personalized mobility counseling, public transportation subsidies, and flexible implementation options for night-shift workers. It is noted that even targeted support for the 0.4 % high-risk population could be delivered at a manageable cost of approximately €6 million at the Grenoble scale, or around €70 million nationwide. In conclusion, LEZs have the potential to enhance healthy living and transportation equity; however, realizing this potential requires the simultaneous enactment of fair and supportive policies that specifically address the needs of vulnerable populations (Blandin et al., 2025).

The health-related discourses analyzed in the case of Ghent reveal that two opposing coalitions have constructed markedly different framings of the LEZ. The environmental coalition presents the LEZ as a policy supporting environmental justice and public health, while the opposing coalition criticizes it in terms of social exclusion, economic inequality, and the loss of mobility rights. The environmental narrative portrays the LEZ as beneficial for vulnerable groups (arguing that these populations already live in more polluted environments and often do not own private vehicles) while emphasizing health benefits such as improved respiratory and child health. In contrast, the opposing discourse argues that LEZs create social exclusion, punish those unable to afford new vehicles, and isolate elderly and disabled individuals from public life. This group frames the health discourse around indirect harms, including psychological stress, restricted mobility, and loss of access. Although both sides claim to speak on behalf of vulnerable populations, their definitions of these groups' needs and their conceptualizations of health diverge fundamentally. Furthermore, both coalitions selectively utilize scientific evidence to support their respective political positions. The study shows that health discourse functions as a tool of legitimacy for environmental actors, whereas for opponents, it serves as a platform for objection. This reflects how environmental and public health policies are debated in society not merely as "technical" issues, but through ideological lenses intertwined with notions of citizenship, elitism, and social equality. Consequently, in interventions such as LEZs, health-related discourses operate not only as channels for information dissemination but also as instruments for political positioning, public persuasion, and legitimacy-building. This underscores the need for public health policies to be grounded not only in scientific evidence but also in social perception, discourse analysis, and inclusive communication strategies to ensure effective and equitable implementation (Vandenhole, 2025).

4. Discussion

This systematic review provides compelling evidence that LEZs, as a policy instrument, have significant implications for both physical and mental health outcomes. The primary objective of LEZ is to reduce exposure to traffic-related harmful air pollutants in particular PM_{10}, $PM_{2.5}$ and NO_2.

4.1 Improvements in air quality and physical health outcomes

A recurring finding across the literature is the demonstrable reduction in air pollutant concentrations following the implementation of LEZs even though they only reduce exhaust emissions and not brake or tyre emissions. Cities such as Rome, Paris, and parts of Germany (Cesaroni et al., 2011; Gehrsitz, 2017; Host et al., 2020; Rohlf et al., 2020; Pestel and Wozny, 2021) reported declines ranging from 5 % to over 50 % in NO_2 and particulate matter, contingent upon the strictness of the intervention. These reductions translated into measurable public health gains, including decreased hospital admissions for cardiovascular and respiratory conditions, reduced pharmaceutical expenditure, and increased life expectancy. In cities with more aggressive LEZ frameworks, such as Paris and Malmö (Host et al., 2020; Flanagan et al., 2022), even infant health indicators and mortality rates showed improvements. However, the magnitude of these effects was heterogenous across regions. For example, early implementations in London (Wood et al., 2015) showed modest improvements in air quality and limited impact on child respiratory health, suggesting that the effectiveness of LEZs may depend heavily on baseline pollution levels, enforcement rigor, and supplementary policy measures such as congestion charges and vehicle renewal incentives.

4.2 Socioeconomic disparities in health gains, mental health and public perception

An important theme that emerged is the unequal distribution of health benefits. Several studies highlighted that individuals from higher socioeconomic strata disproportionately benefited from LEZ, due to better access to compliant vehicles, alternative transportation, and residential areas already characterized by lower pollution levels (Poulhès and Proulhac, 2021). Conversely, low-income and socially vulnerable populations often reside near LEZ boundaries or rely on older, non-compliant vehicles, rendering them more susceptible to exclusion and mobility challenges. Moreover, spatial analyses in cities such as London and Brussels (Verbeek and Hincks, 2022) underscored the necessity of aligning environmental interventions with principles of environmental justice. In Brussels, for instance, the LEZ included high-exposure and low-income zones, which improved health equity. In London, LEZ expansion created new burdens for economically disadvantaged communities, particularly those with poor access to public transportation.

Emerging evidence points to the mental wellbeing consequences of LEZ implementations, especially among residents living near zone boundaries or those directly affected by vehicle restrictions. Short-term reductions in life satisfaction, anxiety due to mobility limitations, and perceptions of social exclusion were recurrent themes (Morton et al., 2021; Sarmiento et al., 2023). Notably, these effects appeared to dissipate over time, indicating a possible adaptation effect. Nonetheless, the psychological burden should not be underestimated, particularly when the policy is implemented without sufficient public consultation, transparency, or support mechanisms. Individuals residing outside LEZ boundaries but regularly commuting into them also experienced a drop in life satisfaction, without gaining the associated health benefits. This suggests that certain groups bear a disproportionate share of the costs.

Public acceptability of LEZ policies is shown to be influenced more by perceptions of fairness, effectiveness, and emotional responses than by technical knowledge (Jiménez-Espada et al., 2023). Communication strategies that emphasize health benefits for children and community wellbeing were found to be especially persuasive (Knamiller et al., 2024). Trust in local governance and availability of viable transportation alternatives also played critical roles in shaping public attitudes.

4.3 Limitations and recommendations for future studies

Despite the breadth of existing research, several gaps remain. First, longitudinal studies are still scarce, especially those that track long-term physical and mental health outcomes post-LEZ implementation. Second, there is a lack of robust data from low- and middle-income countries, where urban air pollution is often more severe and infrastructural inequalities are more pronounced. Third, future studies should aim to incorporate health equity metrics more explicitly to assess not just aggregate improvements, but also distributional justice.

Furthermore, the co-benefits of LEZs such as increased active transportation and reduced noise pollution remain underexplored in quantitative terms. These aspects, particularly when linked with improvements in cardiovascular fitness, mental health, and urban livability, could strengthen the public health justification for expanding LEZ policies.

4.4 Policy implications

The results of this review reinforce that LEZs can serve as an effective policy mechanism to reduce urban air pollution and associated health risks.

However, to ensure sustainable success, policy design must be integrative. This includes:

- equity-sensitive implementation, with support for vulnerable groups (e.g., subsidies, exemptions, and enhanced transit access),
- strong public engagement strategies, with tailored communication efforts based on demographic profiling, and
- integration with other urban mobility policies, such as congestion pricing, pedestrian zones, public transportation improvements, cycling improvements and incentives for low-emission vehicle ownership.

Without addressing these socioeconomic and psychological dimensions, LEZs risk becoming perceived as exclusionary rather than protective. As urbanization intensifies and environmental challenges become more complex, LEZs will need to evolve as part of broader, interdisciplinary frameworks that center on environmental health equity and participatory governance.

5. Conclusion

This review confirms that Low Emission Zones (LEZs) can be an effective tool for improving urban air quality and reducing pollution-related physical health risks, including cardiovascular and respiratory conditions. However, the findings also reveal significant disparities in health benefits, with vulnerable populations often bearing the brunt of social and psychological burdens. Yet these populations are not only generally exposed to higher levels of pollution but also have higher rates of cardiorespiratory diseases. Therefore, with improvements in air quality, they are expected to achieve the greatest physical health gains. Mental health effects, public resistance, and unequal access to alternatives highlight the need for socially inclusive policy design. For LEZs to fulfill their full public health potential, future implementations must prioritize equity, community engagement, and integration with broader mobility and environmental strategies.

References

Andriolli, A.C., Silva, L.T., 2024. Are low emission zones truly embraced by the public? Environments 11 (6). https://doi.org/10.3390/environments11060106.

Attia, M., Alade, T., Attia, S., 2023. The influence of passenger car banning policies on modal shifts: rotterdam's case study. Sustainability 15 (9), 7443. https://doi.org/10.3390/su15097443.

Blandin, L., Bouscasse, H., Mathy, S., 2025. Assessing the ex-ante impacts of a low-emission zone on transport poverty and vulnerability with the VulMob indicator. Case Stud. Transp. Policy 19 (0). https://trid.trb.org/View/2450609.

Broster, S., Terzano, K., 2025. A systematic review of the pollution and health impacts of low emission zones. Case Stud. Transp. Policy 19, 101340. https://doi.org/10.1016/j.cstp.2024.101340.

Cesaroni, G., Boogaard, H., Jonkers, S., et al., 2011. Health benefits of traffic-related air pollution reduction in different socioeconomic groups: the effect of low-emission zoning in Rome. Occup. Environ. Med. 69, 133–139. https://doi.org/10.1136/oem.2010.063750.

Chamberlain, R.C., Fecht, D., Davies, B., et al., 2023. Health effects of low emission and congestion charging zones: a systematic review. Lancet Public Health 8 (7), 559–574. https://doi.org/10.1016/S2468-2667(23)00120-2.

Ellison, R.B., Greaves, S.P., Hensher, D.A., 2013. Five years of London's low emission zone: effects on vehicle fleet composition and air quality. Transp. Res. Part D-Transp. Environ. 23, 25–33. https://doi.org/10.1016/j.trd.2013.03.010.

Ezeah, C., Finney, K., Nnajide, C., 2015. A critical review of the effectiveness of low emission zones (LEZ) as a strategy for the management of air quality in major European cities. J. Multidiscip. Eng. Sci. Technol. 2 (7).

Flanagan, E., Malmqvist, E., Gustafsson, S., et al., 2022. Estimated public health benefits of a low-emission zone in Malmö, Sweden. Environ. Res. 214 (Pt 4), 114124. https://doi.org/10.1016/j.envres.2022.114124.

Gehrsitz, M., 2017. The effect of low emission zones on air pollution and infant health. J. Environ. Econ. Manag. 83, 121–144. https://doi.org/10.1016/j.jeem.2017.02.003.

Göteborgs Stad, 2006. Assessment of environmental zone in Göteborg: A report for the traffic and public transport authority of the city of Göteborg. Göteborg, Sweden.

Griffin, S., Walker, S., Sculpher, M., 2020. Distributional cost effectiveness analysis of West Yorkshire low emission zone policies. Health Econ. 29 (5), 567–579. https://doi.org/10.1002/hec.4003.

Gu, J., Deffner, V., Küchenhoff, H., Pickford, R., et al., 2022. Low emission zones reduced PM10 but not NO2 concentrations in Berlin and Munich, Germany. J. Environ. Manag. 302, 114048. https://doi.org/10.1016/j.jenvman.2021.114048.

Holman, C., Harrison, R.M., Querol, X., 2015. Review of the efficacy of low emission zones to improve urban air quality in European cities. Atmospheric Environ. 111, 161–169. https://doi.org/10.1016/j.atmosenv.2015.04.009.

Host, S., Honoré, C., Joly, F., et al., 2020. Implementation of various hypothetical low emission zone scenarios in Greater Paris: assessment of fine-scale reduction in exposure and expected health benefits. Environ. Res. 185, 109405. https://doi.org/10.1016/j.envres.2020.109405.

Jiménez-Espada, M., García, F.M.M., González-Escobar, R., 2023. Citizen perception and ex ante acceptance of a low-emission zone implementation in a medium-sized Spanish City. Buildings 13 (1). https://doi.org/10.3390/buildings13010249.

Knamiller, C., Rashid, R., Bryant, M., et al., 2024. Who shouts the loudest? A qualitative study exploring barriers and enablers to implementing a low emission zone in a Northern UK city. Transp. Res. Interdiscip. Perspect. 25 (0). https://trid.trb.org/View/2385058.

Ma, L., Graham, D.J., Stettler, M.E.J., 2021. Has the ultra low emission zone in London improved air quality? Environ. Res. Lett. 16 (12), 124001. https://doi.org/10.1088/1748-9326/ac30c1.

Malina, C., Scheffler, F., 2015. The impact of low emission zones on particulate matter concentration and public health. Transp. Res. Part A: Policy Pract. 77, 372–385. https://doi.org/10.1016/j.tra.2015.04.029.

Margaryan, S., 2021. Low emission zones and population health. J. Health Econ. 76, 102402. https://doi.org/10.1016/j.jhealeco.2020.102402.
Moral-Carcedo, J., 2022. Dissuasive effect of low emission zones on traffic: the case of Madrid Central. Transportation. https://doi.org/10.1007/s11116-022-10318-4.
Morfeld, P., Groneberg, D.A., Spallek, M.F., 2014. Effectiveness of low emission zones: large scale analysis of changes in environmental NO2, NO and NOx concentrations in 17 German cities. PLos One 9 (8), 102999. https://doi.org/10.1371/journal.pone.0102999.
Morton, C., Mattioli, G., Anable, J., 2021. Public acceptability towards low emission zones: the role of attitudes, norms, emotions, and trust. Transp. Res. Part A: Policy Pract. 150, 256–270. https://doi.org/10.1016/j.tra.2021.06.007.
Mudway, I.S., Dundas, I., Wood, H.E., et al., 2019. Impact of London's low emission zone on air quality and children's respiratory health: a sequential annual cross-sectional study. Lancet Public Health 4 (1), 28–40. https://doi.org/10.1016/S2468-2667(18)30202-0.
Nishitateno, S., Burke, P.J., 2024. Effects of low emission zones on air quality, new vehicle registrations, and birthweights: evidence from Japan. Environ. Res. Econ. 87 (7), 1955–1992. https://doi.org/10.1007/s10640-024-00875-w.
Pasquier, A., André, M., 2016. Decomposition of low emission zone strategies into mechanisms and methodology for assessing their impacts on air pollution. TAP 2016, 21st International Transport and Air Pollution Conference, 21-p. https://hal.science/hal-01450251/.
Pestel, N., Wozny, F., 2021. Health effects of low emission zones: evidence from German hospitals. J. Environ. Econ. Manag. 109, 102512. https://doi.org/10.1016/j.jeem.2021.102512.
Poulhès, A., Proulhac, L., 2021. The Paris Region low emission zone, a benefit shared with residents outside the zone. Transp. Res. Part D: Transp. Environ. 98 (0). https://trid.trb.org/View/1866703.
Rohlf, A., Holub, F., Koch, N., et al., 2020. The effect of clean air on pharmaceutical expenditures. Econ. Lett. 192, 109221. https://doi.org/10.1016/j.econlet.2020.109221.
Sarmiento, L., Wägner, N., Zaklan, A., 2023. The air quality and well-being effects of low emission zones. J. Public Econ. 227, 105014. https://doi.org/10.1016/j.jpubeco.2023.105014.
Vandenhole, K., 2025. From environmental policy consensus to socio-environmental policy controversy: discursive network dynamics of the Ghentian low emission zone. Environ. Sci. Policy 164, 104013. https://doi.org/10.1016/j.envsci.2025.104013.
Verbeek, T., Hincks, S., 2022. The 'just' management of urban air pollution? A geospatial analysis of low emission zones in Brussels and London. Appl. Geogr. 140 (0). https://trid.trb.org/View/1910803.
WHO Global Air Quality Guidelines, 2021. Retrieved 30 March 2025, from https://www.who.int/news-room/questions-and-answers/item/who-global-air-quality-guidelines.
Wood, H.E., Marlin, N., Mudway, I.S., et al., 2015. Effects of air pollution and the introduction of the london low emission zone on the prevalence of respiratory and allergic symptoms in schoolchildren in East London: a sequential cross-sectional study. PloS One 10 (8), 0109121. https://doi.org/10.1371/journal.pone.0109121.
Xiao, C., Scales, J., Chavda, J., et al., 2024. Children's Health in London and Luton (CHILL) cohort: a 12-month natural experimental study of the effects of the ultra low emission zone on children's travel to school. Int. J. Behav. Nutr. Phys. Activity 21 (1), 89. https://doi.org/10.1186/s12966-024-01621-7.
Zhai, M., Wolff, H., 2021. Air pollution and urban road transport: evidence from the world's largest low-emission zone in London. Environ. Econ. Policy Stud. 23 (4), 721–748. https://doi.org/10.1007/s10018-021-00307-9.

CHAPTER EIGHT

On behaviour change and active travel: Linking interventions, underlying psychological factors and their effectiveness

Michael A.B. van Eggermond[a,*] and Dorothea Schaffner[b]
[a]Faculty of Architecture, Construction & Geomatics, University of Applied Sciences Northwestern Switzerland, Muttenz, Switzerland
[b]Faculty of Applied Psychology, University of Applied Sciences Northwestern Switzerland, Olten, Switzerland
*Corresponding author. e-mail address: michael.vaneggermond@fhnw.ch

Contents

Advances in Transport Policy and Planning, Volume 18
ISSN 2543-0009, https://doi.org/10.1016/bs.atpp.2026.07.003

Abstract

Promoting active travel, such as walking and cycling, offers significant health and environmental benefits. However, behaviour change in this domain remains challenging. This systematic review synthesises evidence on behavioural interventions to increase active travel, focusing on psychological mechanisms that mediate these effects. A systematic search of Web of Science, TRID, and PubMed identified 28 peer-reviewed studies published in English between 2010 and 2025. Studies were included if they evaluated behavioural interventions aimed at increasing active travel and reported pre- and post-intervention measures of both behaviour and psychological factors. The most common intervention functions studied were education, goal setting, planning, and persuasion, primarily 'soft' strategies aimed at shifting attitudes, perceptions, and social norms. Fewer studies examined 'structural' interventions like environmental restructuring or incentives, and these rarely assessed psychological mediators.

The psychological factors most frequently targeted by intervention functions were attitudes, self-efficacy, information and skills, and social influence. Among these, social influence showed the most consistent significant effects, while self-efficacy and information/skills were significantly altered in a substantial share of studies; attitudes showed the weakest and most mixed evidence of change.

Only six out of 28 studies employed formal mediation analyses to test whether intervention effects on behaviour were mediated through psychological factors such as attitudes, motivation, or self-efficacy. This review highlights the need for more theory-driven research into the psychological processes underlying behaviour change in active travel to guide the development of more effective interventions and policies.

1. Introduction

An increased adoption of active modes of transport, such as walking or cycling, is associated with reduced risks of lifestyle diseases and improvements in both physical and mental health. To promote the wider use of these modes of transport, behaviour change is essential. Nevertheless, a second-order meta-analysis revealed that behaviour change interventions have the least effect in the field of transport compared with other outcomes (e.g., littering, recycling, consumption), indicating the challenges that policy-makers and planners face in realising behaviour change (Bergquist et al., 2023).

To promote behaviour change, a range of interventions is available. In academia, a distinction between 'hard' or 'structural' and 'soft' or 'informational' measures has been made to enable a systematic understanding of these interventions (Bamberg et al., 2011; Steg and Vlek, 2009). Hard/structural measures refer to changing the context in which behavioural choices are made (e.g., infrastructure or costs), while soft/informational measures comprise information dissemination, norms, and persuasion. To facilitate further structured analysis, a comprehensive taxonomy that classifies interventions into clearly defined categories has been proposed (Michie et al., 2013). This classification recognizes that interventions can consist of a single component or of multiple components – also called intervention functions – and range from education, incentivisation, and coercion to enablement (Arnott et al., 2014; Michie et al., 2013).

Previous reviews investigating the effectiveness of these behaviour change techniques in different fields reveal only modest or heterogeneous results (Albarracín et al., 2024; Bergquist et al., 2023; Bird et al., 2013). While some of these previous investigations have used a "black box" approach that focuses on the effects of an intervention, neglecting the psychological factors that mediate these effects (Bergquist et al., 2023; Bird et al., 2013), other studies focus on these psychological factors. Such mediating psychological factors include attitudes, habits, knowledge, and awareness, as well as social, cultural, and moral norms (Semenescu et al., 2020). The influence of these psychological factors on behaviour is explained on the basis of theoretical frameworks such as the theory of planned behaviour (Ajzen, 1991), the value-norm model (Stern et al., 1999), and integrated into various process models of behaviour change, for instance the transtheoretical model (Prochaska and Velicer, 1997) and the theory of action phases (e.g. Bamberg, 2013). A further analysis of these mediating psychological factors might contribute to a better understanding which behaviour change techniques are effective.

Enhancing the understanding of mediating factors is relevant not only for advancing academic knowledge but also for informing practical decisions. While several theoretical conceptualisations have incorporated the link between interventions and psychological factors (Bamberg, 2013; Michie et al., 2011; Steg and Vlek, 2009; van Valkengoed et al., 2022), a comprehensive empirical investigation of the connection between interventions, psychological factors, and outcomes in the field of active travel is still missing. However, this knowledge is necessary to systematically evaluate and select effective interventions to promote active travel.

Previous reviews have investigated the implementation of interventions in the context of promoting active travel (Arnott et al., 2014; Bird et al., 2013; Larsen et al., 2024; Roaf et al., 2024). Some of these studies revealed the type of intervention investigated but not their effectiveness (Bird et al., 2013; Larsen et al., 2024). Arnott et al. (2014) and Semenescu et al. (2020) specifically investigated intervention functions and psychological factors, but in the context of reducing car use. The review by Roaf et al. (2024) includes intervention functions and psychological factors in the context of promoting active travel; however, it does not provide evidence on the role of psychological factors as mediators of the effects of the interventions.

In sum, several gaps in the previous literature on understanding behaviour change for active travel can be identified. First, comprehensive knowledge of how interventions influence psychological processes is missing. Second, a review of empirical evidence on the extent to which psychological factors mediate, and therefore explain, the effectiveness of interventions is lacking. Knowledge of the psychological factors and their links to interventions might support decision-makers in practice in choosing and tailoring interventions to address the psychological factors that determine behaviour change (van Valkengoed et al., 2022).

Addressing these gaps in the literature, the objective of this systematic review was to synthesise the available research on the effects of interventions and psychological processes in the context of active travel. In doing so, the review aims to summarise the evidence to answer the following research questions:

1. Which intervention functions and combinations have been investigated to change active travel?

2. Which psychological factors have been studied as explanatory variables for changes in active travel?
3. Which psychological factors are influenced by interventions?
4. Which mediating psychological factors explain the effectiveness of interventions in promoting active travel?

As such, the present review attempts to further advance our understanding of the psychological basis on which the effectiveness of interventions can be explained. Such an understanding might inform policy-makers in making substantiated decisions about which interventions to implement to promote active travel.

The remainder of this review is structured as follows: the next section provides an overview of behaviour change theories, intervention functions, and psychological factors that form the conceptual background for this review. The following section explains the methods and procedures used. Results are then reported and described, followed by a final section that discusses the findings.

2. Background

2.1 Understanding behaviour change: Differentiating between processes and outcomes

Behaviour change interventions are defined as a "coordinated set of activities designed to change specified behaviour patterns", such as increasing active travel or physical activity (Michie et al., 2011). These interventions are characterized by intervention functions or components (Michie et al., 2011). Instead of acting directly on behaviour, the literature recognises that interventions operate by influencing psychological determinants, including, but not limited to, motivation, intention, attitudes, perceived control, and self-efficacy (Michie et al., 2013; Steg and Vlek, 2009; van Valkengoed et al., 2022). These factors, in turn, mediate the relationship between interventions and behaviour change. This logic is foundational in several psychological theories, including the Theory of Planned Behaviour (TPB), as well as the COM-B model and the Behaviour Change Wheel framework.

Thus, interventions can be evaluated not only in terms of behavioural outcomes, but also in terms of the mechanisms of change: whether they successfully altered the psychological mediators or factors they were intended to target, and whether the outcomes or effects of interventions were mediated by the targeted psychological factors.

The different types of links or relationships between interventions, psychological factors, and behavioural outcomes, as they are investigated or discussed in previous research, are highlighted in Fig. 1. Connecting intervention functions on the far left with behavioural outcomes on the far right is Linkage A. This linkage represents the direct effect of an intervention on behaviour and evaluates only whether the intervention changed the target outcome. Linkage B represents the effect of the intervention on psychological factors, such as attitudes, motivation, or perceived control. Linkage C captures the influence of these psychological factors on behaviour. Combined, Linkages B and C represent an indirect pathway, suggesting that interventions operate not by changing behaviour directly, but by altering internal psychological mechanisms which, in turn, influence behaviour. The present research focuses, in addition to existing research, on understanding Linkages B and C, and thereby on the indirect pathway to further explain the effects of intervention functions on outcomes.

2.2 Behaviour change theories

To understand the psychological foundations of these decisions and behaviours, particularly in the context of interventions aimed at promoting

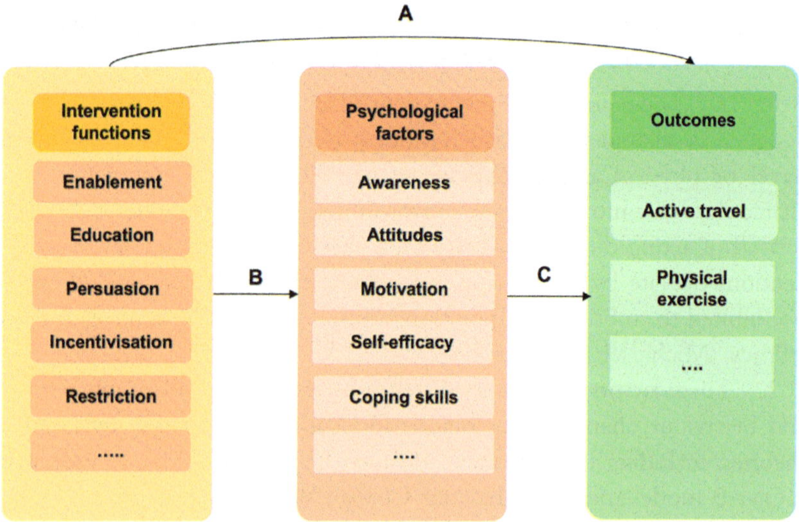

Fig. 1 Conceptual framework linking interventions, psychological factors and behaviour change in active travel. Pathway (A) represents the direct effect of interventions on behavioural outcomes; pathway (B) represents the effect of intervention functions on psychological factors; and pathway (C) represents the effect of psychological factors on behavioural outcomes.

active travel, we draw upon insights from behaviour change theories. One review that maps and synthesises this field is that of Davis et al. (2015) who identified 82 models of behaviour change through expert consultation, database searches, and other strategies. Their analysis revealed that a few theories, namely the Transtheoretical Model of Change (TTM), the Theory of Planned Behaviour (TPB), Social Cognitive Theory (SCT), and the Information–Motivation–Behavioural Skills Model (IMB), dominate the literature. These four theories account for sixty-three per cent of the articles they identified. Davis et al. suggest that factors such as a theory's age, its use in educational settings, and its broad applicability contribute to this dominance.

Building upon their work, we have chosen to focus on TTM, TPB, SCT, IMB, the COM-B model, and the phase model. The COM-B model, a more recent framework, offers a bridge between behaviour change theory and intervention design. Furthermore, given our interest in the transport domain, we include the phase model, which provides valuable insights into the psychological processes underlying travel behaviour.

Behaviour change models attempt to explain and predict behaviour change, often distinguishing between distinct phases or stages. While the specific number and names of these phases vary, they generally include: precontemplation/predecision (becoming aware of the need for change), contemplation/preaction (considering and planning change), action (implementing the change), and maintenance (sustaining the change). Instead of providing a detailed explanation of each model, we focus on eleven psychological factors underlying behaviour change, extracted from these models, and discuss how these factors are addressed within several prominent models. Prior to introducing these factors, we continue with a classification of intervention functions.

2.3 Interventions promoting behaviour change

The literature on behaviour change interventions has proposed several classifications of interventions (Michie et al., 2011; Steg and Vlek, 2009; Bamberg, 2013). More parsimonious classifications differentiate between two types of interventions, such as soft versus hard measures or informational versus structural measures. Both distinctions distinguish between measures that aim at changing motivations, perceptions, cognitions, or social norms from those designed to change the context in which decisions are made (Steg and Vlek, 2009). A more elaborate classification is found in the Behavior Change Wheel approach, differentiating between nine classes of interventions (Michie et al., 2011). As such, all classifications of interventions acknowledge the link between interventions and psychological processes to explain behaviour change. The proposed classification for this review is based on the Behavior Change Wheel (see Table 1). This framework includes nine categories of interventions: education, persuasion, incentivisation, training, restriction, environmental restructuring, modelling, enablement, and coercion. These intervention functions are applied to the context of active travel. Based on the reviewed publications on behaviour change techniques in the field of transport, and within the procedures of the thematic analyses, we inductively complemented this list with four additional intervention functions (see Section 3.7. for an explanation of the procedures). These functions are also reported in related reviews (Bamberg, 2013; Bird et al., 2013). The additionally derived intervention functions are goal-setting, planning, social support, and feedback/monitoring.

2.4 Psychological factors in behaviour change models

For this review we selected psychological factors as determinants of behaviour change in active travel by considering relevant theoretical frameworks. Theoretical approaches have differentiated between several psychological factors that explain behaviour and behaviour change (Ajzen, 2011; Michie et al., 2011). Table 2 provides an overview of these psychological factors to be found in the literature, specifying a definition as well as a link to their theoretical roots. For example, attitudes are incorporated in the Theory of Planned Behaviour, the TTM as decisional balance, in the COM-B model as reflective and automatic behaviour. The SCT considers attitudes likewise to play a role in understanding behaviour change. Considering and discussing psychological factors along these frameworks provides a theory-based understanding of the determinants of behaviour change.

2.5 Combinations of intervention functions and psychological factors

A number of theoretical conceptualisations (Steg and Vlek, 2009; Michie et al., 2011; Bamberg, 2013) propose that behaviour change is determined by psychological factors, which can in turn be influenced by behavioural interventions. In line with these existing publications, we assume that specific intervention functions influence specific psychological factors.

Table 1 Intervention functions based on Arnott et al. (2014) and Michie et al. (2011).

Intervention function	Definition	Examples
Education	Increasing knowledge or understanding of active travel	Campaigns highlighting the health benefits of walking or cycling
Persuasion	Using communication to induce positive or negative feelings or stimulate action towards active travel	Persuasive messages about the dangers of car pollution vs. the joy of cycling or walking
Incentivisation	Creating expectation of reward for active travel	Incentives for cycling to work or school, monetary or intangible rewards for individuals or teams that walk or cycle
Training	Imparting skills to walk or cycle	Cycling classes to train cycling skills, planning skills for convenient or safe walking and cycling routes
Restriction	Using rules to reduce the opportunity to engage in active travel or to increase active travel by reducing the opportunity to use cars	Car free-zones in specific neighbourhoods or in front of schools
Environmental restructuring	Changing the physical or social context in the transportation or urban system	Building more bike lanes and pedestrian-friendly infrastructure
Modelling	Providing an example for people to aspire to or imitate with regards to active travel	Opinion leaders, celebrities or influencers that promoting active commuting or leisure activities
Enablement	Increasing means/reducing barriers to increase capability or opportunity to engage in active travel	Subsidies for purchasing bicycles or free bike-sharing programs

(continued)

Table 1 Intervention functions based on Arnott et al. (2014) and Michie et al. (2011). (*cont'd*)

Intervention function	Definition	Examples
Coercion	Using force, penalties, or negative consequences to change active travel behaviour	Fines for driving in car-free neighbourhoods or school zones during peak hours, mandatory cycling days for employees or students
Goal Setting	Set or agree a goal to promote active travel.	Define a daily walking or cycling goal. Set the goal to use active modes of transportation in 4 out 5 times.
Planning	Formulation of an articulated set of procedures to assist in active travel.	Planning the performance of walking to work at a particular day and time.
Social Support	Advice on, arrange or provide social support (emotional or practical) for the performance of the active travel.	Arrange for as Buddy-system that supports cycling to work.
Feedback and Monitoring	Monitor and provide informative or evaluative feedback on performance of behaviour. Information includes form, frequency, duration or intensity of active travel	Inform a person of how often they used active modes of transport to work or school.

Accordingly, we map the intervention functions to psychological factors using the framework proposed by Michie et al. (2011) (see Table 3).

For example, education could determine problem awareness, attitudes & emotions, intentions, planning & self-regulation, self-efficacy, coping skills & relapse prevention as well as information & skills.

Overall, this reasoning suggests that the effectiveness of the interventions will depend on the extent to which the psychological factors that are targeted by the intervention functions are important determinants of the target behaviour, in our case active travel.

Table 2 Psychological factors in behaviour change models.

Psychological factor	Definition	Theoretical background
Problem Awareness/ Need for Change	This factor involves recognizing the need for behavioural change.	In the Transtheoretical Model (TTM), it's implicit in the progression from the stage *Precontemplation* (unaware/ underinformed) to *Contemplation* (recognizing a problem). Bamberg's model explicitly includes *Problem Awareness* in the *Predecision Phase*. The COM-B model considers how *Opportunity* (both social and physical) can highlight the problem to an individual. Social Cognitive Theory (SCT) acknowledges that the environment can influence awareness. The IMB model addresses this through the *Information* component, which can raise awareness of the problem.
Attitudes	This refers to the positive or negative evaluations of the behaviour.	The Theory of Planned Behavior (TPB) explicitly includes *Attitude toward the Behavior* as a central construct. While not always explicitly named, attitudes are implicitly present in other models. For example, in the Transtheoretical Model (TTM), attitudes influence the *Decisional Balance* and movement through the stages. In Social Cognitive Theory (SCT), attitudes can affect *Outcome Expectations*. In the COM-B model, attitudes contribute to both *Reflective* and *Automatic Motivation*. Bamberg considers attitudes as a component of *Motivational Beliefs*.

(continued)

Table 2 Psychological factors in behaviour change models. (*cont'd*)

Psychological factor	Definition	Theoretical background
Motivation to Change	This encompasses the driving forces behind behaviour change.	TTM uses Decisional Balance and Ambivalence to capture this in the Contemplation stage. Bamberg's model emphasizes Motivational Beliefs, including Outcome Expectancies and Risk Perceptions. TPB considers motivation through Attitudes and Subjective Norms, which influence Intention. COM-B includes Motivation as a core component, distinguishing between reflective and automatic processes. SCT highlights Outcome Expectations and Reinforcement as key motivators.
Intention/ Commitment to Change	This refers to the decision to change.	In TTM, it's represented by Commitment in the Preparation phase. Bamberg's model includes Intention Formation in the Preaction phase. TPB focuses on Intention as a direct predictor of behaviour. COM-B addresses this through Reflective Motivation. SCT considers Intentions as a factor influencing behaviour.
Planning/Self-Regulation:	This involves developing a strategy for change.	TTM includes Plan of Action in the Preparation phase. Bamberg's model considers Planning as a crucial part of the Preaction phase. While TPB doesn't explicitly include it, planning is implied in the formation of Intention. COM-B includes aspects of planning in Reflective Motivation and Psychological Capability. SCT addresses this through Self-Regulation.

Self-Efficacy	This is the belief in one's ability to change.	TTM emphasizes Self-Efficacy in the Action and Maintenance phases. Bamberg distinguishes between Action Self-Efficacy and Maintenance Self-Efficacy. TPB refers to this as Perceived Behavioural Control. COM-B includes it as part of Psychological Capability. SCT also emphasizes Self-Efficacy as a central construct.
Perceived Control/ Barriers	This relates to the perceived ease or difficulty of change.	In TTM, it's implicitly related to Self-Efficacy and the challenges faced in the Action and Maintenance phases. Bamberg implicitly considers it in factors influencing Self-Efficacy. TPB directly addresses this through Perceived Behavioural Control. COM-B considers Physical Opportunity and Physical/ Psychological Capability as related factors. SCT refers to Perceived Barriers/Facilitators.
Social Influence	This refers to the impact of social pressure and expectations.	TTM includes this implicitly in processes like social liberation and normative re-education. Bamberg doesn't explicitly name it. TPB considers this through Subjective Norms. COM-B includes this as Social Opportunity. SCT highlights Observational Learning and Social Norms.
Coping Skills/ Relapse Prevention	This involves strategies for maintaining change and avoiding relapse.	TTM explicitly addresses Relapse Prevention in the Maintenance phase. Bamberg includes Coping Skills in the Postaction phase. TPB does not explicitly address it. COM-B considers it as part of Psychological Capability and Automatic Motivation. SCT includes Coping Responses and Self-Regulatory Strategies.

(continued)

Table 2 Psychological factors in behaviour change models. (*cont'd*)

Psychological factor	Definition	Theoretical background
Habits/Automatic Processes	These are ingrained behavioural patterns.	TTM implicitly considers this in the goal of making new behaviours habitual during Maintenance. Bamberg and TPB do not explicitly address it. COM-B includes it as Automatic Motivation. SCT implicitly considers it as behavioural factors being influenced by past behaviour.
Information & Skills	These are crucial elements for behaviour change. While not core psychological constructs in all models, they are addressed.	TTM implicitly includes these in the processes of change and the Action phase. Bamberg considers them as factors influencing Self-Efficacy. TPB implies their importance for Perceived Behavioural Control. COM-B includes skills as Physical and Psychological Capability. SCT considers these as enabling factors. The IMB model focuses on Information and Behavioural Skills as central and distinct constructs.

Notes: TTM = Transtheoretical Model, COM-B = Capability, Opportunity, Motivation – Behavior; TPB = Theory of Planned Behavior; SCT = Social Cognitive Theory.

2.6 Interventions: Arms, functions and delivery methods

In the literature on behaviour change interventions, different terms are often used interchangeably, such as intervention, intervention function, and treatment or control group. It is useful, however, to distinguish between intervention functions, intervention arms, and delivery methods. Intervention functions (or components) are the mechanisms of action, such as training, incentivisation, or environmental restructuring, that are theorised to influence behaviour.

The term 'intervention' is often used at a more aggregate level to indicate that an intervention has been made, when in reality multiple distinct interventions may have been investigated. By contrast, intervention arms describe the combination of functions (or experimental conditions) in

Table 3 Link between intervention functions and psychological factors based on Michie et al. (2011).

Intervention functions	Psychological factors									
	Problem Awareness	Attitudes & Emotions	Motivation	Intention	Planning & Self-Regulation	Self-Efficacy	Perceived Control & Barriers	Social Influence	Coping Skills & Relapse Prevention	Habits & Automatic Processes	Information & Skills
Education	✓	✓		✓	✓	✓			✓		✓
Goal Setting					✓						
Persuasion	✓	✓	✓	✓				✓		✓	
Planning					✓						
Training					✓	✓			✓		✓
Social Support								✓			✓
Enablement			✓		✓	✓	✓	✓	✓	✓	✓
Feedback & Monitoring			✓								
Incentivisation	✓	✓	✓	✓						✓	
Modelling			✓					✓		✓	
Environmental Restructuring			✓			✓	✓	✓		✓	✓
Coercion	✓	✓	✓	✓						✓	
Restriction							✓				

a specific study (e.g., a control group, informational nudge, planning prompt, or social support condition). In some cases, an intervention arm is also referred to as a 'research group' or 'treatment group'. A single intervention arm may combine several functions, and a control group can itself constitute a form of experimental condition (e.g., minimal information provision). In the remainder of this chapter, we use the term intervention arm to describe this.

Delivery methods refer to the format in which interventions are provided, such as face-to-face sessions, monitoring apps, or online training, but are not further examined in the remainder of this chapter. Distinguishing between these dimensions allows for a more precise mapping of how interventions are designed, delivered, and evaluated, and facilitates comparison across heterogeneous approaches in the literature.

2.7 Methodological implications

To examine whether psychological factors mediate the effect of interventions on behaviour, it is necessary to include two key elements: (1) pre- and post-measurement of behavioural outcomes, and (2) pre- and post-measurement of psychological factors. Accounting for time enables researchers to test whether changes in psychological factors precede, and statistically explain, changes in behaviour. This is illustrated by Linkages A, B, and C in Fig. 1.

- Linkage A represents the direct effect of the intervention on behaviour.
- Linkage B captures the effect of the intervention on psychological factors, such as intention, motivation, or perceived control.
- Linkage C reflects the influence of those psychological factors on behaviour.

When both Linkage B and Linkage C are supported empirically, and the indirect pathway from intervention to behaviour via psychological factors is significant, this constitutes mediation. Statistical approaches such as structural equation modelling (SEM) or bootstrapping methods for indirect effects can be employed to test this. (Hayes, 2017; Preacher and Hayes, 2008) allow for testing of this mediation pathway formally by estimating the size and significance of the indirect effect.

Many studies focus only on Linkage A or report psychological variables as secondary outcomes, without formally linking them to behavioural outcomes. This limits insight into whether interventions worked via the proposed mechanisms. Where full mediation testing is not possible, especially in studies lacking pre-intervention measurement, the inclusion of a control group can help clarify whether observed psychological or behavioural changes are attributable to the intervention. Linkage C is typically tested as an association (moderation or interaction effect). However, in such cases, it only shows whether psychological factors are associated with behaviour, not whether they mediate the effect of the intervention.

3. Methods

3.1 Aim

The aim of this systematic literature review was to summarise the findings from recent studies conducted to increase active travel. The focus is on psychological factors as moderators or mediators of the influence of interventions on behaviour change, in order to provide a better understanding of the processes that explain their effectiveness.

3.2 Protocol and registration

The protocol was registered on PROSPERO at the stage of full text screening (https://www.crd.york.ac.uk/prospero/; CRD420251046808).

3.3 Search strategy

We searched for behavioural interventions in active travel across three databases: Web of Science, TRID, and PubMed. Our keyword search terms were divided into three broad categories: active travel, interventions, and psychological factors. We restricted the publication timeframe to the past 15 years, starting from 2010. Only papers written in English and published in peer-reviewed journals were included in the review. The search was conducted in February 2025. Table 4 lists our search terms.

All references were imported into Covidence for title and abstract screening. Covidence is an online tool that streamlines the systematic review, process from title and abstract screening, through to data analysis and quality appraisal. The platform allows the designation of reviewers for each phase of the review process, ensuring inter-reviewer reliability. A full breakdown of the review process can be seen in Fig. 2. In parallel, all papers for the full-text stage were uploaded to the reference manager Zotero.

Table 4 Key words search terms.

Active travel	Intervention	Psychological factors
Walking	Intervention (general)	Problem Awareness Contemplation
Wheeling		Attitudes
Cycling		Motivation
E-bikes		Beliefs
		Emotion
		Intention
		Commitment
		Self Efficacy
		Perceived Control
		Perceived behavioural Control
		Perceived Barriers
		Social Influence
		Social Norms
		Relapse Prevention
		Coping Skills
		Habits
		Automatic Processes Routine
		Formation
		Knowledge
		Learning
		Capabilities

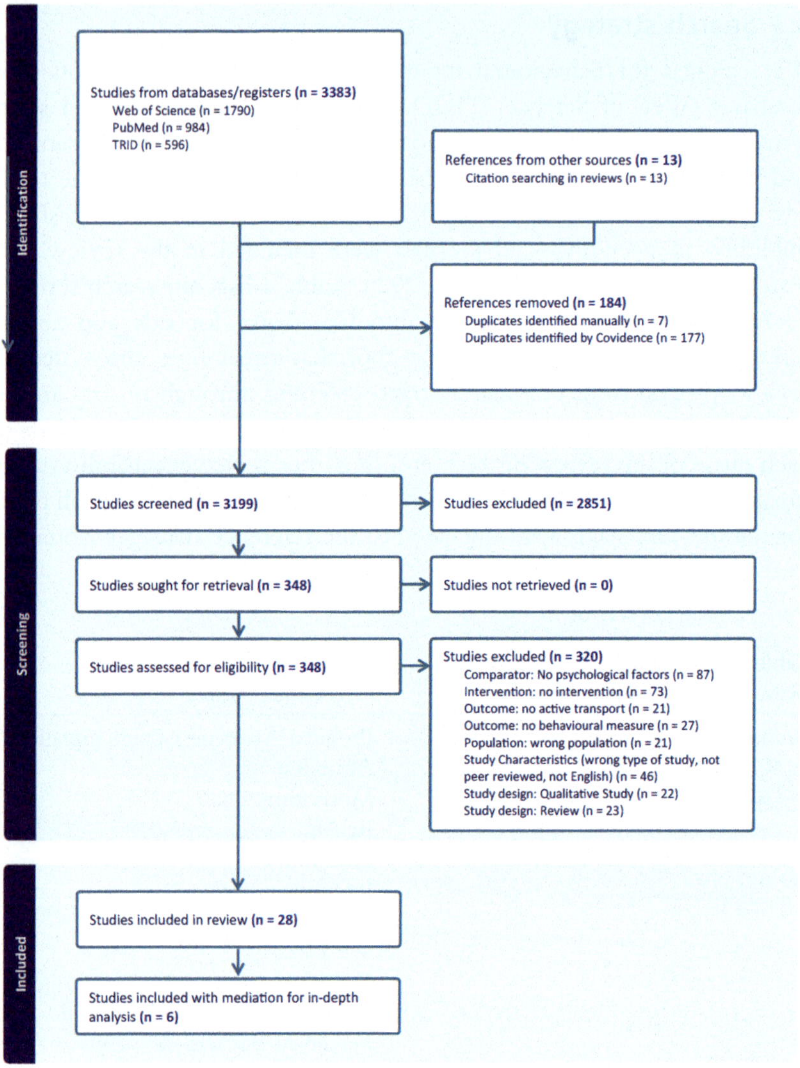

Fig. 2 PRISMA flow chart.

3.4 Eligibility criteria

Inclusion criteria for eligibility of studies to be included in the review were:

Participants/population:

Adults and children were included, patient populations with diseases (e.g. Parkinson, MS) were excluded. Studies that targeted parents, but measured children's behaviour were excluded.

Interventions:

Studies comprising all types of interventions were included. Behavioural interventions were defined as those which targeted a change in behaviour for active travel. Interventions delivered at an individual level or community level were eligible. Studies were eligible if they included a clear intervention aiming at promoting active travel. Interventions that measured only changes in physical activity (such as an increase insteps) or indoor exercise without reference to travel were excluded.

Comparison/study design:

Studies were eligible for the review if the study design was a randomized control trial or included pre-and post-intervention measurements (longitudinal design), quasi experimental or a natural experiment. Studies that used a control, comparison group or graded measures of exposure to the intervention were included, but a control/comparison group was not required.

Studies that were purely descriptive, based on modelled data, or identified correlations only, in the absence of a defined intervention, were excluded. Studies with no interventions were excluded. Likewise, qualitative studies (studies measuring effects based on interviews, focus groups), reviews, reports and protocols were excluded.

Outcome:

Studies were included when they reported on at least two types of outcomes: First, to be included, studies had to assess the effect of an intervention on one or several modes of active travel.

The following modes were classified as active travel:
- Walking
- Cycling
- Wheeling
- E-Bikes

Thereby, we included studies with self-report (e.g. survey, travel diaries) and/or objective data (e.g. data from wearables, device data, observations of walking or cycling, counters, GPS tracking). Measurement of active travel could have been done by frequency (e.g. trips per week), distance (e.g. kilometres travelled), or duration (e.g. minutes walked/cycled per day). Also, we included studies that measured active travel for all types of travel purposes (e.g. commuting, leisure, or exercise).

Second, studies were eligible for the review if the study measured the effect of the intervention on one or several psychological factors. Psychological factors were defined as mediating factors that explain behaviour change based on the theoretical models (see Section 1.4). The measurement of psychological factors was mainly based on self-reported survey data. Studies that did not measure effects of interventions on psychological factors were excluded.

3.5 Study selection

Studies were selected for the review in a two-step process following searches and de-duplication. In the first step, titles and abstracts of all studies were screened against the initial inclusion and exclusion criteria, with the workload divided between the two authors. To ensure consistency, a random sample of all titles and abstracts was independently screened by both authors at the outset of the screening process, and disagreements were resolved through discussion. The remainder of the records were screened by one author, with cases of uncertainty discussed between both authors.

In a second step, the full text publications of studies were accessed. Both authors screened approximately half of the full texts against more detailed inclusion and exclusion criteria, and excluded studies and reasons for exclusion were documented. Again, at the outset of the process, both authors independently screened a sample selected at random and disagreements were resolved through discussion. Studies which were found through alternative means, such as reference crosschecking, were subjected to the same screening process as those which emerged from the searches.

3.6 Data extraction

Selected studies were exported from Covidence and data that summarised the following factors was extracted:

- Population
- Country
- Sample size
- Study design
- Target behaviour
- Measurement of behaviour
- Duration of intervention
- Effect and significance of effect of psychological factor
- Effect and significance of effect of intervention
- Number of intervention arms

- Presence of control group
- Type of measurement for effects (direct effects, moderation, mediation)
- Description of interventions
- Type of interventions
- Type of psychological factor

3.7 Data analysis

A narrative synthesis of the extracted data was conducted by the two researchers. Extracted data was analysed to determine the studies characteristics (countries, population, study designs and target behavior), intervention functions used, and psychological factors measured. Additionally, we analysed significance of found effects. Reports of intervention functions or psychological factors were heterogeneous and based on different theoretical basis. Therefore, we undertook a thematic analysis of each study to categorize intervention functions utilised and psychological factors used based on the deductive categorization scheme derived from previous literature (see Sections 2.4 and 2.5). Further, the deductive categorization scheme for the intervention functions was extended by additional intervention functions as they were found in the empirical literature. Intervention duration was not analysed further due to the expected heterogeneity in reporting. It was expected that not all studies would report on duration, with some focusing on a single day of training while others would concern coaching sessions over a longer span of time or relate to infrastructure improvements. Concerning the significance of the results, we choose to classify results as significant when authors reported significant results, as presented in results tables, at any moment in time. This was chosen because authors did not always report multiple measurement points or provide a clear definition for a short (e.g., 1–3 months), medium (e.g., 6 months), or long-term effect (e.g., more than 12 months).

Exploratory analyses were conducted to consider relations between the presence or absence of specific intervention functions and the effect of interventions on psychological factors, with the aim of determining which interventions are associated with effects. Further, we conducted an in-depth analysis of those studies that included a mediation analysis, investigating the indirect effect of interventions through psychological factors.

Given the heterogeneity across all intervention types, the outcome measures used, study designs employed, a meta-analysis was not deemed an appropriate or feasible method to incorporate into this review Table 5.

Table 5 Psychological factors mediating intervention effects on active travel.

	Measurement of mediation	Intervention functions	Psychological factors (included in mediation analysis)	Sign. Mediation effect	Target behaviour
Darker et al. (2010)	Mediation analysis using bootstrapping	Enablement Goal setting Planning (Combined)	Perceived behavioural control (PBC)	Significant effect	Walking, all trip purposes
			Attitudes	No effect	
			Social Influence	No effect	
			Planning/self-regulation	No effect	
			Intention	No effect	
Fjeldsoe et al. (2013)	Mediation analysis using Sobel	Education Persuasion Enablement Goal setting Planning Social support (combined)	Motivation (outcome expectancy)	No effect	Walking for exercise Physical activity for exercise

			Self-efficacy	No effect	
			Planning/Self-regulation (goal setting skills)	Significant effect	
			Perceived control	No effect	
			Social support	No effect	
Hardeman et al. (2011)	Mediation model using SEM	Persuasion Enablement Modelling (combined)	Intention	No effect	Physical activity Walking for leisure and work-related activity
			Perceived behavioural control (PBC)	No effect	
			Attitude	Not included	
			Social Influence	Not included	
Panter and Ogilvie (2015)	Mediation model using SEM	Environmental restructuring	Attitudes (change in safety)	No effect	Walking and cycling

(continued)

Table 5 Psychological factors mediating intervention effects on active travel. (*cont'd*)

	Measurement of mediation	Intervention functions	Psychological factors (included in mediation analysis)	Sign. Mediation effect	Target behaviour
			Perceived control/ barriers (perception of infrastructure)	No effect	
			Social Influence (perception of social environment)	No effect	
Prestwich et al. (2012)	Mediation analysis using bootstrapping	Three interventions arms:			Walking
		Education Persuasion Social support (collaborative) Planning (implementation intentions)	Attitudes intention Self-efficacy Social Influence	No effect	
		Education Persuasion Social support	Attitudes intention Self-efficacy Social Influence	No effect	

		Education Persuasion Planning (implementation intentions)	Attitudes intention Self-efficacy Social Influence	No effect	
Stark et al. (2018)	Mediation model using SEM	Education Persuasion Enablement Feedback/Monitoring	Attitudes	No effect	Walking and cycling
			Intention	Significant effect (for cycling, partially for walking)	
			Self-efficacy	No effect	
			Social Influence	No effect	

4. Results

A total of 3199 papers were screened for eligibility, with 348 full-text articles assessed for inclusion. Twenty-eight papers underwent further review, which included data extraction and critical appraisal. Six studies that conducted mediation analysis were examined in greater detail. The reasons for excluding the remaining papers were documented. The most common reasons for exclusion were the absence of a psychological factor (or its lack of measurement before or after the intervention), followed by studies that did not report an intervention or did not measure active travel. Fig. 2 shows this process in more detail. A summary of the included studies can be found Table 6.

4.1 Country

The studies included in this review represent an international sample, with contributions from a variety of regions around the world. The largest number of studies were conducted in North America, particularly in the United States (n = 5) and Canada (n = 2).

In Europe (n = 16), the studies were distributed across multiple countries, including the United Kingdom (n = 7), Sweden (n = 2), Germany (n = 1), and others, collectively representing a significant portion of the research. Studies were also conducted in Asia n = 3 and there was additional representation from Australia (n = 2).

4.2 Population

The studies included in this review covered a broad range of populations. The majority of the studies focused on adults (n = 20) including subgroups such as adults aged 45 years or older, parents and postpartum women. Several studies (n = 3) focused specifically on older adults, including those with health conditions such as chronic illness or physical inactivity. Studies involving adults also often targeted working populations, parents, and individuals with particular health profiles, such as sedentary lifestyles or being overweight or obese. In addition to adults, the review included studies on children and adolescents (n = 5), covering age groups from children aged 8–9 years to adolescents with a mean age of 12–14 years.

4.3 Study designs

The included studies employed a range of designs, with Randomised Controlled Trials (RCTs) being the most common (n = 18), defined as

Table 6 Summary of included studies.

Author	Title	Population	Country	Sample size	Study design	Number of arms (incl. control)	Control groups	Target behaviour	Measurement of behaviour	Analysis method	Effect on active travel	Effect on psychological factors
Aranda-Balboa et al. (2022)	The Effect of a School-Based Intervention on Children's Cycling Knowledge, Mode of Commuting and Perceived Barriers: A Randomized Controlled Trial	Adolescents (14–15)	Spain	122 (I=60, C=60)	RCT	2	Yes	Active commuting to school	Self-reported mode choice to school, measured as 'usual mode of transport'	Direct	There was no significant change in the students' usual mode of commuting between baseline and follow-up in either group. Effect size not reported	The cycling group improved in cycling knowledge and showed a reduction in built-environment barriers. Effect size not reported.
Bjørnarå et al. (2019)	From cars to bikes – The effect of an intervention providing access to different bike types: A randomized controlled trial	Adults with children	Norway	35 (I=18, C=17)	RCT	2	Yes	Cycling, all purposes	Mode choice for several trip purposes as days per week Cycling time and distance using a bicycle computer (aggregate values)	Direct	Significant effect of intervention on cycling	Significant effect only with intrinsic motivation, no effect of all other psychological determinants

(continued)

Table 6 Summary of included studies. (*cont'd*)

Author	Title	Population	Country	Sample size	Study design	Number of arms (incl. control)	Control groups	Target behaviour	Measurement of behaviour	Analysis method	Effect on active travel	Effect on psychological factors
Buttazzoni et al. (2019)	Promoting active school travel in elementary schools: A regional case study of the school travel planning intervention	Children (9–14)	Canada	2084	Cross-sectional (two surveys, before and after)	1	No	Active commuting to school	Self-reported active transport, days per week for all trips from/to school	Direct	No significant increases in active commuting trips from baseline to follow-up, although trends toward more active travel and fewer car trips were observed, after controlling for key predictors of school travel	Children reported significant improvements in self-efficacy for walking and cycling. Reductions in barriers (social, convenience, and safety-related) to active school travel were reported. They also perceived fewer physical environment barriers and noted improvements in cycling skills and route features such as access to sidewalks, bike lanes, and tree-lined streets.

Christiansen et al. (2014)	Effects of a Danish multicomponent physical activity intervention on active school transport	Adolescents (mean age 12)	Denmark	1014 (I=598, C=681)	RCT (Level = Schools)	2	Yes	Active commuting to school	Self-reported active transport, days per week for all trips from/to school	Direct	No influence of intervention on behavior change	Only borderline significance of changing attitudes
Darker et al. (2010)	An intervention to promote walking amongst the general population based on an 'extended' theory of planned behaviour: a waiting list randomised controlled trial.	Adults	United Kingdom	118 (I=58, C=60)	RCT	2	Yes	Walking, all purposes	Walking with pedometer, measured as minutes per day Intention to walk	Mediation	The intervention led to a large and significant increase in objectively measured walking time and steps, with participants walking over 60% more per day than controls. While walking levels slightly declined by the final follow-up, they remained *significantly higher* than at baseline, indicating a sustained improvement. Similar patterns were observed in the control group after receiving the intervention later.	The intervention significantly improved control beliefs, attitude, perceived behavioral control (PBC), and intention, with large effect sizes for all except control beliefs (medium). While subjective norms and normative beliefs did not change, PBC and attitude partially mediated the intervention's effect on intention, and PBC alone significantly mediated the intervention's effect on walking behavior. Intention and action planning did not mediate behavior change.

(continued)

Table 6 Summary of included studies. (*cont'd*)

Author	Title	Population	Country	Sample size	Study design	Number of arms (incl. control)	Control groups	Target behaviour	Measurement of behaviour	Analysis method	Effect on active travel	Effect on psychological factors
Ek et al. (2020)	Effectiveness of a 3-Month Mobile Phone–Based Behavior Change Program on Active Transportation and Physical Activity in Adults: Randomized Controlled Trial	Adults aged (20–65 years)	Sweden	208 (I=107, C=111)	RCT	2	Yes	Physical activity, all trip purposes Active transportation, all trip purposes	Accelerometer Active transportation measured through tracking in app	Direct	No difference between control and treatment group at 3 months, significant effects after 6 months.	No significant change in attitudes towards walking and cycling
Fjeldsoe et al. (2013)	Social cognitive mediators of the effect of the MobileMums intervention on physical activity.	Adults (female, post-partum < 12 months)	Australia	88 (61 at follow-up)	RCT	2	Yes	Walking for exercise Physical activity for exercise	Self-reported walking for exercise (multiple items) and physical activity (single item)	Mediation	The intervention led to significant increases in both moderate-to-vigorous physical activity (MVPA) and walking for exercise, particularly during the first six weeks.	The intervention successfully improved some key psychological factors (barrier self-efficacy and goal setting). They did not statistically explain the effect of the intervention on physical activity

Geng et al. (2016)	Impact of information intervention on travel mode choice of urban residents with different goal frames: A controlled trial in Xuzhou, China	Adults	China	392 (Group 1 =165, Group 2 =152, Group 3 =135)	RCT	2	Yes	Walking and cycling, for all trip purposes	Self-reported time spent in different modes of transport for two weeks	Direct	Those previously less engaged in active travel and public transport increased use of all green modes, individuals already frequent users of active travel and public transport showed smaller but consistent increases, and participants whose travel choices were primarily driven by comfort mainly increased non-powered bicycle use.	The information intervention significantly improved cognitive and affective attitudes across all groups. Participants who were previously less engaged in active travel and public transport (Gain-GF) showed the largest attitude improvements, while already frequent users (Green-GF) and those driven mainly by comfort (Hedonic-GF) also reported smaller but consistent attitude gains.
Gilbert et al. (2021)	Do Framed Mental Health Messages on Social Media Influence University Students' Motivation for Physical Activity?	Adults	United Kingdom	147 (GF=50,-LF=49,-C=48)	RCT	3	Yes	Motivation for physical activity; motivation for exercise; motivation for active travel; physical activation	Motivation: Likert scale Physical activity: Self-reported using IPAQ, minutes per weeks	Direct	No significant effect of intervention on walking nor PA	Xignificant effect of intervention on motivation

(continued)

Table 6 Summary of included studies. (*cont'd*)

Author	Title	Population	Country	Sample size	Study design	Number of arms (incl. control)	Control groups	Target behaviour	Measurement of behaviour	Analysis method	Effect on active travel	Effect on psychological factors
Hardcastle et al. (2012)	The effectiveness of a motivational interviewing primary-care based intervention on physical activity and predictors of change in a disadvantaged community.	Adults	United States	207	Longitudinal	1	No	Physical activity and the different components thereof (incl. walking)	Self-reported using IPAQ, minutes per week	Direct	Significant influence of number of sessions on walking time	Significance reported; significant influence of: perceived behavior control, attitudes and social support
Hardeman et al. (2011)	Theory of planned behaviour cognitions do not predict self-reported or objective physical activity levels or change in the ProActive trial.	Adults	United Kingdom	365 (psychological factors: 252)	Longitudinal	3	No	Physical activity Walking for leisure and work-related activity	Physical activity: heart-rate monitoring Walking: self-reported questionnaire (EPAQ2)	Mediation	Significant influence of intervention on PA (brisk walking)	No significant effect on behavior

Huang et al. (2022)	Physical Activity and Social Support to Promote a Health-Promoting Lifestyle in Older Adults: An Intervention Study	Older adults (mean age 70)	Taiwan	60 (I1 =20,-I2 =20,-CG=20)	RCT	3	Yes	Physical activity (walking)	Pedometer using a wristband device	Direct	Supervised group walking led to the highest average daily steps and calorie consumption, particularly on weekdays, followed by independent walking while the control group remained largely sedentary, confirming that structured walking interventions promote healthier activity levels in older adults.	After eight weeks, both intervention groups, especially the supervised group, showed significantly higher scores in social support on the Health Promotion Lifestyle Scale,
Joseph et al. (2023)	Smart Walk: A Culturally Tailored Smartphone-Delivered Physical Activity Intervention for Cardiometa-bolic Risk Reduction among African American Women	adults (female)	United States	60	RCT	2	Yes	Physical activity	Self-reported physical activty (Exercise Vital Sign Questionnaire) Accelerometer	Direct	Significant influence only on self reported PA after 8 months	Significant influence - only on capability

(continued)

Table 6 Summary of included studies. (*cont'd*)

Author	Title	Population	Country	Sample size	Study design	Number of arms (incl. control)	Control groups	Target behaviour	Measurement of behaviour	Analysis method	Effect on active travel	Effect on psychological factors
Kearns et al. (2019)	Increasing cycling for transportation through mentorship programs	Adults	Canada	146	Longitudinal	1	No	Cycling, all trip purposes	Mode usage as expressed as days per week for different modes of transport	Direct	Participants significantly increased their cycling for shopping and work/school trips after the intervention, while walking and public transport as a mode of transport to these destinations decreased.	Participants showed significant gains in cycling confidence, perceived safety, and visibility of women cyclists, with smaller or no changes in utility perceptions and cultural attitudes.
Lanzendorf et al. (2022)	Implementing bicycle-friendly transport policies: Examining the effect of an infrastructural intervention on residents' perceived quality of urban life in Frankfurt, Germany	adults	Germany	274	Cross-sectional (two surveys, before and after)	1	No	Cycling, all trip purposes	Mode use along street with intervention, as expressed as using mode in a given week	Direct	respondents reported higher levels of car use and cycling, lower levels of walking and public transport	Significant influence on attitudes Respondents reported lowerlevels of safety, endangerment and higher levels of quality of life

Lee et al. (2012)	The effect of an intervention combining self-efficacy theory and pedometers on promoting physical activity among adolescents.	Adolescents (female)	Taiwan	94 (I=46, C=48)	RCT	2	Yes	Phsyical activity	Pedometer	Direct	Yes: adolescents in the SPAA-G intervention significantly increased their number of daily aerobic steps compared to the control group, after adjusting for baseline factors, while the control group showed a decrease in steps.	No: no significant differences between groups in perceived exercise self-efficacy.
Moffitt and Mohr (2015)	The efficacy of a self-managed Acceptance and Commitment Therapy intervention DVD for physical activity initiation.	Adults	United States	59 (I = 32, C=27)	RCT	2	Yes	Walking; Physical activity	Pedometer; Self-reported physical activity using IPAQ	Direct	Participants in both groups increased their physical activity over the course of the program, but those in the intervention group showed greater improvements in total activity levels and were more likely to reach recommended guidelines post-intervention. Step count data also showed that intervention participants maintained higher activity levels across the 12 weeks than the control group.	The interventon group showed slightly higher average scores in goal commitment, attainment, and satisfaction, these differences were not statistically significant.

(continued)

Table 6 Summary of included studies. (*cont'd*)

Author	Title	Population	Country	Sample size	Study design	Number of arms (incl. control)	Control groups	Target behaviour	Measurement of behaviour	Analysis method	Effect on active travel	Effect on psychological factors
Nachman and Rodriguez (2023)	Evaluating the Effects of a Classroom-Based Bicycle Education Intervention on Bicycle Activity, Self-Efficacy, Personal Safety, Knowledge, and Mode Choice	Adults	United States	158	Quasi-experimental study	2	Yes	Cycling Physical actitvty (cycling)	Cycling tracking with app; IPAQ for cycling	Direct	No effect of intervention on days cycled or mode choice	Intervention has effect on self-efficacy and knowledge
Olsson et al. (2021)	Integrating Planned Behavior and Stage-of-Change into a Cycling Campaign	Adults	Sweden	172	Quasi-experimental study	3	No	Cycling	Self-reported mode use for commutes	Direct	All three nudges were associated with increased cycling over time, and while the financial nudge appears to have performed slightly better descriptively, the differences between nudge types were not statistically significant.	Changes in perceived behavioral control and initial stage of change significantly predicted progress in stage of change, while the nudging conditions and changes in other psychological factors had no significant effect.

Ory et al. (2018)	Effectiveness of a Lifestyle Intervention on Social Support, Self-Efficacy, and Physical Activity among Older Adults: Evaluation of Texercise Select.	Adults aged 45 years or older	United States	182 at 6 months	Quasi-experimental study	2	Yes	Physical inactivity	Self-reported physical activvy using IIPAQ.	Direct	The intervention group increased their moderate and vigorous activity at both three and six months, while the comparison group showed only a temporary gain in light activity at three months.	The intervention group showed greater improvements in social support and self-efficacy for physical activity than the comparison group, with more participants reporting positive changes.
Panter and Ogilvie (2015)	Theorising and testing environ-mental pathways to behaviour change: natural experimental study of the perception and use of new infrastructure to promote walking and cycling in local communi-ties.	Adults	United Kingdom	967	Longitu-dinal Study	1	No	Walking and cycling for transport for several trip purpose Physical activity	Self-reported journeys; physical activity questionnaire	Mediation	The new infrastructure led to increased walking and cycling primarily through greater use of the new routes by those living nearby (proximity).	While perceptions of improved infrastructure, visibility, and safety were influenced by proximity and linked to route use, these psychological changes explained only a small part of the overall behaviour change.

(continued)

Table 6 Summary of included studies. (*cont'd*)

Author	Title	Population	Country	Sample size	Study design	Number of arms (incl. control)	Control groups	Target behaviour	Measurement of behaviour	Analysis method	Effect on active travel	Effect on psychological factors
Prestwich et al. (2010)	Can implementation intentions and text messages promote brisk walking? A randomized trial.	Adults	United Kingdom	134 (I1 =40, I2 =48, C=46)	RCT	3	Yes	Physical activity	Self-reported physical activty (IPAQ and SWET)	Direct	Yes: Both intervention groups (implementation intentions + plan reminders and implementation intentions + goal reminders) significantly increased the number of days participants met physical activity guidelines compared to the control group. The plan reminder group also showed a marginal increase in overall physical activity. Thus, both text-supported intention strategies improved walking behavior, with the plan reminder condition showing the strongest effect.	Plan and goal recall were assessed in a follow-up recall task. Participants in the plan reminder group remembered their walking plans better than the goal reminder group, while the goal reminder group had better recall of their overall walking goals. Only plan recall was linked to increased brisk walking.

Prestwich et al. (2012)	Randomized controlled trial of collaborative implementa-tion intentions targeting working adults' physical activity.	Adults	United Kingdom	204 pairs	RCT	4	Yes	Phsyical activity	Self-reported physical activty (IPAQ and SWET)	Mediation	Yes: Collaborative implementation intentions resulted in the largest gains in physical-activity frequency and duration across all follow-ups, outperforming both individual plans and partner-only support, while the partner-only condition showed the smallest improvement, behind the control group at six months.	Psychological factors: Partner-based conditions (collaborative and partner-only) boosted perceived social influence, but neither intervention altered enjoyment or self-efficacy; partner groups even showed weaker immediate intentions than individual planners; none of the proposed mediators explained the behaviour changes.
Stark et al. (2018)	The effectiveness of an intervention to promote active travel modes in early adolescence	Adolesce-nts	Austria	169	Experim-ent (RCT)	2	Yes	Walking and cycling, all trip purposes	Self-report mode choice derived from one week travel diary	Mediation	Yes, reported	Yes, reported, significant effect of attitude, PBC, intention only for walking (not cycling).

(continued)

Table 6 Summary of included studies. (*cont'd*)

Author	Title	Population	Country	Sample size	Study design	Number of arms (incl. control)	Control groups	Target behaviour	Measurement of behaviour	Analysis method	Effect on active travel	Effect on psychological factors
Van Hoecke et al. (2014)	The long-term effectiveness of need-supportive physical activity counseling compared with a standard referral in sedentary older adults.	Adults aged 60 years or older	The Netherlands	422	Experiment (RCT)	3	No	Walking; Physical activity	Pedometer; Self-reported physical activity for leisure activities	Direct	All three groups (REFER, WALK, COACH) significantly increased their physical activity levels immediately post-intervention. By follow-up, only WALK and COACH maintained increases in step counts, while REFER showed no change. Despite these improvements, differences between the groups were no longer statistically significant at follow-up.	Perceived need-support was high across all groups, but significantly higher in COACH compared to REFER, reflecting the greater personal interaction and support built into the COACH condition. Autonomous motivation (AM) increased significantly over time across all participants, regardless of group. - differences in AM between groups, and no interaction effect by time and condition.

van Stralen et al. (2010)	Exploring the efficacy and moderators of two computer-tailored physical activity interventions for older adults: a randomized controlled trial.	Older adults	The Netherla-nds	1971	Expe-im-ent (RCT)	3	Yes	Walking and cycling for transport; Physical activity, leisure	Self-reported physical activity, leisure Minutes of two transport activities (i.e., walking and cycling)	Direct	Yes, significant effect of intervention 2	Yes, reported, no significant interaction effects, except for intention.
Walsh et al. (2021)	Commuter Choices: A clustered, quasi-experimental trial of a social cognitive approach to increasing active commuting among office workers	Working adults	Australia	68 (I=48, C=20)	Quasi-Experim-ental Study	2	Yes	Active travel	Main mode: Mode covering the most distance in the reporting week. Active commuting per week: sum of self-reported minutes spent walking, running, or cycling across all commuting trips.	Direct	The intervention group significantly increased average daily active commuting by 9.3 min per day compared to the comparison group; they were also more likely to achieve sufficient physical activity (PA) from commuting, including reaching 80% of PA guidelines through commuting. The comparison group saw a small, non-significant decrease in AC.	The intervention group showed significant increases in self-regulation and social support post-intervention. Self-efficacy was higher in the comparison group both at baseline and post-intervention, with no significant change due to the intervention. - between-group differences were observed in outcome expectations.

(continued)

Table 6 Summary of included studies. (*cont'd*)

Author	Title	Population	Country	Sample size	Study design	Number of arms (incl. control)	Control groups	Target behaviour	Measurement of behaviour	Analysis method	Effect on active travel	Effect on psychological factors
Williams et al. (2015)	The effects of a brief intervention to promote walking on Theory of Planned Behavior constructs: a cluster randomized controlled trial in general practice.	Adults 16–65, sedentary, with chronic conditons	United Kingdom	231 (I=94,-C=137)	RCT	2	Yes	Walking, all trip purposes	Pedometer; intentions to walk	Direct	No effect: There were no significant differences in objectively measured walking minutes between the intervention and control groups at any time point (post-intervention, 6 weeks, or 6 months).	Perceived behavioral control predicted intention to walk more across all time points, with attitude contributing at 6 months, while subjective norms showed no unique effect. There were no significant differences between groups in intention or objectively measured walking at any time point; although the intervention group reported slightly higher walking minutes, the differences were small and not statistically significant.

studies in which participants are randomly assigned to different groups. Longitudinal studies (n = 4) followed the same participants over time to observe changes, while quasi-experimental studies (n = 4) resembled experimental designs but lacked random assignment. Finally, cross-sectional studies (n = 2) measured behaviour at a single point in time across different individuals.

4.4 Target behaviour & measurement

The most frequently studied behaviour was physical activity (n = 14), followed by studies including cycling (n = 5), and walking (n = 5). A smaller number of studies focused explicitly on active travel more broadly (n = 5), typically in the context of school commuting (n = 3). Several studies also examined combined walking and cycling for all trip purposes. Physical activity was often measured in conjunction with walking, followed by cycling.

The methods used to measure these behaviours varied, reflecting the distinct traditions of physical activity and transport research.

For physical activity studies, self-report measures were most common (n = 12), including standardised questionnaires such as the International Physical Activity Questionnaire (IPAQ) and the Self-report Walking and Exercise Tables (SWET), but also single-item scales. Objective measures were also used: pedometers (n = 4) and accelerometers (n = 2) provided step counts or overall activity minutes. Some studies combined self-reports with devices, such as pairing questionnaires with accelerometer data.

For cycling behaviour, self-report tools were again prevalent (n = 4), including trip frequency surveys and cycling diaries. A few studies used objective tools, such as cycling tracking apps (n = 1) or bicycle computers to capture distance and duration (n = 1). Walking was typically measured through pedometers (n = 4) or self-reported trip frequency and purpose (n = 4).

For active travel (walking, cycling, and other modes for utilitarian purposes), self-reported mode choice was the dominant method (n = 4), often recorded via transportation diaries or coded as most prevalent mode of transport. Some studies combined these self-reports with accelerometer data or app-based tracking (n = 2).

When setting the target behaviour and the measurement methods next to each other, it becomes apparent that a distinction can be made between two types of studies: transport-oriented studies and studies focusing on physical exercises.

Transport-oriented studies focused on travel behaviour and modal choice,examining how often and why individuals choose walking or cycling for transport purposes. Measurement methods in these studies typically included self-reported mode choice for specific trips (e.g., commuting to school or work), trip frequency (e.g., days per week walking or cycling for various purposes), travel diaries, or recall surveys for a typical week. Some studies also captured mode usage for specific streets or routes, such as whether participants used a new bike lane (Lanzendorf et al., 2022). A few employed objective tracking tools such as bicycle computers or apps to record cycling time and distance (Bjørnarå et al., 2019; Nachman and Rodriguez, 2023). Other studies in this category include Aranda-Balboa et al. (2022), Buttazzoni et al. (2019), Christiansen et al. (2014), Olsson et al. (2021), and Stark et al. (2018), who focused on self-reported mode choice and trip frequency for walking and cycling. Geng et al. (2016) and Kearns et al. (2019) also examined days per week using various modes; Walsh et al. (2021) assessed active commuting using both main mode and total weekly minutes of active commuting.

Physical activity-oriented studies targeted overall physical activity, often regardless of trip purpose, focusing on total activity levels and health outcomes. Measurement methods in these studies included self-reported physical activity questionnaires (e.g., IPAQ, SWEC).

Some studies addressed both transport and physical outcomes, measuring walking and cycling for transport and leisure purposes with multiple methods. For example, Panter and Ogilvie (2015) and van Stralen et al. (2010) assessed self-reported journeys and physical activity. Ek et al. (2020) used accelerometers alongside app-based tracking to capture comprehensive movement data across purposes.

4.5 Interventions per study and presence of control group

While each study evaluated at least one intervention, several assessed multiple intervention arms. Out of the 28 included studies, 23 examined two or more interventions (i.e. two interventions: n = 15; three interventions: n = 7, four interventions: n = 1). Among these, 20 studies employed a control group, enabling comparative analysis between intervention and non-intervention conditions. The remaining three studies, although lacking a control group, made a clear distinction between two separate interventions. Five studies investigated a single intervention without a control group.

4.6 Employed intervention functions

Table 7 provides an overview of the intervention functions employed in each study. Across all studies, the most frequently used intervention functions were education (n = 18), planning (n = 15), goal setting (n = 14), persuasion (n = 14), followed by training (n = 11), and social support (n = 10). Less frequently used were enablement (n = 8), feedback & monitoring (n = 7), incentivisation and modelling (each n = 5), and environmental restructuring (n = 4). Notably, coercion and restriction were not employed in any of the included studies.

Fig. 3 presents the distribution of intervention function use across all studies and stratified by intervention complexity. We distinguished between studies with a single-function intervention arm and those with a multiple-function intervention arm. In this analysis we included only studies that either had no control group or had just two arms (one active intervention and one control). This approach ensured that the distinction between single and multiple functions was clear without the added complexity of interventions with multiple arms.

The multiple-functions category included 16 studies where the active intervention arm contained more than one function. In contrast, the single-function group was comprised of four studies in which the active intervention was based on a single, standalone function. For comparison, we also show the distribution across the full population of 28 studies included in the analysis. Thus, eight studies were not included in either the single- or multiple-function categories due to their multi-arm study design (Gilbert et al., 2021; Hardeman et al., 2011; Huang et al., 2022; Olsson et al., 2021; Prestwich et al., 2010, 2012; Van Hoecke et al., 2014; van Stralen et al., 2010).

The figure shows that functions such as education, goal setting, and planning were predominantly used in multi-function interventions, whereas enablement and environmental restructuring were among the few that appeared in both multi- and single-function contexts.

Continuing with the studies that employed multiple interventions functions (studies either having no control group or having one intervention and one control; n = 16), the number of intervention functions combined within individual studies varied considerably. Across all included studies, interventions employed between two and eight distinct functions. The most common number of functions used was four, with a total of 44% of studies employing five or more functions. This suggests

Table 7 Summary of intervention functions employed in included studies.

Author	Number of arms (incl. control)	Single or multiple functions per arm	Control groups	Education	Goal setting	Persuasion	Planning	Training	Social Support	Enablement	Feedback & Monitoring	Incentivisation	Modelling	Environmental restructuring	Coercion	Restriction
Aranda-Balboa et al. (2022)	2	Multiple	Yes	✓	—	—	—	✓	—	—	—	—	—	—	—	—
Bjørnarå et al. (2019)	2	Single	Yes	—	—	—	—	—	—	✓	—	—	—	—	—	—
Buttazzoni et al. (2019)	1	Multiple	No	✓	—	✓	—	✓	—	—	—	—	—	✓	—	—
Christiansen et al. (2014)	2	Multiple	Yes	✓	✓	—	—	✓	—	—	—	—	✓	✓	—	—
Darker et al. (2010)	2	Multiple	Yes	—	✓	—	✓	—	—	✓	—	—	—	—	—	—
Duvall (2012)	2	Multiple	Yes	✓	✓	—	✓	—	—	—	✓	—	—	—	—	—
Ek et al. (2020)	2	Multiple	Yes	✓	✓	✓	✓	—	✓	✓	—	—	—	—	—	—

Fjeldsoe et al. (2013)	2	Multiple	Yes	✓	✓	✓	—	—	—	—	—	—	—	—	—	—
Geng et al. (2016)	3	Single	Yes	—	—	✓	—	—	—	—	—	—	—	—	—	—
Gilbert et al. (2021)	1	Multiple	No	—	✓	✓	✓	—	✓	—	—	—	—	—	—	—
Hardcastle et al. (2012)	3	Multiple	No	—	—	✓	—	—	—	✓	—	—	✓	—	—	—
Hardeman et al. (2011)	3	Multiple	Yes	—	—	—	—	—	✓	—	✓	—	—	—	—	—
Huang et al. (2022)	2	Multiple	Yes	✓	✓	✓	✓	✓	✓	✓	—	—	—	—	—	—
Joseph et al. (2023)	1	Multiple	No	✓	✓	—	✓	✓	✓	—	✓	✓	✓	—	—	—
Kearns et al. (2019)	1	Single	No	—	—	—	—	—	—	—	—	—	—	✓	—	—
Lanzendorf et al. (2022)	2	Multiple	Yes	✓	✓	✓	✓	✓	✓	—	✓	✓	—	—	—	—
Lee et al. (2012)	2	Multiple	Yes	✓	✓	—	✓	✓	—	✓	—	—	—	—	—	—

(continued)

Table 7 Summary of intervention functions employed in included studies. *(cont'd)*

Author	Number of arms (incl. control)	Single or multiple functions per arm	Control groups	Education	Goal setting	Persuasion	Planning	Training	Social Support	Enablement	Feedback & *Monitoring*	Incenti-visation	Modelling	Environ-mental restruc-turing	Coercion	Restri-ction
Manca et al. (2022)	2	Single	Yes	✓	—	—	—	—	—	—	—	—	—	—	—	—
Mendoza et al. (2011)	3	Single	No	—	—	✓	—	—	✓	—	—	✓	✓	—	—	—
Moffitt and Mohr (2015)	2	Multiple	Yes	—	✓	—	✓	✓	—	—	—	—	—	—	—	—
Nachman and Rodrigu-ez, (2023)	1	Single	No	—	—	—	—	—	—	—	—	—	—	✓	—	—
Olsson et al. (2021)	3	Multiple	Yes	✓	✓	✓	✓	—	—	—	✓	—	—	—	—	—
Ory et al. (2018)	4	Multiple	Yes	✓	—	✓	✓	—	✓	—	—	—	—	—	—	—
Panter and Ogilvie (2015)	2	Multiple	Yes	✓	—	✓	—	—	—	✓	✓	—	—	—	—	—

Prestwich et al. (2010)	3	Multiple	No	✓	—	—	✓	✓	✓	✓	✓	—	—	—	—	—
Prestwich et al. (2012)	3	Multiple	Yes	—	—	✓	✓	—	—	—	—	—	✓	—	—	—
Stark et al. (2018)	2	Multiple	Yes	✓	✓	—	✓	✓	✓	—	—	—	—	—	—	—
Steffen et al. (2024)	2	Multiple	Yes	✓	✓	✓	✓	—	—	—	—	—	—	—	—	—

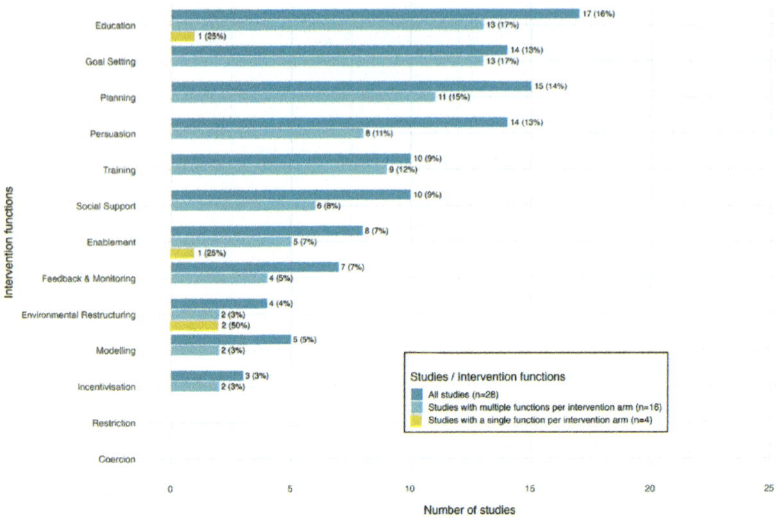

Fig. 3 Intervention functions analysed in the included studies (n = 28), shown for three groups: all included studies, studies with multiple intervention functions per intervention arm, and studies with a single intervention function per intervention arm. Bars indicate the number of studies analysing each intervention function; percentages indicate the proportion of all-intervention funcation assessments within each study group.

that while some interventions relied on a single function, multi-component approaches incorporating multiple behaviour change functions were more typical.

Fig. 4 presents a two-dimensional analysis of the co-occurrence of predefined intervention functions across this selection of studies. Education emerged as the most frequently co-occurring function, appearing alongside a wide range of other functions. It was most often combined with goal setting (n = 10), planning (n = 8), persuasion (n = 7), and training (n = 7), highlighting its central role in multi-component interventions. The most frequent pairing overall was goal setting and planning (n = 11), followed closely by planning and training (n = 7) and goal setting and training (n = 7). Other common combinations included persuasion and planning (n = 5) and education and social support (n = 5), suggesting a pattern of integrating informational strategies with goal-directed and supportive elements.

4.7 Evaluated psychological factors

Across the included studies, we distinguish between studies that measured psychological factors as part of secondary outcomes (i.e., reporting direct

Fig. 4 Combinations of intervention functions of studies employing multiple intervention functions in a single intervention arm (n = 16). Larger bubbles indicate more frequent co-occurence of intervention functions.

effects), and those that conducted formal mediation analysis. While many studies collected data on psychological factors, fewer used mediation analysis to test how these factors explain behaviour change (n = 6). An overview of the factors studied in each study is provided in Table 8. Fig. 5 provides a graphical overview of the studies, stratified by analysis method: studies that reported psychological factors as secondary outcomes (direct effects), and those that conducted formal mediation analyses.

The most frequently investigated psychological factors were attitudes (n = 21), social influence (n = 17), and perceived control and barriers (n = 13). These factors were also often included in mediation analyses. Likewise, self-efficacy (n = 12) was frequently studied. Less frequently investigated factors were motivation (n = 8), information/skills (n = 6), planning and self-regulation (n = 6), and intention (n = 5). The least frequently included were coping skills (n = 3) and habits/automatic processes

Table 8 Measured psychological factors and their significance.

Author	Analysis method	Problem awareness	Attitudes & emotions	Intention	Planning & self-regulation	Self-efficacy	Perceived control & barriers	Social influence	Coping skills & relapse prevention	Habits & automatic processes	Information & skills
Aranda-Balboa et al. (2022)	Direct	—	n.s.	—	—	—	s	n.s.	—	—	s
Bjørnarå et al. (2019)	Direct	—	n.s.	—	—	—	n.s.	—	—	—	—
Buttazzoni et al. (2019)	Direct	—	s	—	—	s	s	s	—	—	s
Christiansen et al. (2014)	Direct	—	s	—	—	—	—	—	—	—	—
Darker et al. (2010)	Mediation	—	m	m	m	—	m	m	—	—	—
Duvall (2012)	Direct	—	n.s.	—	—	—	—	—	—	—	—
Ek et al. (2020)	Mediation	—	—	—	m	m	m	m	—	—	—

Fjeldsoe et al. (2013)	Direct	—	s	—	—	—	—	—	—	—	—
Geng et al. (2016)	Direct	—	—	—	—	—	—	—	—	—	—
Gilbert et al. (2021)	Direct	—	s	—	n.s.	n.s.	s	s	—	—	—
Hardcastle et al. (2012)	Mediation	—	m	—	—	—	m	m	—	—	—
Hardeman et al. (2011)	Direct	—	s	—	—	—	—	s	s	—	—
Huang et al. (2022)	Direct	—	n.s.	—	n.s.	n.s.	s	s	—	—	s
Joseph et al. (2023)	Direct	—	n.s.	—	—	s	—	s	—	—	n.s.
Kearns et al. (2019)	Direct	—	s	—	—	—	—	—	—	—	—
Lanzendorf et al. (2022)	Direct	—	—	—	—	n.s.	—	—	—	—	—

(continued)

Table 8 Measured psychological factors and their significance. (*cont'd*)

Author	Analysis method	Problem awareness	Attitudes & emotions	Intention	Planning & self-regulation	Self-efficacy	Perceived control & barriers	Social influence	Coping skills & relapse prevention	Habits & automatic processes	Information & skills
Lee et al. (2012)	Direct	—	n.s.	—	—	—	—	—	n.s.	—	—
Manca et al. (2022)	Direct	—	—	—	—	s	—	—	—	—	s
Mendoza et al. (2011)	Direct	—	s	—	—	—	s	n.s.	—	—	—
Moffitt and Mohr (2015)	Direct	—	—	—	—	s	—	s	—	—	—
Nachman and Rodrigu-ez (2023)	Mediation	—	m	—	—	—	m	m	—	—	—
Olsson et al. (2021)	Direct	—	—	—	—	—	—	—	—	s	—
Ory et al. (2018)	Mediation	—	m	m	—	m	—	m	—	—	—

Panter and Ogilvie (2015))	Mediation	—	m	m	—	—	m	m	—	—	—
Prestwich et al. (2010)	Direct	—	m	—	m	m	m	m	m	—	m
Prestwich et al. (2012)	Direct	—	—	s	—	—	—	—	—	—	—
Stark et al. (2018)	Direct	—	n.s.	—	s	n.s.	—	n.s.	—	—	—
Steffen et al. (2024)	Direct	—	n.s.	s	—	—	n.s.	s	—	—	—

S = reported significant effect, n.s. = no significant effect, m = measured and evaluated separately (mediation analysis).

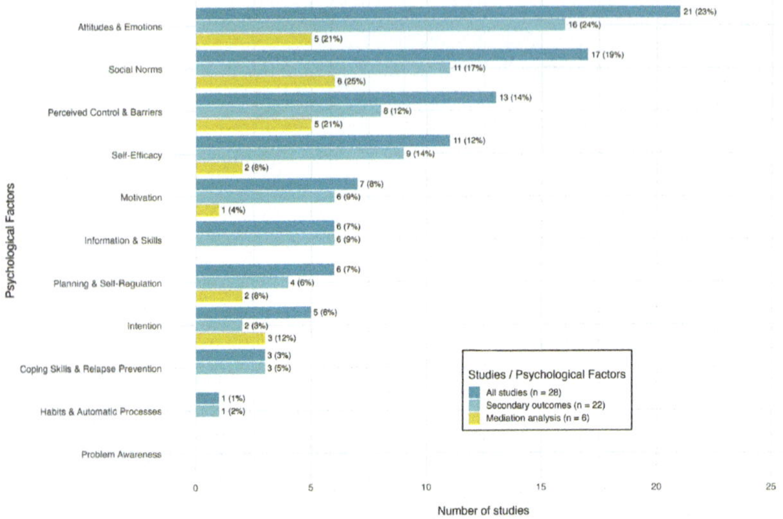

Fig. 5 Psychological factors evaluated in the included studies (n = 28) shown for three groups: all included studies, studies that assessed psychological factors as secondary outcomes, and studies that conducted mediation analysis. Bars indicate the number of studies evaluating each psychological factor; percentages indicate the proportion of all factor assessments within each study group.

(n = 1). With the exception of habits/automatic processes, all of these factors were included at least once in a mediation analysis. Problem awareness was not evaluated in any of the included studies.

4.8 Methods to analyse effects

In evaluating the effectiveness of behaviour change interventions targeting active travel and physical activity, we examined both the overall outcomes and the methods used to identify these effects. Specifically, we classified studies based on whether they assessed direct effects only, that is, whether the intervention led to behaviour change without examining why, or whether they tested mediation models to identify mechanisms of action. For example, a study using bootstrapped mediation analysis (Preacher and Hayes, 2004, 2008) might test whether an intervention increases self-efficacy, which in turn increases walking behaviour. Other studies used structural equation modelling (SEM) to evaluate more complex, simultaneous pathways. Of the included studies, 22 assessed direct effects only without testing mediation, while three studies used bootstrapped mediation analysis, one study applied the Sobel test, and three studies employed structural equation modelling (SEM) to examine mediation pathways.

4.9 Evaluating effects: Intervention functions and primary outcomes

Continuing with the analysis of studies that either had two arms (one of which a control group) and studies with a single intervention arm, Fig. 6 presents a breakdown of intervention functions across the included studies. The left figure shows the number of studies that reported a significant effect on mobility outcomes for each intervention function, while the right-hand side displays the overall number of occurrences of each function in the included studies regardless of statistical significance.

Among studies employing multiple functions (n = 16), some functions were more frequently associated with studies reporting significant effects. For example, planning appeared in 11 studies, with 10 of these reporting significant results. Similarly, goal setting was present in 13 studies, with 11 showing significant effects. Education was also commonly used, featuring in 14 studies, of which nine reported significant outcomes. Other functions, including persuasion, training, and enablement, were also present in studies with and without reported effects, persuasion in eight studies (five significant), training in nine studies (six significant), and enablement in five studies (four significant). Functions such as feedback & monitoring (four studies, three significant) and incentivization (two studies, both significant) were less frequently included but often showed positive results. In contrast, modelling (two studies, one significant) and environmental restructuring (two studies, none significant) appeared less frequently and showed more mixed patterns of effectiveness.

For studies employing single-function interventions (n = 4), the numbers were much smaller. Here, enablement, incentivization, and environmental restructuring each appeared in just one or two studies. While these single-function studies generally reported positive effects, the small sample size makes it difficult to draw broader conclusions.

4.10 Significance of psychological factors as secondary outcomes

Fig. 7 presents the combinations of intervention functions and psychological factors measured across the included studies. A total of 48 function–factor combinations were identified where psychological factors were explicitly measured and considered to be relevant for the intervention functions according to theoretical conceptualization (see Table 3). Of these, 26 combinations reported statistically significant results.

The most frequently targeted factor was attitudes and emotions, measured in 16 combinations, with six showing significant results – mainly

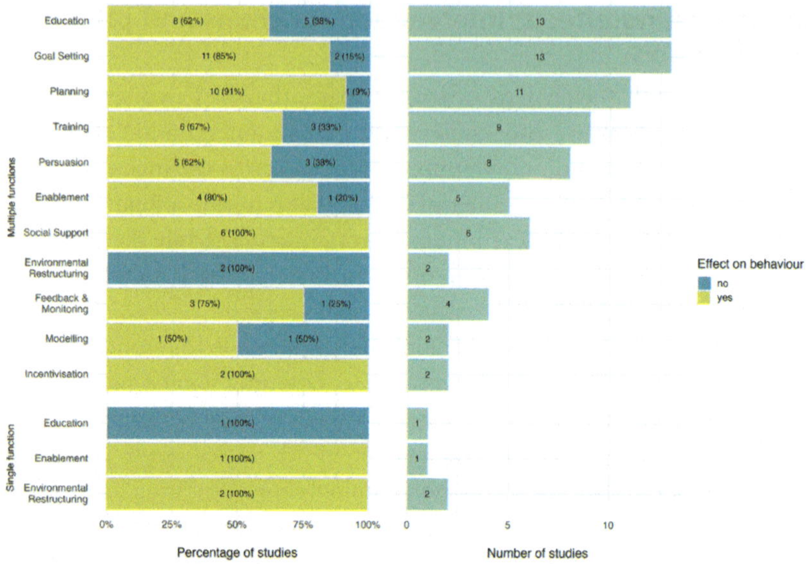

Fig. 6 Effects on behaviour by intervention function, shown separately for interventions with multiple functions and those with a single function. The left panel shows the percentage and number of studies reporting an effect or no effect on behaviour for each intervention function. The right panel shows the total number of studies evaluating each intervention function.

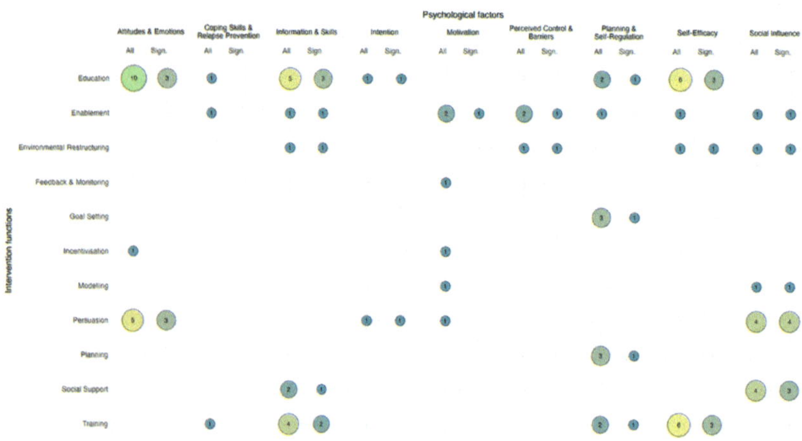

Fig. 7 Combinations of intervention functions and psychological factors in studies only reporting secondary outcomes (n = 16).

using the intervention function education. The second most targeted factor was self-efficacy, measured in 14 combinations across various intervention functions, with seven combinations showing significant effects, targeted either through training or education. Information and skills were measured in 13 combinations, with eight showing significant effects. Planning and self-regulation appeared in 11 combinations, with four showing significant effects. Perceived control and barriers were measured in three combinations, two of which showed significant effects.

Social influence was targeted in 10 combinations, with nine of these showing significant effects – in studies employing persuasion or social support as intervention functions. Motivation was targeted in six combinations, with one study reporting significant effects. Intention was measured in two combinations, both significant. Coping skills and relapse prevention appeared in three combinations, but none showed significant effects.

4.11 Significance of psychological factors with mediation analysis

Out of the 28 studies included in this review six studies investigated mediation of interventions effects through psychological factors on changes in mobility behaviour. These studies are presented in Table 5.

Based on the theoretical conceptions of the TPB, Darker et al. (2010) investigated the influence of an intervention that combined the intervention functions of enablement, goal setting and action planning on walking. The intervention significantly improved attitude perceived behavioural control (PBC), and intention. While subjective norms did not change, PBC and attitude partially mediated the intervention's effect on intention. PBC alone significantly mediated the intervention's effect on walking behaviour. Intention and action planning did not mediate behaviour change.

Fjeldsoe et al. (2013) investigated the impact of mediating psychological variables of multi-component intervention – including the six intervention functions education, persuasion, goal setting, planning and social support. The intervention was designed to increase walking among postnatal women. Both, control and intervention groups received the education intervention function. The intervention successfully improved some key psychological factors (self-efficacy and self-regulation/planning, social support and motivation), but only self-regulation mediated the effect of the intervention on walking. This effect was only found in the short term but not in the longitudinal data.

A TPB-intervention based study investigated the mediating effects of psychological factors on walking among sedentary adults (Hardeman et al., 2011). Based on structural equation modelling this study investigated mediation of the intervention over intention and PBC to explain changes in walking behaviour. Results indicate that none of the factor influenced measured or self-reported behaviour changes.

Panter et al. (2015) investigated the influence of environmental restructuring (improvements in cycling and walking infrastructure) on three types of psychological factors (attitudes, perceived control and social influence). None of these factors contribute to an explanation of effectiveness of the intervention.

Prestwich et al. (2012) analysed the effect of different types of planning, social support and Partner-based conditions (collaborative and partner-only) positively impacted perceived social influence, but neither intervention altered enjoyment or self-efficacy. Partner groups even showed weaker immediate intentions than individual planners. However, none of the proposed mediators explained behaviour changes.

Another TPB based intervention study investigated the impact of a multi-component intervention on walking and cycling among early adolescents (Stark et al., 2018). The results indicate that the intervention effectively influenced attitudes, perceived behavioural control, and intentions. Analysis reveals that changes in attitude, subjective norm, and PBC explained intentions for walking. However, these changes in intention were only weakly associated with changes in self-reported behaviour for walking and cycling.

Overall, only few studies investigated mediation of interventions effects through psychological processes on active travel. Among those studies only a limited number of studies could provide evidence for a significant mediation or moderation of intervention effects through psychological processes.

5. Discussion

We systematically reviewed intervention studies promoting active travel that included psychological factors as determinants of behaviour change. This review discusses the findings of the included studies, comprising 28 studies in total, with 16 studies involving a single intervention arm and only 6 employing formal mediation analyses, and addresses the following research questions: (1) which intervention functions and combinations have been investigated to change active travel, (2) which psychological factors have been studied as explanatory variables for changes in active travel, (3) which psychological factors are influenced by interventions and (4) which mediating psychological factors explain the effectiveness of interventions in promoting active travel, before concluding with reflections on the strengths and limitations of this review.

5.1 Intervention functions and active travel

Answering research question 1, this review reveals that education, goal setting, planning and persuasion are the most frequent intervention functions investigated in combination with psychological factors. One common characteristic of these frequently investigated interventions functions is that they can be classified as 'informational' or 'soft' behaviour change strategies (Steg and Vlek, 2009). This type of intervention strategy aims at changing prevalent motivations, perceptions, cognitions and norms. As a result, academic research including psychological factors has focused on this type of intervention.

Following a similar logic, we find only a few studies that can be categorised as structural interventions. Structural strategies aim at changing contextual factors such as the availability and the actual costs and benefits of behavioural alternatives (Steg and Vlek, 2009). Examples include environmental restructuring, incentivisation, restriction and coercion. These types of intervention functions, presumably, influence psychological processes more indirectly, or the evaluation of such studies are conducted within other disciplines not looking into psychological mediators of behaviour change but only at primary outcomes, such as changes in mode choice, route choice or destination choice.

For example, few studies in our review were classified as employing environmental restructuring as an intervention function. This is unexpected, given that a range of studies has shown that changes in cycling infrastructure or the provision thereof, such as the construction of bike lanes, traffic-calming measures, or improved network connectivity, can lead to increased rates of walking and most of all cycling (Saelens et al., 2003; Pucher et al., 2010; Roaf et al., 2024). One additional reason for this discrepancy may lie in differences in study design or the lack of an accompanying study: infrastructural interventions are often evaluated using aggregate outcome measures such as pedestrian or bicycle counts, rather than individual-level measurements and psychological constructs. These studies typically lack pre–post assessments of individual behaviour or psychological mediators and thus fall outside the inclusion criteria of this review focusing on behaviour change models. Nevertheless, two studies employing environmental restructuring were included in our review. Christiansen et al. (2014) evaluated active travel to school across 14 schools in Denmark, seven of which were in the intervention group that implemented a range of policies to promote active travel. While infrastructure improvements were one of the intervention functions, they were implemented in only two out of the 14 schools. The analysis did not allow for differentiation between the effects of the different intervention functions employed at each school. The study did not find an effect of the intervention on active school travel, which was partially attributed to the lack of infrastructure improvements at all seven schools, but also to the fact that the intervention programme covered many functions. Lanzendorf et al. (2022) conducted a before–after study assessing the effects of the introduction of a bicycle lane in Germany. Attitudes and emotions were measured through perceived quality of urban life, quality of stay, lingering, and safety of children. The study reported improvements across all these measures, with the strongest effects found for perceived safety of children. When analysing subgroups, they found that individuals who already walked or cycled reported higher improvements, whereas the effects for car drivers were not significant or pointed in a negative direction. These findings suggest that interventions may be effective in reinforcing positive attitudes and perceptions among individuals who are already using active travel, while having less impact, or negative effects, on those who primarily rely on car travel. These subgroups differences point to the need to include different perspectives and subgroups in both the design and evaluation of interventions to ensure that strategies are equitable and can engage diverse populations, particularly those less inclined towards active travel. Tailoring interventions to address the attitudes and motivations of different subgroups can result in more inclusive and effective behaviour change strategies.

Environmental restructuring is frequently evaluated by means of visual and stated preference experiments. These experiments are commonly employed to investigate how individuals might respond to hypothetical changes in infrastructure (e.g. Kasraian et al., 2021; Von Stülpnagel and Binnig, 2022) and might concern mode choice, route choice or other choices involving active travel. Surveys occasionally incorporate psychological measurements, such as attitudes toward car use or environmental concern, which are treated as moderators or interaction terms in the models, rather than as mediators that explain how the presented experiment changes behaviour. Consequently, such stated preference and visual experiment studies were not included in our review, as they do not meet the inclusion criteria of interventions with pre- and post-measurement of behaviour and psychological factors.

Similarly, this review identifies only a few studies that investigate the impact of incentivisation to promote behaviour change towards active travel. Studies investigating incentivization interventions, such as rewards, gamification elements, or financial incentives, focus primarily on the uptake and usage of the program and the role of psychological mechanisms than on changes in transport mode choice or active travel frequency. This finding might also be explained based on the psychological foundations of rewards and penalties in behaviourism, a theoretical background that focuses on stimulus-response models rather than using psychological mechanisms to explain behaviour.

Several intervention functions are examined in about a third of the studies: training, social support and enablement. These are intervention functions that are aimed at individuals but do focus on capabilities.

One form of enablement in mobility is the provision of alternative modes of transport, such as e-bikes. Studies consistently show that access to e-bikes can lead to longer cycling distances and more frequent trips by active travel modes (e.g. Bjørnarå et al., 2019; De Kruijf et al., 2018; Bourne et al., 2020; Fyhri and Sundfør, 2020; Söderberg F.K.A. Andersson et al., 2021). However, only one of these e-bike studies, Bjørnarå et al. (2019), was eligible for inclusion in our review based on its measurement of both psychological factors and travel behaviour. Their results revealed a significant increase in intrinsic regulation for cycling in the intervention group compared to the control group after nine months. Furthermore, interest/enjoyment and introjected regulation led participants to feel more responsible to cycle. Cycling increased in the intervention group, while remaining stable in the control group. No significant changes were found for psychological constructs related to car use. These findings suggest that e-bike interventions primarily strengthen internal motivation for cycling, rather than challenge car-related attitudes or norms.

E-bikes also help overcome barriers to cycling, such as physical exertion and distance-related challenges, making cycling a more feasible option for many individuals (de Haas et al., 2022; Kroesen, 2017).

However, the quasi-longitudinal designs of these studies limit the ability to draw conclusions about the psychological mechanisms underlying behaviour change, as they typically lack rigorous pre-post measures of psychological constructs.

The most commonly investigated intervention functions are also often studied in combination. Goal setting is frequently combined with education and planning, while education is also regularly found in combination with planning and training. Combinations between informational and structural strategies are heterogeneous, and no clear pattern emerges (e.g., combining the construction of new cycling infrastructure with a persuasive campaign).

5.2 Investigation of psychological factors in active travel

Continuing with research question 2 'which psychological factors have been studied as explanatory variables for changes in active travel', this review reveals that attitudes and emotions, social influence and perceived control and barriers are the psychological factors evaluated most frequently among the included studies. Notably, these psychological factors are the psychological determinants within one of the most frequently used frameworks explaining behaviour: the Theory of Planned Behaviour (Ajzen, 2011). This framework has received extensive consideration in academic research in general (Armitage and Conner, 2001) as well as in transportation research (e.g. Darker et al., 2010; Hardeman et al., 2011; Sun et al., 2015). Unsurprisingly, these prominent psychological factors are likewise frequently represented in the review at hand. In comparison, intention, as the fourth relevant psychological factor within the Theory of Planned Behaviour was included considerably less often in the investigated studies.

A considerable share of studies included self-efficacy as an explanatory variable. Similar to perceived control and barriers this is a psychological factor that relates to contextual factors such as infrastructure or skills that might be particularly relevant in the transportation sector (see also Chapter 4.1).

This review identifies only a few studies that included coping skills and relapse prevention. This is in line with the literature that points to a gap in the literature regarding studies investigating determinants of maintaining behaviour change (Ohnmacht et al., 2017).

Remarkably, we find only one study that included habit as a psychological determinant. This is surprising, considering that habit has been identified as one of the most relevant determinants of travel behaviour (Verplanken et al., 2008). The small number of studies on habit in our review might be related to the fact that habits in transportation are particularly difficult to change (Walker et al., 2015) or to capture. Interventions aimed at changing habits are often related to actual relocation of participants (Semenescu et al., 2020) and respective field studies often lack the experimental setting that was an inclusion criteria for the review at hand. Moreover, habit is related to automatic processes which are difficult to capture (Aarts and Dijksterhuis, 2000).

5.3 Effect of intervention functions on psychological factors

In addressing research question 3 ‘Which psychological factors are influenced by interventions?’, this review finds that attitudes and emotions are the most frequently targeted psychological constructs in the included studies. As key determinants in several behavioural theories, particularly the Theory of Planned Behaviour, the prominence of attitudes in studies investigating active travel behaviour change is expected. However, the empirical evidence of the effectiveness of this factor based on the studies included in this review is mixed, with only six out of 16 studies reporting a significant effect of interventions on attitudes. Attitudes and emotions were targeted through education and persuasion. Overall, the mixed evidence is in line with previous research that attributes only limited effects of attitudes and the related interventions functions of persuasion and education on behaviour change (Albarracín et al., 2024; Armitage and Conner, 2001; Arnott et al., 2014; Semenescu et al., 2020; van Valkengoed et al., 2022). In addition, with education as one of the most frequently applied intervention functions, it is noteworthy that the link to its targeted psychological factor is often missing.

Self-efficacy was targeted and measured in 14 studies in our review, finding a considerable share of 7 studies with significant effects of the intervention functions education and training. As self-efficacy has been identified as a relevant determinant of behaviour in many transport and health-related behaviours (Semenescu et al., 2020) it is valuable to acknowledge that this psychological factor can be influenced, to some extent, by education and training oriented interventions. Further research, however, is necessary to explain why in a considerable number of investigations these effects cannot be found in intervention studies.

A relatively large number of studies have investigated and found information and skills as significant correlates of different types of interventions functions. This psychological factor was targeted in 13 studies through five different intervention functions: Education, enablement, environmental restructuring and training. This is in line with previous research that provides evidence for this link between skills and promoting new behaviours (van Eggermond et al., 2025). Based on these findings, fostering skills might be a promising avenue to promote active travel.

However, considering the heterogeneous types of interventions to support skills, standardisation of training or education might be helpful to further advance its effectiveness.

Planning and self-regulation were targeted in 11 studies through five intervention functions: education, enablement, goal setting, planning and training. However, only in four out of these 11 studies reported significant effects. With goal setting being one of the most frequently used intervention function found based on this review, it is important to note, that findings on the role of self-regulation and planning to explain the effectiveness of goal-setting remain inconclusive.

The review finds social influence as a relevant psychological determinant that is relatively often significantly linked with a number of intervention functions. In nine out of 10 intervention studies that targeted this factor, a significant effect of an intervention function was reported. This is in line with other studies supporting the relevance of social processes such as social, cultural norms or the behaviour of others (Semenescu et al., 2020). Intervention functions targeting this psychological factor include social support, persuasion, modelling, enablement, and environmental restructuring. However, similar to the domain of skills, the studies employed heterogeneous intervention types to influence these social processes. A more standardised classification and reporting of intervention functions could improve the comparability of studies and help advance the understanding of effective strategies for promoting social and normative changes in active travel behaviour.

5.4 Mediating factors

In our review, only six out of 28 studies employed formal mediation analysis to investigate whether intervention effects on behaviour were transmitted through psychological factors such as attitudes, motivation, or self-efficacy. Among those studies only three studies provided evidence for a significant mediation or moderation of intervention effects through psychological processes. Based on this limited number of studies and the likewise limited effects no general conclusion can be drawn from these studies.

It remains to be discussed, why only a few empirical studies have looked into this important theoretical assumption and why these studies failed to find empirical evidence for mediation.

First, while mediation analysis has a long history in psychology and social sciences (e.g. Preacher and Hayes, 2008; Hayes, 2017) it has been underutilized in transport research, where the focus often remains on behavioural outcomes, such as changes in mode share or trip frequency on an aggregate level, without examining the psychological mechanisms that drive these changes on an individual level.

Secondly, mediation analysis requires study designs that include pre- and post-intervention data collection on both mediators and outcomes at the individual level.

Thirdly, disciplinary traditions may also play a role. While mediation analysis has become common practice in fields like psychology and health behaviour research, transport studies have often focused on revealed and stated preference data, examining travel behaviour as a function of external factors such as infrastructure availability, pricing, or accessibility. These studies, even when including psychological variables like attitudes or perceptions, tend to use them as moderators or interaction terms in discrete choice models, rather than testing them as mediators in a causal pathway between intervention and behaviour.

Finally, the limited use of mediation models may reflect a more pragmatic focus on explaining the effectiveness of an intervention on transport outcomes, increases in cycling, and not on looking into the underlying psychological or causal mechanisms. This leaves the question of why and how interventions work underexplored.

5.5 Contributions, strengths and limitations

This review contributes to the literature in three ways. First, it provides a systematic mapping of intervention functions, psychological factors, and behavioural outcomes in the context of active travel. Second, it identifies a gap in empirical work: the limited use of mediation analysis to test theoretically proposed causal pathways. Third, it highlights under-investigated domains, particularly structural interventions in the context of behavior change research, and points to the need for standardised study designs and outcome measures to strengthen comparability across studies.

A major strength of this review is the comprehensive investigation of intervention functions, psychological factors and behavioural outcomes. Therefore, the review fills a gap in the literature to find empirical substantiations of theoretically proposed causal relations. The review provides an overview of the available body of research that investigates the missing link between intervention functions and psychological factors.

However, the review only finds heterogenous effects and considerable variety in the included intervention functions as well as the measured effects on psychological factors, which makes comparing the results studies as well as drawing conclusions difficult.

This review has several limitations that must be considered when interpreting the findings. First, our search strategy was restricted to studies using the keywords "intervention" and "trial". This narrow scope may have excluded relevant studies from other disciplines or those using alternative terminology, thereby limiting the comprehensiveness of the evidence base.

Second, we did not conduct an in-depth analysis of the specific intervention arms within each study. As result, these studies were excluded in several analyses. Furthermore, the reviewed literature includes only a limited number of studies that investigate potential mediation effects between interventions, psychological factors, and behavioural outcomes. As a result, we can only draw limited conclusions on the role of psychological factors.

A major challenge in synthesizing the evidence was the heterogeneity across intervention studies. There is substantial variation in how interventions are conceptualized, delivered, and measured. This includes differences in study design, outcome measures, intervention duration, measurement points, and the size of study populations. Such inconsistencies complicate comparisons across studies and reduce the ability to draw generalizable conclusions. This is particularly relevant for the question the duration of interventions and when effects are measured, since short term versus long term effect are captured differently and respective differences in measurement might cause bias for the interpretation. This highlights the need for standardisation in both intervention protocols and outcome assessments.

Additionally, many of the studies assessed the effects of combined or multi-function interventions. This makes it challenging to isolate the effects of individual intervention functions on specific psychological outcomes. Moreover, potential interaction effects between intervention functions, such as education and planning, are often unmeasured but may play a significant role in influencing behaviour change, particularly when promoting active travel where often infrastructural measures interact with more informational strategies.

Similarly, this review did not investigate the impact of multi-arm interventions; for several analyses, we only included studies with two arms, one of which was a control group, or studies evaluating a single arm. Future investigations are proposed to consider this issue to better understand the interactions between intervention functions.

On a more practical level, the interventions' effectiveness should also be considered with respect to ethical decisions and their acceptance on the level of policies (Milne, 2012). This relevant issue was beyond the scope of this review but should be considered in future research.

6. Conclusion

This review synthesises existing research on the effectiveness of interventions aimed at promoting active travel, with a particular focus on the psychological factors targeted by these interventions and how changes in these factors influence individuals' decisions to walk or cycle.

The findings indicate that, to date, the theoretically proposed link between interventions, psychological mechanisms, and behavioural change remains largely without empirical support. There are several reasons for this lack of empirical evidence. Firstly, many studies prioritise the measurement of behavioural outcomes, such as mode choice or trip frequency, without assessing psychological constructs such as motivation, attitudes, or perceived control. Secondly, even when psychological factors are measured, they are often treated as secondary outcomes rather than mediators, and formal mediation analyses are rarely conducted.

Notwithstanding this limitation, a few conclusions on psychological factors - i.e. the missing link between interventions and behaviour that can be drawn from this review. Interventions appear to be more effective in influencing social processes, self-efficacy, and cognitive and practical skills.

7. Recommendations

Based on the findings of this review, we recommend the development and implementation of theory-driven interventions to promote active travel. To enhance the comparability and effectiveness of future research, it is crucial to establish standardised definitions of intervention types and to base the selection of targeted psychological factors on established theoretical frameworks. Interventions are advised to be chosen through a systematic analysis of the specific behavioural context, characteristics of the target population, and the behaviours intended for change. Overall, such an approach will facilitate more meaningful comparisons across studies regarding the effectiveness of interventions and their underlying psychological mechanisms.

Additionally, our findings reveal that a majority of the reviewed studies employed multiple intervention functions within a single intervention arm. This common practice suggests that combining different approaches is a promising strategy.

Therefore, we advocate for the integration of multiple intervention functions, combining informational components (e.g., skills training, personalised travel planning) with structural measures (e.g., improvements to walking and cycling infrastructure) to benefit from their combined effects.

Finally, future efforts are recommended to broaden their focus beyond attitudes and emotions to include self-efficacy, social support, skill development, and changes in infrastructure, that in combination enable and sustain active travel behaviours.

Author statement

Financial disclosure

We have received no funding to write this chapter.

CRediT authorship contribution statement

Dorothea Schaffner: Writing – review & editing, Writing – original draft, Validation, Project administration, Methodology, Investigation, Formal analysis, Data curation, Conceptualization.

Michael van Eggermond: Writing – review & editing, Writing – original draft, Validation, Project administration, Methodology, Investigation, Formal analysis, Data curation, Conceptualization.

Declaration of competing interest

The authors declare that they have no known competing financial interests or personal relationships that could have appeared to influence the work reported in this paper.

Appendix: Queries

Web of science

TS= ("active travel" OR cycling OR bicycl* OR wheeling OR walking OR cycle)
AND
TS= (intervention OR trial)
AND
TS= ("Problem Awareness" OR "*Contemplation*"
OR Attitudes
OR Motivation OR Belief OR Beliefs
OR Emotion
OR value
OR "Intention"
OR "Commitment"
OR "Self Efficacy"
OR "Self-Efficacy"

OR "Perceived Control"
OR Planning
OR "Perceived behavioural Control"
OR "Perceived behavioral Control"
OR "Perceived behavior Control"
OR "Perceived behaviour Control"
OR "Perceived Barriers"
OR "Social Influence" OR "Social Norms"
OR "Relapse Prevention" OR "Coping Skills"
OR "Habits"
OR "Automatic Processes" OR "Routine Formation"
OR "Knowledge" OR "Learning"
OR "Capabilities" OR Capability
)
AND
SU= ("Public Health" OR "Transportation" OR "Environmental Sciences" OR "Urban Studies")
AND PY= (2010–2025)

Pubmed

("active travel"[Title/Abstract]
OR "walking" "pedestrian" "walk"[Title/Abstract]
OR "cycling" "bicycl*" "wheeling"[Title/Abstract] OR "cycle"[Title/Abstract]
OR "E-Bike" "pedal-assisted" "Electric bike"[Title/Abstract]
)
AND ("intervention" "trial"[Title/Abstract])
AND ("Public Health"[MeSH] OR "Health Behavior"[MeSH] OR "Urban Health" [MeSH] OR "walking"[MeSH] OR "bicycling"[MeSH] OR "Exercise"[MeSH] OR "Transportation"[MeSH] OR "Health Promotion"[MeSH] OR "psychology"[MeSH])
AND
("Problem Awareness" "Contemplation" Attitudes Motivation Belief Beliefs[Title/Abstract]
OR Emotion value "Intention" "Commitment"[Title/Abstract]
OR "Self Efficacy" "Self-Efficacy" "Perceived Control" Planning[Title/Abstract]
OR "Perceived behavioural Control" "Perceived behavioral Control"[Title/Abstract]
OR "Perceived behavior Control" "Perceived behaviour Control"[Title/Abstract]
OR "Perceived Barriers" "Social Influence" "Social Norms"[Title/Abstract]
OR "Relapse Prevention" "Coping Skills" "Habits"[Title/Abstract]
OR "Automatic Processes" "Routine Formation"[Title/Abstract]
OR "Knowledge" "Learning" "Capabilities" Capability[Title/Abstract])
NOT (
"radiography"[Title/Abstract]
OR "DOHaD"[Title/Abstract]
OR "adolescent health education"[Title/Abstract]
OR "nursing"[Title/Abstract]
OR "headache"[Title/Abstract]
OR "tumor*"[Title/Abstract]
OR "cancer"[Title/Abstract]
OR "pharmacological"[Title/Abstract]
OR "myeloma"[Title/Abstract]

OR "metabolic"[Title/Abstract]
OR "metabolism"[Title/Abstract]
OR "embryo"[Title/Abstract]
OR "opoid"[Title/Abstract]
OR "fungi"[Title/Abstract]
OR "Uterine*"[MeSH Terms]
OR "Brain Injuries/rehabilitation"[MeSH Terms]
OR "bacteria"[Title/Abstract]
OR "animal" "MicroRNA"[Title/Abstract]) AND ("2010"[Date - Publication]: "2025"-[Date - Publication])

TRID

("active travel"
OR "walking" OR "pedestrian" OR "walk"
OR "cycling" OR "bicycl*" OR "wheeling" OR "cycle"
OR "E-Bike" OR "pedal-assisted" OR "Electric bike"
)
AND ("intervention" OR "trial")
AND
("Problem Awareness" OR "Contemplation" OR Attitudes OR Motivation OR Motivations OR Belief OR Beliefs
OR Emotion OR value OR "Intention" OR "Commitment"
OR "Self Efficacy" OR "Self-Efficacy" OR "Perceived Control" OR Planning
OR "Perceived behavioural Control" OR "Perceived behavioral Control"
OR "Perceived behavior Control" OR "Perceived behaviour Control"
OR "Perceived Barriers" OR "Social Influence" OR "Social Norms"
OR "Relapse Prevention" OR "Coping Skills" OR "Habits"
OR "Automatic Processes" OR "Routine Formation"
OR "Knowledge" OR "Learning" OR "Capabilities" OR Capability)

References

Aarts, H., Dijksterhuis, A., 2000. The automatic activation of goal-directed behaviour: the case of travel habit. J. Environ. Psychol. 20 (1), 75–82.

Ajzen, I., 1991. The theory of planned behavior. Organ. Behav. Hum. Decis. Process 50 (2), 179–211. https://doi.org/10.1016/0749-5978(91)90020-T.

Ajzen, I., 2011. The theory of planned behaviour: reactions and reflections. Psychol. Health 26 (9), 1113–1127. https://doi.org/10.1080/08870446.2011.613995.

Albarracín, D., Fayaz-Farkhad, B., Granados Samayoa, J.A., 2024. Determinants of behaviour and their efficacy as targets of behavioural change interventions. Nat. Rev. Psychol. 3 (6), 377–392. https://doi.org/10.1038/s44159-024-00305-0.

Aranda-Balboa, M., Huertas-Delgado, F., Gálvez-Fernández, P., Saucedo-Araujo, R., Molina-Soberanes, D., Campos-Garzón, P., et al., 2022. The effect of a school-based intervention on children's cycling knowledge, mode of commuting and perceived barriers: a randomized controlled trial. Int. J. Environ. Res. Public. Health 19 (15). https://doi.org/10.3390/ijerph19159626.

Armitage, C.J., Conner, M., 2001. Efficacy of the theory of planned behaviour: a meta-analytic review. Br. J. Soc. Psychol. 40 (4), 471–499. https://doi.org/10.1348/014466601164939.

Arnott, B., Rehackova, L., Errington, L., Sniehotta, F.F., Roberts, J., Araujo-Soares, V., 2014. Efficacy of behavioural interventions for transport behaviour change: Systematic review, meta-analysis and intervention coding. Int. J. Behav. Nutr. Phys. Act. 11 (1), 133. https://doi.org/10.1186/s12966-014-0133-9.

Bamberg, S., 2013. Applying the stage model of self-regulated behavioral change in a car use reduction intervention. J. Environ. Psychol. 33, 68–75. https://doi.org/10.1016/j.jenvp.2012.10.001.

Bamberg, S., Fujii, S., Friman, M., Gärling, T., 2011. Behaviour theory and soft transport policy measures. Transp. Policy 18 (1), 228–235. https://doi.org/10.1016/j.tranpol.2010.08.006.

Bergquist, M., Thiel, M., Goldberg, M.H., Van Der Linden, S., 2023. Field interventions for climate change mitigation behaviors: a second-order meta-analysis. Proc. Natl. Acad. Sci. 120 (13), e2214851120. https://doi.org/10.1073/pnas.2214851120.

Bird, E.L., Baker, G., Mutrie, N., Ogilvie, D., Sahlqvist, S., Powell, J., et al., 2013. Behavior change techniques used to promote walking and cycling: a systematic review. Health Psychol. 32 (8), 829–838. https://doi.org/10.1037/a0032078.

Bjørnarå, H.B., Berntsen, S., J te Velde, S., Fyhri, A., Deforche, B., Andersen, L.B., et al., 2019. From cars to bikes – the effect of an intervention providing access to different bike types: a randomized controlled trial. PLoS One 14 (7), e0219304. https://doi.org/10.1371/journal.pone.0219304.

Bourne, J.E., Cooper, A.R., Kelly, P., Kinnear, F.J., England, C., Leary, S., et al., 2020. The impact of e-cycling on travel behaviour: a scoping review. J. Transp. & Health 19, 100910. https://doi.org/10.1016/j.jth.2020.100910.

Buttazzoni, A., Clark, A., Seabrook, J., Gilliland, J., 2019. Promoting active school travel in elementary schools: a regional case study of the school travel planning intervention. J. Transp. & Health 12, 206–219. https://doi.org/10.1016/j.jth.2019.01.007.

Christiansen, L., Toftager, M., Ersboll, A., Troelsen, J., 2014. Effects of a Danish multi-component physical activity intervention on active school transport. J. Transp. & Health 1 (3), 174–181. https://doi.org/10.1016/j.jth.2014.05.002.

Darker, C., French, D., Eves, F., Sniehotta, F., 2010. An intervention to promote walking amongst the general population based on an "extended" theory of planned behaviour: a waiting list randomised controlled trial. Psychol. & Health 25 (1), 71–88. https://doi.org/10.1080/08870440902893716.

Davis, R., Campbell, R., Hildon, Z., Hobbs, L., Michie, S., 2015. Theories of behaviour and behaviour change across the social and behavioural sciences: a scoping review. Health Psychol. Rev. 9 (3), 323–344. https://doi.org/10.1080/17437199.2014.941722.

de Haas, M., Kroesen, M., Chorus, C., Hoogendoorn-Lanser, S., Hoogendoorn, S., 2022. E-bike user groups and substitution effects: evidence from longitudinal travel data in the Netherlands. Transportation 49 (3), 815–840. https://doi.org/10.1007/s11116-021-10195-3.

De Kruijf, J., Ettema, D., Kamphuis, C.B.M., Dijst, M., 2018. Evaluation of an incentive program to stimulate the shift from car commuting to e-cycling in the Netherlands. J. Transp. & Health 10, 74–83. https://doi.org/10.1016/j.jth.2018.06.003.

Duvall, J., 2012. A comparison of engagement strategies for encouraging outdoor walking. J. Phys. Act. Health 9 (1), 62–70. https://doi.org/10.1123/jpah.9.1.62.

Ek, A., Alexandrou, C., Söderström, E., Bergman, P., Delisle Nyström, C., Direito, A., et al., 2020. Effectiveness of a 3-Month mobile phone–based behavior change program on active transportation and physical activity in adults: randomized controlled trial. JMIR mHealth uHealth 8 (6), e18531. https://doi.org/10.2196/18531.

Fjeldsoe, B., Miller, Y., Marshall, A., 2013. Social cognitive mediators of the effect of the MobileMums intervention on physical activity. Health Psychol. 32 (7), 729–738. https://doi.org/10.1037/a0027548.

Fyhri, A., Sundfør, H.B., 2020. Do people who buy e-bikes cycle more? Transportation Res. Part. D: Transp. Environ. 86, 102422. https://doi.org/10.1016/j.trd.2020.102422.

Geng, J., Long, R., Chen, H., 2016. Impact of information intervention on travel mode choice of urban residents with different goal frames: a controlled trial in Xuzhou, China. Transportation Res. Part. A: Policy Pract. 91, 134–147. https://doi.org/10.1016/j.tra.2016.06.031.

Gilbert, G., Williamson, C., Richards, J., Collyer, T., Kelly, P., 2021. Do framed mental health messages on social media influence university students' motivation for physical activity? Int. J. Environ. Res. Public. Health 18 (16). https://doi.org/10.3390/ijerph18168671.

Hardcastle, S., Blake, N., MS, H., 2012. The effectiveness of a motivational interviewing primary-care based intervention on physical activity and predictors of change in a disadvantaged community. J. Behav. Med. 35 (3), 318–333. https://doi.org/10.1007/s10865-012-9417-1.

Hardeman, W., Kinmonth, A., Michie, S., Sutton, S., 2011. Theory of planned behaviour cognitions do not predict self-reported or objective physical activity levels or change in the ProActive trial. Br. J. Health Psychol. 16 (Pt 1), 135–150. https://doi.org/10.1348/135910710×523481.

Hayes, A.F., 2017. Introduction to Mediation, Moderation, and Conditional Process Analysis: A Regression-Based Approach. Guilford Publications.

Huang, W., Huang, H., Wu, C., 2022. Physical activity and social support to promote a health-promoting lifestyle in older adults: an intervention study. Int. J. Environ. Res. Public. Health 19 (21). https://doi.org/10.3390/ijerph192114382.

Joseph, R., Todd, M., Ainsworth, B., Vega-López, S., Adams, M., Hollingshead, K., et al., 2023. Smart walk: a culturally tailored smartphone-delivered physical activity intervention for cardiometabolic risk reduction among African American Women. Int. J. Environ. Res. Public. Health 20 (2). https://doi.org/10.3390/ijerph20021000.

Kasraian, D., Adhikari, S., Kossowsky, D., Luubert, M., Hall, G.B., Hawkins, J., et al., 2021. Evaluating pedestrian perceptions of street design with a 3D stated preference survey. Environ. Plan. B: Urban. Analytics City Sci. 48 (7), 1787–1805. https://doi.org/10.1177/2399808320946050.

Kearns, M., Ledsham, T., Savan, B., Scott, J., 2019. Increasing cycling for transportation through mentorship programs. Transportation Res. Part. A: Policy Pract. 128, 34–45. https://doi.org/10.1016/j.tra.2019.07.014.

Kroesen, M., 2017. To what extent do e-bikes substitute travel by other modes? Evidence from the Netherlands. Transp. Res. Part. D: Transp. Environ. 53, 377–387. https://doi.org/10.1016/j.trd.2017.04.036.

Lanzendorf, M., Scheffler, C., Trost, L., Werschmöller, S., 2022. Implementing bicycle-friendly transport policies: examining the effect of an infrastructural intervention on residents' perceived quality of urban life in Frankfurt, Germany. Case Stud. Transp. Policy 10 (4), 2476–2485. https://doi.org/10.1016/j.cstp.2022.10.014.

Larsen, R., Begg, S., Rudner, J., Verrinder, G., 2024. Behavioural interventions designed to increase commuter cycling: a systematic review. Transp. Res. Part. F: Traffic Psychol. Behav. 100, 388–401. https://doi.org/10.1016/j.trf.2023.11.020.

Lee, L., Kuo, Y., Fanaw, D., Perng, S., Juang, I., 2012. The effect of an intervention combining self-efficacy theory and pedometers on promoting physical activity among adolescents. J. Clin. Nurs. 21 (7–8), 914–922. https://doi.org/10.1111/j.1365-2702.2011.03881.x.

Manca, F., Daina, N., Sivakumar, A., Yi, J.W.X., Zavistas, K., Gemini, G., et al., 2022. Using digital social market applications to incentivise active travel: empirical analysis of a smart city initiative. Sustain. Cities Soc. 77, 103595. https://doi.org/10.1016/j.scs.2021.103595.

Mendoza, J., Watson, K., Baranowski, T., Nicklas, T., Uscanga, D., Hanfling, M., 2011. The walking school bus and children's physical activity: a pilot cluster randomized controlled trial. Pediatrics 128 (3), e537–e544. https://doi.org/10.1542/peds.2010-3486.

Michie, S., Van Stralen, M.M., West, R., 2011. The behaviour change wheel: a new method for characterising and designing behaviour change interventions. Implement. Sci. 6 (1), 42. https://doi.org/10.1186/1748-5908-6-42.

Michie, S., Richardson, M., Johnston, M., Abraham, C., Francis, J., Hardeman, W., et al., 2013. The behavior change technique taxonomy (v1) of 93 hierarchically clustered techniques: building an international consensus for the reporting of behavior change interventions. Ann. Behav. Med. 46 (1), 81–95. https://doi.org/10.1007/s12160-013-9486-6.

Milne, E.M.G., 2012. A public health perspective on transport policy priorities. J. Transp. Geogr. 21, 62–69. https://doi.org/10.1016/j.jtrangeo.2012.01.013.

Moffitt, R., Mohr, P., 2015. The efficacy of a self-managed acceptance and commitment therapy intervention DVD for physical activity initiation. Br. J. Health Psychol. 20 (1), 115–129. https://doi.org/10.1111/bjhp.12098.

Nachman, E., Rodriguez, D., 2023. Evaluating the effects of a classroom-based bicycle education intervention on bicycle activity, self-efficacy, personal safety, knowledge, and mode choice. Front. Sustain. Cities 5. https://doi.org/10.3389/frsc.2023.1098473.

Ohnmacht, T., Schaffner, D., Weibel, C., Schad, H., 2017. Rethinking social psychology and intervention design: a model of energy savings and human behavior. Energy Res. & Soc. Sci. 26, 40–53. https://doi.org/10.1016/j.erss.2017.01.017.

Olsson, L., Friman, M., Kawabata, Y., Fujii, S., 2021. Integrating planned behavior and stage-of-change into a cycling campaign. Sustainability 13 (18). https://doi.org/10.3390/su131810116.

Ory, M., Lee, S., Han, G., Towne, S., Quinn, C., Neher, T., et al., 2018. Effectiveness of a lifestyle intervention on social support, self-efficacy, and physical activity among older adults: evaluation of texercise select. Int. J. Environ. Res. Public. Health 15 (2). https://doi.org/10.3390/ijerph15020234.

Panter, J., Ogilvie, D., 2015. Theorising and testing environmental pathways to behaviour change: natural experimental study of the perception and use of new infrastructure to promote walking and cycling in local communities. BMJ Open 5 (9), e007593. https://doi.org/10.1136/bmjopen-2015-007593.

Preacher, K.J., Hayes, A.F., 2008. Asymptotic and resampling strategies for assessing and comparing indirect effects in multiple mediator models. Behav. Res. Methods 40 (3), 879–891. https://doi.org/10.3758/BRM.40.3.879.

Prestwich, A., Perugini, M., Hurling, R., 2010. Can implementation intentions and text messages promote brisk walking? A randomized trial. Health Psychol. 29 (1), 40–49. https://doi.org/10.1037/a0016993.

Prestwich, A., Conner, M., Lawton, R., Ward, J., Ayres, K., McEachan, R., 2012. Randomized controlled trial of collaborative implementation intentions targeting working adults' physical activity. Health Psychol. 31 (4), 486–495. https://doi.org/10.1037/a0027672.

Prochaska, J.O., Velicer, W.F., 1997. The transtheoretical model of health behavior change. Am. J. Health Promotion 12 (1), 38–48. https://doi.org/10.4278/0890-1171-12.1.38.

Pucher, J., Dill, J., Handy, S., 2010. Infrastructure, programs, and policies to increase bicycling: an international review. Preventive Med. 50, S106–S125. https://doi.org/10.1016/j.ypmed.2009.07.028.

Roaf, E., Lawlor, E.R., Larrington-Spencer, H., 2024. What interventions increase active travel? Adv. Transp. Policy Plan 13. Elsevier, pp. 89–143. https://doi.org/10.1016/bs.atpp.2023.11.004.

Saelens, B.E., Sallis, J.F., Frank, L.D., 2003. Environmental correlates of walking and cycling: findings from the transportation, urban design, and planning literatures. Ann. Behav. Med. 25 (2), 80–91. https://doi.org/10.1207/S15324796ABM2502_03.

Semenescu, A., Gavreliuc, A., Sârbescu, P., 2020. 30 Years of soft interventions to reduce car use – a systematic review and meta-analysis. Transp. Res. Part. D: Transp. Environ. 85, 102397. https://doi.org/10.1016/j.trd.2020.102397.

Söderberg F.K.A. Andersson, A., Adell, E., Winslott Hiselius, L., 2021. What is the substitution effect of e-bikes? A randomised controlled trial. Transp. Res. Part. D: Transp. Environ. 90, 102648. https://doi.org/10.1016/j.trd.2020.102648.

Stark, J., Berger, W., Hössinger, R., 2018. The effectiveness of an intervention to promote active travel modes in early adolescence. Transp. Res. Part. F: Traffic Psychol. Behav. 55, 389–402. https://doi.org/10.1016/j.trf.2018.03.017.

Steffen, J., Hook, H., Witlox, F., 2024. Improving interest in public, active, and shared travel modes through nudging interventions. Transp. Res. Part. F: Traffic Psychol. Behav. 103, 353–367. https://doi.org/10.1016/j.trf.2024.04.020.

Steg, L., Vlek, C., 2009. Encouraging pro-environmental behaviour: an integrative review and research agenda. J. Environ. Psychol. 29 (3), 309–317. https://doi.org/10.1016/j.jenvp.2008.10.004.

Stern, P.C., Dietz, T., Abel, T., Guagnano, G.A., Kalof, L., 1999. A value-belief-norm theory of support for social movements: the case of environmentalism. Hum. Ecol. Rev. 6 (2).

Sun, G., Acheampong, R., Lin, H., Pun, V., 2015. Understanding walking behavior among university students using theory of planned behavior. Int. J. of. Environ. Res. Public. Health 12 (11), 13794–13806. https://doi.org/10.3390/ijerph121113794.

van Eggermond, M.A.B., Schaffner, D., Studer, N., Knecht, L., Johnson, L., 2025. Assessing the effectiveness of an online cycling training for adults to master complex traffic situations. Accid. Anal. & Prev. 211, 107856. https://doi.org/10.1016/j.aap.2024.107856.

Van Hoecke, A., Delecluse, C., Bogaerts, A., Boen, F., 2014. The long-term effectiveness of need-supportive physical activity counseling compared with a standard referral in sedentary older adults. J. Aging Phys. Act. 22 (2), 186–198. https://doi.org/10.1123/japa.2012-0261.

van Stralen, M., de Vries, H., Bolman, C., Mudde, A., Lechner, L., 2010. Exploring the efficacy and moderators of two computer-tailored physical activity interventions for older adults: a randomized controlled trial. Ann. Behav. Med. 39 (2), 139–150. https://doi.org/10.1007/s12160-010-9166-8.

van Valkengoed, A.M., Abrahamse, W., Steg, L., 2022. To select effective interventions for pro-environmental behaviour change, we need to consider determinants of behaviour. Nat. Hum. Behav. 6 (11), 1482–1492. https://doi.org/10.1038/s41562-022-01473-w.

Verplanken, B., Walker, I., Davis, A., Jurasek, M., 2008. Context change and travel mode choice: combining the habit discontinuity and self-activation hypotheses. J. Environ. Psychol. 28 (2), 121–127. https://doi.org/10.1016/j.jenvp.2007.10.005.

Von Stülpnagel, R., Binnig, N., 2022. How safe do you feel? – A large-scale survey concerning the subjective safety associated with different kinds of cycling lanes. Accid. Anal. & Prev 167, 106577. https://doi.org/10.1016/j.aap.2022.106577.

Walker, I., Thomas, G.O., Verplanken, B., 2015. Old habits die hard: travel habit formation and decay during an office relocation. Environ. Behav. 47 (10), 1089–1106. https://doi.org/10.1177/0013916514549619.

Walsh, A., Washington, T., Petrunoff, N., Heesch, K., 2021. Commuter choices: a clustered, quasi-experimental trial of a social cognitive approach to increasing active commuting among office workers. J. Transp. & Health 20. https://doi.org/10.1016/j.jth.2020.100998.

Williams, S., Michie, S., Dale, J., Stallard, N., French, D., 2015. The effects of a brief intervention to promote walking on theory of planned behavior constructs: a cluster randomized controlled trial in general practice. Patient Educ. Counseling 98 (5), 651–659. https://doi.org/10.1016/j.pec.2015.01.010.

CHAPTER NINE

Mobility planning for equitable community recovery and wellbeing

Yegane Ghezelloo[a,*] and Tamiyo Kondo[b]
[a]Department of Architecture, Mie University, Tsu City, Japan
[b]Research Center for Urban Safety and Security, Kobe University, Kobe City, Japan
*Corresponding author. e-mail address: yegane.gh@arch.mie-u.ac.jp

Contents

Abstract

As disasters affect communities, mobility planning plays an important role in disaster recovery, influencing survivors' wellbeing. Post-disaster relocation and displacement to poorly connected areas limit survivors' access to essential services and social networks and create long-term inequities. This review synthesizes literature and case studies on the relationship between mobility planning, mobility disruptions and post-disaster wellbeing, and categorizes findings into three domains: physical, mental-emotional, and social wellbeing. The result shows that mobility barriers undermine overall health by restricting access to medical care and daily activities. In contrast, reliable and inclusive mobility systems reduce stress, encourage social interactions, provide equitable access, and support resilience of the communities. Especially in disaster-affected areas, adequate mobility is tied to equity, and the lack of it disproportionately impacts vulnerable

Advances in Transport Policy and Planning, Volume 18
ISSN 2543-0009, https://doi.org/10.1016/bs.atpp.2026.06.002

groups such as older adults, people with disabilities, and rural populations disconnected from essential services. Our review highlights that accessible, equitable, and context-driven mobility planning can determine recovery outcomes and community resilience for physical, mental-emotional, and social wellbeing. However, a majority of the available research emphasizes social wellbeing compared to other domains, lacks empirical evidence and draws from largely conceptual findings. Future research should further explore empirical studies and context-driven mobility interventions that bridge the gap between physical reconstruction and wellbeing.

1. Introduction

Affected populations often face various challenges in post-disaster recovery processes which extend beyond their immediate physical reconstruction needs. These challenges often disrupt their community wellbeing, including social cohesion, economic stability, and access to essential services, particularly for vulnerable populations who are already disproportionately affected by the disaster (Cutter et al., 2003). Recovery plans often include relocating residential areas to ensure the necessary safety to protect affected communities, but these relocations result in disconnection and displacement of the survivors from their original social networks, familiar environments, and essential services, resulting in delayed community recovery and a worsened sense of dislocation and isolation (Miles and Chang, 2006; Norris et al., 2002; Toyoshima and Iwafune, 2013). These effects may take significant tolls on the physical, mental-emotional, and social wellbeing of the survivors, and necessitate adequate mobility systems reflected in the recovery planning process (Aldrich, 2012; Cheng and Zhang, 2022; Ghannad et al., 2021; Klinenberg, 2018; Meher et al., 2021).

This study aims to investigate the impact of integrating mobility and disaster related mobility disruptions into post-disaster recovery and survivors' physical, mental-emotional, and social wellbeing, offering guidelines for integrating mobility planning into community recovery frameworks. Mobility planning refers to the strategic planning and management of transportation systems to satisfy the mobility needs of people for a better quality of life following disasters. The review includes conceptual analyses and empirically grounded, case-based evidence and focuses on three domains of post-disaster wellbeing in relation to mobility planning: physical wellbeing—the ability to improve functional body health and to go through daily habits and needs; mental-emotional wellbeing—the ability to manage stress and generate positive emotions and feelings; and social wellbeing—the ability to communicate, develop meaningful relationships with others, and maintain a support network (Halleröd and Seldén, 2013; Margolis et al., 2021; Rath and Harter, 2010). This study omits other domains of wellbeing (intellectual, spiritual, vocational, and financial aspects) that are not directly impacted by mobility planning, but rather are outcomes of other aspects of recovery planning (Halleröd and Seldén, 2013).

2. Method

2.1 Search strategy and inclusion criteria

This review synthesizes a wide range of literature on mobility, transportation, accessibility, social capital, resilience, and wellbeing in post-disaster contexts. To examine the role of mobility in post-disaster wellbeing, authors searched three databases between November 2024 and February 2025: Web of Science (WoS), Transport Research International Documentation (TRID), and J-STAGE (Japan Science and Technology Agency, an online platform that distributes Japanese academic journals and research outputs, operated by Japan Science and Technology Agency-JST). Queries combined keywords such as "transportation", "public transportation", "disaster recovery", "community recovery", "relocation", and "wellbeing". Disaster-specific searches were also conducted; publications on studies from Japan such focusing on "Japan 2011 Tsunami Mobility Recovery", and "Kobe Earthquake 1995" between 2000 and 2025 were also obtained for this review.

Studies were included if they: (a) explicitly linked mobility planning to post-disaster contexts; (b) addressed at least one wellbeing dimension (physical, mental-emotional, or social); and (c) provided either empirical evidence or a conceptual analysis. Excluded were duplicates, studies not in disaster contexts, or those without relevance to mobility and wellbeing.

2.2 Screening process and data extraction

The screening process focused on identifying the studies that link community recovery to survivors' wellbeing. Titles and abstracts were first reviewed, followed by full-text screening. From 195 initial records, 61 studies were retained. These included both global syntheses and disaster-specific cases such as 2004 Indian Ocean Tsunami, Hurricanes Katrina 2005 and Sandy 2012 in USA, Christchurch 2010–2012 Earthquakes in New Zealand, and the 2011 Japan Tsunami.

Data extraction documented disaster type, location, and thematic contribution regarding wellbeing domains (physical, mental-emotional, social).

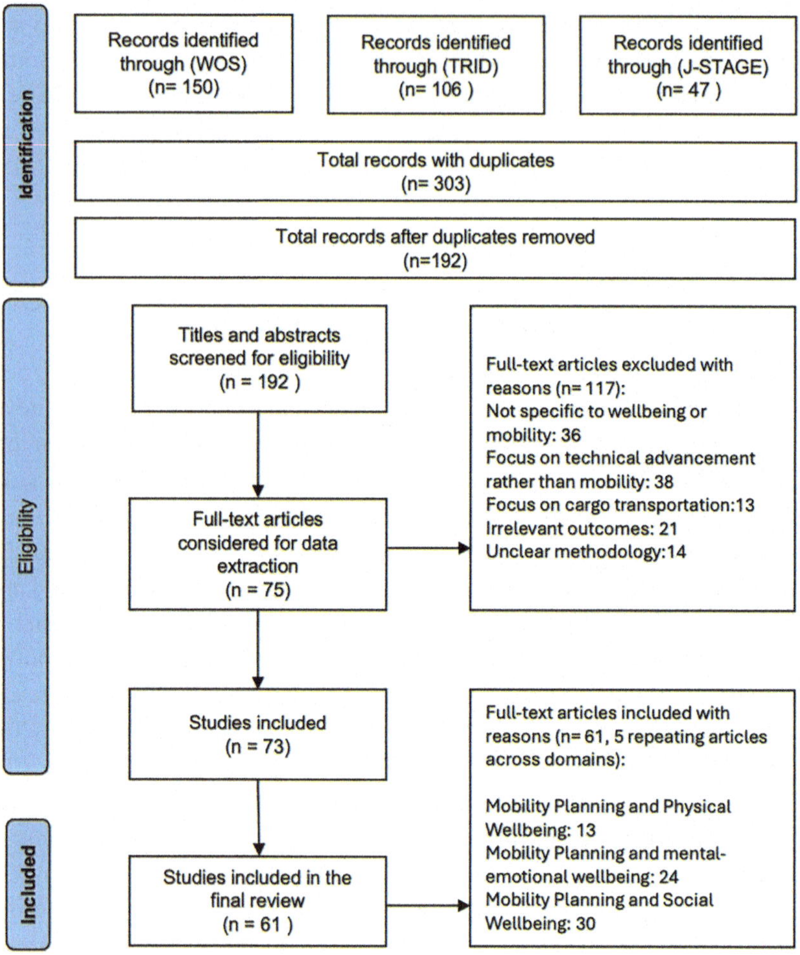

Fig. 1 PRISMA diagram of the screening process.

This process ensured a dataset that highlights how mobility planning shapes post-disaster communities, and wellbeing in disaster-affected areas. Fig. 1 illustrates the screening process in the PRISMA diagram.

3. Results

This study focuses on three domains of post-disaster wellbeing in relation to mobility planning: physical, mental-emotional, and social; Each domain is first explained through conceptual and theory-based studies, followed by examples from disaster specific case-study based research in the context of post-disaster recovery planning and recommendations for better post-disaster mobility planning.

3.1 Mobility planning and physical wellbeing

The importance of mobility in promoting physical health and wellbeing in post disaster contexts is undeniable. Studies reveal that lack of mobility can decrease residents' access to medical institutions, resulting in the compromising of physical wellbeing (Inokuchi, 2021; Kato et al., 2021). Adequate transportation recovery directly affects access to the healthcare, especially for vulnerable groups such as older adults, people with disabilities, and the chronically ill. Disruption in accessibility or poorly designed mobility systems can restrict disaster survivors from essential care, physical activity, and negatively affects their overall physical wellbeing (Yanagihara, 2016; Yang et al., 2024). Barriers to mobility are detrimental for vulnerable populations, especially in various residential environments transitioning from temporary housing to permanent housing. For instance, older adults and residents with disabilities living in one of the temporary housing sites post the 2011 Japan Tsunami have reported having difficulty navigating and using poorly maintained footpaths, which limited their ability to reach shops or public facilities independently and forced them to rely on private cars (Mori and Fujita, 2013). Similarly, some residential areas in Japan after the 2011 Tsunami relocated to higher steep lands or farther from bus routes, increasing the physical burden of daily life and compounding the risk for vulnerable community members. These examples demonstrate how poor mobility design in post-disaster recovery can increase physical strains on community members, especially for those with pre-existing vulnerabilities, forcing social withdrawal, and accelerating dementia caused by heightened physical difficulties (Fuji et al., 2019; Kanamori and Yan, 2024; Takemura, 2012).

Case studies from Miyako and Yamada Town following the 2011 Japan Tsunami report difficulty accessing medical institutions through limited bus services, which required special arrangements such as the use of private transportation for those unable to visit a doctor by themselves (Yanagihara, 2016). Another case study highlights the prolonged physical rehabilitation duration for disaster survivors who were relocated to inland regions, negatively impacting their quality of life (Inohara et al., 2016). Another survey reveals that due to transportation limitations approximately 20 % of residents in coastal areas after the 2011 Japan Tsunami could not access medical institutions, compromising their physical wellbeing (Inokuchi, 2021; Kato et al., 2021). Broader evidence also shows that neglecting inclusive mobility planning can reduce residents' physical activity and physical wellbeing. A study on Māori communities in New Zealand reports worsened vulnerabilities in areas with failed transportation and mobility infrastructure, particularly impacting older adults and people with disabilities (Meher et al., 2021). Research on transportation recovery in New Jersey following 2012 Hurricane Sandy focuses on the need for resilient and inclusive mobility systems for protecting physical safety, as well as continuity of health care in post-disaster contexts (Mudigonda et al., 2019).

3.2 Mobility planning and mental-emotional wellbeing

Accessible public transportation and mobility infrastructure play an important role in reducing isolation and providing a sense of normalcy during recovery by encouraging daily life activities. A study on disaster evacuation preparation found that disaster survivors who could access transportation hubs and could reliably connect to shelters, aids, safety, and social networks reported improved emotional wellbeing (Tipaldo, 2007). In post-disaster recovery efforts, survivors' mental-emotional wellbeing is tied to mobility planning. Limited access to transportation has been shown to increase stress, feelings of isolation, sense of displacement, and psychological strain. Vulnerable populations in rural areas such as seniors who do not have adequate transportation to access mental health facilities face compounded challenges like distance, economic strain, and reduced social contact, resulting in worsened mental-emotional wellbeing (Ghorbanzadeh et al., 2020). In contrast, timely restoration of mobility systems after disasters has been associated with less anxiety and improvement of emotional resilience (Ding, 2024). Additionally, reliable public transportation can support mental health by maintaining social connectivity, reducing isolation and providing disaster survivors with a sense of security during recovery (Blagojević et al., 2022; Xiaobing et al., 2024).

The quality of the recovered transportation infrastructure and mobility systems can influence the mental-emotional wellbeing of the disaster affected communities, as poor or unreliable mobility systems, such as unsafe travel conditions or repeatedly delayed services, have been linked to frustration, anxiety, and increased stress (Tipaldo, 2007; Torales et al., 2024). Restored mobility systems hold values beyond immediate access solutions, and can impact post-disaster tourism by enabling cultural participation, supporting recognition justice, addressing feelings of exclusion, and promoting collective emotional healing (Kurahara, 2013; Martini, 2024).

Following Hurricane Katrina 2005, Mississippi's transportation recovery highlighted the importance of sustainable and accessible transportation systems that are rebuilt alongside community engagement. Such systems contribute to both physical access and the psychological recovery of the survivors (Hassett and Handley, 2006). In another case the response to 2005's Hurricane Katrina and Hurricane Rita revealed that mobility planning is pivotal towards whether disaster survivors experienced isolation, stress, and prolonged disruption in returning to daily life, or instead experienced reconnection with families, the restoration of equitable access, and the assurance of emotional recovery in the short-term and long-term (Mumphrey and Ghara, 2008). Case studies on public transportation recovery following the 2011 Japan Tsunami confirm similar challenges in relocated residential areas and areas with damaged mobility systems (Yoshitaka Motoda, 2011). Case studies following the 2011 Japan tsunami relocation show survivors who relied on available buses that were inconvenient and required reservation-only use reported heightened psychological strains including stress, anxiety, frustration and dependency on temporary alternatives instead (Goto et al., 2023). Other studies on the same disaster found that discontinued public transportation such as bus routes after the disasters led to anxiety and disappointment as its loss was perceived as a loss of social roles by the affected communities (Hajhashemi et al., 2019; Sil et al., 2024; Tanimoto and Minami, 2016). Other cases emphasize how even simple mobility opportunities can support mental wellbeing in residential areas as the disaster survivors expressed higher happiness, social connection and emotional value by having everyday mobility for shopping (Nozaka et al., 2021; Tan et al., 2020). In contrast, poorly planned post-disaster residential areas located on steep slopes could affect vulnerable populations including older adults and members with limited physical health, leading to limited activity, social withdrawal, and even dementia, impacting their long-term mental-emotional wellbeing (Fuji et al., 2019; Monobe and Tokunaga, 2013). These studies underscore that mental-emotional wellbeing in post-disaster recovery are tied to mobility planning: public transportation continuity, inclusivity, and equity can help survivors' daily routines and social participation, promoting psychological resilience (Blake et al., 2019; Faturechi and Miller-Hooks, 2015; Safapour and Kermanshachi, 2021).

3.3 Mobility planning and social wellbeing and equity

Accessible transportation networks are described as the backbone of disaster recovery by ensuring equitable access to services and sustaining connections, and directly supporting the overall wellbeing of the affected populations, and promoting resilience (Trotter and Ivory, 2019). Additionally, resilient mobility systems that can withstand disruptions and provide safe and reliable movements of users in those times ensure continuity of access for all social groups, help reduce inequities, and protect the participation of vulnerable populations in social and economic life (Ding, 2024; Minato and Morimoto, 2012; Tian et al.,. 2023). This evidence places mobility planning as a central contributor to post-disaster wellbeing by enhancing overall quality of life and long-term wellbeing (Ghorbanzadeh et al., 2020; Sil et al., 2024).

Mobility systems promote community connectivity, equity, and social resilience, and could be viewed as a social lifeline. Post-disaster disruptions of mobility decrease walkable accessibility, impact local economic activities, and result in the weakening of social ties and increasing of existing inequalities (Litman, 2003; Rodrigo and Wilkinson, 2021; Yonson et al., 2020).

Social dimensions of mobility are centered around equity and addressing them requires holistic as well as context-driven approaches in recovery processes to increase wellbeing following disasters. During normalcy, users' experience regarding the benefits of mobility systems varies across different social groups. Frequent commuters and empowered members of the society experience more access to discretionary activities compared to vulnerable groups, pensioners and retired people, homemakers, and those who commute occasionally (Dianin et al., 2024; Ghezelloo et al., 2023). Therefore, during disaster recovery periods when more people experience vulnerability and displacement, the existence of transportation planning in recovery plans alone does not bring equitable mobility. Therefore, well-connected transportation nodes are critical for stabilizing social systems and ensuring the continued flow of goods and people and can enhance social resiliency in post-disaster recovery processes where more people experience social isolation (Haxhija et al., 2024; Zhu et al., 2016).

Inclusive mobility systems also promote cultural and social equity, emphasize accessibility and user experience, foster participation in community activities, strengthen social bonds, and sustain equity in recovery (Nakamura, 2024). In addition, integrating social capital into transportation planning can build trust, and enables equitable and resilient recovery (Ritchie, 2017).

Therefore, strategies such as adaptive mobility planning, and prioritizing vulnerable groups' transportation recovery can reduce disparities, promote sustainability and further advance social wellbeing (Fujita et al., 2013; Li et al., 2024; Merschman et al., 2025). Resilient and equitable mobility planning not only restores access, but by emphasizing social connections also functions as a core mechanism for rebuilding social cohesion, equity and wellbeing (Garcia–López et al., 2024; Lichtin et al., 2024; Qviström, 2015).

Case study-based findings of post-disaster related research support these claims. As an example, the Bus Interchange Services following the Christchurch 2010–2011 Earthquakes illustrates that inclusive mobility systems benefit recovery by integrating social, economic, and environmental dimensions to restore equity and wellbeing, and by encouraging equitable community participation essential for effective mobility interventions (Litman, 2003; Rodrigo and Wilkinson, 2021). Case studies from the 2011 Japan Tsunami and 2016 Kaikoura Earthquake in New Zealand both show planning conflicts and poor coordination caused delayed transportation recovery, which interrupted both economic and social revitalization impacted the social wellbeing of the affected residents (Fountain and Cradock-Henry, 2023; Howitt, 2018). Another study on the 2011 Japan Tsunami highlights that mobility preferences shape equity, especially where prioritizing road recovery over railroad and public transportation can deepen the car dependency of the disaster survivors, which limits social fairness and causes an unbalanced use of recovery resources (Nishimura, 2022; Rahimi-Golkhandan and Garvin, 2020). Other studies on the same disaster have highlighted the benefits of contextual and planning mobility solutions such as mobile services, vending vehicles, and shuttle buses provided for residents of the post-disaster relocated housing areas in promoting social interaction and reducing isolation and social withdrawal (Ghezelloo et al., 2022; Iwama et al., 2012; Miyake, 2013; Nakanishi et al., 2013). Also, flexibility in mobility systems such as multimodal transportation including Bus Rapid Transit and inter-city buses which replaced the unrecoverable railroad after the 2011 Japan Tsunami created adaptive mobility solutions helping sustain social wellbeing (Kanamori and Yan, 2018; Tanimoto and Minami, 2016).

3.4 Assessment of evidence on mobility and wellbeing

After the content review, we assessed the methodology through which mobility and wellbeing have been studied in the reviewed research. Table 1 summarizes these findings across the three domains: mobility planning and physical wellbeing, mobility planning and mental-emotional wellbeing, and

Table 1 Summary of assessment of evidence on mobility and wellbeing.

Wellbeing domains	# Of Empirical studies/total (67,6 repeating)	Description
Mobility Planning & Physical Wellbeing	(12/13)	Large-scale surveys: China (Yang et al., 2024); various cases in each, 2011 Japan Tsunami (Miyako City, Iwate Prefecture, Yuriage City, Overall) (Inokuchi, 2021; Kato et al., 2021; Mori and Fujita, 2013; Yanagihara, 2016). Limited number of case studies: various cases in each, 2011 Japan Tsunami (Kesennuma Cirt, Overall) (Fuji et al., 2019; Inohara et al., 2016; Kanamori and Yan, 2024); New Zealand (Meher et al., 2021); Hurricane Sandy, New Jersey (Mudigonda et al., 2019; Tipaldo, 2007); Hurricane Katrina, Mississippi (Hassett and Handley, 2006). Non-empirical: (Takemura, 2012) is conceptual on aging cities (Japan).
Mobility Planning & Mental/ Emotional Wellbeing	(17/24)	Large-scale surveys: urban rail transit, China (Ding, 2024); Hurricane Sandy, USA (Ghorbanzadeh et al., 2020; Hajhashemi et al., 2019); Paraguay (Torales et al., 2024); 2011 Japan Tsunami, Otsuchi Town (Nozaka et al., 2021). Limited number of case studies: NYC, USA (Tipaldo, 2007); Hurricane Sandy, USA (Hajhashemi et al., 2019), Delhi, India (Sil et al., 2024); Shanghai, China (Xiaobing et al., 2024); Canada, simulated disaster recovery (Blagojević et al., 2022); Japan 2011 Tsunami (Kamaishi City, Iwate Prefecture, and overall) (Fuji et al., 2019; Goto et al., 2023; Kurahara, 2013; Monobe and Tokunaga, 2013; Tanimoto and Minami, 2016; Yoshida and Nakamura, 2013; Yoshitaka Motoda, 2011). Non-empirical: Japan 2011 Tsunami (Martini, 2024); China (Tan et al., 2020); reviews/ frameworks (Blake et al., 2019; Faturechi and Miller-Hooks, 2015; Ghorbanzadeh et al., 2020; Mumphrey and Ghara, 2008; Safapour and Kermanshachi, 2021).

Mobility Planning & Social/Social Wellbeing	(21/30)	Large-scale surveys: USA (Rahimi-Golkhandan and Garvin, 2020); Switzerland (Lichtin et al., 2024); Spain (Garcia–López et al., 2024), Limited number of case studies: Christchurch 2011, NZ (Fountain and Cradock-Henry, 2023; Rodrigo and Wilkinson, 2021); Delhi, India (Sil et al., 2024); Kesennuma City, Ishinomaki City and other cases from Japan 2011 Tsunami (Fujita et al., 2013; Ghezelloo et al., 2022; Ghezelloo et al., 2023; Howitt, 2018; Iwama et al., 2012; Kanamori and Yan, 2018, 2024; Minato and Morimoto, 2012; Miyake, 2013; Nakanishi et al., 2013); Kaikōura Earthquake, NZ 2016 (Fountain and Cradock-Henry, 2023); USA (Ghorbanzadeh et al., 2020; Merschman et al., 2025; Zhu et al., 2016); China (Li et al., 2024). Non-empirical: Mostly provide policy/theoretical framing (Dianin et al., 2024; Haxhija et al., 2024; Litman, 2003; Nakamura, 2024; Nishimura, 2022; Qviström, 2015; Ritchie, 2017; Tian et al., 2023; Trotter and Ivory, 2019; Yonson et al., 2020)

mobility planning and social wellbeing. Authors listed each domain with the number of related studies in our database, distinguished empirical studies based on their sample size and case studies and non-empirical studies by their approach. This classification highlights that even though the majority of the research is empirical studies, they mostly include limited and small sample size studies.

4. Summary

Table 2 summarizes the reviewed literature on the impacts of post-disaster recovery through mobility planning on physical, mental-emotional, and social wellbeing and equity. This table reviews wellbeing domains side by side with the consequences of disrupted mobility, such as restricted access, heightened stress, and weakened social cohesion. It

Table 2 Summary of the reviewed literature regarding impacts of disaster and post disaster recovery through mobility on mental health, physical health, and social connectivity.

Wellbeing domains	Consequences	Context-driven solutions	Positive impacts of mobility planning for community recovery
Physical Wellbeing	Reduced access to essential services and public facilities; reduced physical activity; barriers to essential services and daily physical activities (Mori and Fujita, 2013; Yanagihara, 2016)	Customized transportation services in Yamada Town and Ofunato City after the 2011 Japan Tsunami; locally adaptable transit systems in New Jersey post-Hurricane Sandy, and Mississippi transportation recovery after Hurricane Katrina (Ghezelloo et al., 2023; Hassett and Handley, 2006; Mudigonda et al., 2019; Yanagihara, 2016)	Enhanced recovery by maintaining service access; walkable access to nearby facilities and services; improved health outcomes with restored physical mobility and walkability; reduced car reliance (Hajhashemi et al., 2019; Kurahara, 2013; Mumphrey and Ghara, 2008; Yanagihara, 2016)
Mental-emotional Wellbeing	Increased isolation; increased emotional distress; stress from limited access to essential and secondary services; disruption in daily life routines (Inokuchi, 2021; Kanamori and Yan, 2018; Tipaldo, 2007; Toyoshima and Iwafune, 2013; Yanagihara, 2016)	Social-engagement buses in Ofunato City and Yamada Town after the 2011 Japan Tsunami; mobile services and shuttle buses for relocated residents (Ghezelloo et al., 2022; Goto et al., 2023; Kurahara, 2013; Nozaka et al., 2021)	Improved emotional wellbeing from restored continuity, improved access to essential services and facilities (Ding, 2024; Ghorbanzadeh et al., 2020; Kurahara, 2013; Mumphrey and Ghara, 2008; Sil et al., 2024)

Social Wellbeing	Disruption of social ties and daily routines; weakened social cohesion and participation; limited social activities and engagement; decreased civic engagement and social equity (Inokuchi, 2021; Kanamori and Yan, 2018; Ritchie, 2017; Tipaldo, 2007; Yoshitaka Motoda, 2011)	Multimodal systems in Christchurch post-earthquake; community-driven mobility projects in Kaikōura after the 2016 earthquake; vending vehicles and mobile services in post-disaster Japan (Fountain and Cradock-Henry, 2023; Ghezelloo et al., 2022; Iwama et al., 2012; Miyake, 2013; Nakanishi et al., 2013; Rodrigo and Wilkinson, 2021)	Reconnection to community spaces and hubs; strengthened networks and recovery engagement; greater access to events and social gatherings; stronger community bonds and resilience (Ding, 2024; Fountain and Cradock-Henry, 2023; Ghorbanzadeh et al., 2020; Martini, 2024; Nakamura, 2024; Nozaka et al., 2021)

also looks at the context- driven solutions and the positive outcomes achievable through solutions such as inclusive mobility planning, including restored physical activity, emotional resilience, and community reconnection. Based on reviewed case-study based articles, the table presents real-world tailored interventions that provide actionable models for practice.

5. Discussion

This review demonstrates that mobility planning is a critical determinant of post-disaster wellbeing across three domains: physical, mental-emotional, and social (Table 2). Although the findings are categorized for analytical clarity, the impacts frequently overlap across multiple dimensions of well-being and should not be regarded as independent outcomes.

Physical Wellbeing: Case evidence from Japan, New Zealand, and the United States shows that disrupted or poorly designed mobility systems limit access to healthcare, increase physical strain, and reduce daily activity, while resilient and inclusive transportation such as rapid restoration of bus routes or multimodal transit supports health continuity and active living.

Mental-emotional Wellbeing: Survivors facing displacement with limited transportation options report heightened stress, isolation, and anxiety. Conversely, timely mobility restoration and context-driven solutions (e.g., community-driven, neighborhood shuttle buses) reduce psychological strains and help restore a sense of normalcy.

Social Wellbeing and Equity: Mobility planning functions as a social lifeline and enables civic engagement, promotes local economies, and rebuilds trust among community members. Context-Driven solutions and interventions such as mobile services and adaptive multimodal systems can foster equity and strengthen social cohesion.

6. Conclusion

This review confirms that equitable, context-specific mobility systems are fundamental to post-disaster recovery and community wellbeing. Synthesizing evidence from diverse case studies shows that well-designed mobility systems do more than just transit the displaced disaster survivors: they enable continuous access, reduce psychological stress and isolation, and strengthen social networks. Across the three examined domains of wellbeing- physical, mental-emotional, and social- mobility planning emerges as a fundamental factor for rebuilding resilience, bridging the gap between physical reconstruction and the restoration of disaster affected community. These findings confirm that mobility planning in post-disaster contexts operates as a both structural and psychosocial determinant of wellbeing, and inclusive, resilient transportation systems not only promote essential access but also support equity, social participation, and long-term recovery.

6.1 Recommendations

According to the findings of this manuscript, the authors recommend the following applications by planners and stakeholders for improving the field of post-disaster mobility recovery planning and the wellbeing of the residents.

1. Context-sensitive planning can benefit vulnerable groups such as older adults, people with disabilities, or rural residents, by situating routes, stops, and services where they are most needed, thereby enhancing physical, mental-emotional, and social wellbeing.
2. Recovery mobility planning should employ participatory, place-based approaches, allowing residents to help design mobility systems that reflect their daily routines and cultural practices.

3. Planners should integrate multimodal, flexible, adaptive transportation modes such as on-demand buses, temporary transit hubs, and walkable linkages, that can serve as communities transition from disaster surviving to normalcy.

6.2 Avenues for future research

The review found that methodological challenges exist in current post-disaster mobility and wellbeing studies (Table 1). The reviewed cases had the following characteristics:

- Heavy reliance on conceptual frameworks that lack empirical testing.
- Heavy reliance on small-scale, cross-sectional designs that limit extendable impacts.

A major limitation of the existing literature is that, although much of it is described as empirical, most studies are based on small and narrowly focused case-study samples. This constraint reduces the generalizability of observed relationships between mobility planning and post-disaster well-being, and it underscores the need for larger, more diverse research to create guidelines.

Based on the findings, the authors recommend that future mobility planning for post-disaster recovery research should adopt mixed-methods and longitudinal designs and evaluate context-sensitive mobility interventions for their case studies, obtaining larger scale case study samples.

6.3 AI disclaimer

This paper utilized ChatGPT, an AI language model developed by OpenAI, for English language and grammar review.

References

Aldrich, D.P., 2012. Building Resilience: Social Capital in Post-Disaster Recovery. University of Chicago Press.

Blagojević, N., Didier, M., Stojadinović, B., 2022. Simulating the role of transportation infrastructure for community disaster recovery. Proc. Inst. Civ. Eng. - Bridge Eng. 175 (3), 150–159. https://doi.org/10.1680/jbren.21.00018.

Blake, D., Stevenson, J., Wotherspoon, L., Ivory, V., Trotter, M., 2019. The role of data and information exchanges in transport system disaster recovery: a New Zealand case study. Int. J. Disaster Risk Reduct. 39, 101124.

Cheng, Y., & Zhang, Z. (2022). A resilience-based routing planning and scheduling model for post-disaster transportation network recovery with multiple repair teams. 2022 4th International Conference on System Reliability and Safety Engineering (SRSE), 97–103. https://doi.org/10.1109/SRSE56746.2022.10067487.

Cutter, S.L., Boruff, B.J., Shirley, W.L., 2003. Social vulnerability to environmental hazards. Soc. Sci. Q. 84 (2), 242–261.

Dianin, A., Gidam, M., Hauger, G., Ravazzoli, E., 2024. Measuring public transport accessibility to fixed activities and discretionary opportunities: a space–time approach. Eur. Transp. Res. Rev. 16 (1), 9.

Ding, X., 2024. The spatiotemporal evolution mechanism of urban rail transit fault propagation in networked operation modes. Urban Rail Transit 10, 65–88.

Faturechi, R., Miller-Hooks, E., 2015. Measuring the performance of transportation infrastructure systems in disasters: a comprehensive review. J. Infrastruct. Syst. 21 (1), 04014025.

Fountain, J., Cradock-Henry, N.A., 2023. We're all in this together? Community resilience and recovery in Kaikōura following the 2016 Kaikōura-Hurunui earthquake. N. Z. J. Geol. Geophys. 66 (2), 162–176.

Fuji, Y., Okazaki, K., Nakano, H., Wen, Z., Uemura, M., Hirosaki, M., et al., 2019. Effects of social participatory exercise intervention on physically inactive elderly among evacuees living in temporary housing after the Great East Japan Earthquake: a preliminary study. Res. Exer. Epidemiol. 21 (2), 104–112. https://doi.org/10.24804/ree.21.104.

Fujita, M., Mori, K., Oka, M., Suzuki, K., Akiyama, T., Sakagami, T., Amano, K., 2013. Preliminary survey on daily transportation in the disaster-affected areas: a case study of higashimatsushima and ishinomaki districts (special issue: the third report on the great East Japan earthquake recovery — welfare communities, housing, and transportation after the disaster). J. Jpn Assoc. Incl. Soc. 15 (1), 13–17.

Garcia–López, M.-À., Nicolini, R., Sabaté, J.L.R., 2024. Understanding high-frequent bus riders: congestion, education, and riders' preferences. Case Stud. Transp. Policy 16, 101187.

Ghannad, P., Lee, Y.-C., Choi, J.O., 2021. Prioritizing postdisaster recovery of transportation infrastructure systems using multiagent reinforcement learning. J. Manag. Eng. 37 (1), 04020100.

Ghezelloo, Y., Hokugo, A., Maly, E., Shiomi, Y., 2022. Authorization and levels of justice in recovery of gathering spaces after the great East Japan earthquake and tsunami 2011. Prog. Disaster Sci. 13, 100217.

Ghezelloo, Y., Hokugo, A., Tsukihashi, O., 2023. Production of gathering spaces in post-disaster recovery scenarios: case studies from the Great East Japan Earthquake and Tsunami-2011. City, Territ. Archit. 10 (1), 11.

Ghorbanzadeh, M., Kim, K., Ozguven, E.E., Horner, M.W., 2020. A comparative analysis of transportation-based accessibility to mental health services. Transp. Res. Part D: Transp. Environ. 81, 102278.

Goto, J., Sugimoto, C., Tezuka, Y., 2023. Current status and issues of reconstruction town planning in unosumai area, City of Kamaishi focusing on the community living environment. J. City Plann. Ins. Japan 58 (3), 1360–1367. https://doi.org/10.11361/journalcpij.58.1360.

Hajhashemi, E., Murray-Tuite, P.M., Hotle, S.L., Wernstedt, K., 2019. Using agent-based modeling to evaluate the effects of Hurricane Sandy's recovery timeline on the ability to work. Transp. Res. Part D: Transp. Environ. 77, 506–524.

Halleröd, B., Seldén, D., 2013. The multi-dimensional characteristics of wellbeing: how different aspects of wellbeing interact and do not interact with each other. Soc. Indic. Res. 113 (3), 807–825.

Hassett, W.L., Handley, D.M., 2006. Hurricane Katrina: Mississippi's response. Public Works Manag. Policy 10 (4), 295–305.

Haxhija, S., Duran-Rodas, D., Larriva, M.T.B., Wulfhorst, G., 2024. A mobility justice framework to prioritize areas for mobility interventions. Res. Transp. Bus. Manag. 56, 101192.

Howitt, A.M., 2018. Recreating livable communities after catastrophe: Managing the recovery from Japan's Earthquake, Tsunami, and Nuclear Disaster of 2011.

Inohara, S., Watanabe, K., Sugimoto, K., Kato, H., Hayashi, Y., 2016. Evaluation of regional resilience based on the change in the survival and life environment after large-scale disasters. J. Jpn Soc. Civil Eng. Ser. D3 (Infrastruct. Plann. Manag.) 72 (5), I_283–I_291. https://doi.org/10.2208/jscejipm.72.I_283.

Inokuchi, K., 2021. Influences on life of disaster victims under the integrated community care system and group relocation for disaster mitigation in Japan findings of the survey on the great East Japan Earthquake victims. J. Health Welfare Policy 4 (1), 59–84. https://doi.org/10.20690/jhwp.4.1_59.

Iwama, N., Sasaki, M., Tanaka, K., Komaki, N., Asakawa, T., 2012. Recovery process of the food distribution system in a disaster-affected area and living conditions of disaster victims in temporary housing. E-journal GEO 7, 178–196.

Kanamori, T., Yan, W., 2018. Walking accessibility assessment of elderly people in collective relocation and their effects on lifestyle after the great east Japan Earthquake—A case study in Kesennuma City, JAPAN. J. Jpn Soc. Civil Eng. Ser. D3 (Infrastruct. Plann. Manag.) 74 (4), 261–274.

Kanamori, T., Yan, W., 2024. A study of urban structural changes associated with disaster reconstruction and their impact on walkability of collective relocation complexes ——A case study in KESENNUMA city, JAPAN. Jpn J. JSCE 80 (1). https://doi.org/10.2208/jscejj.23-00156. Article 23-00156.

Kato, H., Murao, O., Sakaguchi, T., 2021. The living environment and living style in disaster public housing in Yuriage District during the revitalization period after the Great East Japan Earthquake. J. City Plann. Ins Japan 56 (3), 1501–1508.

Klinenberg, E., 2018. Palaces for the People: How Social Infrastructure Can Help Fight Inequality, Polarization, and the Decline of Civic Life. Crown.

Kurahara, M., 2013. A study on 'NEW PUBLIC COMMONS' in post-earthquake reconstruction activities–a case study of 'model project to support new public commons' in Iwate prefecture. AIJ J. Technol. Des. 19 (41), 309–314. https://doi.org/10.3130/aijt.19.309.

Li, Q., Peng, S., Chen, Z., Du, H., Liu, Y., Li, W., 2024. Resilience evaluation and renovation strategies of public spaces in old communities from a disaster-adaptive perspective. Sustainability 16 (16), 6823.

Lichtin, F., Smith, E.K., Axhausen, K.W., Bernauer, T., 2024. How much should public transport services be expanded, and who should pay? Experimental evidence from Switzerland. Transp. Policy 158, 64–74.

Litman, T.A., 2003. Economic value of walkability. Transp. Res. Rec. 1828 (1), 3–11.

Margolis, S., Schwitzgebel, E., Ozer, D.J., Lyubomirsky, S., 2021. Empirical relationships among five types of well-being. Measuring Well-Being: Interdisciplinary Perspectives from the Social Sciences and the Humanities. Oxford Academic, pp. 460–492.

Martini, A., 2024. Geographies of mobility justice: post-disaster tourism, recognition justice, and affect in Tohoku, Japan. Mobilities 19 (3), 363–378.

Meher, M., Spray, J., Wiles, J., Anderson, A., Willing, E., Witten, K., et al., 2021. Locating transport sector responsibilities for the wellbeing of mobility-challenged people in Aotearoa New Zealand. Wellbeing, space Soc. 2, 100034.

Merschman, E., Doustmohammadi, M., Salman, A.M., Anderson, M., 2025. Post-disaster decision-making framework for roadway networks considering social vulnerability. Travel Behav. Soc. 38, 100910.

Miles, S.B., Chang, S.E., 2006. Modeling community recovery from earthquakes. Earthq. Spectra 22 (2), 439–458.

Minato, N., Morimoto, R., 2012. Collaborative management of regional air transport during natural disasters: case of the 2011 East Japan earthquake and tsunami. Res. Transp. Bus. Manag. 4, 13–21.
Miyake, S., 2013. Various subjects in connection with housing reconstruction by group move etc. J. Rural Plann. Assoc. 31 (4), 549–552. https://doi.org/10.2750/arp.31.549.
Monobe, K., Tokunaga, Y., 2013. A proposal for earthquake reconstruction support by plan and visualization of bus route using gis. J. Jpn Soc. Civil Eng., Ser. F3 (Civ. Eng. Inform.) 69 (2), II_28–II_35. https://doi.org/10.2208/jscejcei.69.II_28.
Mori, K., Fujita, M., 2013. Damage and challenges of transportation in iwate prefecture (special issue: the third report on the great East Japan Earthquake Recovery — Welfare communities, housing, and transportation after the disaster). J. Jpn Assoc. Incl. Soc. 15 (1), 4–8.
Mudigonda, S., Ozbay, K., Bartin, B., 2019. Evaluating the resilience and recovery of public transit system using big data: case study from New Jersey. J. Transp. Saf. Sec. 11 (5), 491–519.
Mumphrey, R.A., Ghara, H., 2008. Hurricanes katrina and rita–Louisiana'S Response and recovery. Sixth National Seismic Conference on Bridges and HighwaysMultidisciplinary Center for Earthquake Engineering ResearchSouth Carolina Department of TransportationFederal Highway AdministrationTransportation Research Board.
Nakamura, F., 2024. Role of public transport in supporting the urban cultural and creative functions. IATSS Res. 48 (3), 342–346.
Nakanishi, H., Matsuo, K., Black, J., 2013. Transportation planning methodologies for post-disaster recovery in regional communities: the East Japan Earthquake and tsunami 2011. J. Transp. Geograp. 31, 181–191.
Nishimura, H., 2022. Restoration and reconstruction of transportation after the Great EastJapan Earthquake and remaining issues. J. Transp. Problems Hum Right 2022 (37-38), 2–10. https://doi.org/10.20611/kotsuken.2022.37-38_2.
Norris, F.H., Friedman, M.J., Watson, P.J., Byrne, C.M., Diaz, E., Kaniasty, K., 2002. 60,000 Disaster victims speak: Part I. An empirical review of the empirical literature, 1981—2001. Psychiatry 65 (3), 207–239.
Nozaka, S., Mugikura, T., Asakawa, T., 2021. Victims' sense of recovery and related background factors after rebuilding their houses following the great East Japan Earthquake: a questionnaire survey of disaster public housing residents in Otsuchi Town. Ann. Reg. Community. Stud. 33.
Qviström, M., 2015. Putting accessibility in place: a relational reading of accessibility in policies for transit-oriented development. Geoforum 58, 166–173. https://doi.org/10.1016/j.geoforum.2014.11.007.
Rahimi-Golkhandan, A., Garvin, M.J., 2020. A socio-economic comparison of urban areas with different transportation system diversity. Constr. Res. Congr. 2020.
Rath, T., Harter, J.K., 2010. Wellbeing: The Five Essential Elements. Simon and Schuster.
Ritchie, L., 2017. Social capital and transportation: critical assets in community resilience. TR News 311.
Rodrigo, N., Wilkinson, S., 2021. Impact of flagship projects on the recovery of a city post-disaster. Int. J. Disaster Risk Reduct. 58, 102191.
Safapour, E., Kermanshachi, S., 2021. Reconstruction of transportation infrastructure with high complexity: mitigating strategies for effective post-disaster reconstruction. Int. Conf. Transp. Dev.
Sil, A., Chowdhury, S., Thoreau, R., 2024. Challenges and barriers for gender-inclusive public transport policies and practice in Delhi, India. Case Studies Transp. Policy 16, 101201.
Takemura, N., 2012. Creating compact cities in a society with a declining and aging population. *Nihon Ronen Igakkai zasshi*. Jpn J. Geriatr. 49 (6), 701–704.

Tan, Z., Xu, M., Meng, Q., Li, Z.-C., 2020. Evacuating metro passengers via the urban bus system under uncertain disruption recovery time and heterogeneous risk-taking behaviour. Transp. Res. Part C: Emerg. Technol. 119, 102761.
Tanimoto, M., Minami, M., 2016. A study on the factors influencing the formation of residents' intentions to maintain public transportation based on a resident awareness survey. Jpn J Transp. Econ. 59, 157–164. https://doi.org/10.32238/koutsugakkai.59.0_157.
Tian, T., Liang, Y., Peng, Z., Cheng, Y., Chen, K., 2023. Assessing the dynamic resilience of Urban rail transit networks during their evolution using a ridership-weighted network. PLoS One 18 (9), e0291639.
Tipaldo, J. M. (2007). New York City's Coastal Storm Evacuation Plan: Implementation, Monitoring and Recovery. In ITE 2007 Annual Meeting and ExhibitInstitute of Transportation Engineers (ITE).
Torales, J., Barrios, I., Melgarejo, O., Amarilla, D., O'Higgins, M., Navarro, R., et al., 2024. The questionnaire on the use of public transportation and well-being (QUPTW): a national survey and validation in Paraguay. J. Transp. Health 38, 101883.
Toyoshima, M., Iwafune, M., 2013. Living environment and residents' health in temporary housing after the great East Japan Earthquake: recommendations based on an empirical study at the personal scale. E-J. GEO 8.
Trotter, M.J., Ivory, V., 2019. A systems-based framework as an engagement tool: adaptation for insight on transport network resilience. Case Stud. Transp. Policy 7 (2), 167–177.
Xiaobing, D., Hua, H., Zhigang, L., Qingquan, M., 2024. The spatiotemporal evolution mechanism of urban rail transit fault propagation in networked operation modes. Urban Rail Transit 10 (1), 65–88.
Yanagihara, H., 2016. Medical relief response by miyako public health center after the great East Japan Earthquake and Tsunami, 2011. Nihon Koshu Eisei Zasshi, Jpn J. Public Health 63 (2), 75–86.
Yang, Z., Guo, Y., Feng, X., Zhou, Y., Zhou, P., Li, X., Qian, X., 2024. Evaluating temporal variations in access to multi-tier hospitals using personal vehicles and public transit: Implications for healthcare equity. Sustain. Cities Soc. 113, 105687.
Yonson, R., Noy, I., Ivory, V.C., Bowie, C., 2020. Earthquake-induced transportation disruption and economic performance: the experience of Christchurch, New Zealand. J. Transp. Geogr. 88, 102823.
Yoshida, M., Nakamura, M., 2013. Damage and challenges of transportation in Miyagi Prefecture (special issue: the third report on the great East Japan Earthquake recovery — Welfare communities, housing, and transportation after the disaster). J. Jpn Assoc. Inclu. Soc. 15 (1), 9–12.
Yoshitaka Motoda, S.U., 2011. Public transportation restoration process at devastated city by tsunami - Case study at Rikuzentakata city - *Proceeding of Infrastructure Planning and Management*. JSCE.
Zhu, Y., Ozbay, K., Xie, K., Yang, H., 2016. Using big data to study resilience of taxi and subway trips for hurricanes Sandy and Irene. Transp. Res. Rec. 2599 (1), 70–80.

CHAPTER TEN

Exploring the health implications of new mobility: Rideshare, automated vehicles, urban air mobility, and beyond

William Riggs*
Management, Urban Affairs and Public Administration University of San Francisco, San Francisco, CA, United States
*Corresponding author. e-mail address: wriggs@usfca.edu

Contents

Abstract

This chapter examines the intersection of transport and public health, focusing on the impact of new mobility solutions, such as rideshare, automated and autonomous vehicles, and urban air mobility. These technologies have the potential to reshape physical activity patterns, environmental exposures, and stress levels. And while these innovations may enhance accessibility, the benefits may be unequally distributed and counteract gains in active modes of travel connected with positive health outcomes

Advances in Transport Policy and Planning, Volume 18
ISSN 2543-0009, https://doi.org/10.1016/bs.atpp.2026.07.005

and urban regeneration. The purpose of this chapter is to advance perspectives on how new mobility systems intersect with health determinants, evaluating opportunities and risks posed by these disruptions. Potential identified risks include: the potential for reduced activity levels; less social cohesion and labor protections; environmental exposure; and reduced psychological well-being. To mitigate these risks various strategies are discussed including health impact assessments, prioritized infrastructure for active modes, clean technologies, and universal access. These ideas, while not exhaustive, aim to provide insight for policy development so that the benefits of new mobility technologies can foster a healthier and more inclusive future for all.

1. Introduction

Rapid technological change during the twenty-first century has dramatically shaped how we travel through urban space. Consumers have more access to transport that is more reliable, convenient, flexible, and digitized than ever before (Rayle et al., 2016). Micromobility has expanded the range that humans can achieve with non-motorized travel via bike and scooters, and platforms like Uber and Lyft have revolutionized rideshare access (Clewlow and Mishra, 2017; Meyer and Shaheen, 2017; Shaheen et al., 2017). At the same time, autonomous vehicles (AV) promise to reduce human error in driving and offer more efficient traffic (Fagnant and Kockelman, 2014; Lipson and Kurman, 2016; Riggs, 2019), yet in the long term pose questions about auto-dependency. And urban air mobility (UAM) could potentially introduce concepts for short-range flight within metropolitan areas that could radically reshape cities (Cohen et al., 2020; Cohen et al., 2021; Holden and Goel, 2016).

These developments raise broader societal impacts, particularly in terms of urban planning – a determinant of public health. Land use and transport are highly connected to health, albeit through a complex web of causality (Krieger, 1994). And transportation has been found to be a key social determinant of health, influencing exposure to pollutants, opportunities for physical activity, and mental well-being (Frank et al., 2006; Jackson et al., 2013). The increasing automation and privatization of transport services might create unanticipated externalities that exacerbate health inequities if not addressed proactively.

This chapter explores how shared mobility, rideshare, autonomous vehicles, and urban air mobility systems could affect health directly and indirectly, with the purpose of advancing a perspective on how new mobility systems intersect with public health and factors planners and policymakers should be considering as we move into the future. I propose a conceptual framework to evaluate these systems based on physical, environmental, and psychosocial health outcomes. To reiterate throughout this chapter, I define 'new mobility' specifically referring to shared mobility, shared micromobility, automated and autonomous vehicles (referred to jointly as AVs), and urban air mobility (UAM). This framework is used to discuss and propose how planners and policymakers might adopt a proactive approach for the healthy design and deployment of these technologies.

2. Conceptual framework

To understand the public health implications of emerging transport technologies, it is important to establish a baseline for healthy transport and map to theories of public health that define individual vs. societal determinants of health (Bircher and Kuruvilla, 2014; Giles-Corti and Donovan, 2002). Conceptual models have framed pathways between public health and transport, most integrating traditional as well as social determinants of health (Giles-Corti and Donovan, 2002; Hahn, 2019). In terms of pathways between land use and transport and public health established frameworks have considered the built environment and infrastructure within the framework of travel behavior, mode choice, and health indicators but they have not fully integrated new mobility (Frank et al., 2019; Glazener et al., 2021, Guo et al., 2024).

While frameworks like Glazener et al. (2021) provide a strong foundation for disruptive technologies, the model does not fully capture several dynamics that are central to new mobility ecosystems, such as: automation-driven behavioral changes and economics; psychosocial stressors related to uncertainty, trust, and human–machine interaction; equity impacts driven by differential exposure to emerging technologies; new spatial, temporal, infrastructural patterns and environmental issues introduced by AV and fleets and aerial mobility. A new conceptual framework is required because existing transport–health models do not fully address automation-driven behavioral changes, equity-mediated exposure differences, human–machine interaction stressors, or emerging environmental pathways.

Fig. 1 provides a conceptual framework mapping these individual-level characteristics to a broader, evaluative framework for new and emerging mobility not merely based on efficiency or innovation but also on their capacity to promote or hinder health across multiple dimensions. This

Fig. 1 A simplified conceptual framework for evaluation of the health implications of new mobility.

framework is used as a guiding theme to introduce new mobility impacts on health in this chapter.

To explain the grounding, first, in the area of *Physical Activity*, just a few minutes of exercise a day can have a vast impact on health. Therefore, transport—particularly through active modes of travel—has been directly connected with increased physical activity. Transit riders have been found to have 15 min more physical activity daily than those that do not use transit (Saelens et al., 2014). Walking, biking, and public transport infrastructure and supportive land uses inherently involve more movement compared to private car use (Frank et al., 2006; Sallis et al., 2016, 2012). Likewise communities that have increased commute mode diversity or modal options have better health outcomes (Frederick et al., 2018). Conversely, a modal shift toward more sedentary options can negatively impact cardiovascular health, contribute to obesity, and increase the risk of chronic diseases (Bauer et al., 2014).

Second, *Environmental* exposure to particulates from transport—particularly to air pollutants, noise, and urban heat—have been associated with, respiratory diseases and increased mortality rates. For example, PM 2.5 is directly associated with increased morbidity (Kioumourtzoglou et al., 2016). Noise pollution from traffic and potential new forms of mobility such as urban air mobility is associated with sleep disturbances, stress, and cardiovascular disease (Basner et al., 2014; Mulero-Pázmány et al., 2017). The adoption of electric, autonomous, and aerial mobility has the potential to reduce some of these exposures, but this depends heavily on energy sources, deployment strategies, and integration with existing infrastructure.

Third, *Psycho-Social* stressors include the time, predictability, and safety of travel. Long commutes and unreliable transport systems elevate stress levels and reduce time for family and community engagement (Clark et al., 2020). On-demand transport and automation may offer psychological relief by reducing travel uncertainty—although they may also create new anxieties about privacy, job displacement, or technology failures. Research from autonomous vehicle pilots shows increased comfort and safety from riders, particularly women report that they are safer in an AV rideshare vs. one driven by human drivers (Riggs, 2024; Riggs et al., 2023). At the same time a large body of work has shown that emergence of rideshare was based largely on economic and community factors, with behavioral economics underlying the psycho-social dimension (Rayle et al., 2014).

The community factors highlighted in Rayle's work bring up the importance of *Equity* as an undergirding force in connection new mobility and health. Cost, reliability and convenience are cited alongside transit frequency, service quality and their link to equitable access to travel (Alemi et al., 2018; Rayle et al., 2016). Research has also found that rideshare meets needs at times and locations where other networks cannot cover (Riggs et al., 2023; Riggs and Cornet, 2024).

3. New mobility and physical activity

Rideshare platforms have become a fixture in urban transport ecosystems, providing flexible, door-to-door service through mobile applications. While their growth has been rapid and pervasive, the health implications of this shift are mixed and highly context-dependent. The services, from rideshare to micromobility, have been shown not only to improve reliability and convenience but to fill network gaps and meet last-mile access for the underserved (Delbosc and Thigpen, 2024; Jackson, 2018; Riggs et al., 2021; Riggs and Cornet, 2026). This is consistent with the *conceptual framework* proposed in Fig. 1 and means that on an individual basis many people choose to ride as either complementing or substituting for public transit. When they complement, they may use it to access or increase their public transit access. When they substitute they may eliminate healthier or more active travel from their daily life (although work previously cited from Saelens (2014) suggests that this may not mean a direct correlation with a less healthy lifestyle since they may substitute another activity elsewhere).

For example research has found that original reports showing that rideshare resulted in runaway vehicle miles travelled (VMT)/vehicle kilometers traveled (VKT) may have been overstated as they did not control for the overall increase in VMT and changes in auto-ownership across the population (Montilla et al., 2025). And while rideshare may have taken ridership away from other modes of transport, academic studies show that the impact has been primarily on private vehicles (Hall et al., 2018; Rayle et al., 2016). Research in Boston for example, showed increased public transit ridership where rideshare companies were able to partner with other companies and public agencies to extend service to audiences that have traditionally not been served by taxicabs (Boston Globe, 2013; MBTA, 2015).

In recent years, this has been replicated across other markets (Young et al., 2020), and has also expended to include many services for older adults and people with disabilities. Services like RideWith24, GreatCall, and GoGo-Grandparent provide ridesourcing for those without a smartphone. For example, GoGoGrandparent allows seniors to hail an Uber or Lyft from a landline, to pre-programming destinations, and get call-back telephone support if needed. Waymo for example, has had significant advocacy from blind and low vision who have seen that their service offers increased opportunity to access travel and parallel research shows that the physical activity benefits of automated mobility are most significant in locations that have concentrated vulnerable populations (Lee and Kockelman, 2022; Waymo, 2025).

Work by Circella and others attributes active-lifestyle-inducing new mobility (in part) to environmental beliefs (Circella et al., 2016). Rideshare use has long been heavily dictated by lifestyle choices, a desire for reliability, convenience and the emergence of new technology to support mobility. For example, a study by the American Public Transportation Association (APTA) found that millennials are more inclined to use alternative modes of transport due to environmental, as well as monetary, considerations than other groups. They many times link to travel modes associated with physical actively; e.g. walking and transit (Gehrke et al., 2019).

At the same time, the convenience of rideshare can reduce reliance on active modes like walking and biking. Several studies have shown that rideshare can displace not just private car trips, but also trips that would have otherwise been made by public transit or active travel (Schaller, 2017), although more recent work by (Montilla et al., 2025) shows that the impacts of this are relatively small when considering overall rates of driving increases. While this substitution effect may not hold in every situation, it does have health consequences: lower physical activity from commutes and lower total activity, assuming that commuters do not substitute activity commutes for daily physical activity (which some literature does suggest). Increases in VMT/VKT associated with rideshare can contribute to congestion and in localized air pollution when clean air vehicles are not involved.

At the same time one of the most significant benefits physical activity and public benefits in the case automated rideshare is safety. Autonomous Vehicles (AVs), Advanced Driver Assistance Systems (ADAS), and Autonomous Driving Systems (ADS) has become a focal point in efforts to mitigate roadway departure crashes and enhance roadside safety infrastructure worldwide—a distinct benefit at the individual level of physical dimension of public health (Crute et al., 2018; Riggs, 2022). To reduce collisions, particularly for vulnerable road usersm AVs are equipped with sophisticated sensors and AI-driven algorithms and can help compliment traditional approaches to roadside safety (Rana and Hossain, 2023; Tengilimoglu et al., 2023).

According the US National Traffic Safety Administration, by removing human error—which accounts for over 90 % of traffic collisions—AVs could dramatically reduce road injuries and fatalities (NHTSA, 2017; NHTSA, 2016). Given these anticipated gains in road safety, there has widespread investment in AV research and pilot programs globally. ADAS, acting as an intermediary between manual driving and full autonomy, already demonstrate promising capabilities in collision prevention and lane-keeping assistance.

And while there is much that we do not know about the future of automated and autonomous driving, the impacts extend far beyond safety into the societal and environmental correlates of health. Most Level-4 autonomous research has shown that autonomous vehicles complement public transport and largely substitute for rideshare with some reduction in cycling behavior (Riggs et al., 2023, 2022). In this light, it could be assumed that autonomous travel might result in some level of reduction in walking and cycling, but it is unclear even whether most business models for autonomous platforms in the near future will be shared fleet due to the cost of deployments and the complications in rapidly scaling fleets (Riggs and Beiker, 2020); for example, as of 2025, the company Waymo has a global fleet of roughly 1500 vehicles and will only add 2000 vehicles in 2026 to spread across all of its operational markets (Hawkins, 2025).

While some academics have speculated that if AVs could become cheap and convenient, they could induce demand for longer commutes and more dispersed land use patterns, contributing to urban sprawl (Milakis et al., 2017), this is not likely to happen in the near future given that the minimum midpoint cost of vehicle hardware is estimated at $167,160 in late 2024 with little room for cost compression anticipated and most AV providers are developing shared fleet models which are more connected to active transport and livable street design (Appleyard and Riggs, 2023; Riggs and Richardson, 2024).

Paralleling trends in automated rideshare there has been a revolution in shared micromobility with a range of small, often electric, powered vehicles emerging on—usually on shared platforms for short trips, including e-scooters, e-bikes, and traditional bicycles. These modes are increasingly visible in cities worldwide and represent a growing segment of urban mobility, and unlike automotive transport modes, micromobility aligns directly with traditional theories of environmental determinants of health. They support active transport at the individual level, and align well with health-promoting urban environments (Lazarus et al., 2020).

While some post-Covid work suggested that e-scooters may appeal to younger users as opposed to bikes as micromobility platforms (Arup, 2022; Bretones et al., 2023), some of which could be linked to more positive acceptability stereotypes that have been perpetuated around shared bikes/e-bikes (An et al., 2023). Research has shown that access to micromobility platforms appears to vary based on location (Brown and Howell, 2024) and quantitative evaluation of e-bike and e-scooter program across 3 countries indicates a fairly natural age distribution (Delbosc and Thigpen, 2024).

Also, despite these advantages, challenges remain. Injury rates for e-scooter users have raised safety concerns, particularly when infrastructure is inadequate or when devices are used improperly (Trivedi et al., 2019). Regulatory inconsistencies, sidewalk clutter, and access inequities have also emerged as policy issues (Riggs et al., 2021). Ensuring that micromobility contributes positively to public health requires coordinated urban design, safety education, and equitable access programs (Brown and Howell, 2024).

And to be clear, the most straightforward benefit of micromobility is physical activity. Even electric-assisted micromobility platforms (e-bikes or e-scooters) require some exertion, and users of shared micromobility often walk-to-and-from docking stations. These movements accumulate into meaningful health gains, particularly in dense urban areas where short-distance travel is common (Gössling, 2020). And while there is limited research on how rideshare and AVs support or replace active transport what is clear is that micromobility can increase it; and it also yields meaningful gains (Bilgin et al., 2025).

4. New mobility and the environment

While the benefits of micromobility are promoted they are also hotly debated. Most micromobility devices have lower emissions per mile than cars (Fishman and Cherry, 2016), and their small size means they take up less road and parking space, potentially freeing up urban land for parks and walkable areas.

However, life-cycle emissions depend on factors like battery manufacturing, charging practices, and fleet turnover (Hollingsworth et al., 2019). And more recent research suggests that micromobility can be detrimental to greenhouse gas emission (GHG) goals with the rebalancing required to make commercial systems work, and over commercialization having led to adverse impacts (Sun and Ertz, 2022). For example, speculation over longer commutes as vehicles become automated, may be balanced over time from an environmental standpoint, as energy sources change. Almost all AVs are being developed as fully electric, and as such not only can reduce tailpipe emissions, but also optimize broader traffic flow (Hua et al., 2026)

Beyond that, drone delivery systems and urban air mobility (UAM) introduce a distinct set of environmental and public-safety risks that differ meaningfully from surface transport (Raza et al., 2025). Research shows that unmanned aircraft experience higher collision probabilities in dense, low-altitude operating environments, where obstacles, uneven wind conditions, and limited air traffic coordination contribute to system failures (Cohen et al., 2021). Loss-of-control incidents—often caused by propulsion or battery malfunction—are well documented in real-world UAM operations and pose risks of ground-impact injuries to residents and bystanders (Clarke and Bennett Moses, 2014). These risks are not evenly distributed across communities, raising questions about equity in exposure, particularly in neighborhoods likely to experience higher volumes of drone delivery traffic.

In parallel, a growing body of ecological research highlights that drones can disturb wildlife and fragment habitat use. Studies demonstrate that UAM operations can alter bird behavior, elevate their physiological stress responses, and in some cases lead to nest abandonment (Mulero-Pázmány et al., 2017). Drone noise—characterized by high-frequency signatures—can disrupt both wildlife and nearby residents, compounding exposure burdens for communities adjacent to parks, waterways, or open-space preserves (Torija et al., 2020; Torija and Clark, 2021).

Without careful routing protocols that intentionally avoid sensitive habitats and migratory corridors, UAM risks reinforcing environmental inequities rather than alleviating them. Together, these findings illustrate that UAM introduces a new exposure regime, and that environmental and ecological considerations should be integrated into early planning, routing design, and regulatory frameworks.

5. New mobility and psycho-social, emotional dimensions

Beyond these advanced new technologies, new mobility also has impacts on psycho-social, and emotional health. Many of the services also can reduce social isolation while offering a safer alternative to driving; for example facilitating access to social venues and healthcare facilities (Greenwood and Wattal, 2017) and. These factors can contribute to improved mental health and community connectivity. For example, many millennials who primarily use rideshare value the opportunity to work and/or socialize online while traveling (APTA, 2013).

From a psycho-social standpoint, AVs may reduce stress associated with driving. As shown in Fig. 2, research has shown that while AVs reduce fears of nighttime safety they also can be associated with increased anxiety about the driving and emotional discomfort (Riggs, 2024). While highly automated vehicles can lead to concerns about the driving and support systems, riders report concerns about emotional comfort with less positive feedback. Other works have emphasized how there is a need for psycho-social support structures moving into the future, and a need for a focus on human factors and emotional design in new mobility disciplines (Cavoli et al. access date; Kong et al., 2018; Riggs, 2024).

In this light, access and equity remain important. While some assume AV development and deployment have so far catered to affluent early adopters, companies have done targeted outreach to communities of concern and vulnerable populations such as blind and low vision communities and the disabled (Waymo, 2025). Still, ensuring that AVs support health requires integrated land-use planning, equity-centered deployment, and regulation that prioritizes both human and environmental well-

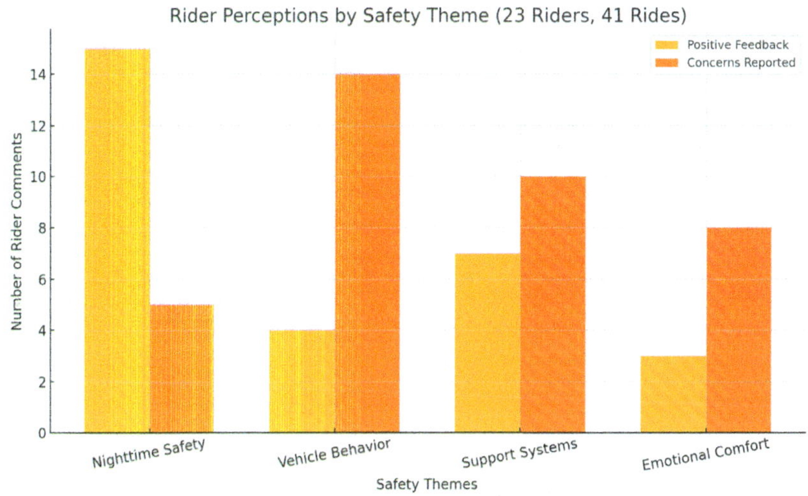

Fig. 2 AV rider perceptions of safety illustrate emotional comfort as a significant concern.

being—something that will only increase as autonomous urban air mobility introduces a radical reimagining of transport.

Concepts such as drone deliveries and electric vertical take-off and landing (eVTOL) vehicles promise rapid point-to-point transport in congested cities. While this could improve access and reduce congestion, the health impacts are largely speculative and under-researched (Cohen et al., 2020; Rajendran et al., 2021). Potential benefits include reduced travel times, especially in emergencies, and less surface congestion, which could improve local air quality and noise levels. However, the noise impacts and visual congestions could pose threats to achieving the benefits of automated mobility and could negatively impact physical and mental well-being. Moreover, vertiports (take-off and landing hubs) may concentrate environmental and acoustic pollution in vulnerable neighborhoods unless carefully planned (Cohen et al., 2021). More research will be needed to assess the health and equit5y implications of automated mobility if it extends to the extensive personalized air travel.

6. New mobility, equity and accessibility

The topic of equity further undergirds the field of public health, and as such new mobility systems must be evaluated not only for their technical sophistication but for their capacity to address or perpetuate health disparities and accessibility. Digital exclusion is one barrier. Rideshare, AV, and UAM services requiring smartphone access and digital literacy, may tend to disproportionately exclude older adults, younger individuals or rural residents. Similarly, geographic access may become uneven. Historically, this has led to mobility gaps that translate into disparities in exposure to environmental stressors and access to health-supporting resources (Moudon et al., 2006; Ulrich et al., 1991).

That said, rideshare services have improved access to mobility for populations previously underserved by traditional transit, such as low-income communities, people with disabilities, and those living in transit deserts (Brown et al., 2020; Brown, 2018). Work from the Federal Reserve of Boston has suggested that rideshare was much more likely to serve areas of the city that had traditionally not been served by the taxi industry (Jackson, 2018). Taxi drivers were 73 % more likely to avoid picking up a Black customer than a White customer, and Black customer who were picked up waited 52 % longer than White riders, with strongest discrimination against women.

The hourly wage of rideshare drivers has long been debated with some suggesting that it was an unsustainable model at less than $10 per hour (Noel, 2018). Rideshare drivers often work long hours without the protections afforded to traditional employees, including healthcare benefits and rest breaks (Riggs, 2019). This can lead to fatigue, stress, and reduced well-being. From a systems perspective, rideshare is a double-edged sword: it can expand access while simultaneously undermining active and sustainable transport practices, and it becomes more complicated in the driverless future. Although automated vehicles can fully account for travel costs in a way where traditional rideshare (on the whole) offers drivers low wages and limited benefits, job retraining and reskilling will be required for many driving jobs in the future.

Policy solutions must correct for these imbalances. These include subsidized fares, universal design standards, accessible app interfaces, and targeted deployment strategies—including full integration for those with disabilities (Riggs and Pande, 2022, 2021)— to achieve true mobility justice. It includes reskilling many for drivers for the new jobs of the automated future so human dignity is retained. Community-based participatory planning can help ensure that innovations meet the needs of all users (Cornet, 2018). This can include developing user personas that map to stakeholders across the economic spectrum (Cornet and Riggs, 2023).

Transportation equity must be a guiding principle in the adoption of emerging technologies. Without it, technological progress will do little to advance public health or social justice.

7. Policy and planning recommendations

In this context, it is important to align new mobility with public health policy goals—since many of the impacts of these new technologies depend on how cities choose to govern them. New mobility innovations require deliberate and coordinated policymaking to anticipate and reduce unintended consequences while maximizing benefits for all. Below are potential recommendations to guide emergent mobility systems that can serve each of the core factors in the conceptual framework: physical activity, environment, psycho-social, and equity.

7.1 Physical activity: Prioritize infrastructure for active modes

Investments in AVs, rideshare, and UAM should not come at the expense of what we already know works for health: safe, continuous infrastructure for walking, cycling, and high-quality public transit. A large body of evidence now shows that active travel is associated with substantial reductions in all-cause mortality, hospitalizations, cardiovascular disease, and even mental health prescriptions compared with non-active commuting (Friel et al., 2024). Recent systematic reviews of active travel interventions also conclude that projects which reallocate space to walking and cycling—protected bike lanes, traffic calming, safer crossings—consistently deliver co-benefits across physical health, emissions, and safety outcomes (Ding et al., 2024; Fitch-Polse and Agarwal, 2025).

That means any deployment of AVs or new mobility services should be bundled with livable and complete streets-style investments rather than widening roadways or preserving auto-priority (Appleyard et al., 2023; Riggs et al., 2020). Low traffic neighborhood policies have been directly correlated with slower speeds and fewer collisions (Furlong et al., 2025). Furthermore automated vehicle technology can integrate with these slow-speed corridors, expanding the net-safety benefit (Schlossberg et al., 2018). Priority should go to networks of connected sidewalks and bikeways, traffic-calmed streets, and transit-priority corridors that make active choices the default; not the exception. Critically, these facilities need to be equitably distributed—not just in high-amenity neighborhoods. Studies on active transport and environmental justice emphasize that lower-income communities often face both higher exposure to traffic risk and fewer high-quality walking and cycling facilities, making intentional redistribution of street space a public health and equity intervention, not just a design choice (Riggs, 2016, 2011).

7.2 Physical activity: Encourage multimodal integration and MaaS

If we are serious about health, AVs and new services should plug into a broader multimodal ecosystem rather than replicate the private-car paradigm. Mobility-as-a-Service (MaaS) platforms offer one way to do this, but they only move the needle if they actively privilege walking, cycling, and transit rather than simply aggregating car-based options. Recent work on MaaS shows that integrated platforms can reduce private car use when they bundle shared mobility with public transport and active modes, supported by real-time information and seamless payment (An and Shen, 2025). At the same time, a systematic review on MaaS and socio-territorial inequalities warns that poorly designed MaaS schemes can actually deepen spatial and social gaps if they mainly serve already-connected populations or require high digital literacy (Lopes et al., 2023).

Policy has to push MaaS toward being a health-promoting, equity-oriented front end for the transport system. That means platforms that surface walking, cycling, and transit first; offer clear information about travel time, cost, and emissions; and integrate targeted subsidies or mobility credits for low-income users. It also means formal coordination between cities, transit agencies, and private operators to ensure coverage in transit deserts, shared branding and user experience, and accessible payment options beyond credit cards and smartphones. When done well, MaaS can become a digital layer that supports mode shift and access to opportunity rather than just another way to package car trips.

7.3 Environmental: Incentivize integration with slow street, low-emission, low-noise technologies

On the environmental side, policies should move toward slower, softer and more sustainable streets—not just to electrify vehicles, but to reduce exposure to harmful emissions and noise at the street level. Evidence from transport and health research is clear: chronic exposure to traffic-related air pollution and noise is associated with higher risks of cardiovascular disease, metabolic disorders, sleep disturbance, and impaired mental health

(Kempen et al., 2018; Minkin et al., 2025; Münzel et al., 2024). The WHO Environmental Noise Guidelines recommends lower thresholds for road and aircraft noise and frame noise as a major public health risk.

This is where AV pilots and new mobility projects should be explicitly tied to slow-street strategies, 15-minute city principles, and low-emission zones (Rojas-Rueda et al., 2024). Rather than adding road based and aerial vehicles into already noisy, high-speed corridors, cities can prioritize electric, low-noise fleets in traffic-calmed networks that support walking and cycling and limit through-traffic in residential areas—treating them for first-order impacts on humans and wildlife (Appleyard, 2020; Riggs, 2022). Regulatory incentives—such as preferential access, curb priority, and fee reductions—can be reserved for operators who meet stringent emissions and noise criteria, with performance verified through independent monitoring and dynamic allocation tools (Binder et al., 2024; Diehl et al., 2021; Pochowski et al., 2022).

7.4 Environmental: Establish data-sharing protocols

To manage exposure and design healthier streets, cities and health agencies can provide good data to support mobility operators with public health research, congestion management, and infrastructure planning. Open, standardized data on vehicle kilometers traveled, speeds, routes, dwell times, and trip purposes can dramatically improve modeling of air pollution, noise, and safety risk. Work from European noise and exposure modeling, for example, shows that detailed traffic and land-use data underpin estimates of population exposure and are now driving EU wide targets to reduce chronic transport noise (European Environment Agency, 2025). Similar approaches are being used for active travel interventions to quantify benefits and costs across health and climate outcomes (Fitch-Polse and Agarwal, 2025).

Cities should commit to clear data governance: how data are stored, who can access them, and how they will be used to support safety, health, and climate goals rather than surveillance or punitive enforcement. When structured correctly, this becomes a reciprocal relationship: operators get better planning and infrastructure, while cities and public health agencies gain the evidence base they need to reduce exposure and evaluate policies.

7.5 Environmental: Mandate health impact assessments (HIAs)

For decades HIAs have offered a standard evaluative tool for transport projects and innovations and their tradeoffs. Case studies San Francisco and elsewhere demonstrate that HIAs can integrate the social and physical determinants of health into environmental planning, influencing roadway design, land use decisions, and mitigation commitments (Corburn, 2007; Corburn and Bhatia, 2007). And by embedding health criteria into the environmental review process, planners can identify the potential for increased pollution, loss of active transport, or mental health stressors before systems are deployed (McAndrews and Deakin, 2020).

For AV, rideshare, micromobility, and UAM deployments, HIAs should be standard—not exceptional. Embedding HIA into environmental review for new mobility pilots would force agencies and operators to grapple with likely changes in traffic volumes, shifts from active to sedentary modes, noise patterns (including aerial noise), and psychosocial stressors associated with automation and surveillance. Critically, HIAs can be structured to prioritize cumulative and distributional impacts, ensuring that proposals are evaluated based on how they affect communities already experiencing high rates of asthma, cardiovascular disease, or injury. This shifts projects away from conversations about "do we meet technical standards?" to "do we move toward or away from health equity?".

7.6 Psycho-social: Promote universal access, inclusive design and emotional design

Psycho-social acuity should be built in to both the hardware and software of new mobility. That means vehicles, streets, and digital platforms that follow universal design principles, supporting users across the spectrum of physical, sensory, cognitive, and emotional abilities. Research on transport and health equity emphasizes that accessible, universally designed public transport reduces exclusion and supports participation in work, education, and civic life (Bringolf, 2024). At the same time, inclusive interface design—multilingual support, low-literacy options, offline functionality, and non-visual cues—has been identified as a key condition for equitable access to digital mobility services and journey planning tools (Ribeiro and Iwona, 2025). Digital-only, English-only, or highly complex interfaces can exacerbate exclusion for older adults, low-literacy users, and people with disabilities (Tiago et al., 2025).

Pilots should therefore incorporate community co-design processes, particularly with disabled people, older adults, caregivers, and communities of color who have historically been marginalized by transport systems. Evaluations should not only track ridership or revenue, but also ask whether these systems are closing or widening gaps in access to jobs, healthcare, healthy food, and social connection. Emerging global frameworks on transport, health, and equity reinforce the idea that emotional safety, trust, and dignity are legitimate health outcomes alongside physical risk (Hosking et al., 2022). Emotional design—vehicles and services that feel safe, legible, and welcoming—should therefore be treated as a core performance metric. It is not just about aesthetics or branding; it is about reducing anxiety, signaling psychological safety, and building trust in systems that can otherwise feel opaque or alienating.

7.7 Equity: Monitor workforce health and labor conditions

Gig workers and AV support staff (including vehicle operators, technicians, and call center staff) are part of the transportation health ecosystem. Evidence from ride-hail and delivery platforms shows that drivers and couriers face long hours, income insecurity, high rates of fatigue, pressure to violate traffic rules, and limited access to basic protections like paid sick leave or health insurance (Christie and Ward, 2019). These conditions are not only a labor issue; they are a public-health and safety issue, affecting crash risk, stress, and economic precarity for workers and for the communities they serve (Taylor et al., 2023). Any health-focused mobility policy should therefore include baseline standards for pay, rest breaks, grievance procedures, discrimination protections, and access to health care for platform and AV-ecosystem workers. Regulators and public agencies can embed these expectations in franchise agreements, procurement contracts, and operating permits so that the pursuit of innovation does not rely on unhealthy work.

7.8 Equity: Build cross-sector institutional capacity

Finally, cities need institutions that are capable of governing this space. Transport, planning, and public health agencies still too often operate in silos, even as global and national frameworks emphasize the need to integrate health and equity into transport decisions (Codes-Johnson et al., 2018; McAndrews and Deakin, 2020). Establishing cross-sector training programs, shared data infrastructures, and joint funding mechanisms can help local governments evaluate and regulate new mobility through a health-equity lens (Douglas et al., 2025). Practical tools—such as health equity frameworks for transport and practitioner toolkits developed by organizations like the WHO—show how agencies can systematically assess distributional impacts, set equity goals, and track progress over time (WHO, 2024). Creating joint offices, interdepartmental task forces, or standing "mobility and health" working groups can move this from a report on a shelf to a lived practice: a governance structure where AVs, micromobility, and UAM are always evaluated in terms of who benefits, who bears the risks, and how those tradeoffs can be redesigned.

Taken together, these strategies represent a proactive, justice-centered mobility policy agenda—one that anticipates change, centers community needs, and protects public health in the face of accelerating technological transformation.

8. Conclusion

The future of new mobility and transport is being written in real time, shaped by the rise of rideshare and automation. These innovations offer great potential to bring about enhanced safety, greater access to transit, and lower emissions through electrification. They also come with risks to physical activity levels, social cohesion, labor protections, environmental exposure, and psychological well-being—risks that may be borne disproportionately by society's most vulnerable.

This duality underscores a central truth: new mobility systems are likely neither good nor bad. Their ultimate impact on public health depends on how we choose to design, govern, and integrate them. If left unchecked, these systems could reinforce patterns of exclusion, increase sedentary behavior, or even compromise mental health through noise, stress, and surveillance. But if approached deliberately—with health, equity, and sustainability as guiding principles—emerging mobility can be a powerful lever for urban regeneration and well-being.

Thus, transport planning must evolve from a narrow focus on speed and efficiency toward a broader paradigm rooted in human dignity. This means adopting rigorous health impact assessments, prioritizing infrastructure for active modes, incentivizing clean technologies, and ensuring universal access. It also means treating digital and environmental justice as inseparable from mobility justice.

Ultimately, the goal should not be to slow technological progress, but to steer it. We must ask not only what our future mobility systems can do, but for whom they will work—and at what cost to health, community, and climate. There are great opportunities before us. And by aligning transport innovation with public health and equity, we can ensure that the next generation can travel in ways that are not only healthier, but also safer, more inclusive, and more humane.

References

Alemi, F., Circella, G., Handy, S., Mokhtarian, P., 2018. What influences travelers to use Uber? Exploring the factors affecting the adoption of on-demand ride services in California. Travel. Behav. Soc. 13, 88–104. https://doi.org/10.1016/j.tbs.2018.06.002.

An, C., Shen, J., 2025. Assessing the impact of Mobility-as-a-Service (MaaS) on sustainable urban travel behaviors: a systematic literature review. Front. Sustain. Cities 7. https://doi.org/10.3389/frsc.2025.1645488.

An, Z., Mullen, C., Zhao, C., Heinen, E., 2023. Stereotypes and the public acceptability of shared micromobility. Travel. Behav. Soc. 33, 100643. https://doi.org/10.1016/j.tbs.2023.100643.

Appleyard, B., 2020. Livable Streets 2.0. Elsevier Science.

Appleyard, B., Riggs, W., 2023. Designing for street livability in the era of driverless cars Transp. Res. Interdiscip. Perspect. 21, 100868. https://doi.org/10.1016/j.trip.2023.100868.

Appleyard, B., Riggs, W., Stanton, J., 2023. Designing transportation and land use coordination: frameworks for measuring, understanding, and realizing sustainability, livability, and equity. Local. Environ. 28, 564–579. https://doi.org/10.1080/13549839.2022.2162026.

APTA, 2013. Millennials and Mobility: Understanding the Millennial Mindset. American Public Transportation Association, Washington DC.

Arup, 2022. National Evaluation of e-Scooter Trials. NatCen Social Research, London.

Basner, M., Babisch, W., Davis, A., Brink, M., Clark, C., Janssen, S., et al., 2014. Auditory and non-auditory effects of noise on health. Lancet 383, 1325–1332.

Bauer, U.E., Briss, P.A., Goodman, R.A., Bowman, B.A., 2014. Prevention of chronic disease in the 21st century: elimination of the leading preventable causes of premature death and disability in the USA. Lancet 384, 45–52.

Bilgin, P., Mattioli, G., Morgan, M., Wadud, Z., 2025. Investigating the effects of ride-sourcing on the dynamics of household car ownership. Transp. Res. Part. D: Transp. Environ. 146, 104886. https://doi.org/10.1016/j.trd.2025.104886.

Binder, R.B., Giuliano, G., Ha, J., 2024. Curb management for more efficient deliveries. In: Ioannou, P., Malikopoulos, A.A. (Eds.), Transportation Mobility in Smart Cities. Springer Nature Switzerland, Cham, pp. 297–319. https://doi.org/10.1007/978-3-031-64769-7_11.

Bircher, J., Kuruvilla, S., 2014. Defining health by addressing individual, social, and environmental determinants: new opportunities for health care and public health. J. Public. Health Pol. 35, 363–386. https://doi.org/10.1057/jphp.2014.19.

Boston Globe, 2013. Spotlight report: Driven to the Edge. The Boston Globe. http://www.bostonglobe.com/metro/specials/taxi (Accessed 12.18.18).

Bretones, A., Marquet, O., Daher, C., Hidalgo, L., Nieuwenhuijsen, M., Miralles-Guasch, C., et al., 2023. Public health-led insights on electric micro-mobility adoption and use: a scoping review. J. Urban. Health 100, 612–626. https://doi.org/10.1007/s11524-023-00731-0.

Bringolf, J., 2024. Universal design for future mobility. Centre for Universal Design Australia. https://universaldesignaustralia.net.au/universal-design-for-mobility/ (Accessed 12.8.25).

Brown, A., Howell, A., 2024. Mobility for the people: equity requirements in US shared micromobility programs. J. Cycl. Micromobility Res. 2, 100020. https://doi.org/10.1016/j.jcmr.2024.100020.

Brown, A., Klein, N.J., Thigpen, C., Williams, N., 2020. Impeding access: the frequency and characteristics of improper scooter, bike, and car parking. Transp. Res. Interdiscip. Perspect. 4, 100099. https://doi.org/10.1016/j.trip.2020.100099.

Brown, A.E., 2018. Ridehail revolution: Ridehail travel and equity in Los Angeles. UCLA Electronic Theses and Dissertations. https://escholarship.org/uc/item/4r22m57k (Accessed 7.6.2016).

Cavoli, C., Phillips, B., Cohen, T., Jones, P. Social and behavioural questions associated with automated vehicles: a literature review. UCL Transport Institute. https://trid.trb.org/View/1457834 (Accessed 7.6.2026).

Christie, N., Ward, H., 2019. The health and safety risks for people who drive for work in the gig economy. J. Transp. & Health 13, 115–127. https://doi.org/10.1016/j.jth.2019.02.007.

Circella, G., Fulton, L., Alemi, F., Berliner, R.M., Tiedeman, K., Mokhtarian, P.L., Handy, S., 2016. What Affects Millennials' Mobility? PART I: Investigating the Environmental Concerns, Lifestyles, Mobility-Related, National Center for Sustainable Transportation Research Report. University of California, Davis, Institute of Transportation Studies. https://ncst.ucdavis.edu/project/ucd-ct-to-11/.

Clark, B., Chatterjee, K., Martin, A., Davis, A., 2020. How commuting affects subjective wellbeing. Transportation 47, 2777–2805. https://doi.org/10.1007/s11116-019-09983-9.

Clarke, R., Bennett Moses, L., 2014. The regulation of civilian drones' impacts on public safety. Comput. Law & Sec. Rev. 30, 263–285. https://doi.org/10.1016/j.clsr.2014.03.007.

Clewlow, R.R., Mishra, G.S., 2017. Disruptive transportation: the adoption, utilization, and impacts of ride-hailing in the United States. University of California, Davis, Institute of Transportation Studies. https://itspubs.ucdavis.edu/wp-content/themes/ucdavis/pubs/download_pdf.php?id=2752.

Codes-Johnson, C., Rattay, K.T., Saperstein, L., 2018. Health in all policies. Dela J. Public. Health 4, 50–53. https://doi.org/10.32481/djph.2018.03.010.

Cohen, A., Guan, J., Beamer, M., Dittoe, R., Mokhtarimousavi, S., 2020. Reimagining the future of transportation with personal flight: Preparing and planning for urban air mobility. UC Berkeley Transportation Sustainability Research Center. https://doi.org/10.7922/G2TT4P6H.

Cohen, A.P., Shaheen, S.A., Farrar, E.M., 2021. Urban air mobility: history, ecosystem, market potential, and challenges. IEEE Trans. Intell. Transp. Syst. 22, 6074–6087.

Corburn, J., 2007. Reconnecting with our roots: American urban planning and public health in the twenty-first century. Urban. Aff. Rev. 42, 688.

Corburn, J., Bhatia, R., 2007. Health impact assessment in San Francisco: incorporating the social determinants of health into environmental planning. J. Environ. Plan. Manag. 50, 323–341.

Cornet, 2018. User-centred design of autonomous mobility forpublic transportation in Singapore. Presented at the International Scientific Conference on Mobility and Transport Urban Mobility – Shaping the Future Together mobil. TUM 2018. Munich, Germany.

Cornet, H., Riggs, W., 2023. Personas for Autonomous Vehicle Deployments. Autonomous Vehicles & the City Working Papers: SSRN. https://doi.org/10.2139/ssrn.4491033.

Crute, J., Riggs, W., Chapin, T., Stevens, L., 2018. Planning for autonomous mobility (No. PAS 592). American Planning Association. Washington DC.

Delbosc, A., Thigpen, C., 2024. Who uses subsidized micromobility, and why? Understanding low-income riders in three countries. J. Cycl. Micromobility Res. 2, 100016. https://doi.org/10.1016/j.jcmr.2024.100016.

Diehl, C., Ranjbari, A., Goodchild, A., 2021. Curbspace management challenges and opportunities from public and private sector perspectives. Transp. Res. Record: J. Transp. Res. Board. 2675, 1413–1427. https://doi.org/10.1177/03611981211027156.

Ding, D., Luo, M., Infante, M.F.P., Gunn, L., Salvo, D., Zapata-Diomedi, B., et al., 2024. The co-benefits of active travel interventions beyond physical activity: a systematic review. Lancet Planet. Health 8, e790–e803. https://doi.org/10.1016/S2542-5196(24)00201-8.

Douglas, M.J., Gale, A., Hrzic, R., Clemens, T., Davis, A.L., 2025. Strategic partnership for health in all policies and sustainable transport in Scotland: a case study evaluation. Public. Health Pract. 9, 100624. https://doi.org/10.1016/j.puhip.2025.100624.

European Environment Agency, 2025. Health impacts of exposure to noise from transport in Europe. EEA: Analysis & Data. https://www.eea.europa.eu/en/analysis/indicators/health-impacts-of-exposure-to-1 (Accessed 12.8.25).

Fagnant, D.J., Kockelman, K.M., 2014. The travel and environmental implications of shared autonomous vehicles, using agent-based model scenarios. Transportation Res. Part. C: Emerg. Technol. 40, 1–13.

Fishman, E., Cherry, C., 2016. E-bikes in the mainstream: Reviewing a decade of research. Transp. Rev. 36, 72–91. https://doi.org/10.1080/01441647.2015.1069907.

Fitch-Polse, D., Agarwal, S., 2025. The benefits of active transportation interventions: a review of the evidence. J. Transp. Land. Use 18, 77–122. https://doi.org/10.5198/jtlu.2025.2468.

Frank, L.D., Iroz-Elardo, N., Macleod, K.E., Hong, A., 2019. Pathways from built environment to health: a conceptual framework linking behavior and exposure-based impacts. J. Transp. & Health 12, 319–335.

Frank, L.D., Sallis, J.F., Conway, T.L., Chapman, J.E., Saelens, B.E., Bachman, W., 2006. Many pathways from land use to health: associations between neighborhood walkability and active transportation, body mass index, and air quality. J. Am. Plan. Assoc. 72, 75–87.

Frederick, C., Riggs, W., Gilderbloom, J.H., 2018. Commute mode diversity and public health: a multivariate analysis of 148 U.S. Cities. Int. J. Sustain. Transportation 12. https://doi.org/10.1080/15568318.2017.1321705.

Friel, C., Walsh, D., Whyte, B., Dibben, C., Feng, Z., Baker, G., et al., 2024. Health benefits of pedestrian and cyclist commuting: evidence from the Scottish longitudinal study. BMJ Public. Health 2, e001295. https://doi.org/10.1136/bmjph-2024-001295.

Furlong, J., Fevyer, D., Armstrong, B., Edwards, P., Aldred, R., Goodman, A., 2025. Low traffic neighbourhoods in London reduce road traffic injuries: a controlled before-and-after analysis (2012–2024). Injury Prev. https://doi.org/10.1136/ip-2024-045571.

Gehrke, S., Felix, A., Reardon, T., 2019. Substitution of ride-hailing services for more sustainable travel options in the greater Boston region. Transp. Res. Rec.: J. Transp. Res. Board. 2673.

Giles-Corti, B., Donovan, R.J., 2002. The relative influence of individual, social and physical environment determinants of physical activity. Soc. Sci. & Med. 54, 1793–1812. https://doi.org/10.1016/S0277-9536(01)00150-2.

Glazener, A., Sanchez, K., Ramani, T., Zietsman, J., Nieuwenhuijsen, M.J., Mindell, J.S., et al., 2021. Fourteen pathways between urban transportation and health: a conceptual model and literature review. J. Transp. & Health 21, 101070. https://doi.org/10.1016/j.jth.2021.101070.

Gössling, S., 2020. Integrating e-scooters in urban transportation: problems, policies, and the prospect of system change. Transp. Res. Part. D: Transp. Environ. 79, 102230.

Greenwood, B.N., Wattal, S., 2017. Show me the way to go home. MIS Q. 41, 163–188.

Guo, C., Loo, B.P.Y., Feng, K., Gao, H.O., Zhang, K., 2024. Fifteen pathways between electric vehicles and public health: a transportation–health conceptual framework. Environ. Health 2, 848–853. https://doi.org/10.1021/envhealth.4c00156.

Hahn, R.A., 2019. Two paths to health in all policies: the traditional public health path and the path of social determinants. Am. J. Public. Health 109, 253–254. https://doi.org/10.2105/AJPH.2018.304884.

Hall, J.D., Palsson, C., Price, J., 2018. Is Uber a substitute or complement for public transit? J. Urban. Econ. 108, 36–50. https://doi.org/10.1016/j.jue.2018.09.003.

Hawkins, A., 2025. Waymo says it will add 2,000 more robotaxis into 2026. The Verge. https://www.theverge.com/news/661025/waymo-fleet-size-factory-arizona-jaguar-robotaxi-zeekr (Accessed 7.13.25).
Holden, J., Goel, N., 2016. Fast-Forwarding to a Future of On-Demand Urban Air Transportation. Community Air Mobility Initiative, San Francisco, CA.
Hollingsworth, J., Copeland, B., Johnson, J.X., 2019. Are e-scooters polluters? The environmental impacts of shared dockless electric scooters. Environ. Res. Lett. 14, 084031. https://doi.org/10.1088/1748-9326/ab2da8.
Hosking, J., Braubach, M., Buss, D., Khayesi, M., Filho, V.P., de Sá, T.H., 2022. Towards a global framework for transport, health and health equity. Environ. Int. 169, 107472. https://doi.org/10.1016/j.envint.2022.107472.
Hua, C., Fan, W.D., Hua, W., Zhang, S., 2026. Environmental sustainability and mobility impacts of connected and autonomous vehicles at urban highways. Expert. Syst. Appl. 295, 128892. https://doi.org/10.1016/j.eswa.2025.128892.
Jackson, O., 2018. The Supply Side of Discrimination: Evidence from the Labor Supply of Boston Taxi Drivers (No. 18–2), Research Department Working Papers. Federal Reserve Bank of Boston, Boston, MA.
Jackson, R.J., Dannenberg, A.L., Frumkin, H., 2013. Health and the built environment: 10 years after. Am. J. Public. Health 103, 1542–1544.
Kempen, E.V., Casas, M., Pershagen, G., Foraster, M., 2018. WHO environmental noise guidelines for the european region: a systematic review on environmental noise and cardiovascular and metabolic effects: a summary. Int. J. Env. Res. Public. Health 15, 379. https://doi.org/10.3390/ijerph15020379.
Kioumourtzoglou, M.-A., Schwartz, J., James, P., Dominici, F., Zanobetti, A., 2016. PM2.5 and mortality in 207 US cities: modification by temperature and city characteristics. Epidemiol 27, 221–227. https://doi.org/10.1097/EDE.0000000000000422.
Kong, P., Cornet, H., Frenkler, F., 2018. Personas and emotional design for public service robots: a case study with autonomous vehicles in public transportation. In: 2018 International Conference on Cyberworlds (Cw). IEEE, pp. 284–287.
Krieger, N., 1994. Epidemiology and the web of causation: has anyone seen the spider? Soc. Sci. & Med. 39, 887–903.
Lazarus, J., Pourquier, J.C., Feng, F., Hammel, H., Shaheen, S., 2020. Micromobility evolution and expansion: understanding how docked and dockless bikesharing models complement and compete – A case study of San Francisco. J. Transp. Geogr. 84, 102620. https://doi.org/10.1016/j.jtrangeo.2019.102620.
Lee, J., Kockelman, K.M., 2022. Access benefits of shared autonomous vehicle fleets: focus on vulnerable populations. Transp. Res. Rec. 2676, 568–582. https://doi.org/10.1177/03611981221094305.
Lipson, H., Kurman, M., 2016. Driverless: Intelligent Cars and the Road Ahead. MIT Press.
Lopes, A.S., Orozco-Fontalvo, M., Moura, F., Vale, D., 2023. Mobility as a service and socio-territorial inequalities: a systematic literature review. J. Transp. Land. Use 16, 215–240. https://doi.org/10.5198/jtlu.2023.2273.
MBTA, 2015. On-Demand Paratransit Pilot Program | The RIDE | MBTA [WWW Document]. https://www.mbta.com/accessibility/the-ride/on-demand-pilot (accessed 30 12.18).
McAndrews, C., Deakin, E., 2020. Public health sector influence in transportation decision-making: the case of health impact assessment. Case Stud. Transp. Policy 8, 1116–1125. https://doi.org/10.1016/j.cstp.2018.02.002.
Meyer, G., Shaheen, S., 2017. Disrupting Mobility: Impacts of Sharing Economy and Innovative Transportation on Cities. Springer.

Milakis, D., Van Arem, B., Van Wee, B., 2017. Policy and society related implications of automated driving: a review of literature and directions for future research. J. Intell. Transp. Syst. 21, 324–348. https://doi.org/10.1080/15472450.2017.1291351.

Minkin, M., Woodland, L., Williams, O.A., Hamilton, S., Hansell, A.L., Vienneau, D., et al., 2025. Revisiting the association between transportation noise and heart disease reported in the World Health Organization Environmental Noise Guidelines for the European Region: a systematic review and *meta*-analysis. Environ. Int. 202, 109667. https://doi.org/10.1016/j.envint.2025.109667.

Montilla, M.A.N., Hui, M., Chatman, D.G., 2025. How ride-hailing services influenced vehicle use and ownership across the Boston metropolitan region. Transportation. https://doi.org/10.1007/s11116-025-10688-5.

Moudon, A.V., Lee, C., Cheadle, A.D., Garvin, C., Johnson, D., Schmid, T.L., et al., 2006. Operational definitions of walkable neighborhood: theoretical and empirical insights. J. Phys. Act. & Health 3, 99.

Mulero-Pázmány, M., Jenni-Eiermann, S., Strebel, N., Sattler, T., Negro, J.J., Tablado, Z., 2017. Unmanned aircraft systems as a new source of disturbance for wildlife: A systematic review. PLOS ONE 12, e0178448. https://doi.org/10.1371/journal.pone.0178448.

Münzel, T., Molitor, M., Kuntic, M., Hahad, O., Röösli, M., Engelmann, N., et al., 2024. Transportation noise pollution and cardiovascular health. Circ. Res. 134, 1113–1135. https://doi.org/10.1161/CIRCRESAHA.123.323584.

NHTSA, 2017. Automated Vehicles 2.0 Activities. US Department of Transportation. https://www.transportation.gov/av/2.0 (Accessed 1.19.21).

NHTSA, 2016. Federal Automated Vehicles Policy: Accelerating the Next Revolution in Roadway Safety. US Department of Transportation. https://www.transportation.gov/sites/dot.gov/files/docs/AV%20policy%20guidance%20PDF.pdf (Accessed 6.7.2026).

Noel, A., 2018. Revised MIT study: uber, lyft drivers make about $10/hour. The points guy. https://thepointsguy.com/2018/03/revised-mit-study-says-uber-lyft-drivers-make-about-8-or-10-per-hour/ (Accessed 12.18.18).

Pochowski, A.L., Crim, S., Liu, L., Trask, L., Sherman Baker, C., Woodworth, S., et al., 2022. Solving the curb space puzzle through the development of a curb space allocation tool. Transp. Res. Rec. 2676, 601–621. https://doi.org/10.1177/03611981221090514.

Rajendran, S., Srinivas, S., Grimshaw, T., 2021. Predicting demand for air taxi urban aviation services using machine learning algorithms. J. Air Transp. Manag. 92, 102043.

Rana, Md.M., Hossain, K., 2023. Connected and autonomous vehicles and infrastructures: a literature review. Int. J. Pavement Res. Technol. 16, 264–284. https://doi.org/10.1007/s42947-021-00130-1.

Rayle, L., Dai, D., Chan, N., Cervero, R., Shaheen, S., 2016. Just a better taxi? A survey-based comparison of taxis, transit, and ridesourcing services in San Francisco. Transp. Policy 45, 168–178. https://doi.org/10.1016/j.tranpol.2015.10.004.

Rayle, L., Shaheen, S., Chan, N., Dai, D., Cervero, R., 2014. App-Based, On-Demand Ride Services: Comparing Taxi and Ridesourcing Trips and User Characteristics in San Francisco University of California Transportation Center (UCTC). University of California, Berkeley, United States.

Raza, W., Renkhoff, J., Ogirimah, O., Bawa, G.K., Stansbury, R.S., 2025. Advanced air mobility: innovations, applications, challenges, and future potential. J. Air Transp. 33, 169–187. https://doi.org/10.2514/1.d0440.

Ribeiro, L., Iwona, A., 2025. From Challenges to Solutions: Building Inclusive Transport for People with Disabilities. Institute for Transportation & Development Policy (ITDP), New York.

Riggs, W., 2024. Advances in Automated Driving: Perceptions of Safety, Operations and Comfort From Riders. Transportation Research Board 105th Annual Meeting. Washington, D.C. https://doi.org/10.2139/ssrn.5318692.

Riggs, W., 2022. End of the Road: Reimagining the Street As the Heart of the City. Bristol University Press, Bristol.

Riggs, W., 2019. Disruptive Transport: Driverless Cars, Transport Innovation and the Sustainable City of Tomorrow, Routledge Equity, Justice and the Sustainable City Series. Routledge, London.

Riggs, W., 2016. Inclusively walkable: Exploring the equity of walkable housing in the San Francisco Bay Area. Local. Environ. 21, 527–554.

Riggs, W., Appleyard, B., Johnson, M., 2020. A design framework for livable streets in the era of autonomous vehicles. Urban, Plan. Transp. Res. 8, 125–137. https://doi.org/10.1080/21650020.2020.1749123.

Riggs, W., Beiker, S.A., 2020. Business models for shared and autonomous mobility. In: Meyer, G., Beiker, S. (Eds.), Road Vehicle Automation 7, Lecture Notes in Mobility. Springer International Publishing, Cham, pp. 33–48. https://doi.org/10.1007/978-3-030-52840-9_4.

Riggs, W., Cornet, H., 2026. Autonomous vehicles and public transit incentives: a case study of Waymo's pilot transit credit program in the San Francisco Bay Area. Transp. Res. Interdiscip. Perspect. 38, 102045. https://doi.org/10.1016/j.trip.2026.102045.

Riggs, W., Cornet, H., 2024. Multidisciplinary dialogues on assessing the automation-readiness of cities. In: Meyer, G., Beiker, S. (Eds.), Road Vehicle Automation 11. Springer Nature Switzerland, Cham, pp. 60–68. https://doi.org/10.1007/978-3-031-67466-2_6.

Riggs, W., Kawashima, M., Batstone, D., 2021. Exploring best practice for municipal e-scooter policy in the United States. Transp. Res. Part. A: Policy Pract. 151, 18–27. https://doi.org/10.1016/j.tra.2021.06.025.

Riggs, W., Niel Shukla, S., Mark, S., 2022. The trip characteristics of a pilot autonomous vehicle rider program: late night service needs and desired increases in service quality, reliability and safety. Autonomous Vehicles & the City Working Papers: SSRN. https://doi.org/10.2139/ssrn.4195380.

Riggs, W., Pande, A., 2022. On-demand microtransit and paratransit service using autonomous vehicles: gaps and opportunities in accessibility policy. Transp. Policy 127, 171–178. https://doi.org/10.1016/j.tranpol.2022.07.024.

Riggs, W., Pande, A., 2021. Gaps and Opportunities in Accessibility Policy for Autonomous Vehicles (No. 2106). Mineta Transportation Institute. https://transweb.sjsu.edu/research/2106-Accessibility-Policy-Autonomous-Vehicles (Accessed 7.6.2026).

Riggs, W., Richardson, E., 2024. Estimating the cost of autonomous vehicles. Autonomous Vehicles & the City Working Papers: SSRN. https://doi.org/10.2139/ssrn.4998828.

Riggs, W., Schrage, N., Shukla, S., Mark, S., 2023. The trip characteristics of a pilot autonomous vehicle rider program: revealing late night service needs and desired increases in service quality, reliability and safety. In: Meyer, G., Beiker, S. (Eds.), Road Vehicle Automation 10, Lecture Notes in Mobility. Springer Nature Switzerland, Cham, pp. 93–107. https://doi.org/10.1007/978-3-031-34757-3_9.

Riggs, W., 2011. Walkability and housing: a comparative study of income, neighborhood change and socio-cultural dynamics in the San Francisco Bay Area. UC Berkeley Electronic Theses and Dissertations. https://escholarship.org/uc/item/5970164x (Accessed 7.6.2026).

Rojas-Rueda, D., Norberciak, M., Morales-Zamora, E., 2024. Advancing health equity through 15-min cities and chrono-urbanism. J. Urban. Health 101, 483–496. https://doi.org/10.1007/s11524-024-00850-2.

Saelens, B.E., Vernez Moudon, A., Kang, B., Hurvitz, P.M., Zhou, C., 2014. Relation between higher physical activity and public transit use. Am. J. Public. Health 104, 854–859. https://doi.org/10.2105/AJPH.2013.301696.

Sallis, J.F., Cerin, E., Conway, T.L., Adams, M.A., Frank, L.D., Pratt, M., et al., 2016. Physical activity in relation to urban environments in 14 cities worldwide: a cross-sectional study. Lancet 387, 2207–2217.

Sallis, J.F., Floyd, M.F., Rodríguez, D.A., Saelens, B.E., 2012. Role of built environments in physical activity, obesity, and cardiovascular disease. Circulation 125, 729–737.

Schaller, B., 2017. Unsustainable? The Growth of App-Based Ride Services and Traffic, Travel and the Future of New York City. Report by Schaller Consulting, Brooklyn NY.

Schlossberg, M., Riggs, W.W., Millard-Ball, A., Shay, E., 2018. Rethinking the street in an era of driverless cars. Urbanism Next. https://rosap.ntl.bts.gov/view/dot/60741/dot_60741_DS1.pdf (Accessed 7.6.2026).

Shaheen, S., Chan, N., Rayle, L., 2017. Ridesourcing's impact and role in urban transportation. Access Magazine. UC Berkeley: University of California Transportation Center. https://escholarship.org/uc/item/5mj3j1n3 (Accessed 7.6.2026).

Sun, S., Ertz, M., 2022. Can shared micromobility programs reduce greenhouse gas emissions: Evidence from urban transportation big data. Sustain. Cities Soc. 85, 104045.

Taylor, K., Van Dijk, P., Newnam, S., Sheppard, D., 2023. Physical and psychological hazards in the gig economy system: a systematic review. Saf. Sci. 166, 106234. https://doi.org/10.1016/j.ssci.2023.106234.

Tengilimoglu, O., Carsten, O., Wadud, Z., 2023. Implications of automated vehicles for physical road environment: a comprehensive review. Transp. Res. Part. E: Logist. Transp. Rev. 169, 102989. https://doi.org/10.1016/j.tre.2022.102989.

Tiago, J., Lopes, A., Carvalho, M.L., Vale, D., 2025. Challenges to inclusive mobility as a service: findings from a stakeholder workshop in Lisbon. J. Urban. Mobil. 8, 100169. https://doi.org/10.1016/j.urbmob.2025.100169.

Torija, A.J., Clark, C., 2021. A psychoacoustic approach to building knowledge about human response to noise of unmanned aerial vehicles. Int. J. Environ. Res. Public. Health 18, 682. https://doi.org/10.3390/ijerph18020682.

Torija, A.J., Li, Z., Self, R.H., 2020. Effects of a hovering unmanned aerial vehicle on urban soundscapes perception. Transp. Res. Part. D: Transp. Environ. 78, 102195. https://doi.org/10.1016/j.trd.2019.11.024.

Trivedi, T.K., Liu, C., Antonio, A.L.M., Wheaton, N., Kreger, V., Yap, A., et al., 2019. Injuries associated with standing electric scooter use. JAMA Netw. Open. 2, e187381.

Ulrich, R.S., Simons, R.F., Losito, B.D., Fiorito, E., Miles, M.A., Zelson, M., 1991. Stress recovery during exposure to natural and urban environments1. J. Environ. Psychol. 11, 201–230.

Waymo, 2025. "They're Connecting People to Community." LightHouse for the Blind SF CEO Shares Why She Rides with Waymo. Waymo. https://waymo.com/community/articles/lighthouse-for-the-blind-sf/ (Accessed 7.13.25).

WHO, 2024. WHO launches new toolkit to advance health equity for persons with disabilities. World Health Organization. https://www.who.int/news/item/26-11-2024-who-launches-new-toolkit-to-advance-health-equity-for-persons-with-disabilities (Accessed 12.8.25).

Young, M., Allen, J., Farber, S., 2020. Measuring when Uber behaves as a substitute or supplement to transit: an examination of travel-time differences in Toronto. J. Transp. Geogr. 82, 102629. https://doi.org/10.1016/j.jtrangeo.2019.102629.

CHAPTER ELEVEN

The Health Economic Assessment Tool (HEAT) for walking and cycling: Reflections from over 10 years of application of a health impact assessment tool in policy and practice

Sonja Kahlmeier[a,b,*], Nick Cavill[c], Francesca Racioppi[a], Nino Sharashidze[a], and Thomas Gotschi[d]

[a]WHO European Centre for Environment and Health, Bonn, Germany
[b]City Health, Zurich, Switzerland
[c]Department of Social & Policy Sciences, University of Bath, Bath, United Kingdom
[d]Institute of Transportation Studies, University of California, Berkeley, United States
*Corresponding author. e-mail address: sonja.kahlmeier@city-health.ch

Contents

Abstract

In recent years, walking and cycling have moved into focus as promising approaches to achieve public health, sustainable transport, climate goals and better urban resilience. However, they are only realistic transport and activity options for a large proportion of the population when they are safe, inclusive and convenient. One way to increase their recognition in transport policy is the inclusion of health impacts of walking and cycling into transport economic appraisals.

Advances in Transport Policy and Planning, Volume 18
ISSN 2543-0009, https://doi.org/10.1016/bs.atpp.2026.06.001

The Health Economic Assessment Tool (HEAT) for walking and cycling calculates: if x people walk or cycle a distance of y on most days, what is the economic value of impacts on premature mortality, taking into account effects of physical activity, air pollution and road fatalities, as well as effects on carbon emissions?. This chapter describes how the HEAT has been used in transport policy and practice in more than 10 years of existence, and identifies lessons learned and challenges

Since its launch in 2009, the HEAT has gained wide recognition as a user-friendly, yet robust, evidence-based tool usable by academics, including for training purposes, policymakers, and practitioners. Originally designed for use in Europe, it has since been expanded for global use. Challenges for a wider uptake of health-impact assessment (HIA) tools including active transport such as HEAT are the dissemination to local practitioners and policy makers also outside European and English-speaking regions and in low- and middle-income contexts, further increasing usability, and more generally the advancement of systematic data collection and impact quantification related to walking and cycling.

1. Introduction

Over recent decades, a lack of physical activity has been recognized as a major determinant of ill health. Insufficient physical activity has been associated with many chronic diseases, including coronary heart disease, stroke, hypertension, cancer and type II diabetes, as well as excess body weight, poor mental health, and reduced independence in old age. Overall, more than 7 % of all-cause and cardiovascular disease deaths and up to 8 % of 13 major non-communicable diseases are attributable to insufficient physical activity (Katzmarzyk et al., 2022). Globally, almost one out of four adults, and four out of five adolescents are not sufficiently active for good health (Guthold et al., 2020, 2018). An increasing number of studies have investigated health impacts from so-called "active travel", i.e. regular cycling or walking for transport, including combined mobility with public transport. Demonstrated health benefits include a 10 % reduction of premature mortality (4–6) and of metabolic risk factors for cardiovascular diseases (Dinu et al., 2019; Zhao et al., 2021), the prevention of diabetes, some cancers and the reduction of cognitive function in older adults (Leyland et al., 2019) and to some degree lower body weight (Dons et al., 2018; Wanner et al., 2012). During the COVID-19 pandemic, cycling and walking have also emerged as travel options that provide physical distancing required by public health measures while at the same time enabling people to remain physically active (World Health Organization, 2020). As a result, many cities around the world have taken steps to promote walking and cycling (India, 2020; Department for Transport, 2021; Schwedhelm et al., 2020; Ville de Paris, 2024). In more recent years, the development of electric bicycles has provided new opportunities to expand the uptake of cycling to cover longer distances, facilitating cycling in hilly environments and maintaining cycling or making it more accessible to older adults (Rérat et al., 2025).

In recent years transport-related physical activity has moved into focus as a promising approach to reach parts of the population who do not find sport amenable, attractive or affordable (Lamb et al., 2014; WHO Regional Office for Europe, 2022). Both the "Eight Investments that work" (International Society for Physical Activity and Health, 2020) and the Global Action Plan on Physical Activity include actions related to promoting safe, active transport (World Health Organization, 2018). In 2021, the first European Masterplan for Cycling was adopted (Cycling Masterplan, 2021), followed by a new Masterplan for Walking (Federal Ministry Republic of Austria for Climate Action, Environment, Energy, Mobility, Innovation and Technology, 2024). There is merit in increasing collaboration between the transport and health sectors to achieve transport goals such as reducing congestion or climate change (Brand et al., 2021; Buehler et al., 2017) as well as public health targets to reduce physical inactivity and disease burden (Gotschi et al., 2015; Götschi et al., 2016; WHO Regional Office for Europe, 2022). For example, in Great Britain, on average only 10 min per day are spent walking for transport, and less than 2 min for cycling. Beyond the 'champions' of active travel such as the Netherlands or Denmark, even in Switzerland, we find over 20 min per day are spent for transport-related walking and 4 5 min for cycling (Gotschi et al., 2015). Such differences in transport behaviour translate into considerable public health impacts (Gotschi et al., 2015; Götschi et al., 2016; WHO Regional Office for Europe, 2022). In addition, evidence from 30 studies from Europe, the United States, Australia and New Zealand shows that the benefits from physical activity clearly outweigh potential harm from air pollution or traffic crashes (Mueller et al., 2015). A similar pattern is seen in evidence from some low- and middle-income settings, such as Brazil (Sá et al., 2017), Mauritius (Thondoo et al., 2020) or India (Woodcock et al., 2009).

For walking and cycling to present realistic transport alternatives for a large share of the population, they need to be safe and convenient (Lamb et al., 2014; WHO Regional Office for Europe, 2022, World Health Organization, 2018; Schwedhelm et al., 2020). Planning practice can draw from a wide portfolio of well-established infrastructure and traffic regulation measures to make active travel modes more palatable. However, the priority given to the promotion of active travel modes in transport planning varies widely, as differences exist between countries, cities, towns, and rural areas (Buehler et al., 2017; Kahlmeier et al., 2021). In addition, issues of inequity and social justice influence the relationship between transport and health by modifying the exposure and severity of health effects and outcomes (Glazener et al., 2021; Martens, 2020; Mizdrak et al., 2023), further stressing the need to estimate variations within and across local populations.

Quantifying the potentially substantial benefits of active travel measures has been recognized early on as a promising approach to elevate the status of walking and cycling within the planning as well as the public health community (de Hartog et al., 2010; Gotschi, 2011; Nordic Council of Ministers, 2005). Cost-benefit analysis is a standard methodology in transport planning: in many countries, a road, bridge or cycle path will not be built unless the benefits can be shown to be greater than the costs. However, traditionally in many cases walking and cycling have not been included in economic valuation of transport projects (Cavill et al., 2008; Nordic Council of Ministers, 2005; van Wee and Borjesson, 2015), putting active forms of travel at a relative disadvantage since the full benefits are not considered. Thus, providing methodological approaches to include the benefits of active travel is one approach to moving walking and cycling up the transport policy agenda. There are several tools available to assess health impacts of active mobility (Brown et al., 2016; Doorley et al., 2015; Mizdrak et al., 2023) They include among the most widely used the Integrated Transport Health Impact Model (ITHIM), supporting modeling of population exposures to physical activity, air pollution and road traffic injury risk (Woodcock et al., 2013; ITHIM), the Propensity to Cycling Tool for modelling cycling uptake and corresponding health and carbon impacts (Lovelace et al., 2017; Woodcock et al., 2021) and the Health Economic Assessment Tool (HEAT) for walking and cycling.

This paper describes, the development of the HEAT, its dissemination and uptake, selected case studies, and potential areas for further development.

2. Key development approaches and steps of the HEAT

In response to the lack of inclusion of active mobility into transport appraisals, in 2005 a multi-phase, open-ended project was established to develop the HEAT for walking and cycling as a user-friendly, harmonized method for economic valuation of health impacts of walking and cycling, based on best available evidence and international expert consensus (Kahlmeier et al., 2011, 2010). Since then, implementation has been steered by a core project group, working in close collaboration with advisory groups, led by the WHO Regional Office for Europe.

The HEAT calculates: if x people cycle or walk y distance on most days, what is the economic value of resulting reductions in mortality? This calculation can serve different types of assessment, for example, of current (or past) levels of cycling or walking, such as showing the value of cycling or walking in a city or country; of changes over time, such as comparing before-and-after situations or scenario A versus scenario B (such as with or without measures taken); and evaluating new or existing projects, including calculating benefit–cost ratios. The tool is intended to be robust but easy to use primarily by transport planners, traffic engineers, economists and special interest groups. The user-friendliness of the tool has been a defining goal in the development of the HEAT that, in its simplest applications, only requires users to input data on the amount of cycling or walking undertaken and the number of people cycling or walking.

In 2007, an approach to calculating the economic value of reduced all-cause mortality from cycling (quantified using the Value of a Statistical Life VSL approach) was adopted at the first HEAT consensus meeting (Kahlmeier et al., 2011, 2010). These international consensus meetings are a core part of the HEAT development to promote critical review, discussion and achievement of consensus on proposed options, including in cases where best expert judgement is needed (Kahlmeier et al., 2010). The HEAT process follows the following key principles:

- Robust and evidence-based Decisions are taken on the best available evidence with the view of providing a scientifically robust tool.
- Easily usable The HEAT is developed for the transport sector as the main target audience, thus for users who are likely to have limited knowledge of epidemiology and public health. Simplicity in application is thus a key consideration for any decision taken.
- Transparent Decisions and any assumptions taken are made transparent.
- Conservative Methodological considerations are taken with an "at-least" approach.
- Adaptable As far as possible, default values are provided for inputs to the tool to facilitate application, which in most cases can be adapted to reflect local conditions and approaches.

- Modular Users can select to run assessments for different modes of transport (i e. walking, cycling and soon e-biking) as well as different impact pathways (physical activity, air pollution, fatal traffic crashes, and carbon emissions). In addition, HEAT is meant for integration into wider cost-benefit analysis as a modular component.

A key feature of the HEAT process is the involvement of experts from a range of fields that are relevant for the development and implementation of walking and cycling measures. To date, next to the coordinating team, more than 120 experts from epidemiology, public health, transport research and planning, health and transport economics, air pollution and environmental sciences, policy making, practice and advocacy from over 30 countries have contributed to the development of the HEAT across the different project phases (WHO Regional Office for Europe, 2023a).

Based on a systematic review of the literature (Cavill et al., 2008), a basic approach designed for the European region was agreed to develop the first HEAT for cycling (Cavill et al., 2007; Rutter et al., 2013), launched in 2009. An updated version of the HEAT for cycling and a new HEAT for walking were finalized at a second consensus meeting and launched in 2011 as a web-based tool (Kahlmeier et al., 2011) with a methods and user guide booklet. In 2013, the third consensus meeting discussed results from another systematic review (Kelly et al., 2014) to update the methods for HEAT walking. A new HEAT version including an option to calculate health impacts from air pollution and road fatalities separately, and to take into account carbon effects of shifting to active modes was launched in 2017 (Götschi et al., 2020; Kahlmeier et al., 2017). In 2021, the first globally applicable version was presented (WHO Regional Office for Europe, 2023b). In 2024, a new version including e-biking and translation into Spanish was launched (WHO Regional Office for Europe, 2024).

Below, we are discussing how the HEAT has been used over its more than 10 years of existence, and identify lessons learned and challenges for the ways in which economic assessments of their health impacts can foster the recognition of walking and cycling in transport policy and practice.

3. Overview of dissemination and uptake

While originally developed for the European region, the HEAT use was widespread beyond Europe: according to web statistics of the HEAT from the Google Analytics tool (Chai, 2023) the top countries in the last 2 years (July 2023–2025) being the United States and the United Kingdom, followed by China, Germany, Sweden, France, Spain, Italy, Canada and Australia, in addition to the use of the tool in cities such as London, Stockholm, Gothenborg, Sydney, Helsinki and Paris.

Despite having been primarily developed for the transport sector, a survey carried out 10 years ago indicated that HEAT was equally used by public health and academics (Cavill and Kahlmeier, 2016; WHO Regional Office for Europe, 2015). As main reasons for not using the HEAT, lack of time or lack of suitable data were quoted. Results were most often used for a presentation, internal or published reports or an academic paper. Main target audiences were a local authority or municipality, a national authority/ministry, a research body or a non-government organization.

Data from different information sources (Brown et al., 2016; Cavill and Kahlmeier, 2016; Doorley et al., 2015; Greenwood et al., 2021; Mueller et al., 2015) collated by spring 2021 yielded a total of 132 documented HEAT applications, including 7 that mentioned HEAT but did not apply it in practice or were incomplete draft reports.

The remaining 125 applications included 52 technical reports and 38 academic publications, as shown in Table 1, as well as 12 government

Table 1 Documented applications of the Health Economic Assessment Tools (HEAT), by type.

Type	Number	Percent	Examples
Reports	52	41.6%	
English	*32*	25.6%	(Cavill et al., 2014; Doll et al., n.d.; Küster and Blondel, 2013)
Non-English	*20*	16.0%	(Hrkal, 2014; Levin et al., 2014; Van Zeebroeck and Charles, 2014)
Academic paper/ abstract	38	30.4%	(Babagoli et al., 2019; Bukovetz et al., 2021; Montes et al., 2012)
Government papers/guidance	12	9.6%	(City of Espoo, 2013; Department for Transport, 2014; Federal Ministry for Agriculture et al., 2015)
Other (case studies, slides, website etc)	23	18.4%	(Thaler and Eder, 2017; WHO calculator)
Total	125	100%	

papers or guidance reports. Twelve of the publications qualified as government papers or guidance, i.e. documents issued by a part of an administration and/or guidance documents that promote the use of HEAT. There were also several reports from academic institutions or consultancies that were developed on behalf of administrative bodies, as well as research reports, in particular by local administrations.

Despite the wide-ranging searches and repeated invitations to report applications to date there is still a limited number of documented uses of HEAT by government agencies, and a majority of those come from the United Kingdom (Cavill and Kahlmeier, 2016; Greenwood et al., 2021; World Health Organization, 2025) This may be due to an English language bias, as the HEAT has only been available in English (despite user guides having also been translated into German, French, Spanish, Finnish and Polish), likely to reflect the differential uptake of the HEAT by certain countries. In addition, it remains challenging to document evidence of the tool's direct impact on policy actions and decision-making (Cavill and Kahlmeier, 2016), not least because the HEAT results are only one factor in an often complex political decision making process. Nevertheless, there are examples such as Transport for Greater Manchester, United Kingdom, that used HEAT as part of its business case to calculate the value of reduced mortality from new cycle trips projected to result from a major cycling investment program (World Health Organization, 2025). The Accra Metropolitan Assembly and Greater Accra Passenger Transport Executive used HEAT to advocate for investment in a comprehensive expansion of walking and cycling infrastructure (Johnson et al., 2023) In the Pan-European Master Plan for Cycling, several results of HEAT-based calculations are used to make the case for the policy goal to double cycling across the Region by 2030 (Cycling Masterplan, 2021). While the HEAT has not been developed as a research tool, usage in almost 40 academic publications confirms its scientific robustness and usefulness in an academic setting, including for training purposes.

In interviews carried out in 2015 with users (Cavill and Kahlmeier, 2016), and more recent analyses of the HEAT's usability (Greenwood et al., 2021; Lushomo, 2024), a number of strengths and weaknesses of the HEAT were identified (see Table 2).

3.1 Examples of applications

In this section we present selected examples of HEAT applications from academia, policy and practice.

Table 2 Strengths and weaknesses of the Health Economic Assessment Tools (HEAT) for walking or cycling.

Strengths	– Allows quantifying the magnitude of the health impacts compared to other (e g. environmental) benefits – Combination of health impacts and economic quantification. – Having a specific number gets people thinking and facilitates discussions and exchange with relevant bodies – Evidence-and consensus-based approach, transparency. – Approach allows integration into existing transport appraisal systems. – Tool's ability to be tailored to the user needs and use case – Can facilitate the exchange between transport and health specialists, where a desire exists – Tool now also adapted for global use – Project coordination by the WHO adds to credibility.
Weaknesses	– In some audiences the use of Value of a Statistical Life and resulting numbers are not easily understood. – Lack of consideration for different social groups – Call for outcomes other than mortality – Risk that further measures might overly complicate the now straightforward structure – HEAT is not well known in local communities where many transport planning decisions take place. – Translations of the English tool and user guide into local languages are needed for uptake, in particular on the local level. – Tool website could be improved in terms of readability, amount of information and simplification of language, user orientation and visual impression – Additional features were missed, e g limited ability to create multiple applications – As long as it is not included in the official national guidance for transport appraisals, it will only be used seldom.

3.1.1 Academia example 1: The untapped health and climate potential of cycling in France

Using individual data from a nationally representative mobility survey for France, this HEAT application assessed, amongst other calculations, the economic benefits of shifting 25 % of short (<5 km) car trips to cycling (Schwarz et al., 2024). They estimated that such a shift would yield approximately a 2-fold increase in premature deaths prevented compared to current levels of cycling, namely about 1800 deaths per year, of an additional societal value of €2 6 billion per year, while also generating important CO_2 emissions reductions (0.257 MtCO2e, UI: 0.231–0.288). In addition, they calculated that on average, €1.02 (UI: 0.59–1.62) of intangible costs were prevented for every km cycled.

3.1.2 Academia example 2: Exploring the health and spatial equity implications of a Bike share system, New York City, USA

In this study, the HEAT was part of the assessment scheme of the New York Citi Bike share system benefit at launch in 2013 and after expansion in 2015 (Babagoli et al., 2019). The study also discussed how further system expansion and utilization by residents in high-poverty communities could affect the potential benefit of the largest bicycle share system in the United States. The results showed that the greatest proportion of Citi Bike stations were located in low-poverty (i.e. wealthier) census tracts (41 % per period), and there were no significant changes in station distribution during expansion. HEAT estimated an increase from two to three premature deaths prevented and an increased annual economic benefit from \$18,800,000 to \$28,300,000 associated with Citi Bike use. The findings underlined the potential for even greater benefits with advancing access in higher-poverty neighbourhoods and communities of colour.

3.1.3 Policy example 1: Austrian masterplans walking and cycling

The Federal Ministry for Climate Action, Environment, Energy, Mobility, Innovation and Technology has been involved in the development of HEAT since the very beginning and sponsored the first HEAT consensus meeting in Graz in May 2007. HEAT is currently promoted in three ways: HEAT and the user guide were translated into German when it was launched as an online tool in 2009 and made available on the ministries' website (WHO calculator). The Ministry also calculated the societal economic value of health effects from current and levels and aspired policy goals for cycling in Austria using the HEAT in 2009 and again in 2014 (Thaler and Eder, 2017); and included a mention of the HEAT into the National Masterplan for Cycling (p. 43) (Federal Ministry for Agriculture et al., 2015). The HEAT results have also been used regularly in presentation and communications of the ministry, e g. in relation to a cycling tour of the former Minister of Environment.

3.1.4 Policy example 2: Making the investment case for cycling and walking in Accra, Ghana

The Greater Accra Passenger Transport Executive and the Accra Metropolitan Assembly committed to having Accra as one of the greenest and healthiest cities in Africa and have focused on the expansion of sustainable transport strategies, including non-motorised transport. Based on this commitment, the expansion of walking and cycling infrastructure in the Greater Accra Metropolitan Area has been assessed, using the HEAT (Johnson et al., 2023). The assessment was based on internal reports and databases at Department of Urban Roads and Accra Metropolitan Assembly. Achieving the policy goal to develop 500 km of safe, comfortable, equitable infrastructure for walking and cycling by 2030, would prevent over 5500 premature deaths over the time span of 10 years, along with over 40 million tons of CO2 emissions, totaling a societal value of US$ 4 2 billion.

The results of the HEAT assessments were discussed with governmental agencies & NGOs at a workshop organized by the World Health Organization. It led to a pledge to develop a non-motorized transport policy for Accra and to review the national Transport Policy. Activities are now underway to secure the necessary funding to implement these ambitious plans.

3.1.5 Practice example: Health impact assessment of fare increases and service cuts on public transport (Boston, Massachusetts, USA)

The Metropolitan Area Planning Council used the HEAT as part of a rapid health impact assessment to calculate the economic costs of potential increases in mortality as a consequence of decreases in regular walking due to two proposals to increase fares and cut services on public transport (James et al., 2014). Results showed that across the two proposals there would be 9–14 additional deaths per year due to decreased physical activity, which could be valued at between $74 9 and $116 5 million per year. This significant cost associated with the proposed fare and service changes was second only to the cost of time lost to congestion. The resulting costs would have by far exceeded the budget shortfall that the proposed changes sought to address. According to the authors, the results contributed to lower fare increases and fewer service cuts than initially proposed.

4. Discussion

With the growing popularity of walking and cycling as healthy and sustainable travel modes, over the past decade, economic assessments of health impacts from walking and cycling have become more established, thanks to practical yet robust tools such as the HEAT or the Integrated

Transport and Health Impact Modelling Tool (ITHIM) (Woodcock et al., 2013). The large number of officially published applications by academia, governments, NGOs and consultancies demonstrates a wide recognition of the HEAT as an established and valued tool to calculate health and carbon impacts from active transport interventions. It was also found to be among the most widely used health-impact assessment tool for active travel by three systematic literature reviews (Brown et al., 2016; Doorley et al., 2015; Mizdrak et al., 2023). Important milestones of this progress have been the endorsement of the HEAT in the Global Action Plan for Physical Activity (p. 69) (World Health Organization, 2018), and most recently in the Pan-European Masterplan for Cycling (p. 21ff) (Cycling Masterplan, 2021) and the Masterplan for Walking (p. 23) (Federal Ministry Republic of Austria for Climate Action, Environment, Energy, Mobility, Innovation and Technology, 2024).

4.1 Success factors and achievements of HEAT

HEAT has been well-received and often characterized as an "eye-opening" tool by a broad audience of transport and health advocates, both within and outside of governmental institutions. This is often due to monetization of health benefits using the value of statistical life approach, which results in benefit estimates that exceed general expectations. On some occasions, this plain quantification of impacts in monetary terms has earned active travel modes "a seat at the table" (Cavill and Kahlmeier, 2016), resulting in more equal consideration of walking and cycling in decision-making processes (World Health Organization, 2025). While examples of a direct impact on policy decisions remain rare, HEAT results have equally resonated in places with low levels of walking or cycling to make a basic case for their benefits, as well as in places with well-established walking or cycling cultures to make more nuanced benefit-versus-cost arguments. This is particularly the case in countries where economic appraisal is an established practice, such as the United Kingdom: here, the HEAT (and its strong backing as a WHO tool) has been critical in sensitizing the Department of Transport for the positive health effects of active mobility, leading to its adoption as a core component the in earlier versions of their WebTAG (Transport Appraisal Guidance) methodology (Cavill and Kahlmeier, 2016; Department for Transport, 2014). Also in the Swiss approach to quantify the external costs and benefits of transport, HEAT served as the basis for the first inclusion of the positive health effects of cycling and walking (Ecoplan, 2014). HEAT also has proven helpful to put benefits from physical activity in perspective to harms from air pollution and insufficient traffic safety while walking or cycling. While research has shown that in general benefits of active travel outweigh the risks (Mueller et al., 2015; Tainio et al., 2021, 2016), HEAT provides users with the possibility to verify or challenge this assumption for their particular local case for example by comparing impacts in a more and a less cycling friendly city (Ilie et al., 2019), helping to counteract perceived fears, or substantiating calls for safety improvements (Garcia et al., 2021). The recognition of the potential role for active travel in efforts to reduce urban carbon emissions (Brand et al., 2021) further increases the usefulness of the HEAT, supporting the inclusion of this argument into appraisals of different policy options.

Being steered by the WHO and making co-creation with leading experts from around the world part of its key approach, the HEAT has earned a status of credibility and scientific robustness by academics, advocates and governments alike. Two national agencies, namely in England and Austria, have officially endorsed the HEAT at some point (Cavill and Kahlmeier, 2016).

Arguably the HEAT tool's greatest success factor is to present the impact assessment as a sequence of clearly delineated steps, when in fact the calculation needs to rely on a fairly complex set of data, methods and assumptions (Götschi et al., 2020; Rutter et al., 2013; WHO Regional Office for Europe, 2023b). Throughout its evolution, the HEAT has made it a top priority to require minimal inputs, while providing as much of the required data and calculations as possible in the background. In the simplest cases, a handful of inputs is sufficient to obtain results. At the same time, over the years the tool has evolved to accommodate both a more diverse set of applications (such as bike sharing or e-biking and an expanded set of input options for the volume of cycling or walking, crash risk estimates or population default values) as well as increasingly diverse audiences and levels of expertise (illustrated by the HEAT use for equity analysis (Babagoli et al., 2019) or its application in Africa (Johnson et al., 2023)). Built-in user-interface options allow users to select a simple, flexible, or full-feature HEAT experience (WHO Regional Office for Europe, 2024).

4.2 Limitations and challenges of HEAT and HIA of active mobility in general

Despite its considerable success, substantial challenges remain for HEAT: investing into modernizing the web-interface and simplifying the explanatory content to improve user experience as well as providing additional features such as the ability to store and create multiple assessments were identified as further fields of development, -Other challenges apply to HIA tools for active transport in general. The most common difficulty reported by HEAT users is how to obtain data on active travel use (Bukovetz et al., 2021; Cavill and Kahlmeier, 2016; Cavill et al., 2017). By design, HEAT leaves the burden of assessing or estimating levels of walking and cycling to its users. While in some circumstances hypothetical calculations based on (often crude) scenario assumptions are sufficient, many users desire to quantify concrete impacts of existing or planned programs or infrastructure projects. However, in particular for small scale projects assessing walking and cycling levels accurately and predicting effects of interventions on future active travel use remains a challenge. Although data collection is outside the immediate scope of HEAT, there is a role for the HEAT project to guide users through the ever-evolving methods for active travel estimation, as the institutional burden to use online surveys or app-based tracking becomes smaller over time.

A limitation of HEAT is that health impacts are assessed based on mortality risk (i.e. premature deaths and road fatalities) only. Although there is ample evidence of impacts of active travel on morbidities (Dinu et al., 2019; Dons et al., 2018; Leyland et al., 2019; Wanner et al., 2012; Zhao et al., 2021), including these in tools such as HEAT would likely increase complexity of use, and thus be at odds with its main goal of providing a simple-to-use tool. Thus, health impact estimates derived by HEAT present relatively crude ballpark estimates and do not allow specific conclusions regarding health outcomes such as mental health or cardiovascular disease.

HEAT uses the VSL to quantify the societal value of reductions in mortality risk. The values are based on a meta-analysis of a large number of studies (OECD, 2012), and recently a methodology was integrated into the HEAT tool to estimate VSL estimates for each country worldwide (Götschi et al., 2020; WHO Regional Office for Europe, 2023b), which has facilitated uptake in countries outside Europe, e.g. in Ghana (Johnson et al., 2023) and in South America (Montes et al., 2012; Wilches-Mogollon et al., 2024). While widely used in transport appraisals and elsewhere, monetization based on this approach does not provide estimates in terms of health care savings or other governmental expenditures, and as such remains hard to explain, particularly to non-transport experts and some local decision-makers.

Despite HEAT having always prioritized user friendliness and simplicity, it often remains a challenge for users to communicate the results effectively to their final target audiences (i.e. decision makers). To that effect, results export features and results visualizations have been added. However, it remains true for HEAT, as well as all other HIA tools, that effective application of such tools requires investments in capacity building and dissemination to foster integration of the findings into the policy discourse.

4.3 Outlook

The primary goal of HEAT and other HIA tools for active travel modes is to provide decision-making processes that affect walking and cycling with robust, quantitative inputs. This goal has been pursued through a three-pronged strategy: (a) provide a scientifically robust tool broadly accepted by experts and governmental institutions, (b) provide a simple-to-use tool easily picked up by practitioners within and outside of governmental institutions, and (c) disseminate the tool and related success stories as widely as possible. While tool development remains ongoing (eg recent integration. of e-biking), with the launch of the globally applicable version the priority has shifted towards wider dissemination and capacity building, e.g. through webinars and presentations. Looking into integration of disease endpoints, complementing VSL with an approach taking better account of life years (Smith et al., 2021) and guiding users through the evolving methods for active travel estimation are part of the wider development agenda.

As with many innovations, successful adoption of the HEAT has been greatly helped by enthusiastic "early adopters" who see its potential and make the effort to try it out and then advocate for it. More strategically developing and supporting networks of such advocates will be a key task for building capacity and increasing the use of the tool in the future. Options are, for example the Transport, Health and Environment Pan-European Partnership or the Partnership for Healthy Cities (a global network, supported by Bloomberg Philanthropies, the WHO and Vital Strategies). The challenge is identifying the right people, getting them to spend time to apply it to a specific scenario or case study and to promote it at a national and/or local level.

Continued strategic communication, capacity building and dissemination, and further user research are thus key tasks for the future, along with translation of the tool into more languages, user guide and the website, particularly making it amenable outside of Europe, e g. Spanish (currently only available for the website and online tool), Portuguese or Arabic. Another element is to collate more case studies that are applicable to low- and middle-income contexts supporting a more global uptake of the HEAT, particularly considering the recent adaptation of the tool for global use.

Finally, lack of systematically collected data on walking and cycling was identified as a key barrier to use of HIA tools such as the HEAT. Users stated that trying the HEAT often had an unexpected outcome of helping them realise the gaps in their data. Supporting international, national and sub-national transport authorities in collecting better data on walking and cycling should be another key component of a future HEAT dissemination strategy.

In conclusion, the contribution of walking and cycling to addressing public health, sustainable transport and climate goals are substantial, particularly in settings facing increasing levels of urbanisation and motorisation. Therefore, integrating health impacts into transport economic assessments should be a standard approach for all transport planning approaches to ensure that the most cost-effective and thus sustainable investments are made.

Acknowledgments

We gratefully acknowledge the support received by Sophia Röckel, Pia Andersen and Christian Schweizer, Division of Communicable Diseases, Health Security and Environment, WHO Regional Office for Europe, in carrying out the HEAT user survey and collating information on use of the HEAT. We also thankfully acknowledge the project lead by Dr Randy Rzewnicki, formerly European Cyclists' Federation, in the 2015 HEAT user survey. We further thank Kitty Greenwood, Yingjie Huang (Charlotte), Talia Shehadeh and Oscar Schilly, kindly supervised by Audrey de Nazelle, Faculty of Natural Sciences, Centre for Environmental Policy, Imperial College London, for their review of the HEAT tool and identification of case studies.

The authors alone are responsible for the views expressed in this article and they do not necessarily represent the views, decisions or policies of the WHO or other institution with which they are affiliated.

Funding

The HEAT user survey was co-funded under a LIFE + grant to the European Cyclists' Federation from DG Environment, European Commission.

Conflict of interest

The authors declare that the research was conducted in the absence of any commercial or financial relationships that could be construed as a potential conflict of interest. The authors alone are responsible for the views expressed in this article and they do not necessarily represent the views, decisions or policies of the institutions of WHO or other institutions with which they are affiliated.

References

Babagoli, M.A., Kaufman, T.K., Noyes, P., Sheffield, P.E., 2019. Exploring the health and spatial equity implications of the New York City Bike share system. J. Transp. & Health 13, 200–209. https://doi.org/10.1016/j.jth.2019.04.003.

Brand, C., Götschi, T., Dons, E., Gerike, R., Anaya-Boig, E., Avila-Palencia, I., et al., 2021. The climate change mitigation impacts of active travel: evidence from a longitudinal panel study in seven European cities. Glob. Environ. Change 67, 102224. https://doi.org/10.1016/j.gloenvcha.2021.102224.

Brown, V., Diomedi, B.Z., Moodie, M., Veerman, J.L., Carter, R., 2016. A systematic review of economic analyses of active transport interventions that include physical activity benefits. Transp. Policy 45, 190–208. https://doi.org/10.1016/j.tranpol.2015.10.003.

Buehler, R., Pucher, J., Gerike, R., Götschi, T., 2017. Reducing car dependence in the heart of Europe: lessons from Germany, Austria, and Switzerland. Transp. Rev. 37, 4–28. https://doi.org/10.1080/01441647.2016.1177799.

Bukovetz, J., Shuntova, K., Spiroski, I., Memeti, S., 2021. Assessment of health and economic benefits of walking in the Republic of North Macedonia using Health Economic Assessment Tool (HEAT). Arch. Public. Health 13, 17–29. https://doi.org/10.3889/aph.2021.6010.

Cavill, N., Kahlmeier, S., 2016. Turn up the HEAT - Recommendations to Increase the use of the World Health Organization's Health Economic Assessment Tool for Cycling Across Europe. European Cyclist Federation (ECF), Brussels.

Cavill, N., Kahlmeier, S., Rutter, H., Racioppi, F., Oja, P., 2007. Economic Assessment of Transport Infrastructure and Policies: Methodological Guidance on the Economic Appraisal of Health Effects Related to Walking and Cycling. WHO Regional Office for Europe, Copenhagen.

Cavill, N., Kahlmeier, S., Rutter, H., Racioppi, F., Oja, P., 2008. Economic analyses of transport infrastructure and policies including health effects related to cycling and walking: a systematic review. Transp. Policy 15, 291–304 https://doi.org/10.1016/j.tranpol.2008.11.001.

Cavill, N., Rutter, H., Gower, R., 2014. Economic Assessment of the Health Benefits of Walking on the Wales Coast Path. Natural Resources Wales, Cardiff, United Kingdom.

Cavill, N., Kahlmeier, S., Crone, D., Goudas, M., 2017. Measuring the value of an Urban Active Environment (UActivE) including case study examples from the EU SPACE (Supporting Policy and Action for Active Environments) project. University of Gloucestershire, Co-funded by the Erasmus+ Program of the European Union. ISBN 978-1-86174-237-7. https://cesie.org/media/SPACE-output-3-Measuring-value-of-an-Urban-Active-Environment_EN.pdf.

Chai, W., 2023. What is Google analytics and how does it work? [WWW Document]. Business Analytics. https://www.techtarget.com/searchbusinessanalytics/definition/Google-Analytics (Accessed 1.16.23).

City of Espoo, 2013. Cycling promotion program 2013–2024 [Pyöräilyn edistämisohjelma 2013–2024]. Espoo, Finland.

de Hartog, J.J., Boogaard, H., Nijland, H., Hoek, G., 2010. Do the health benefits of cycling outweigh the risks? Env. Health Persp. 118, 1109–1116. https://doi.org/10.1289/Ehp.0901747.

Department for Transport, 2014. Transport Analysis Guidance: An Overview of Transport Appraisal (WebTAG). Department for Transport, London.

Department for Transport, 2021. The impact of the coronavirus pandemic on walking and cycling statistics, England: 2020 [WWW Document]. GOV.UK. https://www.gov.uk/government/statistics/walking-and-cycling-statistics-england-2020/the-impact-of-the-coronavirus-pandemic-on-walking-and-cycling-statistics-england-2020 (accessed 1.16.23).

Dinu, M., Pagliai, G., Macchi, C., Sofi, F., 2019. Active commuting and multiple health outcomes: a systematic review and meta-analysis. Sports Med. 49, 437–452. https://doi.org/10.1007/s40279-018-1023-0.

Doll, C., Hartwig, J., Senger, F., Schade, W., Maibach, M., Sutter, D., et al., n.d. Economic aspects of non-technical measures to reduce traffic emissions: Summary (No. Report No. (UBA-FB) 001728). Federal Environment Agency, Dessau-Roßlau, Germany.

Dons, E., Rojas-Rueda, D., Anaya-Boig, E., Avila-Palencia, I., Brand, C., Cole-Hunter, T., et al., 2018. Transport mode choice and body mass index: cross-sectional and longitudinal evidence from a European-wide study. Env. Int. 119, 109–116. https://doi.org/10.1016/j.envint.2018.06.023.

Doorley, R., Pakrashi, V., Ghosh, B., 2015. Quantifying the health impacts of active travel: assessment of methodologies. Transp. Rev. 35, 559–582. https://doi.org/10.1080/01441647.2015.1037378.

Ecoplan, INFRAS, 2014. Externe Kosten des Verkehrs 2010: Monetarisierung von Umwelt-, Unfall- und Gesundheitseffekten. Studie im Auftrag desBundesamtes für Raumentwicklung, n.d. Bundesamt für Raumentwicklung, Bern.

Federal Ministry for Agriculture, Forestry, Environment and Water Management, 2015. Masterplan Cycling [Masterplan Radfahren] 2015–2025. Federal Ministry for Agriculture, Forestry, Environment and Water Management, Vienna.

Federal Ministry for Climate Action, Environment, Energy, Mobility, Innovation and Technology (2021). Pan-European Master Plan for Cycling Promotion. 5th High-level Meeting on Transport, Health and Environment Vienna, Austria.

Federal Ministry Republic of Austria for Climate Action, Environment, Energy, Mobility, Innovation and Technology, 2024. Pan-European Master Plan on Walking. Federal Ministry Republic of Austria for Climate Action, Environment, Energy, Mobility. Innovation and Technology, Vienna.

Federal Ministry for Agriculture, Forestry, Environment and Water, 2020. WHO-calculator for the health effects from cycling [WWW Document]. [WHO-Kalkulator für Gesundheitseffekte durch Radfahren]. https://www.klimaaktiv.at/service/tools/mobilitaet/HEATforCycling.html.

Garcia, L., Johnson, R., Johnson, A., Abbas, A., Goel, R., Tatah, L., et al., 2021. Health impacts of changes in travel patterns in Greater Accra Metropolitan Area, Ghana. Environ. Int. 155, 106680. https://doi.org/10.1016/j.envint.2021.106680.

Glazener, A., Sanchez, K., Ramani, T., Zietsman, J., Nieuwenhuijsen, M.J., Mindell, J.S., et al., 2021. Fourteen pathways between urban transportation and health: a conceptual model and literature review. J. Transp. & Health 21, 101070. https://doi.org/10.1016/j.jth.2021.101070.

Gotschi, T., 2011. Costs and benefits of bicycling investments in Portland, Oregon. J. Phys. Act. Health 8, S49–S58. https://doi.org/10.1123/jpah.8.s1.s49.

Gotschi, T., Tainio, M., Maizlish, N., Schwanen, T., Goodman, A., Woodcock, J., 2015. Contrasts in active transport behaviour across four countries: how do they translate into public health benefits? Prev. Med. 74, 42–48. https://doi.org/10.1016/j.ypmed.2015.02.009.

Götschi, T., Garrard, J., Giles-Corti, B., 2016. Cycling as a part of daily life: a review of health perspectives. Transp. Rev. 36, 45–71. https://doi.org/10.1080/01441647.2015.1057877.

Götschi, T., Kahlmeier, S., Castro, A., Brand, C., Cavill, N., Kelly, P., et al., 2020. Integrated impact assessment of active travel: expanding the scope of the Health Economic Assessment Tool (HEAT) for walking and cycling. Int. J. Env. Res. Public. Health 17, 7361. https://doi.org/10.3390/ijerph17207361.

Greenwood, K., Huang, Y., Shehadeh, T., Schilly, O., 2021. Comprehensive Review of the Web Presence of WHO's Health Economic Assessment Tool (HEAT) and Identification and Possible Implementation of Improvements. Imperial College, London, London.

Guthold, R., Stevens, G.A., Riley, L.M., Bull, F.C., 2018. Worldwide trends in insufficient physical activity from 2001 to 2016: a pooled analysis of 358 population-based surveys with 1·9 million participants. Lancet Glob. Health 6, e1077–e1086. https://doi.org/10.1016/S2214-109X(18)30357-7.

Guthold, R., Stevens, G.A., Riley, L.M., Bull, F.C., 2020. Global trends in insufficient physical activity among adolescents: a pooled analysis of 298 population-based surveys with 1·6 million participants. Lancet Child. Adolesc. Health 4, 23–35. https://doi.org/10.1016/S2352-4642(19)30323-2.

Hrkal, J., 2014. Monitoring of cycling in the area Elbe Trail [Monitoring cyklotouristiky na úseku Labské stezky] (Diploma thesis). Faculty of International Relations, College of Economics, Prague.

Ilie, A., Oprea, C., Ruscă, A., Dinu, O., Olteanu, S., Burciu, Ş., 2019. Health impact assessment study on active travel in large urban areas. Procedia Manufacturing, 12th International Conference Interdisciplinarity in Engineering, INTER-ENG 2018, 4–5 October 2018, Tirgu Mures, Romania 32, 944–951. https://doi.org/10.1016/j.promfg.2019.02.307.

India, ITDP, 2020. In: Post-lockdown guidelines to create cycle-friendly citiesIDTP, New York. https://itdp.in/wp-content/uploads/2020/06/COVID-Response-Post-lockdown-guidelines-to-create-cycle-friendly-cities.pdf.

International Society for Physical Activity and Health ISPAH, 2020. ISPAH's eight investments that work for physical activity.[WWW Document]. https://ispah.org/resources/key-resources/.

James, P., Ito, K., Buonocore, J.J., Levy, J.I., Arcaya, M.C., 2014. A health impact assessment of proposed public transportation service cuts and fare increases in Boston, Massachusetts (USA). Int. J. Env. Res. Pub He 11, 8010–8024. https://doi.org/10.3390/ijerph110808010.

Johnson, A., Nhar, E., Santos, A.C., 2023. Health and economic impact assessment of walking and cycling interventions in Accra, Ghana: an investment case using the WHO HEAT tool.Word Health Organization. Ghana Office and World Health Organization Headquarters, Department of Health Promotion, Physical Activity Unit, Geneva. https://www.afro.who.int/sites/default/files/2023-10/HEAT%20Report%202023.pdf.

Kahlmeier, S., Boig, E.A., Fernandez, A.C., Smeds, E., Benvenuti, F., Eriksson, U., et al., 2021. Assessing the policy environment for active mobility in cities-development and feasibility of the PASTA cycling and walking policy environment score. Int. J. Env. Res. Public. Health 18, 986. https://doi.org/10.3390/ijerph18030986.

Kahlmeier, S., Cavill, N., Dinsdale, H., Rutter, H., Götschi, T., Foster, C., et al., 2011. Health Economic Assessment Tools (HEAT) for Walking and for Cycling. Methodology and User Guide. WHO Regional Office for Europe, Copenhagen.

Kahlmeier, S., Götschi, T., Cavill, N., Castro, A., Brand, C., Rojas Rueda, D., et al., 2017. Health economic assessment tool (HEAT) for walking and for cycling. Methods and User Guide on Physical Activity, Air Pollution, Injuries and Carbon Impact Assessments. WHO Regional Office for Europe, Copenhagen.

Kahlmeier, S., Racioppi, F., Cavill, N., Rutter, H., Oja, P., 2010. "Health in All Policies" in practice: guidance and tools to quantifying the health effects of cycling and walking. J. Phys. Act. Health 7, S120–S125.

Katzmarzyk, P.T., Friedenreich, C., Shiroma, E.J., Lee, I.-M., 2022. Physical inactivity and non-communicable disease burden in low-income, middle-income and high-income countries. Br. J. Sports Med. 56, 101–106. https://doi.org/10.1136/bjsports-2020-103640.

Kelly, P., Kahlmeier, S., Gotschi, T., Orsini, N., Richards, J., Roberts, N., et al., 2014. Systematic review and meta-analysis of reduction in all-cause mortality from walking and cycling and shape of dose response relationship. Int. J. Behav. Nutr. Phys. Act. 11, 132. https://doi.org/10.1186/s12966-014-0132-x.

Küster, F., Blondel, B., 2013. Calculating the economic benefits of cycling in EU-27. European Cyclist Federation ECF. Brussels, Belgium.

Lamb, M., Halbesma, N., Wild, S., 2014. Cycling as a mode of transport: a possible solution for the increasing burden of type 2 diabetes? Practical Diabetes 30, 286–289. https://doi.org/10.1002/pdi.1793.

Levin, K., Neergaard, K., Nilsson, A., 2014. Effects on Climate, Public Health and Social Economy of Region Skåne's Orientation for Continued Bicycle Development in Skåne [Effekter på klimat, folkhälsa och samhällsekonomi av Region Skånes inriktning för fortsatt cykelutveckling i Skåne]. Trivector Traffic, Lund, Sweden.

Leyland, L.-A., Spencer, B., Beale, N., Jones, T., van Reekum, C.M., 2019. The effect of cycling on cognitive function and well-being in older adults. PLoS One 14, e0211779. https://doi.org/10.1371/journal.pone.0211779.

Lovelace, R., Goodman, A., Aldred, R., Berkoff, N., Abbas, A., Woodcock, J., 2017. The propensity to cycle tool: an open source online system for sustainable transport planning. JTLU 10. https://doi.org/10.5198/jtlu.2016.862.

Lushomo, 2024. HEAT Website: UX Research Summary, On behalf of the WHO European Centre Environment and Health, Bonn, Germany. Lushomo, Leatherhead, United Kingdom.

Martens, K., 2020. Chapter eight - A justice perspective on transport and health. In: Nieuwenhuijsen, M.J., Khreis, H. (Eds.), Advances in Transportation and Health. Elsevier, pp. 197–221. https://doi.org/10.1016/B978-0-12-819136-1.00008-5.

Mizdrak, A., Tatah, L., Mueller, N., Shaw, C., Woodcock, J., 2023. Assessing the health impacts of changes in active transport: An updated systematic review. J. Transp. & Health 33, 101702. https://doi.org/10.1016/j.jth.2023.101702.

Montes, F., Sarmiento, O.L., Zarama, R., Pratt, M., Wang, G.J., Jacoby, E., et al., 2012. Do health benefits outweigh the costs of mass recreational programs? An economic analysis of four ciclovia programs. J. Urban. Health 89, 153–170. https://doi.org/10.1007/s11524-011-9628-8.

Mueller, N., Rojas-Rueda, D., Cole-Hunter, T., de Nazelle, A., Dons, E., Gerike, R., et al., 2015. Health impact assessment of active transportation: A systematic review. Prev. Med. 76, 103–114. https://doi.org/10.1016/j.ypmed.2015.04.010.

Nordic Council of Ministers CBA of cycling. Secretary of the Nordic Council of Ministers, Copenhagen. https://www.norden.org/en/publication/cba-cycling.

OECD, 2012. Mortality risk valuation in environment, health, and transport policies. Paris.

Rérat, P., Marincek, D., Ravalet, E., 2025. How do e-bikes compete with the other modes of transport? Investigating multiple dimensions of a modal shift. Appl. Mobilities 10, 85–98. https://doi.org/10.1080/23800127.2024.2332006.

Rutter, H., Cavill, N., Racioppi, F., Dinsdale, H., Oja, P., Kahlmeier, S., 2013. Economic impact of reduced mortality due to increased cycling. Am. J. Public. Health 44, 89–92.

Sá, T.H., Tainio, M., Goodman, A., Edwards, P., Haines, A., Gouveia, N., et al., 2017. ealth impact modelling of different travel patterns on physical activity, air pollution and road injuries for São Paulo, Brazil. Environ. Int. 108, 22–31. https://doi.org/10.1016/j.envint.2017.07.009.

Schwarz, E., Leroutier, M., De Nazelle, A., Quirion, P., Jean, K., 2024. The untapped health and climate potential of cycling in France: a national assessment from individual travel data. Lancet Regional Health - Europe 39, 100874. https://doi.org/10.1016/j.lanepe.2024.100874.

Schwedhelm, A., Li, W., Harms, L., Adriazola-Steil, C., 2020. Biking Provides a Critical Lifeline During the Coronavirus Crisis [WWW Document]. World Resources Institute, Washington. https://www.wri.org/insights/biking-provides-critical-lifeline-during-coronavirus-crisis.

Smith, R., Thomas, C., Squires, H., Götschi, T., Kahlmeier, S., Goyder, E., 2021. The price of precision: trade-offs between usability and validity in the World Health Organization Health Economic Assessment Tool for walking and cycling. Public. Health 194, 263–269. https://doi.org/10.1016/j.puhe.2021.03.016.

Tainio, M., de Nazelle, A.J., Gotschi, T., Kahlmeier, S., Rojas-Rueda, D., Nieuwenhuijsen, M.J., et al., 2016. Can air pollution negate the health benefits of cycling and walking? Prev. Med. 87, 233–236. https://doi.org/10.1016/j.ypmed.2016.02.002.

Tainio, M., Jovanovic Andersen, Z., Nieuwenhuijsen, M.J., Hu, L., de Nazelle, A., An, R., et al., 2021. Air pollution, physical activity and health: a mapping review of the evidence. Env. Int. 147, 105954. https://doi.org/10.1016/j.envint.2020.105954.

Thaler, R., Eder, M., 2017. HEAT for cycling application in Austria. Federal Ministry of Agriculture. Forestry, Environment and Water Management, Vienna, Austria.

Thondoo, M., Mueller, N., Rojas-Rueda, D., de Vries, D., Gupta, J., Nieuwenhuijsen, M.J., 2020. Participatory quantitative health impact assessment of urban transport planning: a case study from Eastern Africa. Environ. Int. 144, 106027. https://doi.org/10.1016/j.envint.2020.106027.

University of Cambridge, MRC Epidemiology Unit, 2025. Integrated transport and health impact modelling tool (ITHIM) [WWW Document]. MRC Epidemiology Unit, Cambridge. https://www.mrc-epid.cam.ac.uk/research/research-areas/public-health-modelling/ithim/ (accessed 8.19.25).

van Wee, B., Borjesson, M., 2015. How to make CBA more suitable for evaluating cycling policies. Transp. Policy 44, 117–124. https://doi.org/10.1016/j.tranpol.2015.07.005.

Van Zeebroeck, B., Charles, J., 2014. Impact and potential of bicycle use for the economy and employment in the Brussels Region [Impact en potentieel van fietsgebruik voor de economie en de werkgelegenheid in het Brussels Gewest]. Ministry Brussels-Capital Region, Brussels, Belgium.

Ville de Paris, 2024. A new cycling plan for a 100% bikeable city [WWW Document]. https://www.paris.fr/en/pages/a-new-cycling-plan-for-a-100-bikeable-city-28350 (accessed 8.19.25).

Wanner, M., Götschi, T., Martin-Diener, E., Kahlmeier, S., Martin, B.W., 2012. Active transport, physical activity, and body weight in adults: a systematic review. Am. J. Prev. Med. 42, 493–502. https://doi.org/10.1016/j.amepre.2012.01.030.

WHO Regional Office for Europe, 2015. Factsheets on Health-Enhancing Physical Activity in the 28 European Union Member States of the WHO European Region. WHO Regional Office for Europe, Copenhagen, Denmark.

WHO Regional Office for Europe, 2022. Walking and Cycling: Latest Evidence to Support Policy-Making and Practice. World Health Organization, Geneva,Switzerland.

WHO Regional Office for Europe, 2024. Health economic assessment tool (HEAT) for walking and for cycling. Methods and User Guide on Physical Activity, Air Pollution, Road Fatalities and Carbon Impact Assessments: 2024 update. (Copenhagen).

WHO Regional Office for Europe, 2023a. General acknowledgements [WWW Document]. HEAT Health economic assessment tool. https://www.heatwalkingcycling.org/?&heat_locale=en-US&heat_lang=en#homepage.

WHO Regional Office for Europe, 2023b. Health economic assessment tool (HEAT) for walking and for cycling: methods and user guide on physical activity, air pollution, injuries and carbon impact assessments: 2022 update. Copenhagen, Denmark.

Wilches-Mogollon, M.A., Sarmiento, O.L., Medaglia, A.L., Montes, F., Guzman, L.A., Sánchez-Silva, M., et al., 2024. Impact assessment of an active transport intervention via systems analytics. Transp. Res. D: Transp. Environ. 128, 104112. https://doi.org/10.1016/j.trd.2024.104112.

Woodcock, J., Aldred, R., Lovelace, R., Strain, T., Goodman, A., 2021. Health, environmental and distributional impacts of cycling uptake: the model underlying the propensity to cycle tool for England and Wales. J. Transp. & Health 22, 101066. https://doi.org/10.1016/j.jth.2021.101066.

Woodcock, J., Edwards, P., Tonne, C., Armstrong, B.G., Ashiru, O., Banister, D., et al., 2009. Public health benefits of strategies to reduce greenhouse-gas emissions: urban land transport. Lancet 374, 1930–1943. https://doi.org/10.1016/S0140-6736(09)61714-1.

Woodcock, J., Givoni, M., Morgan, A.S., 2013. Health impact modelling of active travel visions for England and Wales using an Integrated Transport and Health Impact Modelling Tool (ITHIM). PLoS One 8, e51462. https://doi.org/10.1371/journal.pone.0051462.

World Health Organization, 2018. Physical Activity for Health - More Active People for a Healthier World: Draft Global Action Plan on Physical Activity 2018–2030. WHO Discussion Paper (9 April) WHO, Geneva, Switzerland.

World Health Organization, 2020. Supporting Healthy Urban Transport and Mobility in the Context of COVID-19. World Health Organization, Geneva, Switzerland.

World Health Organization, 2025. Examples of Applications of the Health Economic Assessment Tool for Cycling and Walking. World Health Organization, Geneva, Switzerland.

Zhao, Y., Hu, F., Feng, Y., Yang, X., Li, Y., Guo, C., et al., 2021. Association of cycling with risk of all-cause and cardiovascular disease mortality: a systematic review and dose-response meta-analysis of prospective Cohort studies. Sports Med. 51, 1439–1448. https://doi.org/10.1007/s40279-021-01452-7.

CHAPTER TWELVE

Conclusion - Transport policy and health: What have we learned and where do we go next?

Dena Kasraian[a,*], Ahmadreza Faghih Imani[b], and Stephen Watkins[c]
[a]Department of the Built Environment, Eindhoven University of Technology, Eindhoven, the Netherlands
[b]Centre for Environmental Policy, Imperial College London, London, United Kingdom
[c]Transport and Health Science Group, 4, St Andrew's Place, London, United Kingdom
*Corresponding author. e-mail address: d.kasraian@tue.nl

Contents

Abstract

This chapter synthesises the findings of the ten review chapters, offering insights into how transport policies and interventions influence health, wellbeing and equity. Throughout the volume, contributors highlight that health impacts depend not only on the type of intervention but also on design, implementation, governance, context, and the distribution of benefits and burdens. The chapter identifies cross-cutting themes related to equity, behavioural and psychosocial mechanisms, public acceptance, wider societal impacts, unintended consequences and the limits of existing evidence. It ends by emphasizing priorities for future research and policy, such as enhancing longitudinal and comparative studies and considering broader health and wellbeing impacts. It also underscores the need to increase equity considerations in transport appraisal and to develop better decision-support tools that can capture more health co-benefits.

Advances in Transport Policy and Planning, Volume 18
ISSN 2543-0009, https://doi.org/10.1016/bs.atpp.2026.07.010

This volume set out to review how transport policies and interventions influence health, wellbeing and equity. It brings together chapters on transport infrastructure and services, land-use planning and the allocation of urban space, pricing and regulatory measures, behavioural interventions, mobility in disaster recovery, emerging mobility technologies and health impact assessment. Across these chapters, health is understood broadly: not only as the absence of disease or injury, but also in terms of physical activity, access to opportunities, social participation, mental wellbeing, environmental quality and the fair distribution of benefits and burdens. The volume therefore reinforces a core message of the *Health on the Move* series: transport policy is health policy. This chapter presents a synthesis of the key findings and cross-cutting insights across chapters.

1. Key findings

The chapters in this volume demonstrate that transport policy influences health through a wide range of pathways and across different policy instruments. McMillan et al.'s chapter on buses shows that **transport infrastructure and service provision** can contribute to public health and health equity when services are affordable, reliable, accessible and well integrated. These improvements in access, social participation and physical activity emerge as important benefits, while air pollution, noise, injuries, personal safety and occupational health remain important concerns.

The chapters on street placemaking, pedestrianisation, and Ciclovías demonstrate the considerable health potential of **land-use planning** interventions, while recognising that the evidence base remains uneven. Taken together, these reviews suggest that redesigning car-dominant urban spaces can support physical activity, social interaction, perceived safety, wellbeing and environmental quality. However, the strength of evidence varies across intervention types, and the reviews also identify implementation challenges related to accessibility, gentrification, public acceptance and the uneven distribution of benefits and burdens. Participatory planning and equity-sensitive design therefore emerge as recurring conditions for success.

Chapters on fare-free transportation and Low Emission Zones show how **pricing** and **regulatory** instruments can influence health through access, affordability, and environmental exposure. Fare-free transportation initiatives can improve access to healthcare, social participation and mobility opportunities, particularly for groups facing financial or mobility barriers. The chapter also suggests that benefits may arise through psychosocial mechanisms, including reduced financial stress, a sense of mobility independence, and the ability to participate more fully in social life. Low Emission Zones can reduce exposure to traffic-related air pollution and associated physical health risks. Still, they may also create financial, mobility and psychological burdens for some groups, including lower-income households, owners of non-compliant vehicles and people living near or outside zone boundaries. The review also points to the need for complementary measures that help maximise benefits while reducing potential negative distributional effects. These include equity-focused implementation, meaningful public engagement, and stronger links with public transport, walking, and cycling initiatives.

The behaviour change chapter adds a different perspective by focusing on how active travel interventions work. It shows that **behavioural interventions** are often evaluated in terms of changes in walking, cycling or physical activity, while the psychological mechanisms through which they are expected to work are less consistently measured and tested. This points to the need for more theory-driven evaluations that examine not only whether interventions increase active travel, but also how changes in attitudes, self-efficacy, perceived control, social influence and planning contribute to behaviour change. More broadly, the chapter reinforces the idea that infrastructure and policy interventions may be more effective when accompanied by strategies that support behaviour change.

The chapters on post-disaster mobility planning and new mobility broaden the discussion to exceptional and future contexts. Although focusing on very different contexts, both chapters emphasise the importance of anticipating and managing change. The disaster recovery chapter shows how transport systems shape wellbeing in recovery contexts. It shows how disrupted or poorly planned mobility can restrict access to healthcare and essential services, increase stress and isolation, and weaken social networks. In contrast, accessible and context-sensitive mobility planning can support physical, mental-emotional and social wellbeing, particularly for populations that are more vulnerable to displacement and poor transport access. The new mobility chapter extends this discussion to emerging technologies and services whose health impacts are still evolving. Innovations in **infrastructure and service provision** enabled through **ICT** systems such as rideshare, shared micromobility, automated vehicles and urban air mobility, may create new opportunities for access, safety and environmental improvement, but also new risks related to reduced active travel, harmful environmental and noise exposure, psychosocial stress, poor labour conditions and unequal

Table 1 Cross-cutting themes emerging across the chapters.

Cross-cutting theme	Chapters where this is most visible	What chapters show	Implication for research, policy and practice
1. Evidence strength and intervention effectiveness vary across policy areas	All chapters, but especially 5, 6, 8, 9, and 10	Some areas, such as LEZs and bus services, have stronger, more established evidence, while others, such as Ciclovías, fare-free transport, and post-disaster mobility, rely on small samples, short-term studies, or observational designs. Across policy areas, the chapters also show that intervention effectiveness is difficult to assess because health impacts occur through multiple, overlapping pathways and depend on design, context and implementation.	More longitudinal, comparative, and counterfactual evaluations are needed, alongside larger samples and greater attention to how, where, and under what conditions interventions are most effective. Evaluations should avoid focusing on a single outcome and should consider the full range of health pathways.
2. Behavioural and psychosocial mechanisms matter	6, 7, 8, 9, and 10	Health impacts may arise not only from changes in environmental exposures or travel behaviour, but also from psychological and social mechanisms such as perceived control, stress, dignity, entitlement to mobility, trust, safety, and emotional comfort.	Future evaluations should examine mechanisms of behaviour change, using theory-driven, qualitative and mixed-methods approaches alongside quantitative outcome measures.
3. Health benefits and burdens are unevenly distributed	2, 3, 4, 5, 6, 7, 9, and 10	Several chapters show that the benefits and burdens of transport policies vary by factors such as income, age, disability, gender, geography, and digital access.	Equity considerations should be embedded in the planning, design, implementation, appraisal, and monitoring of transport policies.

4. Geographical and contextual diversity remains limited	All chapters, but especially 3, 4, 5, 6, 7, 9, and 10	Much of the evidence is concentrated in the Global North or is from single-city case studies. The chapters also show that local context, governance arrangements, spatial distribution and implementation conditions can shape outcomes.	Evidence needs greater geographical and contextual diversity, including comparative studies across cities, regions and countries, and greater attention to transferability across settings.
5. Policies have wider societal impacts and spillover effects	3, 4, 6, 7, 9, and 10	Transport policies may generate wider co-benefits (e.g., urban cooling and climate resilience); unintended socio-spatial, economic and environmental consequences (e.g., gentrification, traffic redistribution, wildlife disturbance); and spillover effects (e.g., in the neighbouring communities)	Evaluations should consider wider social, environmental and economic impacts, including unintended consequences and spill-over effects beyond direct users and intervention locations.
6. Appraisal and decision-support tools can make health more visible	11; also relevant across all intervention chapters	Tools such as HEAT can help translate health impacts into forms that are more visible within transport appraisal and investment decisions, particularly for walking and cycling.	Health impact assessment and economic appraisal should be strengthened, while also expanding beyond mortality to include broader health, wellbeing and equity outcomes.
7. Public acceptance matters for implementation	3, 4, 6, 7, and 10	Several chapters show that public acceptance can shape intervention implementation and outcomes. Acceptance may depend on perceived benefits and burdens, trust in decision-makers, accessibility concerns, place attachment, stakeholder interests and the spatial distribution of impacts.	Public acceptance should be examined as part of implementation and equity analysis, including how support or opposition varies across population groups, stakeholders and places.

access. Together, these chapters suggest that transport planning must become more adaptive and forward-looking while explicitly considering health and equity impacts.

Across the chapters, a recurring theme is the need for stronger evidence, more robust evaluation methods, and better integration of health into transport decision-making. The HEAT chapter then turns to the tools needed to make health impacts more visible in transport decision-making. It shows how the economic valuation of the health and environmental benefits of walking and cycling can help integrate health considerations into transport appraisal, particularly by estimating the value of reductions in premature mortality associated with physical activity, air pollution, and road fatalities as well as carbon impacts of shifting to active modes. The chapter also identifies several key challenges, such as gaps in walking and cycling data and limited attention to morbidity. In addition, it highlights difficulties in communicating economic valuation findings and the need to strengthen dissemination and capacity-building efforts beyond European and English-speaking settings.

Overall, the chapters showed that transport policies influence health through multiple, often overlapping pathways and are affected by broader equity issues. Table 1 summarises the key findings across the chapters.

2. Avenues for future research

The chapters in this volume demonstrate the growing maturity of the transport and health field. Nevertheless, important gaps remain regarding the effectiveness, distributional impacts, implementation, and evaluation of transport policies. We need to move beyond documenting associations between transport and health to develop a deeper understanding of causal mechanisms, contextual conditions, as well as broader and long-term outcomes. The cross-cutting themes emerging from this volume's chapters (Table 1) point towards the following avenues for future research.

2.1 Evaluating intervention effectiveness

Although the evidence linking transport interventions to health outcomes continues to grow, uncertainties remain regarding intervention effectiveness. Future research should examine whether interventions are effective over time, how they perform relative to alternative policy measures or non-intervention settings, which components drive observed outcomes, and which combinations of measures are most effective.

Several chapters highlight the limited availability of longitudinal evidence and the frequent reliance on participation or usage measures, such as attendance at Ciclovías, public transport use, or use of streets and public spaces. While such measures provide useful information on reach and uptake, they offer limited insight into whether changes in travel behaviour translate into sustained health benefits. More robust longitudinal, comparative and counterfactual study designs are therefore needed to strengthen causal inference and assess how the impacts of interventions evolve and whether their benefits are sustained over time.

Future studies should also disentangle the effects of individual intervention components within multi-component policies. Interventions such as pedestrianisation, street redesign and placemaking initiatives often combine traffic restrictions, greening, public seating, street closures and changes to the public realm. At the same time, research should examine how different policy components interact, since transport interventions are often most effective when implemented as part of wider policy packages that combine incentives, restrictions, infrastructure, and behavioural change (Aldred et al., 2024; Pucher et al., 2010; Winters et al., 2017).

A further limitation identified across several reviews is the lack of appropriate comparators. Many studies evaluate changes in health outcomes following the introduction of an intervention but provide limited evidence on how those outcomes compare with alternative transport modes (e.g., bus versus car use), intervention designs (e.g., full versus partial pedestrianisation), or non-intervention settings (a city with LEZs compared to one without). More comparative studies in future would allow stronger inferences regarding the relative effectiveness of each transport intervention. To better understand causal mechanisms, counterfactual evaluation designs are needed to determine what health outcomes would have occurred in the absence of an intervention.

2.2 Understanding behavioural and psychosocial mechanisms

Stronger evidence is needed on the behavioural and psychosocial mechanisms through which transport interventions influence health. Future research should more closely examine the relationships among intervention functions, psychological determinants, and subsequent behaviour change. In particular, research is needed to investigate the role of factors such as attitudes, self-efficacy, perceived control, social influence, planning, and motivation in driving behaviour change towards active travel and its associated health benefits.

The need to understand psychosocial mechanisms also extends beyond active travel. Fare-free transportation may generate health benefits not only through improved access and physical activity but also through reduced financial stress, dignity, an entitlement to mobility, and the ability to participate more fully in social life. Similarly, emerging mobility technologies highlight the need to understand better the roles of trust, perceived safety, emotional comfort, surveillance concerns and human-machine interaction in behaviour change towards their adoption and associated health impacts. Addressing these knowledge gaps will require more theory-driven evaluations, supported by qualitative and mixed-methods research to explain through which behavioural and psychosocial mechanisms transport interventions affect health.

2.3 Advancing health equity and distributional analyses

A consistent finding across the reviews is that transport interventions can generate benefits and burdens that are unevenlly distributed across populations. Future research should therefore continue the trend of moving beyond average effects and examine how impacts vary by gender, age, socioeconomic status, ethnicity, disability, and geography. Groups that remain under-represented in the literature include carers, people with specific mobility needs, and sexual minorities. Approaches based on distributive justice principles, such as minimum standards approaches, may help assess whether interventions effectively serve populations with the greatest need. Furthermore, public acceptance evaluation could be part of the equity analysis of transport interventions during implementation, helping to identify differences in how benefits and burdens are perceived across population groups (see item 7).

Emerging mobility technologies also highlight digital justice as an increasingly important dimension of transport equity. Many new mobility services rely on smartphones, digital payment systems and digital literacy, potentially excluding older adults, people with disabilities, low-income populations, and others with limited access to such technologies. Future research should examine how digital access and literacy, platform design, and data governance shape transport services and, consequently, health outcomes. Such work can help ensure that technological innovation advances rather than undermines mobility justice, particularly for populations already experiencing transport disadvantage.

2.4 Broadening geographical and contextual diversity

The evidence base remains mostly concentrated in high-income countries and in a relatively small number of urban contexts. Further research could evaluate interventions across multiple cities, regions and countries. Greater attention is needed in rapidly urbanising regions in low- and middle-income countries, as well as for rural and remote areas where travel patterns, infrastructure constraints, and health impacts may differ substantially from those observed in large urban settings. Comparative studies would shed light on how contextual factors, such as urban form, governance, transport infrastructure, social inequality, and baseline travel behaviour, shape health and equity outcomes. Such studies would also help distinguish between largely transferable findings and those that are specific to particular contexts. In addition, evidence is needed from contexts of mobility disruption, including extreme weather events, infrastructure failures, strikes, disaster recovery, post-conflict reconstruction, and other situations where transport systems operate under challenging social, political, or environmental conditions.

2.5 Assessing wider societal impacts: Negative externalities, co-benefits and spill-over effects

Several chapters identify significant gaps in understanding the wider societal impacts of transport interventions. Areas our reviews have identified as potential unintended consequences include social and economic impacts, such as gentrification, affordability pressures, digital exclusion, and labour conditions; spatial impacts, including traffic redistribution and changes in the use of public space; and environmental impacts related to construction and wildlife.

At the same time, positive co-benefits of transport policies across health, environmental, social and economic domains remain insufficiently examined. Pedestrianisation, street placemaking and redesign, for example, may not only improve safety and air quality, but also support social interaction and mental wellbeing. When combined with greening measures, these interventions can further enhance mental wellbeing while also contributing to urban cooling, biodiversity, and climate resilience. Identifying, quantifying, and, where appropriate, monetising these co-benefits helps to strengthen the public health and economic case for transport interventions.

Future research should also examine spill-over effects beyond the immediate users or areas targeted by interventions. Low Emission Zones, for example, may affect not only residents within regulated areas but also commuters, neighbouring communities, and people living near zone boundaries. Similarly, changes to bus services, fare policies, or street design may have wider community-level effects that are not captured by studies focused solely on direct users.

Finally, we also need to look beyond passenger health to examine occupational health outcomes among transport workers (e.g., bus and ride-share drivers), including musculoskeletal conditions, mental health, workplace exposures, and the potential health impacts associated with employment.

2.6 Improving evaluation methods and decision-support tools

Future research should continue improving the frameworks and methods used to evaluate the health impacts of transport policies and interventions. We are observing a welcome increase in studies that move beyond traditional physical health outcomes and increasingly examine mental health and social benefits associated with transport interventions. Evaluation approaches should capitalise on this progress by incorporating these broader outcomes into health impact assessments. This also means moving beyond mortality alone to include morbidity and broader wellbeing outcomes where evidence and data allow.

Further efforts are also necessary to ensure that the distributional and long-term health impacts of transport are better captured. This requires detailed data and the capacity to monitor long-term impacts. Efforts should particularly focus on improving data on walking and cycling, as well as on methods for estimating levels of active travel. In addition, global data-sharing platforms could help facilitate the evaluation of transport interventions across different contexts and populations (Giles-Corti et al., 2020; Lowe et al., 2022).

Hand in hand with improved impact evaluation, decision-support and economic appraisal tools should better translate this broader evidence into policy and investment decisions. Dimensions that are not yet fully explored and monetised include improvements in employment, social participation, and mental wellbeing. Social return-on-investment approaches, together with improved communication and visualisation of results, may help demonstrate the broader value of transport interventions and strengthen the integration of health considerations into transport decision-making.

2.7 Assessing the public acceptance of interventions

The success of many transport interventions depends not only on their effectiveness but also on their acceptability (van Wee et al., 2023). Public acceptance is increasingly recognised as a critical factor in transport policy, and many interventions, including LEZs, pedestrianisation schemes, and emerging mobility technologies, face implementation challenges related to public perceptions, acceptance, and support.

There is a need to move beyond just measuring support and opposition and explore the factors that shape public acceptance. Evidence from pedestrianisation schemes suggests that perceived benefits and costs, travel habits, accessibility concerns, place attachment, trust in decision-makers, and proximity to interventions influence levels of public acceptance. Public support also varies across stakeholder groups, with people who walk and cycle more often, business owners, and visitors often experiencing interventions such as pedestrianisation in very different ways. Future research should therefore investigate how people's experiences shape their attitudes to policy measures. More specifically, research is needed on how perceived exposure to intervention effects such as perceived impacts of traffic redistribution, and perceived changes in accessibility shapes the public acceptance of policy measures. Here, mixed methods can be particularly beneficial for understanding why benefits and burdens are perceived differently across population groups.

3. Towards health-oriented transport policy

A central message emerging from this volume is that transport policy should be viewed not only as a means of moving people and goods, but also as a powerful determinant of public health and health equity. A recent review of sustainable urban mobility plans in 230 cities across Europe found that health is increasingly present in transport plans. Still, the focus is mostly on minimising the detrimental health impacts of transport rather than on opportunities to enhance health (Kasraian et al., 2024). Reviews in this volume, such as chapters on fare-free transport, Ciclovías, Low Emission Zones, and pedestrianisation schemes, demonstrate that there are substantial opportunities not only to reduce transport-related harms but also to actively promote health and wellbeing. Collectively, the chapters in this volume highlight the need to integrate health throughout transport planning, appraisal, implementation, and evaluation processes.

A second recurring theme is the importance of health equity. Many of the interventions reviewed generate different benefits and burdens across population groups. For example, public transport services and fare-free transport initiatives can improve accessibility for vulnerable populations. At the same time, Low Emission Zones and pedestrianisation schemes may influence communities outside the intervention area. Policymakers should therefore move beyond average population impacts and consider who benefits, who may be disadvantaged, and how transport interventions affect different social groups. Embedding equity objectives within transport planning and monitoring frameworks can help ensure that mobility systems contribute to reducing rather than reinforcing existing health inequalities.

The reviews also highlight the need to consider the full range of health pathways and wider societal impacts associated with transport interventions. While transport policy has traditionally focused on outcomes such as congestion, travel time, air pollution, and road safety, the evidence reviewed in this volume points to a broader set of impacts including social interaction, community cohesion, mental wellbeing, access to services, and the quality of public space. Many interventions also generate important co-benefits across environmental, social, and economic domains. For example, pedestrianisation and street redesign schemes can improve not only safety and air quality but also social interaction, wellbeing, urban cooling, climate resilience, and biodiversity when combined with urban greening measures. Recognising these multiple impacts can strengthen the case and secure public support for transport policies that simultaneously advance public health, sustainability, and quality of life.

Finally, the findings emphasise the importance of strengthening health impact assessment, economic appraisal, and monitoring systems. Despite the growing evidence base linking transport and health, health considerations remain insufficiently embedded in many transport decision-making processes. Tools such as the Health Economic Assessment Tool (HEAT) demonstrate how health impacts can be quantified and monetised, allowing health outcomes to receive greater consideration alongside traditional transport objectives. More comprehensive assessment frameworks, supported by appropriate monitoring systems and health-related indicators, can help ensure that the health consequences of transport policies are systematically considered. Stronger collaboration among the transport, planning, public health, and environmental sectors will be essential to translating the growing evidence base into healthier, more equitable, and more sustainable mobility systems.

References

Aldred, R., Goodman, A., Woodcock, J., 2024. Impacts of active travel interventions on travel behaviour and health: results from a five-year longitudinal travel survey in outer London. J. Transp. & Health 35, 101771. https://doi.org/10.1016/J.JTH.2024.101771.

Giles-Corti, B., Lowe, M., Arundel, J., 2020. Achieving the SDGs: evaluating indicators to be used to benchmark and monitor progress towards creating healthy and sustainable cities. Health Policy 124 (6), 581–590. https://www.sciencedirect.com/science/article/pii/S016885101830441X.

Kasraian, D., Murdock, H.E., Faghih Imani, A., Yu, Y., de Nazelle, A., Stead, D., et al., 2024. Health in mobility planning: an assessment of how health is considered in sustainable urban mobility plans. J. Transp. & Health 39, 101919. https://doi.org/10.1016/J.JTH.2024.101919.

Lowe, M., Adlakha, D., Sallis, J.F., Salvo, D., Cerin, E., Moudon, A.V., et al., 2022. City planning policies to support health and sustainability: an international comparison of policy indicators for 25 cities. Lancet Glob. Health 10 (6), e882–e894. https://doi.org/10.1016/S2214-109X(22)00069-9.

Pucher, J., Dill, J., Handy, S., 2010. Infrastructure, programs, and policies to increase bicycling: an international review. Preventive Med. 50 (Suppl.), S106–S125. https://doi.org/10.1016/J.YPMED.2009.07.028.

van Wee, B., Annema, J.A., van Barneveld, S., 2023. Controversial policies: growing support after implementation. A discussion paper. Transp. Policy 139, 79–86. https://doi.org/10.1016/J.TRANPOL.2023.05.010.

Winters, M., Buehler, R., Götschi, T., 2017. Policies to promote active travel: evidence from reviews of the literature. Curr. Environ. Health Rep. 4 (3), 278–285. https://doi.org/10.1007/S40572-017-0148-X/TABLES/2.

Printed and bound by CPI Group (UK) Ltd, Croydon, CR0 4YY
14/09/2026
02216284-0003